PROPERTY-TAX EXEMPTION
FOR CHARITIES

D1263911

Evelyn Brody, editor

PROPERTY-TAX EXEMPTION FOR CHARITIES

Mapping the Battlefield

THE URBAN INSTITUTE PRESS
Washington, D.C.

THE URBAN INSTITUTE PRESS
2100 M Street, N.W.
Washington, DC 20037

Library of Congress Cataloging in Publication Data
   Property-tax exemption for charities : mapping the battlefield /
   Evelyn Brody, editor.
          p. cm.
   Includes bibliographical references and index.
       ISBN 0-87766-706-3 (pbk.)
       1. Charities—United States. 2. Tax exemption—United States. 3.
   Property tax—United States. I. Brody, Evelyn.
       HV91 .P765 2002
       361.7′632′0973—dc21

                                                            2002002496

ISBN 0-87766-706-3 (paper, alk. paper)

Printed in the United States of America

THE URBAN INSTITUTE is a nonprofit policy research and educational organization established in Washington, D.C., in 1968. Its staff investigates the social, economic, and governance problems confronting the nation and evaluates the public and private means to alleviate them. The Institute disseminates its research findings through publications, its Web site, the media, seminars, and forums.

Through work that ranges from broad conceptual studies to administrative and technical assistance, Institute researchers contribute to the stock of knowledge available to guide decisionmaking in the public interest.

Conclusions or opinions expressed in Institute publications are those of the authors and do not necessarily reflect the views of officers or trustees of the Institute, advisory groups, or any organizations that provide financial support to the Institute.

Editor's dedication:
To my parents,
Warren and Elizabeth Brody

Contents

Introduction

Evelyn Brody

The exemption from property tax for charities, despite its long history, has been little studied and is poorly understood. Recently, threats from revenue-starved municipalities and other local governments have mounted, whether as frontal attacks on the charity exemption or as demands for payments in lieu of taxes.[1] Meanwhile, property-owning charities such as hospitals, universities, and even cultural institutions seem to have transformed themselves into big businesses, making the public receptive to modifying the exemption. This book places the debate about the exemption in a larger context. The chapters that follow describe the economic, legal, social, and political forces at work, presenting different points of view and speculating on the future directions of reform.

In this age of global electronic commerce and the Internet's assault on sovereign borders, a study of the property-tax exemption for charitable organizations may seem quaint. However, just as a tossed ball poised at the height of its flight appears to have stopped, the issues in this study will accelerate in importance in the coming years. The same economic forces undermining the traditional income- and sales-tax bases will also magnify the importance of the property tax, whose base is fixed and easily measured (Youngman 1998).[2] More subtly, economic and social changes put increasing pressure on our accepted notions of the boundaries of the nonprofit sector.

The few previous books on the nonprofit property-tax exemption surfaced in times of economic and social strain. From the earliest years of our republic, fears of a voraciously expanding religious sector have sporadically produced furious debates over the extent to which churches should render unto Caesar—or even own property at all (see Robertson 1968). The near-bankruptcy of New York City in the late 1960s and 1970s prompted Alfred Balk's influential work, *The Free List* (1971), and Peter Swords' response, *Charitable Real Property Exemption in New York State* (1981). Most studies of tax benefits for charity, when they consider property-tax at all, include it along with the range of special income-tax rules for charities. (See, for example, John Colombo and Mark Hall's stimulating *The Charitable Tax Exemption,* 1995, considered by Grimm in chapter 13 of this volume.) Similarly, a popular recent work based on a series of articles in the *Philadelphia Inquirer* found little data on property-tax exemption, and, instead, aimed its anti-exemption guns on income-tax exemption (see Gaul and Borowski 1993). The occasional state and municipal studies of the effects of property-tax exemption—one as long ago as 1922 (Adler), but most dating from the 1970s and 1990s—also lament the paucity of data while expressing concern over an eroding tax base.

In recent years, as the number and economic influence of nonprofit organizations have grown, academic research has struggled to keep up. Some of the questions are definitional: What makes nonprofit organizations distinct from businesses and governmental entities? Some involve policy implications: Do mutual-benefit nonprofits merit less public support—and narrower tax exemptions—than charitable nonprofits? Some are simply matters of data gathering: How many nonprofit organizations are there? None of these questions is easy to answer.

Despite this surge in academic interest, the issue of property-tax exemption has remained in the anecdotal dust. The topic suffers from a myriad of research handicaps. As a threshold matter, the property tax itself is of bewildering complexity and variation due to deliberate reliance on local decisionmaking and administration.[3] Compared with the federal income tax, the property tax—with its amalgamation of thousands of local (sometimes overlapping) jurisdictions and combinations of caps and equalization formulas—is nearly impenetrable, and administration can vary dramatically from the law that appears on the statute books. Property-tax exemptions, too, follow definitions and limitations somewhat different from exemptions under the federal income tax, and can seem ad hoc. Finally, assessors have little or no incentive to assess the value of property held by nontaxpayers, so even valuations that do exist can lack reliability.

To remedy the scholarship gap, this book brings together authors from a range of disciplines to assess what we know—and why we cannot yet know more—about the property-tax exemption for charities. The 13 chapters present legal, economic, political, historical, and municipal-administration perspectives. Several of the authors disagree on some basic premises, so this book offers a variety of perspectives rather than a synthesis of views.[4]

Most important, the chapter authors demonstrate how public perception differs sharply from reality. Three features characterize the current property-tax exemption for charities. First, the data, while sparse, suggest that exemptions granted to nonprofit organizations constitute only a small fraction of total exemptions. Notably, the largest category of exempt property belongs to governments. Second, municipal demands for "voluntary" payments in lieu of taxes (PILOTs) occur only sporadically; even where PILOT programs exit, they raise comparatively little revenue. Third, and paradoxically, the press treats the charity exemption as front-page news.

How do we reconcile these findings? The title of this book suggests that a war rages over this issue—so where are the battles occurring? If "all politics is local," then no tax system is more political than the property tax. Averages mask the widely varying impact of exemptions on particular communities and of taxes or PILOTs on particular nonprofits. Moreover, the property tax falls on narrowly defined local populations, while the benefits of a particular charity's activities may be enjoyed more broadly. Finally, as charities engage in a wider range of activities—some indistinguishable from those engaged in by taxpaying entities—public support for exemption crumbles. Much to the nonprofit sector's consternation, tax exemption has come to be viewed as a subsidy granted by government, rather than an inherent entitlement of the organizational form.

Illustrating these issues, the Fairfax County, Virginia, board of supervisors recently amended guidelines to permit national charities, as well as local ones, to apply for property-tax exemption. In December 1999, the board approved exemption, worth over $300,000 a year, to the National Wildlife Federation, which has an annual budget of $82 million. One county supervisor praised the Federation for being a good citizen by providing local environmental and educational programs. A dissenting supervisor, however, contended, "We're just giving away taxpayer money to an organization that doesn't need it and shouldn't get it. . . . I'm delighted they do what they do, and I'm delighted they're in Fairfax County. And I think, like everybody else, they ought to pay their taxes." Similarly, a member of the Virginia General Assembly, whose approval would still be required, commented, "We have typically turned down people who have got large staffs and salary commitments as inappropriate for government assistance. . . ." The Federation's spokesman defended its application: "We think that the conservation, education, and advocacy work that the organization does is exactly the kind of exemplary work that the state of Virginia and the county of Fairfax want to encourage. . . . Yes, it's a bigger exemption, but I think that means we're also doing that much more good." Finally, the president of Citizens for Sensible Taxation complained, "Are [county officials] going to cut spending by $300,000? If they aren't, who is going to pay it? It's going to be Joe Citizen" (O'Hanlon 1999; Stokeld 2000).[5]

In general, property-tax exemption for charities has long been a story in the Northeast, whose cities are strictly bounded, lack open land, and host large nonprofit sectors. In recent years, though, the twin pressures of school-finance reform and tax-limitation initiatives (such as Proposition 13 in California and Proposition 2-1/2 in Massachusetts)[6] have increased the focus on exempt-property classifications across the country. Most recently, we saw the collapse of a high-level effort to find a federal solution to electronic commerce's threat to state coffers (Johnston 2000; Rigsby 2001). These developments suggest that the property tax will become more important as a source of state and local government finance—and that exemptions for charities will grow as an area of contention.

Chapter Findings

Part I: Framework and Structure

This book sets the stage with two initial chapters laying out the legal and political landscape of property-tax exemption for nonprofit organizations. In chapter 1, Janne G. Gallagher, deputy general counsel of the Council on Foundations, describes the basic legal structure of the exemption, including the relationship between the states and their local governments in recognizing or conditioning exemption. As a threshold matter, property-tax exemption is granted at the state level (often in the state constitution), but the effects are felt locally. While state laws vary in their terminology and details, they have several features in common: In general, exempt property must be owned and operated by a church or a nonprofit educational, charitable, or, in some states, health care institution, exclusively for exempt purposes. While states sometimes exempt benevolent organizations, the nonprofit tax exemption is essentially a charity tax exemption. Federal section 501(c)(3) status often helps, but such status is not always sufficient, and chapter 1 explores different state definitions of "charity." In addition, exemption is generally not available for property leased (but not owned) by a charity, nor is it available for (most) investment property; some states deny exemption for "excess" property; and some states apportion tax for property used in part in an unrelated business. Finally, Gallagher introduces the range of local government demands for payments in lieu of taxes and in-kind services in lieu of taxes (SILOTs), and discusses the differences between taxes and special assessments and user fees.

While economic analysis and legal interpretation are crucial to understanding the status and effects of tax exemptions, the decision to relieve specific property from a general tax burden is inherently and primarily political. As Joan M. Youngman, Lincoln Institute of Land Policy senior fellow, shows in chapter 2, the political debate is made all the more contentious by the impact of large national trends, such as changes in the health care industry, on the most local of taxes on tangible, visible property. The chapter analyzes current political issues concerning property-tax exemptions from two perspectives. First, Youngman examines questions arising from the nature of the tax itself—its hybrid nature as a general levy and as a payment for property-related services, the uncertainties of the valuation process, and the proliferation of tax abatements of various types. Second, she considers recent developments that have exacerbated contemporary conflicts over nonprofit property-tax exemptions, including changes in the role of cultural institutions, growth in the size and professionalization of the nonprofit sector, and increasing public scrutiny of nonprofit operations. Because these trends also affect the governmental and business sectors just as much as, if not more than, they affect nonprofits, the chapter concludes that the vigorous political debate does not necessarily indicate any diminution in public support for charity property-tax exemptions.

Part I concludes with two chapters examining the economics of the issues. As New York University economics professor Dick Netzer explains in chapter 3, the importance of property-tax exemptions for charities as a matter of public-finance policy—and as an economic benefit to the exempt charities—depends on how important the property tax is in local government finance and on what has happened to the base of the tax (i.e., the value of taxable property). The property tax declined as a source of local government revenue from roughly two-thirds of the total in 1932 to one-fourth in 1980, but it has stabilized since then. The factors that produced the decline seem not to be major grievances any longer, so the tax will likely remain an important revenue source for years to come, rather than a trivial tax whose burden charities would barely feel. On the other hand, the base of the tax has narrowed, in part because of the enactment of tax preferences for individuals, designed to reduce the tax's unpopularity. Indeed, effective—even harsh—state limitations on local tax rates and levies are now widespread. Accordingly, exemption for charities may rankle more today.

Netzer explains that the property tax is, and always has been, a tax that finances identifiable benefits to local residents (and to some businesses), and in so doing increases rather than reduces land values. To the extent that this is the case, exemptions for charities seem no more reasonable than exempting them from paying for the private goods and services they use, if we view property-tax exemptions as justified by a "base-defining" concept (see Brody, chapter 6 of this volume). However, if we view exemptions as a form of subsidy (and one that is easier operationally than direct cash payments), then exemption could be justified regardless of the benefits that property taxes finance. An important consideration, however, is that the subsidy is financed by specific local governments and paid to charities whose services may benefit mainly people who do not live in that city.

Finally, Netzer asks whether the property owned by charities constitutes a rising share of potentially taxable property. The aggregate data do not show this to be true. Data for the few places in which such data are readily available (and at least somewhat reliable) show that, on a statewide basis, exempt nonprofit property is a very small percentage of taxable property (for example, 2.5 percent in California), and very small, indeed, relative to government-owned property, much of which belongs to federal and state agencies. However, the percentages are much higher in some cities, notably (again) in the Northeast. A significant share of the tax-exempt property of charities typically is owned by religious organizations, including both houses of worship and religiously affiliated health and social service organizations.

The available data are explored further in chapter 4 by Joseph J. Cordes, professor of economics at George Washington University and research affiliate at the Urban Institute, and his co-authors, Marie Gantz and Thomas Pollak, of the Urban Institute. Again acknowledging that hard data are scarce, the authors arrive at a rough "order of magnitude" of between $8 and $13 billion nationally for the annual value of charity property-tax exemption, or between 1.3 percent and 2.1 percent of the total revenue received by public charities that filed federal tax returns. The authors find wide variation by state and across jurisdictions within states. In addition, they estimate that this dollar amount should be increased by an additional one-third to represent real estate owned by churches.

Because only charities that own the property they occupy enjoy the exemption, these authors also examine the own-versus-rent question. A tax-exempt organization cannot use income-tax deductions for either depreciation or rent. Thus the financial benefit from ownership exactly equals the value of the property tax that the entity need not pay. However, other things being equal, nonprofit organizations have an incentive to rent rather than own when the property-tax rate is low and when the depreciation system is relatively generous. Many economists believe that, unlike the situation in the early 1980s, current depreciation rules approximate economic depreciation, so today the property-tax exemption provides an unambiguous incentive to own rather than rent. In addition, chapter 4 discusses the impact of exemption on nonprofit organizations' decisions about where to locate. While the tax exemption has no effect on the locational decisions of nonprofits that rent, nonprofits that own do not have a tax incentive to avoid jurisdictions with high property taxes.

Lastly, chapter 4 examines whether the property-tax exemption encourages nonprofits to undertake commercial ventures and allows nonprofits to compete unfairly with for-profit businesses. The authors cite both theory and empirical evidence that imply that the property-tax exemption can provide a financial incentive for some nonprofits to engage in commercial ventures they might otherwise avoid, but the authors conclude that the driving force behind investments in commercial activities is the ability to earn superior financial returns, rather than the ability to enter a market and "unfairly" undercut the competition.

Part II: Contrasting Theories of Exemption Law

The next three chapters examine the development of the current structure of the nonprofit property-tax exemption. In chapter 5, Stephen Diamond, a professor at the University of Miami School of Law, explores the history of the property tax and of property-tax exemption for charities. The origins of the philanthropic tax exemption are problematic: What is an exemption when there is no theory of universal taxation? Did the exemption flow from the state support of churches? Did the exemption reflect the absence of income, similar to the frequent exemption for undeveloped land?

Diamond finds that the exemption initially reflected a clear qualitative desire that exempt institutions should not disappear through tax liens, although no one made a quantitative assessment of the institutions' value to the community. It was only after the Civil War, when Protestants noted that elaborate Catholic churches were receiving a larger benefit, that the exemption was conceptualized as a quantifiable subsidy. The national debate over church exemptions in the 1870s, and again in the 1890s, belied the notion that such exemptions were covert subsidies. They were not subject to annual review, but neither were many direct grants. In sum, Diamond concludes that, over time, we have seen the commodification of the tax exemption.

Chapters 6 and 7 delve into the legal rationales for exemption. First, Evelyn Brody, professor of law at Chicago-Kent College of Law and associate scholar at the Urban Institute, presents contrasting theories of property-tax exemption. The base-defining theory views exemption not as a grant but rather as the correct treatment of what the property-tax system is seeking to tax. This theory views the state as respecting the independence of the charitable sector by refraining from taxation. Alternatively, property-tax exemption can be viewed as a subsidy that should be subject to the same scrutiny as direct subsidies. Nevertheless, she points out, if exemption is a subsidy, it is an odd form of subsidy: The exemption is worth the most to charities that own the most property in the most heavily taxed jurisdictions. To Brody, either the base-defining theory or the subsidy theory might best be understood under a "sovereignty" perspective—that the civil government treats the charitable sector as something akin to an independent sovereign entitled to operate without being taxed.

The base-defining theory appears to offer the higher wall against attack, but charities' unwillingness to debate the fairness and efficiency of exemption frustrates municipalities, which may respond by challenging exemptions. Under a subsidy rationale, states might feel more free to tinker with the types of activities they wish to subsidize. In practice, some charities compromise by making voluntary payments in lieu of taxes. Fiscal pressure can also be relieved by having the states compensate municipalities that host exempt charities (see Carbone and Brody, chapter 10 of this volume). For churches, Brody finds, the constitutional attitude has evolved from a laissez-faire accommodation of religion to a subsidy theory of exemption, in which religious organizations merge into the larger universe of exempt organizations and thus are both subject to neutrally applied tax regimes and entitled to neutrally granted exemptions.

In chapter 7, Deirdre Dessingue, associate general counsel at the U.S. Catholic Conference, discusses the "wall" between church and state, and the ramifications of recent Supreme Court cases on public financing of parochial schools. She explores the specific types of religious organizations that actually enjoy exemption *as churches*, including places of worship, seminaries, central administrative headquarters, and parsonages; youth and adult clubs, mission societies, and conventions or associations of churches; charitable, educational, and social welfare agencies serving the general public as well as members; and all other religious organizations, particularly those not affiliated with any church or group of churches.

Part III: The Economic War within the States: Exemption Battles and PILOTs

The book next turns to mechanisms adopted by local municipalities to offset some of the revenue lost because of exempt properties. Chapter 8 contains the results of the first nationwide study of the use of nonstatutory, negotiated payments in lieu of taxes by nonprofit organizations. The author, Pamela Leland of the YWCA in Wilmington, Delaware, used written and telephone communications with municipal finance directors and community leaders in the 73 sampled cities. The sample comprised the 50 largest cities in the United States, plus the largest city in any state not already included. Leland found that, at least in the large cities, PILOTs seem to be neither widespread nor growing rapidly, as charities fear. However, she cautions, it is difficult to discern informal arrangements between local governments and charities. Moreover, the picture might be different in small college towns and other municipalities where a large nonprofit institution owns a disproportionate share of property.

We next turn to the municipal perspective, focusing on cities in the Northeast. In chapter 9, David B. Glancey, chair of Philadelphia's Board of Revision of Taxes, describes the Philadelphia Voluntary Contribution Program, a 1994 initiative of the mayor's office. From the city's viewpoint, this program was a cautious response to a national phenomenon: the dramatic expansion and changing character of the tax-exempt nonprofit sector. The program recognized that while nonprofits play a vital role in Philadelphia's economy, they also increase service demands on the city's already over-burdened local tax base. The Voluntary Contribution Program, which was officially terminated at the end of 1999, attempted to encourage tax-exempt nonprofit organizations to return to the city a limited measure of what the city provided them in essential tax-supported services.

While this arrangement worked over its initial five-year term, by renewal time the economic picture for both the city and the nonprofit sector had changed, with nonprofit hospitals coming under particular stress. Meanwhile, in 1997, the Pennsylvania legislature had adopted a statute designed to reaffirm charity exemption, while encouraging charities to enter into voluntary agreements with municipalities. As a result, Philadelphia—effectively waiving its share of the voluntary payments in favor of the school district—offered to reduce by 50 percent the annual contributions requested of health care institutions, and will consider individual hardship cases. Cash renewals have fallen from $5 million to $800,000 (with service levels remaining constant).

In chapter 10, Nicholas R. Carbone, director of the Connecticut Institute for Municipal Studies, and Evelyn Brody provide a case study of Hartford, Connecticut, and explain the development of an innovative state-level solution. The leader of the Hartford City Council in the 1970s, Carbone initiated the expansion of Connecticut's PILOT program to cover nonprofit hospitals and universities. The state had already been compensating municipalities for the presence of state-owned exempt property, but since 1978 it has paid PILOTs for these private parcels as well. Over the years, the legislature has been increasing the rate at which the PILOTs are paid; because of recent budget surpluses, the state now pays 77 percent of the tax that would otherwise be paid by exempt non-profit hospitals and universities. (This is, as in the past, a higher rate than that paid on state-owned property.) While the state payments, as increased, have gone a long way to smoothing town-gown relations, the PILOT program depends on annual legislative appropriations, and nothing guarantees that Connecticut will continue to spend any surplus this way. Connecticut's pioneering policy of paying PILOTs for nonprofit hospitals and schools has been copied only (and not to the same degree) by neighboring Rhode Island.

Chapter 10 also describes additional approaches adopted by Hartford to make up for tax revenues lost because of local charities. First, the city has engaged in ad hoc negotiations with churches, in the 1970s to obtain the use of church premises for senior services, and more recently to recruit parishioners as volunteer tutors. Second, and controversially, Hartford has placed a moratorium on zoning approvals for new social service charities in the central business district, which it is trying to "gentrify." Third, Trinity College has joined a growing trend by center-city nonprofit property owners—notably universities—to pour funds into local community development. This represents a reversal of the traditional "siege mentality" of universities located in undesirable neighborhoods, and reflects, no doubt, some self-interest on the part of schools competing to attract young students (Grunwald 1999).

Chapter 11, by historian Peter Dobkin Hall, Hauser lecturer in public policy at Harvard University's John F. Kennedy School, explores the contingent character of tax exemptions through a historical case study of New Haven, Connecticut. The fiscal dilemmas of this well-studied city represent those of municipalities in which commercial and manufacturing enterprises have been replaced by a nonprofit service economy. The chapter considers the evolving use of tax exemptions in five periods: 1750 to 1819, 1820 to 1879, 1880 to 1940, 1940 to 1960, and 1960 to the present. The discussion examines how the tax treatment in each period was shaped by the following "contingencies": (1) the scope, scale and role of governments; (2) recognized boundaries between public and private actions, and the legal capacity of entities; (3) organizational populations and ecologies; (4) the public's sensitivity to taxes, corporate citizenship, and accountability; (5) the distribution of benefits provided by various levels of government and by exempt entities; and (6) social differentiation and the role of exempt entities.

Part IV: Exploring Future Directions

The book concludes with two chapters that speculate on future possible approaches to property-tax exemption for charities.

In chapter 12, Woods Bowman, associate professor of economics at DePaul University's Public Services Graduate Program, explores how financial relief to municipalities might be achieved short of total repeal of the charity exemption. As an alternative to PILOTs, he proposes a one-time charge on exempt property, analogous to oft-utilized development impact fees, that would be assessed when property is taken off the rolls. The charge would be equal to the assessed value removed, which he demonstrates equals the net economic impact on the host community. He likens the impact of exemption to an "exit tax" on capital leaving the community.

In addition, Bowman urges that policymakers design such a community-impact compensation program to include government-owned property, which is worth two-and-a-half times as much as charitable property; after all, a great deal of public property is dedicated to charitable purposes (e.g., universities, community colleges, and hospitals). Finally, he explores the desirability of instead allowing charities to provide negotiated services in lieu of taxes, which could be a superior solution for both sides.

In our concluding chapter, Robert T. Grimm, Jr., of the Indiana University Center on Philanthropy, looks at the ramifications of proposals to narrow the types of owners entitled to exemption. In chapter 13, he explores the justifications and impact of narrowing the property-tax exemption to charities that produce a significant amount of public/collective goods (instead of including self-supporting commercial charities that often produce mostly private goods). His study applies nuanced models for determining a nonprofit's production of public goods to five major nonprofit industry groups in Indianapolis: arts, culture, and humanities; education; environment and animal-related; health; human services; and public benefit. Grimm also addresses commercial nonprofits' particular issues. Most notably—and not surprisingly, to those who have followed the trend in charity financing—Grimm finds that if a reasonably high level of support from donations (such as 50 percent, or even 30 percent) were imposed as a condition to property-tax exemption, few of the best-known charities would remain exempt.

Commentaries

To supplement the issues and perspectives set out in the main chapters, at the end of this volume we present commentaries from Daniel Salomone, David Sjoquist, Edward Zelinsky, Peter Swords, and Richard Pomp.

Daniel Salomone, executive director of the Minnesota Taxpayers Association, uses examples from Minnesota to illustrate the difficulties of applying the property-tax law. The lack of an accepted rationale for the tax, not to mention the exemptions, raises problematic practical issues as well as political disagreements over fairness, efficiency, and administrability. The lesson he draws is, essentially, that in the clash between charities and municipalities, "charities win"—although, as he comments, the charity exemption means little when so many other types of exemption exist. As part of a larger tax reform proposal, the administration of Minnesota governor Jesse Ventura recently proposed rationalizing the ad hoc and uneven use of PILOTs by adopting a standardized, statewide formula for measuring the cost of basic local services, and permitting municipalities to choose to assess these fees on nonprofit property. However, political pressures forced the administration to abandon this aspect of the governor's plan, illustrating the difficulty of achieving reform.

David Sjoquist, professor in the School of Policy Studies at Georgia State University, applies a public-choice framework to the chapters in part III to explain how municipalities, charities, and their supporters will behave. He identifies specific factors, in addition to the general free-riding tendencies and other collective problems of organizing a lobbying effort, that affect behavior. Demands for taxation or PILOTs, he finds, depend on the amount of tax involved and its importance relative to other revenue sources; the level of existing fiscal stress and the need for the next dollar; the degree to which local residents benefit from the nonprofits' activities; the lobbying strength of those served by or contributing to the nonprofits; the nature of nonprofit services, and whether they are available from for-profit providers; the distribution of nonprofits throughout the state; and the lobbying power of those adversely affected. Factors influencing nonprofit resistance to taxation or PILOTs include the amount of tax or PILOTs at issue; the extent to which local nonprofits own rather than rent their property; fears of the slippery slope, and the effects on other favored treatments from an erosion of exemption; the public relations value of being seen as contributing to the community; and the fear of worse treatment in the future.

Edward A. Zelinsky, professor of law at Yeshiva University's Benjamin N. Cardozo School of Law, puts the exemption for charities in the context of the larger property-tax system designed to accommodate a variety of pressures. He describes such devices as exemptions, caps, circuit breakers, income-tax credits, state transfer payments to municipalities, and PILOTs, all of which operate to ameliorate the full tax theoretically imposed on property owned by farmers, the elderly, homeowners, and others. As a practical result, political opposition to the property tax has been blunted, thus "[immunizing] the tax from outright abolition."

Peter Swords, executive director of the New York Coordinating Committee, expands on the base-defining theory of exemption. As a matter of tax policy, the tax base properly comprises only money and wealth used and available for private, personal ends, such as residences and industrial and commercial property. (By "tax base" he means amounts above the costs of compensating the government for services provided to property, including exempt property.) However, at some point, tax policy merges with democratic theory: When should people be taxed on income or wealth transferred to privately controlled charities? In the end, Swords concludes, this is a moral choice: Upon whom and what is it fair to lay the burden of tax?

Richard Pomp, professor of law at the University of Connecticut Law School, begins by celebrating the political skills of author Nicholas Carbone. Pomp served as academic advisor in the efforts led by Carbone (described in chapter 10) to address the fiscal pain caused by the expansion of exemptions from the Hartford tax base. As a scholar of state and local taxation, Pomp explains the virtues of statutory clarity, vigilant enforcement, and an examination of the scope of existing exemptions. He believes exemptions should be narrowed unless the state is willing to make compensating payments, as he helped achieve in Connecticut. Moreover, Pomp favors replacing the property-tax exemption with explicit cash subsidies, in order to avoid the "irrationalities" that result under current law. Short of such a radical reconfiguration, in order to allow municipalities to protect their tax base when nonprofits acquire taxable property, Pomp proposes an array of legislative options: case-by-case local denial of exemption; phase-ins and phase-outs of exemption; acreage and dollar limits; and user charges.

Future Research

While nominally focused on a narrow issue, this book serves more broadly as a case study of many of the political, economic, and legal challenges facing the nonprofit sector today. Indeed, we hope that this book will stimulate nonprofit researchers to expand the scope of their inquiries and draw formerly uninvolved researchers into the conversation. Private philanthropy can exist uneasily in democratic society, raising basic questions about how wealth is earned and allocated. The increasingly complex regulatory and funding ties between governments and nonprofit organizations blur the sectoral boundaries (see Boris and Steuerle, eds., 1999; Salamon 1995). Nor can nonprofit entities be easily distinguished from for-profit or public entities on the basis of activities, since many groups tend to be involved in the same activities, from hospital care and nursing homes to education and certain forms of entertainment (Weisbrod, ed., 1998). Politically granted outcomes, including special legal treatment for nonprofit organizations under property-tax laws, ultimately depend on social legitimacy.

Acknowledgments

This volume grew out of a panel of papers that I presented with Woods Bowman and Robert Grimm on "Property-Tax Exemptions and Payments in Lieu of Taxes" at the 26th Annual Conference of the Association for Research on Nonprofit Organizations and Voluntary Action (in Indianapolis, Indiana, December 6, 1997). Urban Institute Senior Scholar C. Eugene Steuerle, who chaired that panel, encouraged me to develop the topic into this collection. I am also grateful for the support of the Urban Institute's Center on Nonprofits and Philanthropy, and the enthusiasm of its director, Elizabeth Boris. This book is made possible by additional project funding from the Lincoln Institute of Land Policy. The authors appreciate comments and suggestions from attendees at a June 2000, book conference in Washington, D.C., especially from our discussants: David Brunori, Daniel Salomone, Richard Steinberg, John H. Bowman, Jay Rotz, David A. Brennen, Richard D. Pomp, David Sjoquist, Jeffrey Chapman, Bill Stafford, and Ingrid Stafford. Finally, all participants in this project appreciate the organizational skills of the Urban Institute Center on Nonprofits and Philanthropy's Sarah Wilson.

NOTES

1. While this volume does not deal explicitly with the sales and use tax, exemptions for charities raise similar concerns. At one 1995 conference for nonprofit organizations,

"Panelists told the assembled charity and foundation representatives horror stories of soup kitchens, nursing homes, colleges, and religious organizations losing their property-tax and sales-tax exemptions and even of attempts to slap taxes on Girl Scout cookies" (Stokeld 1995, 924).

2. "Randy, governments will always find ways to collect taxes. If worse comes to worst, the IRS can just base everything on property taxes—you can't hide real estate in cyberspace" (Stephenson 1999, 841). As Vito Tanzi recently discussed, the pressures for open economies to confine their coverage to immobile factors could lead to reduced capital income taxes, and hence reduced public welfare spending (Tanzi 1995).

3. As Glenn Fisher observed, "achieving uniform taxation required a degree of centralization and professionalization of administration that conflicted with deeply held political values" (Fisher 1996, 6).

4. Indeed, it is sometimes difficult to agree even on rhetoric. At the June 2000 book conference for this volume, charity partisans were heard characterizing PILOTs (payments in lieu of taxes) as "extortion," while municipality supporters used the term "contributions."

5. A bill exempting the Federation's property was signed by the governor on March 24, 2001, effective July 1, 2001 (HB 72, incorporated into HB 2128), shortly after the opening of the Federation's $20 million headquarters building (Rein 2001).

Meanwhile, in Massachusetts, Harvard University came under withering local criticism after it acquired a $162 million office complex called the Arsenal, a Superfund site cleaned up with the help of $100 million in taxpayer money (Kocian 2001). The town, fearing that Harvard will convert the property from taxable to exempt purposes (such as dorms or classrooms), "angrily rejected Harvard's first draft payment-in-lieu-of-taxes offer" (ibid.). Increasing the pressure on Harvard to negotiate is a state bill, currently in committee, that would permit a municipality to require a nonprofit to pay taxes on any new property that accounts for at least 1 percent of its tax category (ibid.).

6. See generally O'Sullivan, Sexton, and Sheffrin (1995).

REFERENCES

Adler, Philip. 1922. "Historical Origin of the Exemption from Taxation of Charitable Institutions." In *Tax Exemptions on Real Estate: An Increasing Menace*, part I (1–84). White Plains, N.Y.: Westchester County Chamber of Commerce.

Balk, Alfred. 1971. *The Free List: Property Without Taxes.* New York: Russell Sage Foundation.

Boris, Elizabeth, and C. Eugene Steuerle, eds. 1999. *Nonprofits and Government: Collaboration and Conflict.* Washington, D.C.: Urban Institute Press.

Colombo, John D., and Mark A. Hall. 1995. *The Charitable Tax Exemption.* Boulder, Colo.: Westview Press.

Fisher, Glenn W. 1996. *The Worst Tax? A History of the Property Tax in America.* Lawrence, Kans.: University Press of Kansas.

Gaul, Gilbert M., and Neill A. Borowski. 1993. *Free Ride: The Tax-Exempt Economy.* Kansas City: Andrews and McMeel.

Grunwald, Michael. 1999. "Colleges Embrace Towns They Once Avoided." *Washington Post*, June 6, A3.

Johnston, David Cay. 2000. "Agreement on Internet Taxes Eludes Deeply Divided Commission." *New York Times*, March 31, C1.

Kocian, Lisa. 2001. "Looking for Deal on Taxes Harvard, Town in Talks over Arsenal Complex Plan." *Boston Globe*, August 16, Globe West 1.

O'Hanlon, Ann. 1999. "Wealthy Nonprofit Gets Tax Break from Fairfax; Detractors Warn of a Costly Precedent." *Washington Post*, December 8, B1.

O'Sullivan, Arthur, Terri A. Sexton, and Steven M. Sheffrin. 1995. *Property Taxes and Tax Revolts: The Legacy of Proposition 13.* Cambridge, U.K.: Cambridge University Press.

Rein, Lisa. 2001. "Va. Bill Has Big Tax Break for Wildlife Federation." *Washington Post*, February 13, B1.

Rigsby, Deborah. 2001. "Internet Moratorium Extended Two Years: Congress Fails to Resolve Tax Collection Issues." *Nation's Cities Weekly*, Nov. 26, 1.

Robertson, D.B. 1968. *Should Churches Be Taxed?* Philadelphia: Westminster Press.

Salamon, Lester M. 1995. *Partners in Public Service: Government-Nonprofit Relations in the Modern Welfare State.* Baltimore: Johns Hopkins University Press.

Stephenson, Neal. 1999. *Cryptonomicon.* New York: Avon Books.

Stokeld, Fred. 2000. "Proposed Property Tax Exemption for National Wildlife Federation Stirs Debate." *Tax Notes* 86: 157.

———. 1995. "Charities Face Exemption Challenges at All Levels, Panel Warns." *Exempt Organization Tax Review* 11: 924–25.

Swords, Peter. 1981. *Charitable Real Property Exemption in New York State.* New York: Association of the Bar of the City of New York and Columbia University Press.

Tanzi, Vito. 1995. *Taxation in an Integrating World.* Washington, D.C.: The Brookings Institution.

Weisbrod, Burton A., ed. 1998. *To Profit or Not to Profit: The Commercial Transformation of the Nonprofit Sector.* Cambridge, U.K.: Cambridge University Press.

Youngman, Joan M. 1998. "Property, Taxes, and the Future of Property Taxes." In *The Future of State Taxation,* edited by David Brunori. (111–27). Washington, D.C.: Urban Institute Press.

PART I
Framework and Structure

The Legal Structure of Property-Tax Exemption

Janne Gallagher

P roperty tax consistently ranks as one of the most unpopular taxes in America. It is highly visible, can be inconvenient to pay, and is based on an assessment process that may be, or seem to be, biased and unfair. Nevertheless, property-tax revenue has the virtue of being a revenue source for local governments that is not only stable but also peculiarly under their jurisdiction and control. Accordingly, this traditional mainstay of local-government finance is likely to remain so in the future.

Basic Legal Standards for Charitable Tax Exemption

The law of American property-tax exemption is firmly rooted in the special treatment that British law afforded bequests for charitable purposes. American settlers carried with them the process of forming charitable corporations to carry on religious and educational work.[1] Tax exemption was part of this package, and as property taxation became an increasingly important source of revenue for local government, property-tax exemption for religious, charitable, and educational institutions became the norm (see Diamond, chapter 5 of this volume). Today, all 50 states and the District of Columbia have constitutional or statutory provisions exempting property that these organizations own and use to carry out their charitable missions. While some significant differences in the scope and wording of exemption provisions do exist, state laws reflect the basic premise that charitable property should not be burdened with taxation.

State Constitutions

State constitutional exemptions for charity generally are permissive. They allow, but do not require, the legislature to enact exemptions within defined categories.[2] For example, sections 2(a)(i) and 2(a)(vi) of Article 8 of the Pennsylvania constitution authorize the legislature to exempt, among others, "actual places of regularly stated religious worship" and "institutions of purely public charity." However, exemption for institutions of purely public charity may extend only to "that portion of real property of such institution which is actually and regularly used for the purposes of the institution" (ibid.). The legislature may adopt a narrower provision, but it may not exempt property that is not within one of the enumerated categories. As the Pennsylvania Supreme Court declared, "The legislature is constitutionally limited to exempt only those charitable organizations which are 'institutions of purely public charity,' and we cannot constitutionally interpret that statutory language to exempt an organization which is not a 'pure' public charity" (*Hospital Utilization Project v. Commonwealth*, 507 Pa. 1, 12, 487 A.2d 1306, 1312 (1987)).

A few state constitutions contain mandatory provisions—that is, the constitutional provision directly grants the exemption. The legislature may neither broaden nor narrow it. Section 170 of the Kentucky constitution, for example, directly exempts "institutions of purely public charity" from paying ad valorem taxes. Because this provision is self-executing, the legislature has not been called on to enact exemption legislation.

Not all states provide for charitable exemptions in their constitutions. Some state constitutions, such as that of Massachusetts, simply permit the legislature to grant such exemptions as it chooses. There is no need for special guarantees for charitable exemptions in such states. In the few states where the constitution is silent on the matter of exemption, the courts have ruled that granting exemption is within the inherent power of the legislature. Thus, the Maine court held that the legislature had discretion to grant exemptions for the property of literary, benevolent, and charitable institutions because such exemptions had long been accepted (*State v. Hamlin*, 86 Me. 495, 30 A. 76 (1894)).

State Laws

States generally have laws exempting the property of churches, schools, and "charitable" organizations. Explicitly religious exemptions usually are limited to houses of worship. Other property of religious institutions qualifies for exemption only if it fits within the state's exemptions for charitable or educational institutions. Schools, colleges, and universities occupy a special place in the hearts of state legislatures. Virtually every state guarantees exemption to these institutions.[3] Exemption for educational institutions that do not grant degrees is less common. Some states explicitly exempt property belonging to museums, libraries, performing arts organizations, and similar entities that broadly educate the public, but in most states these and other institutions that do not grant degrees are exempt only if they are charitable in nature.

Arts organizations sometimes face challenges under state property-tax exemption laws, often with mixed results. One key issue, especially for amateur theater groups, is whether the organization's efforts primarily benefit the public, for which exemption is appropriate, or whether the group is more of a social club, for which exemption is not allowed. However, exemption also can hinge on the interpretation of key words in the state's exemption statute. For example, an Oregon theater company ultimately prevailed in a challenge to its property-tax exemption, but only after the state supreme court decided that the state's exemption for "literary" institutions extended to words that are spoken aloud as well as those that are written (*Theater West of Lincoln City v. Department of Revenue*, 319 Or. 114, 873 P.2d 1083 (1994)).

Health care institutions have posed special problems when local governments have challenged their right to tax exemption, and the challenged hospitals have often sought explicit recognition of their exemptions from state legislatures. However, even being named as exempt in a state statute is not sufficient protection if a court determines that the health care entity is not "charitable." Thus, a Utah statute provided that property used for a hospital would be deemed to be used for charitable purposes. Nevertheless, in *Utah County v. Intermountain Health Care*, 709 P.2d 265 (Utah 1985), the Utah court ruled that the hospital must prove that it was operating for charitable purposes. Other states, such as Texas, have imposed special "community service" requirements on nonprofit health care.[4]

States are particularly suspicious of charitable entities that provide long-term housing. Seeing the clear contrast between, for example, elderly people who live in their own homes and pay taxes, and those who live in property owned by a charitable institution that does not, many courts have held housing providers to a particularly strict standard of proof.[5]

A state's authority to exempt nonprofit organizations that are not religious, charitable, or educational depends on the wording of the state's constitution. Most states carefully enumerate the exemptions the legislature is permitted to grant,[6] and there is a general trend toward denying charitable exemptions to groups that are not charitable. Thus, in *Board of Equalization v. York Rite Bodies of Freemasonry*, 209 Ga. App. 359, 433 S.E. 2d 299 (1993), the Georgia Appeals Court ruled that Masonic lodges do not qualify under the state's exemption for property of institutions of purely public charity. Although the court agreed that the Masons pursue many charitable activities, it also found that group resources are used to benefit their members, a group that is limited to males over the age of 21 who believe in a single God. Similarly, the Idaho court denied charitable exemption to property owned by a motorcycle club and used for racing (*Owyhee Motorcycle Club v. Ada County*, 855 P.2d 47 (Idaho 1993)).

In some states whose constitution allows more latitude, the legislature has acted to grant exemption to noncharitable nonprofits. The Virginia legislature, for example, has exempted numerous such groups, from garden clubs to war veterans' posts (Va. Code Ann. §§ 58.1-3607 through 58.1-3620 and §§ 58.1-3650.1 through 58.1-3650.847). Arizona recently added property-tax exemption for war veterans' organizations that qualify for federal tax exemption under sections 501(c)(3) or 501(c)(19) of the Internal Revenue Code. The most frequent beneficiaries of such exemptions are membership organizations that do not qualify for charitable status under section 501(c)(3) because they are selective in their membership but that carry on some charitable activities or are seen as promoting the welfare of the community.[7]

Formal Requirements for Exemption

Identity of Ownership and Use

Generally, property must be both owned by an eligible organization and used by that organization to further the purposes for which it was granted exemption. Accordingly, charitable institutions that lease office and other space from a private owner usually gain no benefit from tax exemption because they do not meet the ownership requirement. For example, the Illinois Court of Appeals ruled against exemption for property leased by a church to use for religious and educational purposes. The court held that the church could not gain exemption because the individual who owned the property was motivated by profit (*Victory Church v. Illinois Department of Revenue*, 637 N.E.2d 463 (Ill. App. 1994)). Similarly, the Vermont court ruled against exemption for property leased from private individuals for use as group homes for persons with developmental disabilities (*Lincoln Street, Inc. v. Town of Springfield*, 159 Vt. 181, 615 A.2d 1028 (1992)).

By the same token, property leased by a charity to others is also generally taxable, because it fails the requirement that it be used for the owner's exempt purposes. Accordingly, property held for investment purposes is routinely subject to tax.

When a charity owns property, occupies part of it for its charitable purposes, and leases the remainder, the impact on taxation can vary wildly. At one extreme, even limited use of otherwise-exempt property by a taxable entity can result in complete loss of exemption. Thus, a congregate-care facility lost its property-tax exemption in Maine when it rented some space to physicians and leased a few housing units at market rates. The court refused to apportion the tax between the taxable and nontaxable uses (*City of Lewiston v. Marcotte Congregate Housing, Inc.*, 673 A.2d 209 (Me. 1996)). At the other extreme, a small amount of noncharitable use may be disregarded, with the property continuing to be fully exempt. Colorado, for example, will overlook the nonexempt use of otherwise-exempt religious property as long as the nonexempt use does not exceed 208 hours a year or produce more than $10,000 in gross rental income (Colo. Rev. Stat. § 39-3-106.5). More commonly, however, the tax on mixed-use property is allocated based on a formula that takes into account both exempt and nonexempt uses. A South Dakota case offers a good example of the considerations that come into play in arriving at an appropriate formula. In *Lutherans Outdoors in South Dakota, Inc. v. State Board of Equalization*, 475 N.W.2d 140 (S. Dak. 1991), the court's formula based the amount of tax owed on the number of days that the property (a camp) was used for nonexempt purposes, compared with the number used for exempt activities. The court excluded idle days, when the camp was not used for any purpose, from the denominator, thereby rejecting the camp's argument that idle time should be considered an exempt use. However, the court also rejected the county's argument that the allocation should be based on the proportion of income derived from the various activities, rather than the days of use, because it found that an income formula failed to adequately account for the subsidies built into the camp's exempt operations.

California has adopted a sophisticated statutory formula to apportion tax exemption for property that falls within the state's "welfare" exemption—that is, property used for religious, hospital, scientific, or charitable purposes (Cal. Rev. & Tax Code, § 214). For purposes of the formula, a use is unrelated to the property's exempt purpose only if it produces unrelated business taxable income, as defined in section 512 of the Internal Revenue Code. If the organization uses a reasonably ascertainable portion of the property to produce the unrelated income, the tax obligation for that piece will be apportioned based on the amount of income it derives from taxable versus exempt activities at that location. If the exempt activity does not produce income, the tax will be apportioned based on the amount of time devoted to taxable versus exempt activities at that location. If there is no ascertainable portion of the property used to produce the taxable income, the assessor applies the same formula to the entire property (Cal. Rev. & Tax Code, § 214.05).

Property owned by one charity and leased to another charity presents special problems. If the lessee charity is using the property to further its exempt purposes, denying exemption due to the lack of formal identity between ownership and use seems overly formalistic. Denying exemption can also encourage inefficiency by discouraging charities from sharing excess space. But the fact that the lessee is another charity does not preclude the lessor charity from realizing an investment return on its assets.

States have developed a variety of responses to this problem. Some simply disregard situations in which one charity permits another to occupy a small percentage of its space, treating such uses as incidental. As the trend toward apportioning space between taxable and nontaxable uses has grown, however, courts and legislatures have been forced to fashion equitable solutions. A common one is to permit exemption only when the lease arrangements are at or below cost. Nonetheless, courts often remain hostile to these legislative solutions. One court, for example, denied property-tax exemption for a building that a Catholic church leased to a shelter for pregnant women and their children. The court refused to apply a state statute allowing one charity to lease *part* of its space to another, because the church leased an *entire* building to the shelter (*In re Archdiocese of Philadelphia*, 617 A.2d 821 (Pa. Commw. 1992)).

The requirement that distinctions be made between ownership and use has caused some nonprofits to lose exemption when corporate restructurings have placed ownership of the property in one corporation and the charitable activity in another. The opinions issued in some of these cases suggest strong judicial hostility to charitable entities that, because of their size and complex corporate structure, appear to be acting like commercial businesses.[8] Exemption loss also can occur when property is owned by a real estate partnership that includes profit-motivated investors.

Actual Use

All states deny exemption to property that a charity does not use for its exempt purposes. Thus, a charity may not purchase land for future development and hold it off the tax rolls while the organization decides whether to build on it. Even if the charity does not use the property for commercial gain during the interim, it must pay the property tax. This principle frequently leads to litigation over such issues as whether property is being "used" for an exempt purpose when construction or renovation begins, and the precise point at which this occurs. For example, courts have been called on to rule on whether the drawing up of plans or the application for permits constitutes the formal commencement of the construction process.

A corollary to the law on use is that the law will not extend exemption to more property than is needed for the exempt purpose. This issue most frequently arises in cases involving summer camps and religious institutions, and generally involves undeveloped acreage that may be lightly used or used only a few times a year. For example, the Nevada court upheld exemption for only 146 acres of a 1,300-acre parcel owned by a church, finding that the remainder was not actually used for religious purposes (*Simpson v. International Community of Christ* (Nev. 1990)). Some legislatures have dealt with this issue directly by limiting the acreage for which exemption may be sought. Michigan, for example, limits property owned by YMCA, YWCA, Boy Scout, Girl Scout, Camp Fire, and 4-H organizations to not more than 400 acres (Mich. Comp. Laws Ann. § 211.7d).[9]

Some property not directly used to carry out an exempt purpose may still be exempt if its use is ancillary to and reasonably necessary for the exempt function. Parking lots, for example, are frequently exempt from tax because the operation of a parking lot is necessary to enable people to make use of an exempt facility. Faculty housing, or housing for a camp caretaker, is another example of property that may qualify for exemption on this basis.

Defining Charity

Since state constitutions exempt "charities" or "public charities" or "institutions of purely public charity," defining what is meant by charity has been a key issue in the development of state tax-exemption law. This work began in the 19th century with the adoption of state constitutional provisions and has continued ever since. It is important to keep in mind that the development of state charitable-exemption law predated the adoption of the federal Internal Revenue Code, and that property-tax exemption, rather than being derived from federal law, was the basis for many of the concepts that found their way into the income-tax regulations and rulings. Although some present-day amendments to state statutes make exemption under section 501(c)(3) of the Internal Revenue Code a prerequisite to property-tax exemption, possession of federal exempt status is no guarantee that a charity will be exempt from tax on its property.

The Courts

States generally may be divided into those that base their rationale for tax exemption on the principle that charities relieve a government burden and those that accept the rationale that exemption is granted because the work of the charity confers a benefit on the community. States that strictly apply the government burden rationale generally apply more stringent criteria. This can be carried to extremes, however. Pennsylvania's Commonwealth Court, for example, denied exemption to a nonprofit publisher of religious materials, finding that it could not be said to relieve a government burden because the government is barred from religious activities (*Scripture Union v. Deitch*, 572 A.2d 51 (Pa. Commw. 1990)). The common law of many states includes a requirement that a charity seeking an exemption must embody some aspect of "gift or giving." This can mean that charitable contributions must form part of an organization's financial support and that it must offer at least some of its services free or below cost. Other factors that courts frequently take into account include whether the organization serves a charitable class, confers private benefits on its founders or insiders, or relieves a government burden. Although not always explicitly discussed, the presence of federal subsidies that can be used to cover the tax payment is sometimes a factor in court rulings that a property fails to qualify for exemption because it lacks the element of gift or giving. Thus, exemption has been denied where federal rent subsidies brought the rent paid by tenants up to fair market value (*In re Nassau County Hispanic Foundation*, 603 N.Y.S.2d 174 (N.Y. App. Div. 1993)).

Some state courts have explicitly adopted multipart tests for charitable tax exemption. Thus, Minnesota uses a six-part test that looks to (1) the stated purpose of the undertaking; (2) whether the organization is supported by charitable contributions; (3) whether recipients of charity are required to pay for its services; (4) whether income received produces profit; (5) the identity of the charity's beneficiaries; and (6) whether dividends or assets upon dissolution are available to private interests (*North Star Research Institute v. Hennepin County*, 236 N.W.2d 754 (Minn. 1975)).

Some states have been evolving a "commerciality" doctrine, in which the courts look to whether a charity behaves differently than a business offering similar goods and services. Thus, a New York court distinguished a YWCA residence facility, where residents paid rent, from commercial low-cost hotels because the YWCA offered counseling services and was safer and more secure (*YWCA v. Wagner*, 409 N.Y.S.2d 167 (N.Y. 1978)). However, several courts have ruled that the mere fact of competition with a commercial establishment is not sufficient to cause loss of exemption.[10]

The Legislatures

Many state legislatures have tried to define the group of organizations that will be tax exempt because they are charitable. Such efforts most often take the form of the specification of particular organizations, or classes of organizations, that will be exempt; examples range from scouting organizations to groups providing housing for the elderly. Some states have developed lengthy lists of statutorily exempt charities. Virginia is the most extreme in this regard, naming more than 800 nonprofit organizations or groups as exempt (Va. Code §§ 58.1-3650.1 through 58.1-3650.847). The existence of numerous statutory categories often reflects legislative action to overturn court decisions denying exemption.

A few states allow some level of local control over exemption decisions, at least for some types of charities. Thus, Vermont requires town-meeting approval for charitable tax exemption. The initial vote grants exemption for 10 years, with 5-year renewals if the town continues to vote favorably.[11]

The consent of local authorities is a prerequisite in Massachusetts to gaining exemption for facilities serving the mentally ill (Mass. Ann. Laws ch. 59 §5 *Third* (c)). Virginia's complex process for seeking a legislative exemption requires the assistance of elected officials.

More recently, several states have enacted laws that require health care organizations either to provide minimum levels of uncompensated care or to produce annual reports describing their community service. Although generally not directly tied to tax-exemption requirements, these laws represent legislators' efforts to grapple directly with the issue of whether charitable organizations must care for the poor, and, if so, to what degree.

Modern Challenges to Tax Exemption

Two 1985 decisions set the stage for the current round of challenges to charitable property-tax exemption. In *Utah County v. Intermountain Health Care Inc.*, 709 P.2d 265 (Utah 1985), county assessors convinced the Utah Supreme Court that two hospitals were insufficiently charitable to qualify for property-tax exemption. In *Hospital Utilization Project v. Commonwealth*, 507 Pa. 1, 487 A.2d 1306 (1985), the Pennsylvania Supreme Court found that a jointly owned hospital support facility was not an institution of purely public charity and so could not qualify for sales-tax exemption in Pennsylvania. Both courts emphasized two key points that have come to dominate much of the state-level discussion of charitable tax exemption. One is whether all charities must provide a significant level of service to the poor. The other is the extent to which charitable exemptions should be limited to those organizations that directly relieve a government burden in the narrowest sense of the term—undertaking a task that the government is legally obligated to provide.

Following these decisions, Utah and Pennsylvania took divergent paths. After losing an effort to amend the Utah constitution, the state's charitable hospitals and nursing homes worked with the Utah State Tax Commission to develop objective standards for deciding exemption cases involving these organizations. The resulting standards require that hospitals and nursing homes maintain charity-care plans, demonstrate how they publicize the availability of subsidized care, and show that the total of their unreimbursed gifts to the community exceeds the value of their property-tax exemption. Nine years after the original *Intermountain*

Health Care decision, the Utah Supreme Court upheld the constitutionality of the Tax Commission's standards (*Howell v. County Board of Cache County*, 881 P.2d 880 (Utah 1994)).

Pennsylvania, in contrast, became mired in 10 years of litigation over the meaning of the five tests for charitable tax exemption that the court announced in the *HUP* decision. To gain tax exemption, the *HUP* court ruled, an institution of purely public charity must

- Advance a charitable purpose;
- Donate or render gratuitously a substantial portion of its services (footnote 9 of the opinion states that the word "substantial" does not imply any particular percentage, but the organization must make a bona fide effort to serve primarily those who cannot afford the usual fee);
- Benefit a substantial and indefinite class of persons who are legitimate subjects of charity;
- Relieve the government of some of its burden; and
- Operate entirely free from private profit motive.

The Commonwealth Court of Pennsylvania subsequently issued a series of decisions that denied exemption to virtually every charity that came before it.[12] In these decisions, the court adopted very stringent interpretations of the five *HUP* tests. Surpluses were considered evidence of a private profit motive. Groups that received government funding could not be said to be reducing a government burden. Serving the elderly did not fulfill a charitable purpose, unless recipients were also poor and received financial assistance. Religious activities could not be charitable because the U.S. Constitution bars governments from offering religious services.

Eventually, the state supreme court issued a series of corrective decisions. In *St. Margaret Seneca Place v. Board of Property Assessment Appeals and Review*, 536 Pa. 478, 640 A.2d 380 (1994), the court reversed the Commonwealth Court's ruling that a nursing home with a large population of Medicaid patients failed all five of the *HUP* tests. In deciding the case, the Pennsylvania Supreme Court clarified the following important issues:

- An organization may receive payments from the government and still relieve a government burden, at least if the organization can demonstrate that it absorbs part of the cost of caring for those receiving a government subsidy.

- An organization can meet the "donate or render gratuitously" standard by subsidizing part of the cost of caring for some with excess revenue from services to others. Further, services do not need to be entirely free to be "gratuitous." It is enough if the charges are below the actual cost of providing the services.

- A surplus of revenue is not the same as a private profit motive if the surplus is used to maintain and operate the facility and not used to pay excessive salaries or benefits to corporate officers. Charities may factor in capital indebtedness in determining whether they have a surplus.

More recently, the state supreme court issued a second important decision affirming a decision by the Commonwealth Court that Washington & Jefferson College, a small independent school in the western part of the state, met all five parts of the *HUP* test. The most significant aspect of this decision is that an institution that is open to all benefits a charitable class (*City of Washington v. Board of Assessment Appeals*, 704 A.2d 120 (Pa. 1997)). In an unfortunate accident of timing, the court issued this decision just a few days before the legislature's vote on the Institutions of Purely Public Charity Act, Pa. Act 55 (uncodified), leaving charities little time to assess the decision's significance or the continuing need for the legislation in light of the court decision.

Pennsylvania's 1997 Institutions of Purely Public Charity Act defines each of the state's constitutional requirements for tax exemption. The act includes particularly complex provisions that spell out how a charity can satisfy the requirement that it donate or render gratuitously a substantial portion of its services. There are no fewer than seven ways a charity can meet this test, with most depending, in turn, on an equally complex definition of the services that may be considered to be uncompensated.

Alternative Revenue Measures

PILOTs/SILOTs

Payments in lieu of taxes, commonly known as PILOTs, are cash and in-kind contributions that a tax-exempt entity makes more or less voluntarily to a taxing body.[13] Some jurisdictions use the term SILOTs, or services in lieu of taxes, to refer to in-kind contributions.

PILOTs are not restricted to nonprofits. Larger governments sometimes pay PILOTs to smaller governments, as when a state or the federal government contributes to a local government that hosts a disproportionate amount of state or federal property. Some businesses, granted temporary tax exemptions as an incentive to relocate, also pay PILOTs to local governments.

Although the most pressing financial problems occur in the large urban cities, rural areas may seek PILOTs as well. A large charitable institution located in a small town will have a disproportionate effect on both the town's tax base and on the services the town must provide. Even the suburbs are not immune from financial problems: For example, although the school-age population is growing, older people seem reluctant to support the expansion of the public school system. Suburbs also are experiencing an influx of less-affluent people and, in some areas, a marked expansion of immigrant communities.

Local governments generally use a carrot-and-stick approach in soliciting PILOTs. Some governments appeal to charities' sense of fairness, arguing that since nonprofits benefit from taxpayer-funded services, such as fire and police protection, it is only fair that they pay a share of those costs. Other governments accompany their requests with thinly veiled threats that noncompliance may trigger a challenge to the organization's property-tax exemption or make it more difficult to obtain a building permit or a zoning waiver. Some subtlety is required, however. A New York court ruled that a city could not deny a special-use permit solely because an applicant was exempt from property tax and refused to agree to make a payment in lieu of taxes (*Pacer Inc. v. City of Middletown*, 635 N.Y. S.2d 704 (App. Div. 1995)).

There is nothing novel about PILOTs. Under a law of the Massachusetts Bay Province, Harvard College was one of the first New World institutions to gain tax exemption. More than 200 years later, it was the first institution of higher education to enter into a formal agreement with respect to PILOTs. As early as 1929, Harvard University agreed to make PILOTs to Cambridge for 20 years. That agreement was renewed in 1949.[14] The university and the city signed a 10-year agreement in 1968 that was renewed in 1978 and again in 1990. Currently, Harvard pays Cambridge about $1.1 million per year on $71 million worth of tax-exempt property. MIT reportedly pays Cambridge another $767,000.[15]

Boston appears to have been the first city to create a systematic program soliciting PILOTs. The so-called "Boston plan," instituted in the late 1980s, seeks PILOTs from nonprofit property owners whenever they attempt to take currently taxable property off the tax rolls or request city permits and waivers to expand or improve their existing property. The city advocates a loose formula for determining payments that takes into account such factors as the cost of providing city services, the intended use of the property, and the services provided by the organization. Receipts were estimated at around $10 million for 2001.[16]

Pennsylvania communities have been particularly successful in their efforts to negotiate PILOTs. The state supreme court's decision in the *HUP* case, coupled with the string of adverse rulings by the Commonwealth Court, led cities, counties, townships, and school districts across Pennsylvania to solicit PILOTs under threat of challenges to charitable tax exemptions. While initially directed mainly at hospitals and health care facilities, the tax challenges later expanded to include a variety of institutions, including colleges and universities, YMCAs, museums, and some independent schools. One researcher found that at least two-thirds of Pennsylvania counties sought taxes, PILOTs, and voluntary contributions from nonprofits. She believes that more than 1,000 charities—probably a significant underestimate—either were contacted for payments or had their exempt status revoked.[17]

Other localities have not been shy. But despite the widespread nature of the activity, there has been very little effort to evaluate PILOT programs from the point of view of either local government or nonprofits (but see Leland, chapter 8 of this volume). The disorganized and scattershot nature of many of the efforts makes evaluation difficult. However, one recent effort questioned whether PILOT solicitations make sense as a matter of public finance. That report concluded that even the more organized programs, such as those in Boston and Philadelphia, "are piecemeal in nature, unevenly enforced, difficult to administer, and produce very little revenue in relation to the city's overall tax base" (Louisiana Bureau of Governmental Research 1996, 17).[18]

User Fees

Transforming services that are funded from general tax revenues into services for which fees are charged is another route for shifting part of the cost of local government to tax-exempt institutions.[19] While finding ways to increase municipal revenue without raising "taxes" is the primary motivation behind this trend, adding tax-exempt groups to the base of fee payers is an additional benefit.

A tax is classically defined as an "enforced contribution to provide for the support of government" (*United States v. LaFranca*, 282 U.S. 568, 572 (1931)). The obligation to pay taxes generally arises automatically from ownership of property, the receipt of income, or the decision to purchase tangible property. User fees, in contrast, are separate charges for goods or services provided. Typical examples are fees for the use of a public park, or water and sewer charges.[20] A true user fee is not imposed as a tax, is not enforced as a tax, and is generally based on the amount of goods or services received. Moreover, the usual penalty for failure to pay a user fee is denial of access to the desired good or service. Charitable institutions generally pay user fees, even if they are exempt from property tax.

Recent litigation on user fees has involved charges for the treatment of storm-water runoff. Two jurisdictions—Oregon and Florida—have upheld these charges as user fees over churches' objections that the fees infringed on their property-tax exemption. The Florida Supreme Court found that the treatment of storm water conferred a direct benefit on developed property, similar to the benefit provided by solid-waste collection (*Sarasota County v. Sarasota Church of Christ*, 667 So. 2d 180 (Fla. 1995)). The Oregon Tax Court ruled that the fee was a valid user charge because it was pegged to the amount of impermeable surface a property contained, not to the property's value (*Multnomah County v. Department of Revenue*, No. 3650, 1995 WL 76 1416 (Or. Tax, June 1995)).

Special Assessments

The use of special assessments to pay for improvements that benefit some properties, but not others, dates back to colonial days. Special assessments are commonly used to pay for services such as sewer hookups and sidewalks, although some localities also use them to fund parks and beautification projects that benefit particular neighborhoods or to build parking garages that benefit downtown businesses.

A variant on this theme is the use of special assessments to pay for higher levels of services in defined areas of a city, particularly services designed to preserve and enhance the city's commercial downtown. The creation of a special-benefits district lets downtown businesses purchase a higher level of services, such as more frequent street sweeping, safety patrols using private security guards, and amenities such as flower boxes and marketing campaigns, than the city would otherwise provide. Using the power of government to impose special assessments on all similarly situated property within the district avoids the free-rider problem that inevitably arises if concerned businesses undertake these steps voluntarily.

How do special assessments affect nonprofits? Legislatures may exempt the property of nonprofits from special assessments, and some states have done so. However, nonprofits are generally not exempt from special assessments. Moreover, even if nonprofits are exempt, they may be subject to intense pressure to make voluntary payments if they own property within the special district. For example, the state legislation that authorized the city of Baltimore to create the Charles Village district exempted nonprofits from assessments to the extent they were exempt from ordinary property taxes. However, the operating plan for the district was premised on nonprofits' making voluntary payments to support the district's work, and district supporters put considerable pressure on area nonprofits to make contributions. Ultimately, both Johns Hopkins University and a local hospital agreed to contribute to the effort. Johns Hopkins' contribution included both cash and an agreement to hire another security guard to patrol the neighborhood. In addition, both the university and the hospital joined in conducting a yearlong assessment of community needs and ways to meet them.

Municipal Services Fees

Some communities with large concentrations of tax-exempt property have pressured state legislators to support measures that would allow the communities to impose user fees on tax-exempt entities. The details differ from state to state, but most proposals would require nonprofits to make payments to cities and towns for such services as police and fire protection, street maintenance and repair, and sanitation services. Over the course of the decade, at least seven states—Kansas, Iowa, Maine, Massachusetts, New Hampshire, Oregon, and Wisconsin—have rejected these proposals, but efforts continue.

Municipal services fees have many of the characteristics of a property tax. Unlike true user fees, they are incurred because of ownership of property, not the consumption of services. The amount paid is generally a function of the value of the property, even when there has been an effort to base the amount of the fee on budgeted expenditures for the particular services.[21] Frequently, the legislative proposal states that the "fees" will be assessed only against exempt property, with other property owners continuing to support the same services through their tax payments. In addition, the fees would be enforced through liens on property in the same manner as property taxes. In essence, local governments are urging a partial repeal of property-tax exemption: Charities would pay the portion of the tax deemed to benefit property, while remaining exempt from the part that is allocated to education and social services.

Proponents of mandatory municipal services fees use the same arguments as supporters of PILOTs in justifying their proposals: namely, that they are simply seeking recompense for services they provide directly to property. Supporters generally argue that they are not trying to repeal property-tax exemption for nonprofits. Rather, they assert that they are trying to collect fees for services in much the same way that governments collect water bills.

Business and Government Payments in Lieu of Taxes

The frequency of PILOTs paid by the federal and some state governments may be a factor behind payment demands from local governments. As local governments grow used to the idea that tax-exempt property can generate some revenue, albeit not the full tax payment, it becomes increasingly difficult to articulate a reason why charities also should not make such payments. Indeed, two states have extended their compensatory-payment programs to include some nonprofit property, although such programs generally are underfunded (see Carbone and Brody, chapter 10 of this volume).

PILOTs paid by businesses that have been granted tax relief as part of an economic incentive package are another factor supporting the concept that tax-exempt property can nonetheless be expected to contribute something to local costs. In fact, the frequent use of tax incentives to induce or prevent relocation by large businesses may be contributing to a general perception that property-tax payments are something to be negotiated. The concept that tax payments are a matter for negotiation further undermines support for traditional forms of tax exemption.

Conclusion

The trend toward closer scrutiny of tax exemptions for charitable institutions will certainly continue, if not accelerate, as local governments shoulder the costs associated with population increases, the need for infrastructure repairs, and an increasing portion of the burden of providing for those in need. The population of school-age children is growing rapidly, taxing the ability of many school districts to provide both buildings and teachers. Federal devolution of welfare responsibility to the states will likely devolve further to local government as individuals and families lose federal benefits. Suburban areas will feel the pinch—as will their urban and rural counterparts—as the number of poor people living in suburbs grows. If charities are not able to persuade the public that the historic practice of charitable tax exemption is justified, the long-term trend may be toward abolishing or limiting the value of that exemption.

NOTES

1. Throughout this chapter, the term "charity" is given its broad legal meaning— that is, charity encompasses the relief of poverty, the advancement of education, the advancement of religion, the promotion of health, governmental or municipal purposes, and "other purposes the accomplishment of which is beneficial to the community" (Restatement (Second) of Trusts § 368).

2. As part of the property-tax reform movement of the 19th century, many states adopted constitutional provisions requiring that property be taxed fairly and uniformly. Constitutional permission to exempt religious and charitable entities precluded challenges that such exemptions rendered the tax invalid by destroying uniformity.

3. A few states even exempt private schools that operate for profit. However, these exemptions tend to be narrowly construed. For example, Alabama denied exemption to a privately owned child care center because it was not subject to regulation or licensing by the Department of Education, its teachers were not certified, and attendance was not compulsory (State v. Kinder-Care Learning Centers, Inc., 418 So. 2d 859 (Ala. 1982)).

4. Strictly speaking, the Texas community-care requirements, which can be found in chapter 61 of the Texas Health and Safety Code, are a condition of hospital licensure, not property-tax exemption. However, Pennsylvania authorities used them as a model when drafting the community-service provisions of Act 55, the 1997 statute addressing property-tax exemption for institutions of purely public charity.

5. See, for example, Waterbury First Church Housing v. Brown, 170 Conn. 556, 367 A.2d 1386 (1976); and National Church Residences of Chillicothe v. Lindley, 18 Ohio St.3d 53, 479 N.E.2d 870 (1985).

6. For example, the California constitution places exemptions applicable to nonprofit organizations in sections 3 and 4 of Article 13. Section 3, which is mandatory on the

legislature, exempts, among other things, property used for libraries and museums that are free and open to the public; buildings, land, equipment, and securities used exclusively for educational purposes by a nonprofit institution of higher education; buildings, land on which they are situated, and equipment used exclusively for religious worship; and property used or held exclusively for the permanent deposit of human dead or for the care and maintenance of the property or the dead, except when used or held for profit. Section 3 property also is exempt from special assessment.

Section 4 permits, but does not require, the legislature to exempt from property taxation, among other things, property used exclusively for religious, hospital, or charitable purposes and owned or held in trust by corporations or other entities that are organized and operating for those purposes, that are nonprofit, and no part of whose net earnings inures to the benefit of any private shareholder or individual; property owned by the California School of Mechanical Arts, California Academy of Sciences, or Cogswell Polytechnical College, or held in trust for the Huntington Library and Art Gallery, or their successors; and real property not used for commercial purposes that is reasonably and necessarily required for parking vehicles of persons worshipping on land exempt by Section 3(f).

7. Although not described in section 501(c)(3), these organizations are exempt from federal income tax under other subsections of section 501(c). In addition, some of them—fraternal groups, some war veteran posts, and cemeteries—are eligible recipients of tax-deductible contributions under section 170(c)(3), (c)(4), and (c)(5). Cemetery associations and war veteran groups must observe a prohibition against private inurement. Fraternal orders may accept deductible gifts only for use for exclusively charitable purposes.

8. See, for example, *In re Coles-Cumberland Professional Development Corp.*, 672 N.E.2d 391 (Ill. App. 1996); and *In re Northwestern Group*, 665 A.2d 856 (Pa. Commw. 1995).

9. The property-tax cost to the organization for excess land is often quite low. Generally the property is not improved, meaning that the tax is calculated on the bare value of the land. Moreover, the property may be eligible for further reductions if the charity is willing to grant conservation easements or make use of other special tax rates for which rural property may be eligible.

10. See, for example, *Book Agents of the Methodist Episcopal Church v. State Board Of Equalization,* 513 S.W.2d 514, 521 (Tenn. 1974).

11. Vt. Stat. Ann. tit. 32, § 3840. A consequence of requiring town approval has been that most charitable organizations seek exemption as "public" organizations—a permissible exemption category under section 3802(4) of title 32, but one that does not require a town vote. See, for example, *American Museum of Fly Fishing, Inc. v. Town of Manchester,* 557 A.2d 900 (Vt. 1989).

12. Institutions denied exemptions included hospitals (e.g., *School District of the City of Erie v. Hamot Medical Center,* 602 A.2d 407 (Pa. Commw., 1992)); nursing homes (e.g., *St. Margaret Seneca Place v. Board of Property Assessment Appeals and Review,* No. 882 C.D. 1991, Feb. 20, 1992, rev'd, 536 Pa. 478, 640 A.2d 380 (Pa. Commw. 1994)); private schools (e.g., *Wyoming Valley Montessori Association v. Board of Assessment Appeals of Luzerne County,* 532 A.2d 931 (Pa. Commw. 1987)); a religious publisher (*Scripture Union v. Deitch,* 572 A.2d 51 (Pa. Commw. 1990)); a residential program for troubled youth (*Community Service Foundation v. Bucks County Board of Assessment,* No. 36 C.D.

1995 (Pa. Commw., Feb. 28, 1996)); and even a Head Start program (*Butler County Children's Center Inc. v. Board of County Commissioners*, No. 1982 C.D. 1990 (Pa. Commw., Feb. 21, 1992 (unpublished)).

13. See, for example, *Sprik v. Regents of the University of Michigan*, 43 Mich. App. 178, 204 N.W.2d 62 (1972).

14. L. Richard Gabler and John F. Shannon (1977).

15. *New York Times* (1990, B9).

16. City of Boston (1997); financial data from telephone conversation with Jeffrey Austin, Assessing Department, October 17, 2001.

17. Leland (1995), cited with permission. The survey did not include demands by townships and school districts, and other local government entities.

18. See also Worcester Municipal Research Bureau (1997, 10).

19. Netzer, chapter 3 of this volume, table 1 goes to 1996.

20. See, for example, *National Cable Television Association v. United States*, 415 U.S. 336, 341 (1974); *United States v. City of Columbia*, 914 F.2d 151 (8th Cir. 1990); and *Emerson College v. City of Boston*, 391 Mass. 415, 462 N.E.2d 1098 (1984).

21. Charges in Maine, for example, would have been based on a formula that divided the cost of providing the enumerated services by the total assessed value of all property. The result would then have been multiplied by the assessed value of each exempt property. The resulting charge would have been capped at not more than the lower of 1.5 percent of gross receipts or 25 percent of the tax that would be due if the property were fully taxable.

REFERENCES

City of Boston, Assessing Department. 1997. "Payment in Lieu of Taxes Program: Guidelines for Tax-Exempt Institutions."

Gabler, L. Richard, and John F. Shannon. 1977. "The Exemption of Religious, Educational, and Charitable Institutions from Property Taxation." In *Research Papers of the Commission on Private Philanthropy and Public Needs* (IV: 2535–72). Washington, D.C.: Department of Treasury.

Leland, Pamela J. 1995. "The Extent of the Challenge to Property-Tax Exemption in Pennsylvania: A Survey of 67 Counties." In *Nonprofit Organizations as Public Actors: Rising to New Public Policy Challenges* (471–99). Working Papers of the Independent Sector 1995 Spring Research Forum.

Louisiana Bureau of Governmental Research. 1996. "Property Taxes in New Orleans: Who Pays? Who Doesn't? And Why?" October. Text (without tables and figures) available in LEXIS, Fedtax library, State Tax Notes file, as 96 STN 227–22 (November 26, 1996).

New York Times. 1990. "Harvard Will Pay More to Cambridge in Accord." November 26. B9.

Worcester Municipal Research Bureau. 1997. "Should Nonprofit Organizations Make Payment in Lieu of Taxes? The Case For and Against." Report No. 97-4, June 24. Worcester, Mass.

2

The Politics of the Property-Tax Debate

Political Issues

Joan M. Youngman

Of the many settings in which challenges to a property's tax-exempt status may arise, the realm of politics is the most lively, unpredictable, and multifaceted. Legal cases look primarily to statutory interpretation and judicial precedent, and estimates of economic impact rest on specific quantitative data, but political opinion reflects subjective reactions, value judgments, media coverage, social developments, and cultural trends. Instability in any of these areas increases the likelihood of controversy and dispute. Some elements in the political debate on exemptions, such as concepts of public ownership, homeownership, and agricultural use, are relatively stable, with general agreement as to their status and definition. As a result, exemptions and immunities for government-owned property, homestead allowances for owner-occupied residences, and the exemption of large amounts of agricultural land value through current-use assessment are not politically controversial, however much they may be criticized on economic or policy grounds.

By contrast, the exemption for property held by charitable organizations is a source of continual political controversy, largely because of the inherently unsettled nature of a number of its central concepts, including elements as basic as charity, public welfare, ownership, value, and even the definition of the tax itself. In this situation, ambiguities as to the purpose, scope, and effect of the exemption provide a rich medium for dispute. This chapter will consider various facets of this debate from two perspectives, one dealing generally with the structure of the property tax, the other with questions specific to the exemption of property held by charitable organizations.

Ambiguities in the Operation of the Property Tax

Three characteristics of the real-property tax lend special complexity to political and policy debates concerning its structure and operation. The first is the hybrid nature of a tax that also has many characteristics of a fee for property-related services. Nonprofit organizations are on stronger ground both politically and legally in claiming an exemption from taxes than in seeking to avoid paying fees. The second characteristic of the tax concerns the definition and valuation of property subject to taxation. This has important implications for the taxable status of property with mixed charitable and commercial uses, and also for the valuation of unique and specialized property, such as churches. Finally, the proliferation of partial exemptions and preferential assessments for residences, agriculture, and businesses adds an element of uncertainty to the expectations of taxability against which debates on exemption take place.

Fees for Services

The historical evolution of the property tax has never included a clear statement of the tax's nature and goals (see Diamond, chapter 5 of this volume). In the form of a general tax instrument, the tax incorporates many elements of a charge for property-related services, while its base of real property value suggests that this value serves as either an index of ability to pay or as a measure of benefits received.

These rationales are not explicit; in fact, they are in many respects inconsistent and in some cases fallacious. Gross real-property value is not necessarily an index of net real-property wealth, and net real-property wealth is not necessarily an index of net wealth. Even an accurate measure of net wealth could be politically unacceptable as a tax base if it required homeowners to borrow against or even sell their residences to pay the tax. In terms of property-related benefits, elaborate residences and costly modern commercial buildings may impose fewer demands on police and fire services than do poorly maintained structures of low value.

It is not surprising, then, that disagreements flourish as to the nature of the tax, the purpose of tax exemptions, and the role to be played by nontax revenue instruments, particularly fees. Because an exemption from property taxation does not necessarily imply an equivalent exemption from special assessments or fees,[1] local governments often attempt to tax nonprofit institutions through fees, and nonprofit institutions just as frequently respond by charging that the fees are disguised taxes. Even the distinction between fees and special assessments is itself grounds for dispute.[2] A shift from legal to political modes of debate may produce such mutations as coerced voluntary payments—as when the mayor of Ithaca, New York, halted construction on the Cornell campus until the university increased its voluntary contributions to the city (*New York Times* 1995; Glaberson 1996).

These disputes reflect the tension between a fundamental consensus that charitable organizations should be tax-exempt, an equally basic belief that local governments should be reimbursed for the property-related services they render, and a sense that property wealth indicates an ability to pay either taxes or some form of fees. This tension is greatest at the local level, where tax revenue is most likely to fund property-related services and where there may be resentment against state-mandated exemptions that reduce the local tax base.[3]

The familiar sequence in which fees replace taxes in financing local services when direct taxation is restricted illustrates the tenuous distinction between taxes and fees. After the passage of many tax-limitation measures in the 1970s, localities sought to replace property-tax revenue with user fees, special assessments, impact fees, linkage fees, and other innovative instruments that combined regulatory, service-provision, and taxation characteristics. One California city even attempted to impose a "view tax" to finance beach maintenance, using assessments based on parcel size, view, proximity, and beach access (Fulton 1991). Fees that are ultimately held to constitute taxes are invalidated if they fail to conform to statutory and constitutional provisions governing taxes, such as requirements for uniformity, equality, and voter approval.[4] The characterization of specific levies as taxes or fees has been the subject of a plethora of cases dealing with every conceivable type of charge. The unpredictable and contradictory results of such cases only emphasize how uncertain the distinction between taxes and fees can be. For example, the Massachusetts Supreme Judicial Court found a Boston fee for fire protection to be an unconstitutional tax (*Emerson College v. City of Boston,*

462 N.E.2d 1098 (Mass. 1984)), while the West Virginia Supreme Court found a fire and flood protection fee not to be a tax (*City of Huntington v. Bacon*, 473 S.E.2d 743 (W. Va. 1996)), and the Montana Attorney General found fire protection fees to constitute a benefit assessment (*Opinions of the Montana Attorney General* 46: 7 (1995)).

One of the most dramatic measures to replace property taxes in post–Proposition 13 California was the Mello-Roos Community Facilities Act of 1982. The act permitted the establishment of special districts to finance services such as police and fire protection, schools, parks, and water and sewer construction—functions for which special assessments had traditionally been held invalid. For example, in a decision invalidating a library fee, the Washington Supreme Court noted that "no other state has attempted to authorize the construction of a public library financed by local improvement district special assessments" (*Heavens v. King County Rural Library District*, 404 P.2d 453, 456 (Wash. 1965)). Mello-Roos financing rose from approximately $100 million in 1985 to nearly $1 billion in 1990 (O'Sullivan, Sexton, and Sheffrin 1995, 107). In 1994 the Howard Jarvis Taxpayers Association sued Los Angeles County to invalidate a library fee as a disguised tax, charging, "The Mello-Roos 'fee' imposed by the county is in actuality a property tax. It is levied as an incident of property ownership and not as an incident of actual library use. The tax will appear on the property tax bill" (Doerr 1996a, 880). The lawsuit was dropped when the board of supervisors rescinded the fee and funded the library from general revenue, although the board retained the new special district (Doerr 1996b).

Business-improvement districts represent another important innovation for funding local services (Briffault 1999, 448), a mechanism more akin to special assessments than to taxes but even less restrictive in application.[5] In 1999, a California court held that business-improvement district assessments fall outside the limitations of Proposition 218, which requires taxpayer approval of any new or increased taxes or assessments (*Howard Jarvis Taxpayers Association v. City of San Diego*, 84 Cal. Rptr. 2d 804 (Cal. Ct. App. 1999)).

Definition and Value of Taxable Property

Ambiguities in the concepts of ownership and property have a special impact on charitable organizations holding partial interests in real estate that is also used for nonexempt purposes. These ambiguities often produce disputes as to the definition and taxability of "possessory interests," partial interests that rise to the level of real property for tax purposes (*United States v. County of Fresno*, 429 U.S. 452 (1977)). At various times, California courts have found taxable possessory interests in the form of a defense contractor's right to use a government shipyard (*Kaiser Co. v. Reid*, 184 P.2d 879 (Cal. 1947)), a forest ranger's right to occupy government housing (*United States v. County of Fresno*, 123 Cal. Rptr. 548 (Cal. Ct. App. 1975), *aff'd*, 429 U.S. 452 (1977)), a refreshment company's right to operate concession stands in a public stadium (*Stadium Concessions, Inc. v. City of Los Angeles*, 131 Cal. Rptr. 442 (Cal. Ct. App. 1976)), a media company's right to run cable lines through public rights of way (*Cox Cable San Diego, Inc. v. County of San Diego*, 229 Cal. Rptr. 839 (Cal. Ct. App. 1986)), a business owner's right to operate amusement machines in a public airport (*Freeman v. County of Fresno*, 178 Cal. Rptr. 764 (Cal. Ct. App. 1981)), and a concessionaire's right to rent television sets to patients in a county hospital (*Wells National Services Corp. v. County of Santa Clara*, 126 Cal. Rptr. 715 (Cal. Ct. App. 1976)).

The complex mixture of uses to which institutional properties—from church parking lots and day care centers to hospital gift shops and doctors' office buildings—are put provides a basis for political battles between those opposed to unwarranted extensions of an exemption and those who object to narrow and inflexible interpretations of its scope. Divided legal interests afford grounds for similar disputes, whether the state law requires charitable ownership, charitable use, or both. One California assessor, for example, refused to recognize an exemption if the owner of the property was not the user, even if both ownership and use were admittedly charitable; the position was ultimately overturned by an appellate court (*Christ The Good Shepherd Lutheran Church v. Mathiesen*, 146 Cal. Rptr. 321 (Cal. Ct. App. 1978)).

The perceived impact of tax exemptions—and thus, to some extent, political reactions to them—varies dramatically according to assumptions as to the market value of taxable property. A number of extraneous factors may influence these calculations. Some jurisdictions' debt limits are based on property value, including the value of tax-exempt property (American Law Reports 1997). This encourages overvaluation of exempt property, with no countervailing incentive for the exempt owner to contest this estimate. Historically, state boards of equalization were established in part to correct for the opposite influence, the incentive for jurisdictions to understate property value in order to qualify for greater amounts of state aid or to be responsible for lower amounts of state property tax (Seligman 1913, 21–22).

The amount of the tax base lost to exemptions, and of the revenue that would be raised by their elimination, depends on the market value of exempt buildings. Many of the buildings, particularly those owned by religious and educational institutions, do not have a standard market in terms of numerous buyers and sellers of comparable properties. In the case of highly specialized industrial and manufacturing facilities, courts have occasionally been willing to consider replacement cost instead of actual sale value as the basis for the tax. However, there is considerable resistance to this substitution, which James Bonbright referred to as "a tour de force by which to bridge the gap between the realization value of a property and its value to the owner" (Bonbright 1937, 60).

The classic case of "specialty" valuation concerned the New York Stock Exchange, whose owners went to court in 1927 to protest a $9 million assessment on the grounds that the building was so uniquely suited to the Exchange's purposes that no purchaser could have a use for it (*New York Stock Exchange Building Co. v. Cantor*, 223 N.Y.S. 64 (N.Y. App. Div. 1927)), *aff'd mem.*, 162 N.E. 514 (N.Y. 1928)). Therefore, the Exchange contended, the building should be assessed only on the value of its land, reduced by the demolition costs the hypothetical purchaser would incur.

The New York courts rejected that position, and began a line of valuation cases that took into account value to the owner, as measured by depreciated reproduction cost, for useful but unmarketable property.[6] This approach has coexisted uneasily with a literal reading of the statutory market-value standard, and in recent years it has been considerably restricted.[7]

These cases, which deal primarily with industrial manufacturing and assembly buildings, have clear implications for the debate over the impact of tax exemptions. Any calculation of the amount of property tax lost to exemptions must necessarily hypothesize a market value for much property that is unique. For example, the New York State Board of Real Property Services provides an annual estimate of the percentage of the state's property value that is exempt (Heidelmark 1999). The tenuousness of such figures is illustrated by church challenges to historic-preservation restrictions that prevent them from altering buildings that no longer serve their congregations' needs.[8] In these battles of "mission or maintenance," much attention has been directed toward the financial burden of preserving architecturally significant structures. As one case noted,

> Physically, the condition of the building is deteriorating. The Sunday school rooms are inadequate and space is lacking for retreats, seminars and other religious and charitable programs. The balcony of the sanctuary has been closed because it deteriorated to the point of being too dangerous for use. The plumbing facilities are "decrepit," lighting is poor and there are no elevators for handicapped individuals. As for the exterior, extensive repairs to the roof and masonry are required. Falling stones and masonry fragments are a danger to pedestrians. In addition, leaks in the roof drainage system have rotted large sections of wall. (*Church of St. Paul and St. Andrew v. Barwick*, 496 N.E.2d 183, 194 (N.Y. 1986) (dissenting opinion).)

Although, as in this case, churches have been largely unsuccessful in their legal battles for "de-landmarking,"[9] it is likely that they would meet with a far more sympathetic response if they were seeking to reduce a tax payment, rather than to replace a piece of a city's architectural heritage with new construction. As these buildings would not be replicated today if lost, even the more skeptical approach of the *New York Stock Exchange* case might view them as "tear-down propositions" for tax purposes.

Expansion of Exemptions

The least precise but perhaps most pervasive ambiguity involving the property tax concerns the definition of fully taxable property. The difference between taxable real estate and exempt property must now be determined in a system in which the homestead exemption and tax freezes for senior citizens reduce the taxable value of private residences, current-use valuation exempts large amounts of agricultural and open-space land, and property-tax relief plays a major role in state and local competition for business. This is not a definitional issue, but rather a significant shift in perception as to the baseline norm of taxability against which exemption disputes take place. Alfred Balk's 1971 analysis of exemptions was prescient in this regard, for it considered homestead allowances, preferential assessments, and tax exemptions for nonprofit organizations as one integrated category (Balk 1971).

These developments affect the charitable exemption in conflicting ways. On the one hand, erosion of the tax base places additional revenue pressure on local governments and can easily lead to new challenges to existing exemptions. At the same time, the now-familiar exchange of tax incentives for the promise of job creation and economic growth is available to charitable organizations as well as private industry. In 1971, the *Boston Globe* editorialized against "the demand that private institutions of higher education be required to pay real estate taxes":

> Massachusetts' independent colleges and universities are in many ways the state's proudest possession and tradition. They are also a very big business. Every nickel spent here by out-of-state and foreign students is a net gain to the commonwealth's economy. So is every nickel attracted from government and foundations. . . . The "ed biz" does not pollute significantly. . . . It employs thousands of people, from professors to dishwashers. Its endowments feed a steady stream of cash into the state's economy. . . . (*Boston Globe* 1971)

The tradition continues almost 30 years later, as shown by two 1999 *Boston Globe* headlines: "Harvard Touts Its $2B Impact on Economy" (Weiss 1999) and "Harvard Study Touts Its Economic Impact" (Bailey 1999). Moreover, political acceptance of widespread tax incentives, preferential assessment provisions, and special allowances undermines the perception that the charitable exemption is either a striking departure from the norm or an example of special favoritism.

Issues Specific to Charitable Organizations

In addition to the many ambiguities inherent in the property tax itself, a number of uncertainties in the specific treatment of property held by nonprofit organizations destabilizes the exemption's political status. Various aspects of charitable work, even those of a clearly noncommercial nature, have taken on new and more politicized forms in response to contemporary social challenges, from the support of defiantly unorthodox artistic expression to the promotion of highly traditional cultural values. At the same time, special questions arise as to the very meaning of a charitable institution in an era when new modes of operation undermine earlier distinctions between commercial and nonprofit business methods.

Public uneasiness with the size and influence of tax-exempt institutions can be seen in exposés such as the *Philadelphia Inquirer's* 1993 six-part series, "Warehouses of Wealth: The Tax-Free Economy." This influential investigation did not emphasize violations of the law, but rather the quasi-commercial activities, lavish expenditures, and wealth of nonprofit organizations. The series was later published as a book and sent to every member of Congress (Gaul and Borowski 1993; *Connecticut Law Tribune* 1996). The authors were awarded a $25,000 prize for investigative reporting from the Kennedy School of Government at Harvard (*New York Times* 1994). In cases of actual malfeasance or misappropriation of charitable funds, the larger amounts available for charitable work enhance both the opportunity for and the impact of such scandals.

The lack of clarity as to the definition of charitable activity stems in part from the diverse state standards governing property taxation. Many uses of property that are exempt in some states are taxable in others (Clotfelter 1989, 679). State law can also make such disputes easier to bring to court. Unlike the restrictive federal law of taxpayer standing, which generally bars private groups from challenging an organization's exempt status,[10] states often permit individual taxpayers to initiate such proceedings (American Law Reports 1999). A 1999 staff recommendation to the Tennessee State Board of Equalization that the YMCA of Middle Tennessee lose its property-tax exemption followed a complaint by Nashville health clubs (Tennessee State Board of Equalization, *Complaint of Club Systems of Tennessee, Inc.*, May 28, 1999). The complaint was brought pursuant to a statute that allows the board to initiate proceedings for revoking an exemption after a determination of probable cause "upon the written complaint of any person" (Tenn. Code Ann. sec. 67-5-212(b)(5)).

The two sides of this political struggle are fairly evenly matched. Local governments suffering from reduced federal aid, limitations on property taxes, and rising costs of public services naturally look to nonprofit institutions as a potential source of revenue. Yet the strength of public support for nonprofit tax exemptions remains impressive. In the widely publicized 1996 Colorado referendum on an amendment that would have rendered the property of many nonprofit and religious organizations taxable, the measure failed by more than 4 to 1, defeated in every county in the state (Wherry 1996).

The Culture Wars

Charitable exemptions' vulnerability to shifting state and local political sentiment is greatly increased when the very nature of this charitable activity changes and a new consensus must develop as to its taxable status.

In one example that attracted considerable attention, the California State Board of Equalization withdrew the property-tax exemption for the Rev. Robert Schuller's Crystal Cathedral in 1983 because

> concerts featuring Lawrence Welk, Victor Borge and Fred Waring had been staged there and the church had been used for a variety of other secular enterprises,

including profit-making weight reduction classes and psychological counseling programs. "There's been nothing like it, nothing as commercialized as this," William Grommet, an investigator for the Equalization Board, said in an interview. "They were charging people $12, $17 for tickets. They even had a Ticketron there; the first time I saw it, I thought: 'You mean you have to buy a ticket to go to church?'" (Lindsey 1983)

A compromise was reached in that particular case, allowing the exemption to continue on the "strictly religious portions of the sanctuary" (*San Diego Union-Tribune* 1986 and 1984). But the diversity of religious practice in the United States prevents any ready distinction between the commercial and the strictly religious in such cases. When some courts recognize that legitimate religious practice may entail use of peyote (*People v. Woody*, 394 P.2d 813 (Cal. 1964)) or the sacrifice of chickens (*Church of the Lukumi Babalu Aye, Inc. v. City of Hialeah*, 508 U.S. 520 (1993)) and the general public accepts that standard religious practice may entail the sale of tickets for services (Torkelson 1997), no general public consensus can be assumed as to what constitutes "strictly religious" use of a building. If David "danced before the Lord with all his might" (2 Samuel 6:14), and tent-revival meetings have been recognized by the Supreme Court as models of religious practice (*Murdock v. Pennsylvania*, 319 U.S. 105 (1943)), then it is not at all clear that self-improvement, concerts, and ticket sales may not also be part of the contemporary religious landscape.

This pluralism presents special challenges when nontraditional sects take large amounts of property off the tax rolls for headquarters, camps, and retreat facilities in rural areas, such as western Massachusetts and upstate New York. Ulster County, New York, much of whose area is in Catskill Park, has experienced this phenomenon over the past two decades. There, the assessor of the town of Hardenburgh responded by exempting nearly all the town's residential property as religious under charters from the Universal Life Church. A 1981 New York case described

the dramatic increase in the number of parcels of land accorded tax-exempt status by respondent Kerwick, the Assessor of the Town of Hardenburgh, in 1977. It is undisputed that this increase was due to the enrollment, en masse, of 88 percent of the town's landowners as officers in an allegedly religious denomination known as the Universal Life Church. It appears that all Universal Life Church members who sought an exemption received one. The facts in the petition, which for present purposes are assumed to be true, state that on April 27, 1977, Kerwick telephoned petitioner James Dudley and informed him that if [Dudley] failed to become a Universal Life Church follower he, along with 12 percent of the remaining landowners, would have to pay the full $500,000 annual governmental expense of the town. (*Dudley v. Kerwick*, 421 N.E.2d 797 (N.Y. 1981))[11]

This case brought to life the well-worn tale, attributed to various sources, of the tavern owner who declares his premises a church after an influx of exempt organizations reduces his town's tax base (Balk 1971, 28; Larson and Lowell 1976, 243).

The close connection between religious and political concerns also guarantees some degree of political reaction when religious leaders take public positions on highly controversial issues, such as gay rights, abortion, or welfare reform. The complexity of this determination was illustrated by the New York Court of Appeals decision allowing the Unification Church a religious tax exemption, reversing both the trial court and the Appellate Division, which had found it to be a primarily political organization with some religious elements.[12]

Uncertainty about the line between political and charitable activity is not limited to the religious sphere. The punitive private-foundation provisions of the 1969 Tax Reform Act were strongly motivated by political resentment of Ford Foundation support for activities such as the Congress of Racial Equality's voter-registration programs (Smith and Chiechi 1974, 43). Nor are these controversies limited to one side of the political spectrum, as evidenced by the decade-long effort by abortion-rights groups to strip the Catholic Church of its tax-exempt status.[13] Although a ruling against the plaintiffs on grounds of standing ended that specific legal challenge, it did not end such controversies. In 1993, for example, former Internal Revenue Service Commissioner Jerome Kurtz criticized plans by the Catholic Church and the Christian Coalition to jointly endorse candidates for New York City school board elections, saying, "The undertaking of these religious groups, directed toward bringing their religious convictions to bear on the administration of public schools, is the classic case that the Internal Revenue Code's prohibition of religious organizations participating in political campaigns is designed to prevent, and it should be prevented" (Kurtz 1993, A16). The Internal Revenue Service formally denied federal tax-exempt status to the Christian Coalition in 1999 as a result of its political activity (Rosenbaum 1999).

Controversial positions on social, economic, and cultural issues will inevitably attract hostile attention to any public subsidy or tax preference benefiting the positions' proponents. The 1999 contretemps between the Brooklyn Museum of Art and New York Mayor Giuliani over the aptly named "Sensation" exhibit brought many of these elements together in a volatile mix. The mayor, objecting to perceived religious slights in the avant-garde artwork, threatened both to end the museum's municipal funding and to terminate its lease of city property. These legal actions were eventually dropped (Feuer 2000), but not before months of controversy and embarrassing investigations of museum practices, from the extent to which private collectors and auction houses control museum shows (Dobrzynski 1999) to demands by some museums for commissions on private art sold after exhibit there (Dobrzynski 2000). The drama encouraged caustic and satirical attacks that implicitly or directly questioned municipal funding for the museum. One reporter described guests at a Brooklyn Museum reception as "nibbling shrimp and baby lobster tails, talking on cell phones and solemnly contemplating such works of art as a sink and plumbing nestled in what looked like a musician's case" (Kifner 1999). Conservative columnist William Safire charged that the "museum's serenely elitist board members are either incredibly stupid or knew—and did not care—that this would (a) offend the religious, (b) anger and divide the city, (c) make a ton of money for the exhibition's owners, and (d) make the museum's staff the heroes of free expression with their own set" (Safire 1999).

The National Endowment for the Arts (NEA) has encountered similar problems repeatedly over the past two decades, receiving nearly equal measures of criticism for being too avant-garde, too timid, too elitist, and too populist (Brenson 1998; Miller 1997). One commentator wrote of "a tension at the very heart of the NEA: How can a national agency in a democracy make decisions that are, in their very essence, anti-democratic? . . . But if the NEA is not elitist, what do we need it for?" (Rothstein 1997, §2, 1). The difficulty of promoting public funding for activities that disturb public sensibilities has led some commentators to despair of government patronage of the arts: "One is tempted to say the hell with it, let it go down, if only to end these endless, boring disputes about the immorality of American artists and their nefarious efforts to pick the pockets of poor hardworking taxpayers" (Brustein 1997, 31). Ironically, the great private museums that are often cited as the alternative to publicly funded arts organizations are themselves beneficiaries of substantial governmental support, not least through their property-tax exemptions. Therefore it is not surprising that they should encounter some measure of the turbulence that accompanies direct public funding.

Charity and Commerce

One cultural development that has affected the form as well as the function of many nonprofit organizations over the past two decades has been the emergence of free-market triumphalism, with its concomitant esteem for deregulation, businesslike procedures, entrepreneurial attitudes, and private-sector initiatives. At a time when nonprofit institutions have found themselves under pressure to operate more efficiently, rely less on public funding, and emulate business practices, new uncertainty has necessarily arisen as to the definition of "charitable" activity.

The most dramatic instance of this reconfiguration concerns the health care industry—the very term indicating the new influence of market forces. The continuing national debate over the appropriate balance of public and private roles in this sector obviates any fixed and settled norms for institutional operations. Although "the growing market power of health care payers is shrinking hospital managers' residual discretion to pursue non-market purposes" (Bloche 1995, 388), nonprofit health care providers must distinguish themselves from commercial ventures.

A formal legal challenge by the state of Texas to the tax-exempt status of Houston's Methodist Hospital, the nation's largest private nonprofit hospital, typified this phenomenon. After the hospital successfully defended its exemption, one Texas legislator remarked, "Methodist's contention that getting paid to care for rich people is as charitable as caring for poor people for free is offensive" (Taylor 1993). The *Boston Globe* reported a more wide-ranging approach to a similar controversy in Massachusetts: "Secretary of State William F. Galvin said yesterday he will give the state's health maintenance organizations until November to institute sweeping consumer-friendly reforms or he will move to strip them of their nonprofit status" (Cassidy 1999, A1).

One analysis considers the property-tax exemption part of the cross-subsidization that allows nonprofit hospitals to treat those unable to pay for their care:

> In at least one regard, nonprofits exploit everyone, although by cheating on cost rather than quality. If the nonprofit hospital views its role as providing health care to those in need, everyone pays the cross-subsidy for charges which they did not incur. Because our society is not willing to pay for universal health insurance, the nonprofit hospital attempts to recover unreimbursed costs from two smaller groups: the citizens that live within the local taxing district and the insurance companies of patients. This system has been defended as a second-best solution. The reasoning goes something like this: Health care is akin to a right; society is unwilling to pay for that right; the nonprofit hospitals do well by cross-subsidizing; and make the "right" a reality. (Hyman 1990, 371)

Hyman continues indignantly, "This is absurd," citing Articles I, II and III of the Constitution for the proposition that legislative, executive, and judicial powers are vested in the federal government and that hospitals do not have the power to create or implement rights (ibid., 371).

This contrast between the literal precision of theory and the ambiguities of practice is another source of the conflicting public expectations for nonprofit operations. An advocate for affordable housing acknowledged a parallel conflict in support for tax incentives to private developers: "In the present political climate, which is witnessing increasing demands for lower taxes and less government spending, visibility and political accountability must be counted as liabilities. . . . While tax incentives are not the most equitable, effective, or efficient method of providing an adequate supply of low-income housing, at present they are the only method" (Stevenson 1979, 118–19). The author's reference to the "present political climate" is two decades old, but the situation is unlikely to change soon.

The now-perennial challenges to tax exemptions for YMCA and hospital-based fitness centers evidence the competitive pressures on both tax-exempt and commercial organizations. These disputes vividly highlight the uncertain, varied, and subjective criteria that influence exemption determinations. The Oregon YMCA left itself open to easy rebuttal by arguing that "physical development facilities such as weight rooms, track and basketball courts, as well as its monitored exercise program for cardiac patients, relieve the government of the cost of providing such facilities" (*The Young Men's Christian Association of Columbia-Willamette v. Department of Revenue*, 784 P.2d 1086, 1093 (Or. 1989)), but a Tennessee court was equally dismissive of the argument that a hospital gift shop "is not a necessary component of the treatment of the sick, ill or infirm":

> It may be true, as the State contends, that "The purchase of a sweatshirt or Christmas tree ornament certainly in no way assists in the recovery of a broken leg or the cure of cancer," but our analysis must take into account the total effect of the operation of the gift shop on the mission of the hospital, rather than focussing on the dubious therapeutic value of some of the items in its stock. (*Middle Tennessee Medical Center v. Assessment Appeals Commission*, 1994 Tenn. App. Lexis 43, 1994 WL 32584 (Tenn. App. 1994))[14]

In light of the political sensitivity to commercial activity by nonprofit organizations, it is ironic that nonprofits have adopted commercial formulations in describing their operations. For example, the abortion-rights groups challenging the Catholic Church's exempt status characterized themselves as competitors to its positions of advocacy, similar to economic competitors harmed by favoritism to a rival. The Second Circuit rejected this argument in part because "affording standing on that basis would lack a limiting principle, and would effectively give standing to any spectator who supported a given side in public political debate" (*Abortion Rights Mobilization v. United States Catholic Conference*, 885 F.2d 1020, 1030 (2d Cir. 1989), *cert. denied*, 495 U.S. 918 (1990)).

More recently, the 1997 *Camps Newfound* case overturned a Maine law that restricted exemptions to institutions primarily benefiting state residents, holding that the law discriminated against interstate commerce. The court found that the charitable summer camp challenging the statute "unquestionably engaged in commerce," and held that "for purposes of Commerce Clause analysis, any categorical distinction between the activities of profit-making enterprises and not-for-profit entities is therefore wholly illusory" (*Camps Newfound/Owatonna, Inc. v. Town of Harrison*, 520 U.S. 564, 586 (1997)). As Evelyn Brody pointed out, "Paradoxically, though, the charities' posture in *Camps Newfound*, while bolstering their constitutional argument, might undermine their political support. The public appears uneasy about, if not hostile to, the increasing nonprofit commercialism" (Brody 1997, 452). A report on the 1997 annual meeting of the Federation of Tax Administrators summarized the Federation's view of this case: "Nonprofits are in business in the same way as for-profits. They just zero out income" (Adams 1997, 16).

Uneasiness about the nonprofit sector's size and influence greatly compounds when this power is exercised in commercial activities. New York University won the court battle over tax-exempt income from its ownership of Mueller Spaghetti Company (*C. F. Mueller Co. v. Commissioner*, 190 F.2d 120 (2d Cir. 1951)) but lost that particular war when political reaction led to federal taxation of unrelated business income (Wellford and Gallagher 1988, 82–83). In the current era of nonprofit affinity cards and off-site museum stores,[15] when an association of Christian retailers has begun offering seminars on "How to Start and Run a Successful Church Retail Store" (Miller 1999), it is not unusual to encounter public releases of this sort:

> In the last half-century, and especially in the last 30 years, the nonprofit sector has grown much faster than either the business or governmental sectors as a percentage of national income and percentage of national workforce. According to the IRS report, between 1975 and 1990, while the nation's GDP grew 52 percent, nonprofit revenue grew 227 percent, both figures adjusted for inflation. Nationally, nonprofit organizations employ 10 million people, more than the federal government and state governments combined, excluding the military. In the state of California, the nonprofit economy equals the size of the state budget, about $60 billion. Dona-

tions to charity each year equal the combined profits of the Fortune 500 corporations. Nonprofits are big business. (O'Neill 1997)

This statement was intended to celebrate the success of nonprofit organizations, but it echoes many earlier writings that warned of such an increase in nonprofits' economic power. Those predictions were often used
to attack the charitable tax exemption. It was not a new theme even in
1875, when President Ulysses S. Grant warned in his State of the Union
message of "an evil that, if permitted to continue, will probably lead to
great trouble in our land before the close of the nineteenth century. It is
the accumulation of the vast amount of untaxed church property"
(Robertson 1968, 79).

School for Scandal

Like many aspects of contemporary life, the political climate for tax exemptions has been shaped by media scrutiny. Even if the incidence of actual
wrongdoing is no greater than in the past, the intensified journalistic sur-
veillance and coverage, together with the larger amounts of money at the
disposal of the nonprofit sector, ensure that the scandals that do occur are
likely to be on a larger scale and to receive more extensive publicity.

Unfortunately, charitable organizations have not stinted in contributing to this spectacle. The 1990s alone saw charges of sexual misconduct
against the president of Covenant House (Goodstein 1990) and the executive director of the NAACP (Jordan 1994). The head of the Foundation
for New Era Philanthropy was charged with 83 counts of mail fraud
(Walsh 1996). Evangelist Jim Bakker spent more than five years in prison
(Smothers 1994), the assets of his PTL ministry having been sold to an
investor with "interests in real estate, clothing, garbage collection and
landfills" (*New York Times* 1988). William Aramony went from leading
the United Way of America to serving a seven-year prison sentence for
defrauding the organization of more than $1 million, yet in 1998 a federal
judge upheld his United Way pension of more than $4 million on grounds
that "a felon, no matter how despised, does not lose his right to enforce a
contract" (*Aramony v. United Way of America*, 28 F. Supp. 2d 147, 153
(S.D.N.Y. 1998), *affirmed in part, reversed in part, and remanded, Aramony v. United Way Replacement Benefit Plan*, 191 F.3d 140 (2d Cir. 1999).
This led to headlines such as "Imprisoned Charity Chief Wins $2.3M"
(Smith 1998) and "Judge Gives Thief Who Headed United Way $2 Mil-
lion Pension" (Wee 1998).[16]

Stanford President Donald Kennedy lost his post after an investigation of billing practices found that Stanford had charged the government for flowers, furniture, parties, a grand piano, football tickets, and depreciation on a yacht as "indirect research costs" (Cooper 1991). Although initial reports claimed Stanford had overcharged the federal government by more than $200 million, the dispute was ultimately settled for an amount between $3 million and $4 million, with an acknowledgement that the issue concerned a contract dispute and not fraud or misuse of funds (Celis 1994). Even after this settlement, the *Washington Post* editorialized, "The harm done to universities' credibility by this idiotic behavior—at a time when higher education was loudly lamenting its poverty and calling for more government funds—was topped only by the dimness of university officials who insisted this was the sort of mistake anybody could make" (*Washington Post* 1994). An article in the *New York Times* then drew a connection between these charges and allegations of drug use, sexual harassment, and plagiarism (Deutsch 1991). After Kennedy returned to teaching, his course on ethics was noted by the *Washington Post* in an article entitled "The Year of the Weird" (Shepherd 1993).

In 1998, Dr. Peter Diamandopoulos, who had been forced from the presidency of Adelphi University amid charges of overcompensation and mismanagement (including a 62 percent drop in enrollment during his tenure), took a position at Boston University, whose chancellor and former president, John Silber, was an Adelphi trustee until he and other board members were removed by the New York State Board of Regents. The two had been "friendly competitors for the rank as the nation's highest-paid university president" (Lambert 1998).

Government prosecutors and investigative committees are important elements in the search for scandal. Donald Kennedy's accounting difficulties attracted national attention after congressional hearings by Rep. John D. Dingell (D-MI). Dingell's earlier investigation of the Nobel Prize–winning biologist David Baltimore for alleged research fraud had caused Baltimore to lose the presidency of Rockefeller University (Kevles 1998). Similarly, in 1997, the New York attorney general sued the former trustees of Adelphi University to recover millions of dollars spent on wrongful contracts, the trustees' legal defense, and "a lavish lifestyle for the college's president" (Lambert 1997). The suit was settled in 1998 when the former trustees agreed to pay Adelphi $1.23 million and assume responsibility for more than $400,000 in legal bills (Halbfinger 1998). Even the Girl Scouts were investigated by the Connecticut attorney general after a local troop leader complained about the allocation of revenues from cookie sales (Grubman 1994).

This climate of scrutiny does not require allegations of illegal behavior. A 1999 *Wall Street Journal* profile of Richard Koshalek, director of the Los Angeles Museum of Contemporary Art, had the air of an exposé:

> While the Los Angeles Museum of Contemporary Art pays its director a healthy $225,000 annually and gives him access to tens of thousands of dollars more for entertainment and fund-raising expenses, it still takes much more than that for Mr. Koshalek to keep pace with the multimillionaires he courts. . . . "The amount of support from museum trustees for my lifestyle in this role would startle people," says Mr. Koshalek, who estimates that trustees and donors shell out about $500,000 each year to host museum dinners and events. But trustees say living the high life is simply part of Mr. Koshalek's duties: "I would feel Richard isn't doing his job if I didn't see him in places like this," says museum trustee Dean Valentine, president of Viacom Inc.'s UPN television network, seated at a nearby table at Spago. (Langley 1999, A1)

This approach leads to articles investigating "deluxe hotels . . . posh establishments . . . dinner parties that cost thousands of dollars" with headlines such as "Do Limousine Service, Luxury Hotel Rooms and a $5,500 Dinner Belong on the San Diego Museum of Art's Balance Sheets?" (Turegano 1995).

Just as these incidents must be considered in the context of overall nonprofit activities, the impact of their coverage can be evaluated only in the larger setting of intense media scrutiny of all type of institutions, public and private. After a *U.S. News & World Report* cover story attacked nonprofit businesses under the headline "Tax Exempt! You Pay Uncle Sam, How Come Thousands of American Corporations Do Not?" (Pound, Cohen, and Loeb 1995), *Time* magazine devoted an entire special issue to similar investigations of for-profit operations (Barlett and Steele 1998). Just as the expansion of property-tax exemptions weakens the perception of the charitable exemption as a notable departure from uniformity, so tireless journalistic attention to scandal diminishes the impact of any single instance of such coverage.

Conclusion

The unsettled political climate confronting charitable institutions is not the result of any single factor, nor is it confined to the nonprofit sphere. It reflects instabilities inherent in the structure of the property tax, a changing cultural understanding of charitable works, and a political environment receptive to challenge and confrontation. Charities encounter difficulties because of this situation, but also contribute to and benefit from it. Greater resources and more efficient management undermine earlier distinctions between business and charity but are clearly an advantage to the nonprofit sector, even as they force the sector to clarify its noncommercial goals and mission. An irreverent and skeptical tone of public debate may deprive religious and charitable organizations of the deference and respect they could command in an earlier era, but it also permits unconventional and challenging explorations that a prior age would not readily have tolerated into religion, social inquiry, or the arts. A period suspicious of taxation and big government, a period that not only permits but encourages minute investigation of any allegations of official wrongdoing, will often be an uncomfortable one for large institutions that undergo such scrutiny. Yet mistrust of public and commercial enterprises also enhances the relative standing of churches and private charities that are perceived as more honest, more compassionate, or more efficient providers of social services.

The charitable exemption from the property tax touches on too many deeply felt and contentious issues ever to be free of political disputes. At any given time, the form of those disputes will reflect pressing contemporary concerns and unresolved ambiguities in social goals, behavioral expectations, and cultural norms. Confronting and coming to terms with these conflicts is one way in which the nonprofit sector engages with the public life of its age.

NOTES

1. See, for example, *Loyola Marymount University v. Los Angeles Unified School District*, Cal. Rptr. 2d 424, 432 (Calif. Ct. App. 1996); and *State Highway Commission of Kansas v. City of Topeka*, 393 P.2d 1008 (Kan. 1964).

2. *San Marcos Water District v. San Marcos Unified School District*, 720 P.2d 935 (California 1986).

3. This may be particularly likely when state legislation addresses specific local exemptions. For example, one 1998 Virginia law designated as exempt specific properties held by the Fairfax Good Shepherd Housing and Family Services, the Virginia Congress of Parents and Teachers, Shen-Paco Industries, the Robert E. Rose Memorial Foundation, Shalom Et Benedictus, Zulekia Court Number 35, L.O.S.N.A., Riverfront Management Corporation, Sophia House, Hospice Support Care, the Audubon Naturalist Society of the Central Atlantic States, the Avenel Foundation, the National D-Day Memorial Foun-

dation, the Williamsburg Land Conservancy, the Beth Sholom Home of Eastern Virginia, Lend-A-Paw Relief Organization, the Jewish Foundation for Group Homes, the Gainesville Ruritan Club, and the Northern Virginia Family Service (Tax Analysts 1998).

4. *Bolt v. Lansing*, 587 N.W.2d 264 (Mich. 1998); *Oil Company v. State Tax Commission*, 942 P.2d 906 (Utah 1996).

5. *Federal Reserve Bank v. Metrocentre Improvement Dist. #1*, 657 F.2d 183 (8th Cir. 1981).

6. *County of Suffolk v. Van Bourgondien, Inc.*, 392 N.E.2d 1236 (N.Y 1979); *Great Atlantic & Pacific Tea Co. v. Kiernan*, 366 N.E. 2d 808 (N.Y. 1977); *Jos. E. Seagram & Sons, Inc. v. Tax Commission*, 200 N.E.2d 447 (N.Y. 1964); and *Xerox Corp. v. Ross*, 421 N.Y.S.2d 475 (N.Y. App. Div. 1979).

7. *FMC Corp. v. Unmack*, 699 N.E.2d 893 (N.Y. 1998); *Niagara Mohawk Power Corp. v. Assessor of Geddes*, 699 N.E.2d 899 (N.Y. 1998); and *Saratoga Harness Racing, Inc. v. Williams*, 697 N.E.2d 164 (N.Y. 1998).

8. See, for example, *Church of St. Paul and St. Andrew v. Barwick*, 496 N.E.2d 183 (N.Y. 1986); and *Rector, Wardens, & Members of Vestry of St. Bartholomew's Church v. New York*, 914 F.2d 348 (2d Cir. 1990).

9. See, for example, *City of Boerne v. Flores*, 521 U.S. 507 (1997).

10. For example, *Abortion Rights Mobilization, Inc. v. United States Catholic Conference*, 885 F.2d 1020 (2d Cir. 1989), *cert. denied*, 495 U.S. 918 (1990).

11. Three years after the Court of Appeals upheld the constitutionality of the law requiring exclusive use for religious purposes as a condition of exemption (*Town of Hardenburgh v. State*, 421 N.E.2d 795 (N.Y. 1981), *appeal dismissed*, 454 U.S. 958 (1981)), the *New York Times* reported, "Today, resident taxes in Hardenburgh are down nearly 50 percent, to 1974 levels, Town Assessor Robert Kerwick reports. What has happened, he says, is that the state has bought for parkland and put back on the tax rolls 3,200 acres owned by the Catskill Center for Conservation and 1,776 acres held by the Boy Scouts of America. The state is now Hardenburgh's biggest payer of the property tax. 'They represent 75 percent of the tax base,' Mr. Kerwick says. 'The exemptions that are on the rolls at present are quite minimal'" (*New York Times* 1983). For another case involving the Universal Life Church, see *County of Sheboygan v. Research Universal Life Church*, 555 N.W.2d 410 (Wis. Ct. App. 1996), which permitted no religious exemption for family residences or for a tire store.

12. *Holy Spirit Association for the Unification of World Christianity v. Tax Commission of the City of New York*, 435 N.E.2d 662 (N.Y. 1982).

13. *Abortion Rights Mobilization, Inc. v. United States Catholic Conference*, 885 F.2d 1020 (2d Cir. 1989), *cert. denied*, 495 U.S. 918 (1990).

14. The Internal Revenue Service has found an exempt purpose in a hospital wellness center whose fees permitted a "significant segment of the population" to participate (IRS 1990).

15. It is tempting for commentators to compare this culture of commerce to an earlier period when culture and commerce did not converge. "Once upon a time, museum retailing was a fringe operation, limited to merchandise that really did relate to the institution's historic mission: postcards of great art, catalogs, reference books" (Gibson 1999, W17). In Revenue Rulings 73-104 and 73-105 (IRS 1973a, 1973b), the Internal Revenue Service held the sale of items related to the educational purposes of a

museum to be related to the museum's exempt purpose. Cultural disputes over controversial programming and exhibits also extend to goods sold at museum shops, as when the Brooklyn Museum of Art "raised eyebrows" with items at its gift shop based on works by "animal-corpse sculptor Damien Hirst" (Bensinger 1999, B1).

16. After many subsequent hearings, a $3.2 million pension payment ordered by the trial court was overturned on appeal (*Aramony v. United Way of America*, 86 F. Supp. 2d 199 (S.D.N.Y. 2000), *rev'd*, 254 F.3d 403 (2d Cir. 2001)).

REFERENCES

Adams, Sally. 1997. "FTA 65th Annual Meeting Focuses on Taxing Transactions in a Shifting Technology Environment." 58 *CCH State Tax Review* 58: 12–16.

American Law Reports. 1999. "Standing of One Taxpayer to Complain of Underassessment or Nonassessment of Property of Another for State and Local Taxation." *American Law Reports 4th* 9: 428.

———. 1997. "Inclusion of Tax-Exempt Property in Determining Value of Taxable Property for Debt Limit Purposes." *American Law Reports 2d* 30: 903.

Bailey, Doug. 1999. "Harvard Study Touts Its Economic Impact." *Boston Globe*, September 30, B2.

Balk, Alfred. 1971. *The Free List: Property Without Taxes.* New York: Russell Sage Foundation.

Barlett, Donald L., and James B. Steele. 1998. "Corporate Welfare: A *Time* Investigation Uncovers How Hundreds of Companies Get on the Dole—And Why It Costs Every Working American the Equivalent of Two Weeks' Pay Every Year." *Time*, November 9. Special issue.

Bensinger, Ken. 1999. "Scandal Spills Over (Check The Gift Shop) at Brooklyn Museum." *Wall Street Journal*, October 4, B1.

Bloche, M. Gregg. 1995. "Health Policy Below the Waterline: Medical Care and the Charitable Exemption." *Minnesota Law Review* 80: 299–405.

Bonbright, James. 1937. *The Valuation of Property*, vol. 1. New York: McGraw-Hill.

Boston Globe. 1971. "Colleges and Taxes." Editorial. August 30, 8.

Brenson, Michael. 1998. "Washington's Stake in the Arts." *New York Times*, April 12, sec. 2, 1.

Briffault, Richard. 1999. "A Government for Our Time? Business Improvement Districts and Urban Governance." *Columbia Law Review* 99: 365–477.

Brody, Evelyn. 1997. "Hocking the Halo: Implications of the Charities' Winning Briefs in *Camps Newfound/Owatonna, Inc.*" *Stetson Law Review* 27: 433–56.

Brustein, Robert. 1997. "Mend It, Don't End It." *The New Republic*, October 6, 31.

Cassidy, Tina. 1999. "Galvin Tells HMOs to Reform by November." *Boston Globe*, September 7, A1.

Celis, William. 1994. "Navy Settles a Fraud Case on Stanford Research Costs." *New York Times*, October 19, A16.

Clotfelter, Charles T. 1989. "Tax-Induced Distortions in the Voluntary Sector." *Case Western Reserve Law Review* 39: 663–703.

Connecticut Law Tribune. 1996. "Challenging Times Ahead For Charities." October 14, 21.

Cooper, Kenneth J. 1991. "Antique Commode as Overhead Expense; House Sub-committee Examines Stanford's Questionable Billings for Government Research." *Washington Post*, March 14, A23.

Deutsch, Claudia H. 1991. "Academia Fails the Ethics Test." *New York Times*, November 3, sec. 4A (education supplement), 26.

Dobrzynski, Judith H. 2000. "A Possible Conflict by Museums in Art Sales." *New York Times*, February 21, E1.

———. 1999. "Private Collections Routine at Museums." *New York Times*, October 1, B6.

Doerr, David. 1996a. "California Taxpayers Sue to Invalidate Los Angeles County Library Tax." *State Tax Notes* 7: 880 (October 3).

———. 1996b. "Los Angeles Supervisors Rescind Library Tax; Lawsuit Is Dropped." *State Tax Notes* 7: 1226 (October 31).

Feuer, Alan. 2000. "Giuliani Dropping His Bitter Battle with Art Museum." *New York Times*, March 28, A1.

Fulton, William. 1991. "Another Legacy of Proposition 13." *Los Angeles Times*, December 1, M6.

Gaul, Gilbert M., and Neill A. Borowski. 1993. *Free Ride: The Tax-Exempt Economy*. Kansas City: Andrews and McMeel.

Gibson, Eric. 1999. "I Went to the Met and They Sold Me This Lousy T-Shirt." *Wall Street Journal*, October 1, W17.

Glaberson, William. 1996. "In Era of Fiscal Damage Control, Cities Fight Idea of 'Tax Exempt.'" *New York Times*, February 21, A1.

Goodstein, Laurie. 1990. "Priest's Misconduct Detailed; Sexual Activity Cited by Covenant House." *Washington Post*, August 3, A3.

Grubman, Cathy. 1994. "Challenge, Change, Controversy." *Washington Post*, January 3, B5.

Halbfinger, David M. 1998. "Lawsuits Over Ouster of Adelphi Chief Are Settled." *New York Times*, November 18, B1.

Heidelmark, William J. 1999. *Exemptions from Real Property Taxation in New York State*. Albany: New York State Office of Real Property Services.

Hyman, David A. 1990. "The Conundrum of Charitability: Reassessing Tax Exemption for Hospitals." *American Journal of Law and Medicine* 16: 327–80.

Internal Revenue Service. 1990. Private Letter Ruling 91-10-042.

———. 1973a. Letter Ruling Rev. Rul. 73-104, 1973-1 C.B. 263.

———. 1973b. Revenue Ruling 73-105, 1973-1 C.B. 264.

IRS. *See* Internal Revenue Service.

Jordan, Emma Coleman. 1994. "Prisoners of Sex; Will the NAACP Get the Message That Equality Begins at Home?" *Washington Post*, August 21, C3.

Kevles, Daniel J. 1998. *The Baltimore Case: A Trial of Politics, Science, and Character*. New York: Norton.

Kifner, John. 1999. "Art Lovers Peruse Exhibit and Defy Giuliani." *New York Times*, October 1, B1.

Kurtz, Jerome. 1993. "Churches Risk Their Tax Exemption." *New York Times*, May 17, A16.

Lambert, Bruce. 1998. "President Who Was Forced From Job at Adelphi is Hired at Boston." *New York Times*, December 6, sec. 1, 58.

———. 1997. "State Sues to Recover Funds Spend by Adelphi's Ex-Trustees." *New York Times*, March 25, B5.

Langley, Monica. 1999. "Hanger-On: A Museum Director Finds Wooing the Rich Means 'Living the Life.'" *Wall Street Journal*, May 26, A1.

Larson, Martin A., and C. Stanley Lowell. 1976. *The Religious Empire*. Washington: R.B. Luce & Co.

Lindsey, Robert. 1983. "Evangelist's 'Cathedral' Loses Tax Exemption." *New York Times*, January 26, A13.

Miller, Judith. 1997. "Study Links Drop in Support to Elitist Attitude in the Arts." *New York Times*, October 13, A1.

Miller, Lisa. 1999. "Registers Ring in Sanctuary Stores." *Wall Street Journal*, December 17, B1.

Montana Attorney General. 1995. *Opinions of the Montana Attorney General* 46: 7.

New York Times. 1995. "Ithaca's Mayor Blocks Cornell Construction Projects." May 3, B9.

———. 1994. "Reporters Win $25,000 Prize." March 12, sec. 1, 47.

———. 1988. "PTL Reports Deal of $115 Million for Assets." October 5, A28.

———. 1983. "Tax Rebellion." March 13, sec. 1, 49.

O'Neill, Michael. 1997. Institute for Nonprofit Organization Management, University of San Francisco, "Growing Pains: The Conflict Over Nonprofits and Public Policy." http://www.tmcenter.org/cwc/cwc-oneill2.html.

O'Sullivan, Arthur, Terri A. Sexton, and Steven M. Sheffrin. 1995. *Property Taxes and Tax Revolts: The Legacy of Proposition 13*. Cambridge: Cambridge University Press.

Pound, Edward T., Gary Cohen, and Penny Loeb. 1995. "Tax Exempt! You Pay Uncle Sam, How Come Thousands of American Corporations Do Not?" *U.S. News & World Report*, October 2, 36.

Robertson, D.B. 1968. *Should Churches Be Taxed?* Philadelphia: The Westminster Press.

Rosenbaum, David E. 1999. "Tax-Exempt Status Rejected, Christian Coalition Regroups." *New York Times*, June 11, A5.

Rothstein, Edward. 1997. "Where a Democracy and Its Money Have No Place." *New York Times*, October 26, sec. 2, 1.

Safire, William. 1999. "Manichaean Madness." *New York Times*, September 30, A29.

San Diego Union-Tribune. 1986. "Cathedral Wary on Event Plans After Tax Woes." August 16, A13.

———. 1984. "IRS Mails Tax Bill to TV Evangelist." March 9, A21.

Seligman, Edwin R.A. 1913. *Essays in Taxation* (8th ed.). New York: Macmillan.

Shepherd, Chuck. 1993. "1993: The Year of the Weird." *Washington Post*, December 26, C3.

Smith, Greg B. 1998. "Imprisoned Charity Chief Wins $2.3M." *New York Daily News*, October 23, 34.

Smith, William H., and Carolyn P. Chiechi. 1974. *Private Foundations: Before and After the Tax Reform Act of 1969*. Washington, American Enterprise Institute for Public Policy Research.

Smothers, Ronald. 1994. "Ex-Television Evangelist Bakker Ends Prison Sentence for Fraud." *New York Times*, December 2, A18.

Stevenson, D. 1979. "Tax Reform and Real Estate Tax Shelters: Consequences for Low-Income Housing." *University of Cincinnati Law Review* 48: 99–119.

Taylor, Gary. 1993. "Lawsuit Dismissal Doesn't Resolve Care Issue." *National Law Journal*, March 15, 10.

Tax Analysts. 1998. "Virginia Final SB 5 Grants Property Tax Exemptions to Certain Organizations." *State Tax Today*, 98 STN 82-17 (April 29).

Torkelson, Jean. 1997. "Good Reasons for 'Pay to Pray.'" *Denver Rocky Mountain News*, October 11, 12D.

Turegano, Preston. 1995. "Do Limousine Service, Luxury Hotel Rooms and a $5,500 Dinner Belong on the San Diego Museum of Art's Balance Sheets?" *San Diego Union-Tribune*, October 8, E1.

Walsh, Sharon. 1996. "Head of Charity Charged with Fraud; New Era Philanthropy Foundation Said to Have Collected $350 Million." *Washington Post*, September 28, C1.

Washington Post. 1994. "The Research Bill at Stanford." Editorial. October 29, A18.

Wee, Eric L. 1998. "Judge Gives Thief Who Headed United Way $2 Million Pension." *Washington Post*, October 24, 3A.

Weiss, Joanna. 1999. "Harvard Touts Its $2B Impact on Economy." *Boston Globe*, September 27, B1.

Wellford, W. Harrison, and Janne G. Gallagher. 1988. *Unfair Competition? The Challenge to Charitable Tax Exemption.* Washington, D.C.: National Assembly of National Voluntary Health and Social Welfare Organizations.

Wherry, Robert A., Jr. 1996. "Colorado Voters Spare Nonprofits from a Property Tax." *State Tax Notes* 11: 1336.

3

Local Government Finance and the Economics of Property-Tax Exemption

Dick Netzer

The Role of the Property Tax in Local Government Finance

At the outset of the Great Depression, the property tax provided about two-thirds of all local government revenue (table 3-1), and local governments were by far the most important providers of public services in the American federal system. By 1950, the property tax provided less than half of local government revenue, mainly because of a substantial increase in state aid to local governments—that is, a shift to state-levied taxes on income and sales (table 3-2). Immediately after the war, there was a significant increase in local government reliance on taxes other than the property tax (mainly in California, Illinois, Ohio, and Pennsylvania) and on user charges and other nontax revenue sources. Then, from roughly 1950 to the mid-1960s, the role of the property tax in local finance stabilized, as rapid increases in local government expenditure were matched by increases in both property values and effective property-tax rates.

The Great Society ushered in a sharp 15-year decline in the role of the property tax, which was providing only 26 percent of local revenue by 1980. The main factor was a significant increase in the federal and state roles, combined with smaller increases in the roles of nontax revenue and local taxes other than the property tax. The "revolt" against rising effective property-tax rates had begun, with modestly effective restrictions in several states by 1970, further and more effective property-tax

Table 3-1. *Percentage Distribution of Total Local Government Revenue, Excluding "Insurance-Trust" Revenue*[a]

Revenue Source	1932	1950	1960	1970	1980	1990	1996
Property taxes	68	44	43	37	26	27	26
Revenue from state and federal government	13	28	28	34	40	34	35
Nontax revenue[b]	17	22	23	22	26	30	30
Nonproperty taxes	2	6	6	7	8	9	9

Sources: State and local tax revenue data for 1932, 1950, 1960, and 1970 from the *Historical Statistics* volume of the *1977 Census of Governments;* for 1980 and 1990 from the Census Bureau annual releases, *Government Finances in 1979–80* and *in 1989–90.* Data for 1996 downloaded from the Census Bureau Web site (http://www.census.gov), July 1999.

[a] "Insurance-trust" revenue of local governments consists almost entirely of employee contributions to retirement funds and earnings of those funds.

[b] Nearly 80 percent of nontax revenue in 1995–96 comprised charges for services of various kinds. The remainder was mainly interest earnings.

Table 3-2. *Property Tax as a Percentage of Total Tax Revenue and Gross Domestic Product, by Year*

Year	Property Tax as Percentage of	
	Total Tax Revenue	Gross Domestic Product
1932	72.8	7.74
1950	46.2	2.56
1960	45.4	3.12
1970	39.2	3.29
1980	30.5	2.46
1990	31.0	2.71
1996	30.4	2.74

Sources: State-local tax revenue data for 1932, 1950, 1960, and 1970 from the *Historical Statistics* volume of the *1977 Census of Governments;* for 1980 and 1990 from the Census Bureau annual releases, *Government Finances in 1979–80* and *in 1989–90.* Gross domestic product data from *Statistical Abstract of the United States,* various issues. Tax revenue data for 1996 downloaded from the Census Bureau Web site (http://www.census.gov), July 1999.

"relief" measures in the 1970s, and then California's Proposition 13, a hugely effective restriction that became law on July 1, 1978, about three weeks after being approved by the voters.

But despite new restrictions reflecting the "revolt" in numerous states, the role of the property tax has changed little nationwide since 1980. The decline in federal aid, especially in federal aid directly to local governments (rather than through the states), that began in 1980 was not offset by increases in state aid in most states—state taxes as well as local ones became objects of the tax revolt. The role of user charges continued to expand so that, by 1996, intergovernmental aid and locally generated nontax revenue were both more important revenue sources than the property tax (see Netzer 1992 for more on the increased reliance on user charges in the 1970s and 1980s). In 1950 and again in 1965, an informed observer might well have predicted that the American property tax would soon become as unimportant as property taxes then were in much of the rest of the world. Even among the English-speaking countries, whose local governments had traditionally been sustained by the property tax, the property tax is close to vestigial. But of all the OECD (Organization for Economic Cooperation and Development) countries, only the United States has a property tax that is now marginally higher relative to GDP than it was in 1950 (table 3-2).

It is somewhat misleading to speak of "the" property tax; since colonial times, each state has had a distinctive property tax policy. As with other differences among the states, some property-tax differences can be explained in part by fairly distinctive factors, but the origin of and rationale for some of the differences are mysterious. In any event, table 3-3 shows the regional differences in property-tax revenue, as a percentage of both total state and local tax revenue and state personal income, in 1962 (before the slide in the role of the property tax) and in 1994–95. Historically, the northeastern and midwestern states have relied relatively heavily on the property tax and the southern states relatively lightly, with the western region about average. But there were and continue to be wide variations within regions. Superficially, there seems to have been some convergence among the states over time, except for among the western states, where Proposition 13 appears to have spread. However, the standard deviation of the two measures relative to their means actually increased somewhat between 1962 and 1994–95.

Table 3-3. *Property-Tax Revenue as a Percentage of State-Local Tax Revenue and Personal Income, by Region (1962 and 1994–95)*

| | Property Tax Revenue as Percentage of | | | |
| | Total State-Local Tax Revenue | | Personal Income | |
	1962	1994–95	1962	1994–95
United States	**47.9**	**30.8**	**4.33**	**3.54**
Northeast	57.0	34.3	4.62	4.32
CT	53.6	37.7	4.57	4.60
DC	37.0	30.0	2.68	4.14
DE	20.5	14.6	1.58	1.63
MA	60.6	34.9	6.03	3.97
MD	41.7	26.9	3.48	2.96
ME	52.8	41.4	5.44	5.35
NH	63.6	64.1	5.73	6.10
NJ	64.7	46.9	5.41	5.45
NY	44.4	31.9	4.74	4.78
PA	34.7	28.4	3.01	3.16
RI	47.8	43.2	4.40	5.20
VT	45.2	44.7	5.32	5.52
Midwest	53.0	32.4	4.82	3.71
IA	56.6	35.0	5.94	4.34
IL	53.4	38.3	4.56	4.20
IN	56.2	33.2	4.83	3.56
KS	56.1	31.8	5.99	3.66
MI	49.3	28.0	4.84	3.06
MN	54.9	31.1	6.14	4.12
MO	42.6	25.6	3.37	2.69
ND	52.8	28.3	4.89	3.41
NE	70.5	37.7	5.57	4.48
OH	51.7	28.8	4.24	3.28
SD	58.4	40.4	5.97	4.17
WI	55.6	36.4	5.80	4.93
South	34.4	28.1	3.09	2.95
AL	20.3	12.6	1.68	1.19
AR	28.3	14.8	2.63	1.55
FL	41.2	35.9	3.91	3.77
GA	31.8	28.2	2.77	3.09
KY	30.3	16.2	2.68	1.92

Table 3-3. *Property-Tax Revenue as a Percentage of State-Local Tax Revenue and Personal Income, by Region (1962 and 1994–95) (Continued)*

	Property Tax Revenue as Percentage of			
	Total State-Local Tax Revenue		*Personal Income*	
	1962	*1994–95*	*1962*	*1994–95*
LA	22.6	16.6	2.61	1.70
MS	29.9	23.4	3.27	2.65
NC	27.9	21.9	2.51	2.47
OK	31.2	16.6	3.06	1.80
SC	24.3	29.2	2.14	3.14
TN	33.3	22.8	2.84	2.07
TX	45.3	36.7	4.12	3.81
VA	35.9	30.5	2.66	3.10
WV	27.2	19.4	2.60	2.25
West	*46.3*	*27.9*	*4.78*	*3.23*
AK	12.0	25.1	1.83	4.81
AZ	47.7	29.3	4.95	3.58
CA	50.2	27.8	5.25	3.14
CO	47.7	31.2	5.02	3.24
HI	27.8	16.9	1.75	2.16
ID	66.2	26.4	4.89	3.07
MT	56.8	43.2	5.88	5.09
NM	25.2	11.9	2.53	1.52
NV	31.1	20.7	2.84	2.38
OR	47.4	34.2	4.55	3.91
UT	44.1	24.9	4.49	3.03
WA	30.9	29.5	3.14	3.61
WY	53.4	40.2	5.54	4.82

Sources: 1962, Dick Netzer, *Economics of the Property Tax* (1966), Table 5-1, pp. 90–91. 1994–95, calculated from SLfin951.x, downloaded from the Bureau of the Census Web site.

There also are differences in the two measures. For example, as measured by the share of state-local tax revenue, the property tax as a share of state-local tax revenue has declined significantly in Massachusetts, Connecticut, New Jersey, and New York, but only in Massachusetts (among these states) was there a large decline in the tax relative to personal income. That is true of other regions as well.

The Changing Property-Tax Base

In its 19th-century heyday, the "general property tax" was indeed general in its coverage: All property, real and personal, owned by households and business entities was subject to the tax, in law if not in practice (there was some difficulty involved in discovering many assets less conspicuous than land and buildings). By the early 20th century, reformers agreed that the tax ought to be limited to those assets that actually could be discovered and valued by local assessors. So intangibles and household goods were exempted by law, as well as in practice, in the great majority of states by World War II. But half the states continued to apply the property tax to the one form of personal property for which there are reliable market value data: motor vehicles. All but four states continued to tax the value of business machinery and equipment until the 1960s, as was true also of non-farm business inventories and farm equipment and livestock. However, most states have subsequently exempted inventories from the tax, and some have exempted machinery and equipment as well. Tangible personal property related to business is being removed from the base in part for the familiar administrative reasons dating from the 19th century, in part in the belief that the step will foster economic development, and in part as a populist response to noisy complaints by small businesses. (It is impossible to overestimate the extent to which decisions on the property tax are based on widespread voter perceptions about aspects of the tax—for example, how heavy a burden it is compared to the past—which may be strikingly inconsistent with the facts.)

As of 1991, various types of personal property were generally taxable (that is, throughout a state):[1] business inventories (taxed by 15 states); commercial and industrial machinery and equipment (39 states); agricultural equipment and/or inventories (29 states); household personal property not used in the production of income (2 states); motor vehicles (13 states); and some types of intangible personal property (9 states) (U.S. Department of Commerce 1994). In 1961, personal property amounted to 16 percent of total taxable assessed value nationwide; by 1991, the percentage had declined to 8.8 percent (ibid., xv).

By 1980, the property-tax base in most states consisted of most real property owned by households and businesses; business machinery and equipment (including farm machinery); transportation; communications and public utility real and personal property; and, sometimes, motor vehicles. For much of the 20th century, the share of property-tax revenues derived from transportation, communications, and public utilities (the so-called TCPU sector) was large: 12.6 percent of total property-tax revenue and about 30 percent of property-tax revenue from nonfarm business property in 1957, when the sector accounted for about 11 percent of gross product originating in nonfarm business.[2] There were two reasons for this extraordinary share. First, the industries are capital intensive, and second, in nearly all states, utility property has been assessed by state agencies as entire operating systems, valued on a basis that reflects market value much more adequately than the methods used to assess ordinary commercial and industrial property. The result has been relative overassessment and overtaxation of utility property.

In recent years, this has changed considerably, and the utility share of the tax base has declined in many states. Nationally, the TCPU share probably is no more than 6 percent of the taxable property base now, less than half its share in 1957.[3] One reason is federal intervention, in the form of legislation that prohibits states from subjecting interstate transportation carriers to discriminatory taxation; the first of these laws, applying to railroads, took effect in 1979.[4] A second factor has been technological and regulatory changes in the telecommunications industry. There is now much less physical property actually owned and operated by telecommunications companies than there used to be, and much service is provided by firms that cannot be reached readily by a state's tax collectors. In 1957, the TCPU sector accounted for 42 percent of the total value of structures and equipment used in all industries; by 1997, that had declined to 27 percent. In 1957, it took $5.24 worth of structures and equipment to produce $1.00 of output in that sector; by 1997, it took only $3.49 to do so.[5]

In some states, there are substantial economic development tax incentives for business real property. Indeed, in some large central cities (notably New York), no new commercial structures are built without such preferences (not surprising, given that the target effective property-tax rate for commercial real property is 4.5 percent; City of New York Department of Finance 1998). However, in many if not most places, such preferences are more than offset by the preferential tax treatment of residential property in general (and for elderly and low-income owners more specifically) and of agricultural land, through comprehensive classification schemes (in which the different classes are taxed explicitly on the basis of values that are different fractions of market value) or by the use of specific preferences. Simultaneously, extralegal preferences to favored classes (that is, systematic underassessment not sanctioned by law of residential and other classes) has been much reduced in many parts of the country.[6]

In some states, the residential share of the tax base—about 41 percent in 1957 (Netzer 1966, 20)—was increased inadvertently by ineptly drafted property-tax caps, especially California's Proposition 13 and its imitators, that were intended mainly to protect homeowners. Property-tax laws and practice frequently distinguish between existing and new owners of real property. Politics dictates favoring existing owners, so the severe restrictions on increases in assessed values in Proposition 13 do not extend to home buyers. (Economics would dictate doing just the opposite, advising governments to provide incentives at the margin for additional investment in the local community; this is often done with regard to economic development preferences for business property.) But because the turnover of owner-occupied houses is far greater than for any other type of real property, especially in places where the population is growing rapidly, over time owner-occupied housing would become a larger fraction of the taxable property base under a Proposition 13-type arrangement.

The Uses of Property-Tax Revenue

It might seem obvious that the property tax is used for whatever it is that local governments do. However, because the property tax provides virtually all local school-district tax revenue, lesser shares of the own-source revenue of general-purpose local governments (county and municipalities), and very small shares of the own-source revenue of most special-purpose local government units, the obvious answer is not quite accurate.

Table 3-4 contains information from the 1992 Census of Governments (U.S. Department of Commerce 1994),[7] and estimates based on those data. Roughly 42 percent of property-tax revenue is collected by school districts, and, of course, is applied entirely to financing education. In New England; in five cities in New York, Maryland, and Virginia; and in a few other places, general-purpose local governments are responsible for schools. These local governments accounted for 19 percent of local government expenditure for education in 1991–92 and devoted an estimated 10 percent of total property-tax collections to financing the local share of their education expenditure. Thus, about 52 percent of total local government property-tax revenue was devoted to education, apparently only a slightly smaller share than it was 40 years ago.

What of the other 48 percent of property-tax revenues? Most American local governments are small. In 1991–92, counties, cities, and towns (or

Table 3-4. *The Property Tax in Local Government Finance, 1991–92, by Type of Government Unit*

	Amount ($ in billions)	Percent of Own-Source General Revenue	Estimated Locally Financed Education Expenditure[a]	Estimated Property-Tax Revenue Used For Education[b]
All local governments	171.3	47.4	111.9	89.5
School districts	72.6	79.2	90.8	72.6
General-purpose governments (counties, municipalities, town-ships or towns)	93.2	39.8	21.1	16.9
Special districts	5.4	15.2	*	*
Counties 250,000+ population	25.2	46.6	3.9	3.1
Cities 200,000+ population	19.0	30.3	5.7	4.6
Used for education	89.5			
Used for other purposes, except in large cities and counties	45.3			
Subtotal	134.8	Presumed "benefit" portion of property tax revenue		
Noneducation use, in large cities and counties	36.5			

Source: 1992 Census of Governments, Volume 4, *Government Finances,* various numbers.

* Less than $0.05 billion (0.05 percent).

[a] Local expenditure for education less intergovernmental revenue for education. This is an inexact estimate because of timing differences in specific types of expenditures and the revenue to finance them and the treatment in Census data of debt service and retirement contributions.

[b] Estimate based on the assumption that, on average, the property tax accounts for roughly 80 percent of the share of local financing of education by general-purpose local governments. Examination of data for numerous places suggests that this is not far from the truth.

townships) *other than* the 174 counties with populations over 250,000 people and the 76 cities with populations over 200,000 people, collected about $45.3 billion in property taxes (26 percent of total U.S. property-tax revenue of local governments) and applied the money to noneducation purposes. These local governments' principal expenditures not financed from user charges or intergovernmental revenue, and thus financed largely by the property tax, are public safety, highways, and governmental administration.[8] Although ordinary citizens may not feel that spending for governmental administration provides measurable benefits to them individually, it seems appropriate to view local property taxes outside large urban places as being essentially benefits taxes. This may also apply to property taxes for schools in larger places as well, as table 3-4 suggests. On the other hand, ordinary citizens may not view much of the 21 percent of the property tax used for nonschool purposes in larger urban places as benefits taxes, although if such expenditures are perceived to buy especially "good government," that will be capitalized into higher property values, benefiting property owners.

Perhaps a better way of putting it is as follows. Local governments in large cities spend their property-tax revenue in four ways: for schools; for services that are redistributive by design or required because of poverty and social malaise; for services that provide valuable collective benefits that, while not redistributive in any real way, are not specific to any one household or individual; and for services that afford benefits to individual households and individuals. Some, if not all, of the last type of benefits could be financed from user charges but, instead, are financed from general revenues.

What the Data Imply for the Theory of the Local Property Tax

In 1956 and 1972, two articles published in economic journals revolutionized how economists thought about the local property tax. The first, by Charles M. Tiebout (Tiebout 1956), offers a model of efficient decision-making in a system of local governments. The essence of the model is its assumption that people sort themselves among suburban political jurisdictions on the basis of their preferences for local public services. The idea that citizens vote with their feet, when combined with some other strong assumptions, generates a perfect competitive market for local government services in large urban areas.

Ordinarily, economic efficiency cannot be maximized in public-sector decisionmaking, in part because consumers will not fully reveal their individual preferences by actually paying for the services they consume, and decisions made by majority vote will sacrifice individual preferences to political compromises. In a Tiebout world, in which there is an infinite supply of potential new residential communities, each of which is an autonomous political jurisdiction, households will locate only in jurisdictions that offer the package of public services that each household truly prefers, so there is no efficiency loss related to choosing a compromise solution based on majoritarian decisionmaking. The choice of residential location will be made with the full knowledge that there can be no free riding. If you choose to live in a community that offers a public-service package that costs 10 percent more than any other possible location, then you will pay 10 percent more in local tax. In effect, each jurisdiction is a club that households join and continue as members of only if the price and services are suitable.

The Tiebout model requires a number of rather restrictive assumptions, none of which completely holds in urban America, so at first the Tiebout paper was not treated very seriously by economists (nor did Tiebout himself treat it as the breakthrough it was). But during the 1960s, economists noticed that a Tiebout-type solution seemed consistent with the data on local government finance (except for school districts) in parts of some large metropolitan areas characterized by quite small suburban jurisdictions, notably relatively affluent suburban wedges in the Chicago, New York, Boston, and Los Angeles areas.[9] The theory predicts that the variation in tax rates will be positively associated with the scope and quality of public services among local government units within a given metropolitan area. That does seem to be the case for dormitory suburbs—at least with respect to nonschool expenditures and taxes—of those large metropolitan areas with many small local governments. However, this is not the case for school spending and taxes or for nonschool public finance when the presence or absence of business property is considered: Then the relative size of the tax base, rather than the level of spending, is the main determinant of tax rates. So the theory is reflected in part in real-world experience.

By the 1970s, the Tiebout theory was being taken seriously, so much so that the one key assumption that was not real—the use of head taxes (i.e., poll taxes) as the sole local tax—became disturbing. When the conventional property tax is substituted for the head tax, the model breaks down, for free riding becomes possible: One can enter a high-service jurisdiction and free ride if one owns a very modest house and thus pays little in local taxes. In a series of papers, economist Bruce W. Hamilton closed the system (Hamilton 1978, 1976a, 1976b, 1975). Hamilton pointed out that there are, indeed, property taxes in the real world of American suburbia, but there also are local land-use controls—"zoning," for short—that can and do prevent the would-be free-riding household from living in a mobile home on a minuscule lot in a high-spending jurisdiction. Zoning, Hamilton showed, is an essential ingredient of a Tiebout world, so such worlds are now known as Tiebout-Hamilton worlds.

In a Tiebout-Hamilton world, within a jurisdiction that is virtually all residential, the property tax is a benefits tax. Property-tax rates, as such, are not "high" or "low" but resemble the prices of ordinary consumer goods: They buy more or less luxurious goods and services. As we move closer to reality—there are limits on the creation of new communities, there is commuting to work, and there is some nonresidential property to tax within many suburban communities—the property tax remains a benefits tax, although it becomes less pure. Moreover, as William Fischel has pointed out, the local fiscal system quickly becomes one in which a major policy objective is to increase local property values by offering combinations of services and taxes for which outsiders will pay premiums (Fischel 1998, 1992).

But in the 1970s the benefits-tax story was complicated by work on the theory of the property tax that dealt with the incidence of the burden of the property tax, which to economists usually means the distribution of the burden by income class. The first person to deal with issues touching on the burden of property tax was Arnold C. Harberger, who had been writing since 1962 about the incidence of national taxes—notably the corporate income tax—on income from capital (Harberger 1962; Cragg, Harberger, and Mieszkowski 1967; Harberger and Neil 1976).[10] Harberger began by noting that, in a very large economy like the United States or in a smaller, mostly closed economy, the supply of capital is relatively fixed: In the aggregate, saving does not respond much to changes in the rate of return on saving. The highest estimates of the elasticity of saving with respect to price are +0.2 or less, usually much less. If a general tax on the income from capital is imposed (or increased) over the entire economy, the supply of capital will change little, so the effect of the tax will be almost entirely to reduce the average rate of return on capital. If the tax falls unevenly on the income from different types of capital, there will be shifts in the use of aggregate capital, and the rate of return will fall less on lightly taxed capital and more on heavily taxed capital. But the return on capital taxed at the average rate will decline by the amount of the tax at its standard rate.

In 1967, Peter M. Mieszkowski, a junior co-author with Harberger, circulated a paper in which he explicitly applied the Harberger approach to the property tax. The paper caused a great stir even before its publication (Mieszkowski 1972), and its position quickly became known as the "New View" of the property tax: On a national basis (and the American property tax does exist everywhere in the country), the tax lowers the rate of return on capital by an amount equal to the average property-tax rate on all capital (including capital that is not subject to the tax). Deviations from the average property-tax rate have "excise-tax effects," both positive and negative. For instance, lower property-tax rates reduce the user cost of that type of capital or in that place, causing inflows of those types of capital that will face low local property taxes. Conversely, higher-than-average property taxes raise the user costs of that type of capital or in that place, causing outflows of capital from the high-tax areas.[11]

The position in Mieszkowski's 1972 paper, that the property tax in the real world is a mixture of capital tax and positive and negative excise taxes, has been the accepted one since the late 1970s (see Heilbrun 1983).[12] There has been some debate about what this signifies for the conception of the property tax as a benefits tax, à la Tiebout-Hamilton. Mieszkowski and his colleague George Zodrow argue that the economic distortions of the excise effects of the property tax largely conflict with the benign view of the Tiebout-Hamilton model, and that it is wrong to think of the property tax as being, on balance, equivalent to a benefits tax (Mieszkowski and Zodrow 1989, 1986). Fischel is perhaps the strongest advocate of the opposing benefits-tax view, but even Fischel allows that the benefits-tax view may not be applicable to local governments operating within the boundaries of large central cities.

There is an alternative formulation, cast in the context of cities that are by no means dormitories and addressed to the issue of the extent to which high city property taxes have negative effects on the location of economic activity. (This is best expressed in Brazer 1961; he attributed his formulation to the views submitted to a British royal commission in 1899 by the great English economist and policy adviser Alfred Marshall.) Clearly, there can be no harmful excise effects to the extent that the tax rate in the city in question does not exceed the rate in most conceivable alternative locations. Nor can there be harmful effects to the extent that the city has unique locational advantages for particular types of activity, such that the city government can share in the "location rents" that measure those advantages. Thus, a 4.5 percent tax on the value of commercial and high-end residential property in Manhattan, in the face of a national average property-tax rate of a little more than 1 percent, does not exceed the location rents for at least some businesses and households—and that no doubt would be true for some nonprofits if they lost their property-tax exemptions.[13] Beyond that, the property tax does buy some services that mobile taxpayers value, for nonprofits that are exempt from the property tax as well as for taxable businesses and households.

Even in these places, most of the property-tax revenue is clearly being spent for services that provide benefits to residents, business property-tax payers, and, to a lesser extent, commuters and other nonresidents. But the connection between the taxpayer's payment and her sense of the benefits from that tax payment is obscure, and it is hard to claim that the tax is a benefits tax in such a way that it affects citizens' voting and residential choices. If the tax is not a benefits tax from those perspectives, then the local tax, to the extent that it differs from the national average, is a distorting excise of the Mieszkowski-Zodrow type, imposing a substantial excess burden. It is likely to be regressive to the extent that, in a given place, it is above the national average, because the losses from the outflow of capital occasioned by the high tax will rest on the owners of local factors of production that are relatively immobile, notably unskilled labor and owners of structures that have substantial life left in them.

But as the earlier discussion suggests, a substantial share of property-tax revenue is raised in places where the decisionmaking units of government are relatively small. Here the property tax tends to be a benefits tax, as in the Tiebout-Hamilton model. Property-tax and local-expenditure decisions are framed, often quite explicitly, with the objective of increasing the value of real property within the jurisdiction, a consideration Fischel considers central (see especially Fischel 1998).

Tax-Exempt Property: How Much?

Is the share of potentially taxable property owned by entities that are normally tax-exempt increasing? One would think, from the vociferousness of the complaints of local officials, that increasing shares of the property-tax base are becoming tax-exempt and are in the hands of charitable organizations.

The aggregate data do not show this. Table 3-5 contains Federal Reserve Board balance sheet estimates for the real estate owned by households, nonfinancial corporate businesses, and nonprofit organizations between 1963 and 1998.[14] While these estimates are the most careful ones that exist, observers have raised questions about them, particularly in regard to the implicit valuation of land. The table shows that the value of the real estate

Table 3-5. *Value of Real Estate Owned by the Household and Nonfarm Nonfinancial Corporate Business Sectors in the Federal Reserve "Flow of Funds" Accounts (Dollar amounts in billions)*

End of Year	Value of Real Estate Owned by Households, Excluding Nonprofit Organizations	Value of Real Estate Owned by Nonfarm Nonfinancial Corporate Business	Total of these 2 Sectors	Value of Real Estate Owned by Nonprofit Organizations	Value of Real Estate Owned by Nonprofits, as Percentage of Total
1963	$553.9	$378.5	$932.4	$76.4	7.6%
1964	580.4	394.7	975.1	83.1	7.9
1965	606.2	419.1	1,025.3	91.5	8.2
1966	649.6	447.4	1,097.0	100.5	8.4
1967	686.3	478.8	1,165.1	109.4	8.6
1968	768.8	519.7	1,288.5	122.5	8.7
1969	833.1	574.7	1,407.8	138.3	8.9
1970	875.0	633.6	1,508.6	153.5	9.2
1971	957.8	702.3	1,660.1	173.0	9.4
1972	1,099.3	779.4	1,878.7	196.8	9.5
1973	1,252.2	895.3	2,147.5	227.9	9.6
1974	1,261.8	1,047.2	2,309.0	258.5	10.1
1975	1,414.2	1,170.8	2,585.0	277.4	9.7
1976	1,590.6	1,284.9	2,875.5	297.4	9.4
1977	1,887.5	1,419.9	3,307.4	331.6	9.1
1978	2,212.0	1,600.2	3,812.2	375.5	9.0
1979	2,604.8	1,824.1	4,428.9	430.0	8.9
1980	2,944.6	2,079.9	5,024.5	477.2	8.7
1981	3,294.9	2,342.9	5,637.8	518.9	8.4
1982	3,449.8	2,514.4	5,964.2	549.6	8.4
1983	4,181.0	2,587.7	6,768.7	575.8	7.8
1984	4,629.8	2,731.9	7,361.7	611.5	7.7
1985	5,235.3	2,853.9	8,089.2	643.1	7.4

(Continued)

Table 3-5. *Value of Real Estate Owned by the Household and Nonfarm Nonfinancial Corporate Business Sectors in the Federal Reserve "Flow of Funds" Accounts (Dollar amounts in billions) (Continued)*

End of Year	Value of Real Estate Owned by Households, Excluding Nonprofit Organizations	Value of Real Estate Owned by Nonfarm Nonfinancial Corporate Business	Total of these 2 Sectors	Value of Real Estate Owned by Nonprofit Organizations	Value of Real Estate Owned by Nonprofits, as Percentage of Total
1986	5,719.3	2,936.3	8,655.6	678.6	7.3
1987	6,176.7	3,983.4	10,160.1	711.5	6.5
1988	6,712.6	3,288.5	10,001.1	758.2	7.0
1989	7,296.0	3,471.9	10,767.9	801.1	6.9
1990	7,405.1	3,440.5	10,845.6	796.6	6.8
1991	6,716.0	3,254.5	9,970.5	761.0	7.1
1992	6,948.8	3,011.8	9,960.6	715.4	6.7
1993	7,105.0	2,900.7	10,005.7	699.9	6.5
1994	7,281.9	3,073.8	10,355.7	735.8	6.6
1995	7,631.1	3,203.2	10,834.3	766.9	6.6
1996	8,031.2	3,353.9	11,385.1	801.7	6.6
1997	8,620.4	3,756.2	12.376.6	896.5	6.6
1998	9,242.8	4,202.7	13,445.5	995.2	6.9
Standard deviation/ mean	74.8%	59.9%	69.1%	59.3%	13.6%
Average annual growth rate	8.4%	7.1%	7.9%	7.6%	

Source: Federal Reserve Board, *Flow of Funds Accounts of the United States, Annual Flows and Outstandings*, release Z.1, dated June 11, 1999, downloaded from the Federal Reserve Board Web site, August 1999.

owned by the two sectors whose property is usually taxed has grown slightly more rapidly than that of nonprofit organizations. Until the mid-1970s, the rate of growth had been higher for the nonprofits, but the non-profits' share of the total has declined considerably since 1974.

Table 3-6 uses data from the Bureau of Economic Analysis's (BEA) "fixed reproducible tangible wealth" accounts, for structures only (i.e.,

Table 3-6. *Change in the Current Value of Structures of Types Ordinarily Subject to Property Taxation as Real Property when Privately Owned, by Ownership, 1977–97 (Dollar amounts in billions)*[a]

Type of Structure	1977	1997	Percent Increase
Private and generally taxable			
Nonresidential buildings[b]	$1,356	$2,855	110%
Residential buildings[c]	1,879	6,816	263
Total	3,236	9,670	199
Buildings mostly owned by nonprofits[d]	191	658	245
Government buildings			
Federal, national defense	86	129	49
Federal, other	29	117	300
Total Federal	116	246	112
State and local buildings	377	1,380	266
Total government buildings	493	1,625	230

Sources: "Fixed Reproducible Tangible Wealth in the United States: Revised Estimates for 1995–97 and Summary Estimates for 1925–97," *Survey of Current Business*, September 1998, pp. 36–48, for 1997 data. Comparable data for 1977 derived from files downloaded from the Bureau of Economic Analysis Web site (http://www.bea.gov), July 1999.

[a] "Value" means depreciated replacement value, based on the "perpetual-inventory" method used by the Bureau of Economic Analysis, U.S. Department of Commerce, in making national-wealth estimates.

[b] Some nonbuilding structures, such as mining structures, are taxable as ordinary real property, but often are valued in quite different ways than ordinary buildings; most privately owned infrastructure, other than that owned by utilities, is not taxed.

[c] Mobile homes typically are not taxed as real property but as personal property, and often at quite modest rates. The data shown here apply to residential buildings on permanent sites.

[d] Religious buildings, educational buildings, hospitals, and institutional buildings.

excluding land). The table shows that the depreciated replacement value of both nonprofit and state and local government structures increased far more rapidly than the value of private nonresidential buildings between 1977 and 1997, and about as rapidly as private residential buildings. The BEA estimating method is inherently unreliable with regard to structures, relative to reasonable estimates of market value for those parts of the stock of structures for which there is market-value evidence. Nonetheless, these data provide no support for the claims that the growth rate in the value of tax-exempt, nonprofit real property is extraordinarily rapid for the nation as a whole. Still, the value of tax-exempt property could be rising relative to the actual value of the privately owned real property that is taxable, because of the exemptions and tax preferences for residential and business property on the tax rolls.

So much for the limited data on tax-exempt property in the aggregate. For a relatively small number of states, data on the value of tax-exempt property—that is, the assessed values on the tax rolls—are available, sometimes only on state government Web sites, but the data are usually highly suspect.[15] First, local assessors are part of the property-tax money-raising process: Their main duty is to value taxable properties correctly, so as to avoid missing any value that is taxable. Spending time valuing tax-exempt properties is wasteful, since it serves no public purpose (unless there is a PILOT program in which the annual PILOTs are directly linked to the assessed value of the tax-exempt property, which is not widespread practice). Few assessors pay any attention to tax-exempt property; the values on the rolls may be very old, at the extremes reflecting construction costs and land values from over a century ago.

Second, for properties recently added to the tax-exempt part of the roll, the probable error may be in the opposite direction: The building may have no conceivable taxable uses, except after extremely high-cost conversion, and it might be extremely expensive to demolish the structure to free the site for other uses. Third, while the value of the land under the structures is usually similar to the surrounding land values, that may not always be the case.

There are analogies to the "blockage" concept used in the valuation of estates for wealth-transfer taxes. When assets that are rarely, if ever, sold are valued on the assumption that all of them are offered for sale on the same day, it is plausible to assume that the realized prices of those assets will be greatly diminished by the simultaneous sales. The U.S. Tax Court has accepted this reasoning in a number of cases, some of the most notable in connection with estates that included large numbers of works by a single artist. One can imagine parallel situations in the valuation of the real property of large tax-exempt organizations. For example, New York University (NYU) was on the edge of financial collapse in early 1972, with a negative unrestricted endowment, substantial short-term debt, and projected large operating losses. Had that collapse happened, the value of adjacent land and of buildings in the Washington Square area would have collapsed, too. NYU owned about 1 million square feet of largely vacant loft buildings whose value, as well as that of several million square feet in privately owned loft buildings in the area, would have been negative without NYU's demand. The university also owned a substantial amount of dormitory space, at a time when the hotel occupancy rate in the city was extremely low and when students were fleeing dormitory living at many colleges across the country.

Tables 3-7 through 3-13 provide recent data on the value of tax-exempt property for three states—Wisconsin, Oregon, and California—and two cities, New York and Washington, D.C. The Wisconsin data come from special reports required from local assessors beginning in 1998; the reports may be new estimates of value by assessors and thus perhaps more reliable. The Oregon data are highly aggregated estimates by the staff of the state Department of Revenue, made in the course of preparing the biennial tax-expenditure report. The data for the other three jurisdictions are the assessed values that appear on the local tax rolls, for what they are worth. The following summarizes the relation between the assessed value of exempt private property as a percentage of the assessed value that is taxable:

Jurisdiction and year	Percentage of exempt private property	Percentage of exempt nonprofit property
Wisconsin, 1988	5.9	5.9
Oregon, 1997–98	2.3	2.3
California, 1998–99	4.2	2.5
New York City, 1998–99	21.4	12.5
Washington, D.C., 1995	23.0	13.1

Source: See tables 3-7 through 3-13.

In the three states shown, the assessed value of tax-exempt property of nonprofit organizations is so small a share of taxable assessed values that, were these exemptions eliminated and the formerly exempt organizations required to pay the standard property tax (without making any changes in their economic behavior, such as selling off real property), the reduction in property taxes paid by existing taxable property would be negligible. This is also the case for the larger counties in California: In no case would the reduction be more than 3 percent.[16] In New York City and Washington, D.C., however, tax-exempt nonprofit property is carried on the tax rolls at values that add up to about one-eighth

Table 3-7. *Tax-Exempt Private Property in Wisconsin, as of January 1, 1998*

	Tax-Exempt Private Property as a Percentage of	
Type of Tax District	Total Taxable Property	Total Exempt Private Property
Town	2.3	n/a
Village	5.1	n/a
City	8.4	n/a
Statewide	5.9	n/a
Type of exempt property		
Religious, not included below	n/a	30.6
Nursing and retirement homes[a]	n/a	16.6
Educational facilities[a]	n/a	12.1
Medical facility	n/a	16.8
Housing	n/a	3.7
Other[b]	n/a	12.8

Source: Wisconsin Department of Revenue Web site (http://www.dor.state.wi.us/html/stats.html).
[a] Includes religious homes and schools.
[b] Includes property owned by YMCAs/YWCAs, scouting organizations, and similar organizations.

of the value of taxable property, so the reduction in property taxes paid by others would be large.

Of course, the real property of tax-exempt organizations is not evenly distributed across a state. Such property is likely to be concentrated in the central cities of metropolitan areas, in state capitals (e.g., for nonprofits that have old and symbiotic relations with state governments, such as state historical museums), and in small cities that are the homes of large private universities and colleges, such as New Haven. Table 3-14 shows the uneven geographic concentration of nonprofits in Oregon, one of the states for which there are good data. The value of the property of the charitable nonprofits (the "social welfare" exemptions) is 2.6 times as important relative to taxable property in Multnomah County (Portland) as in the three outlying counties of the metropolitan area for which there are data, and 3.4 times as important in Multnomah as in the rest of the state. One would expect the disparity to be even greater for central cities that are quite small relative to their metropolitan areas, such as Boston, St. Louis, and Pittsburgh, and for state capitals that are small relative to the populations of their states and metropolitan areas.[17] Moreover, the relative size of tax-exempt property is likely to be quite a bit higher in much of the Northeast

Table 3-8. *Value and Impact of Nonprofit Exemptions Listed in Oregon's* 1999–2001 Tax Expenditure Report *(Dollar amounts in millions)*

Type of Property	1997–98 Assessed Value of Exempt Property	1997–99 Revenue Impact		
		Loss[a]	Shift[b]	Total
Charitable, literary, and scientific	$1,500.0	$38.1	$7.1	$45.2
Fraternal organizations	200.2	5.2	1.0	6.2
Religious organizations	2,000.0	53.1	9.9	63.0
Schools and day care	106.0	2.8	0.5	3.3
Other[c]	43.6	0.8	0.2	0.9
Total	3,849.8	100.0	18.7	118.6
Revenue impact, as percent of actual property-tax revenue in the 1997–99 biennium		2.34%		
Exhibit: Public property				
State and local	21,000.0	541.0	101.0	642.0
Public ways	16,300.0	420.0	78.0	498.0
Federal property	91,700.0	2,363.0	440.0	2,830.0
Total, public property	129,000.0	3,324.0	619.0	3,970.0

Source: Report downloaded from http://www.dor.state.or.us/statistical/

[a] "Loss" refers to the amount that would be collected if this property were fully taxable, the tax-exempt organization's behavior were unchanged, and the state constitution permitted the increased tax levy (which it does not, under "Measure 50," effective in 1997–98).

[b] "Shift" refers to the amount that would be collected if this property were fully taxable and the tax-exempt organization's behavior were unchanged; the Department of Revenue calculates that tax rates on taxable properties could rise by these amounts, even under "Measure 50."

[c] Includes fraternities, sororities, and cooperative student housing; libraries; senior services centers; and nonprofit water associations.

than elsewhere in the country, because of the importance of real-property-intensive, private institutions of higher education and (to a lesser extent) nonprofit hospitals in that region.[18]

The tables (except table 3-7, for Wisconsin) suggest that the concern for the large amount of exempt property that is politically visible in many places may arise from the large amount of tax-exempt property that is *not* in the hands of private nonprofit organizations. In Oregon, for example,

Table 3-9. *Taxable and Exempt Private Property in California, 1988–89 to 1998–99*

Year	Total Assessed Value ($ in billions)	Exemptions		"Other" as Percentage of Total Assessed Value
		Homestead ($ in billions)	Other[a] ($ in billions)	
1988–89	1,301.5	31.8	25.9	1.99
1989–90	1,442.3	32.1	28.8	2.00
1990–91	1,610.1	32.5	32.2	2.00
1991–92	1,738.3	32.9	35.5	2.04
1992–93	1,828.3	33.5	38.5	2.11
1993–94	1,883.1	34.3	43.2	2.29
1994–95	1,906.8	35.2	43.4	2.28
1995–96	1,922.7	35.5	46.7	2.43
1996–97	1,947.0	35.6	49.6	2.55
1997–98	2,004.7	35.9	54.0	2.69
1998–89	2,100.8	36.0	56.6	2.69

Source: Table 4, Appendix to State Board of Equalization, *1997–98 Annual Report.*
[a] Veterans exemptions and various charitable exemptions.

Table 3-10. *Value of "Other" Exemptions in California, 1998–99*

Type of Exempt Property	Value ($ in millions)	Percentage of Total Exempt Value
Veterans	1,149	2.0
College	7,395	13.1
Church	1,066	1.9
Religious	7,909	14.0
School below college grade	1,452	2.6
Hospitals	14,205	25.2
Other charitable properties[a]	23,158	41.1
Total	56,354	100.0

Source: Table 8, Appendix to State Board of Equalization, *1997–98 Annual Report.*
[a] "General welfare agencies, youth service agencies and religious properties other than churches."

Table 3-11. *Exemptions in California's Largest Counties, 1998–99*

County	Total Assessed Value ($ in millions)	Exempt Value ($ in millions)	Exempt Value as Percent of Total
Los Angeles	529,017	17,635	3.33
Orange	191,464	3,205	1.67
San Diego	162,732	4,724	2.90
Santa Clara	150,226	5,705	3.80
Alameda	93,823	2,365	2.52
San Bernardino	76,159	2,067	2.71
Riverside	75,789	1,562	2.06
Contra Costa	72,119	1,555	2.16
San Francisco	64,806	2,515	3.88

Source: Table 7, Appendix to State Board of Equalization, *1997–98 Annual Report.*

the estimated value of public property is more than 30 times the value of tax-exempt nonprofit property; in New York City, the multiplier is nearly 5.0; and it is 3.4 in the District of Columbia. Moreover, politically popular property-tax relief programs—for homeowners, senior citizens, veterans, and economic development—can have large impacts relative to the non-profit exemption, as the data in the text table for New York City and D.C. show. But property-tax relief programs—especially those in the form of drastic rate limitations (as in California and Massachusetts)—can, by restraining the growth in tax rates or the taxable value of ordinary private property, or both, make the tax-exempt charities more conspicuous targets than they were when tax-base growth and discretion in tax rates were the expectations in local government budgets.

The proportion of the nonprofit exemptions that benefits religious entities is large, as shown where data provide the breakdown of the non-profit exemptions: about 50 percent in Wisconsin and Oregon, 40 percent in California, and 70 percent in New York City.[19] That surely complicates policy solutions that entail taxes or compulsory PILOTs to be paid by now-exempt nonprofits.

Tax Exemption and the Property Tax as a Benefits Tax

In chapter 6, author Brody raises a fundamental question as to whether the ultimate rationale for the property-tax exemption is that charities are

Table 3-12. *Property-Tax Exemptions in New York City, Fiscal 1999*

Type of Property	Assessed Value ($ in millions)	Percent of Total Assessed Value	Percent of Exempt Assessed Value	Percent of Taxable Assessed Value
Total assessed value	140,927.9	100.0	n/a	n/a
Subject to tax[a]	77,698.7	55.1	n/a	n/a
Exempt[b]	63,229.2	44.9	100.0	n/a
Exempt property:				
Public property	46,618.6	33.1	73.7	n/a
Federal and foreign governments	2,378.0	1.7	3.8	n/a
State and local government[c]	44,240.6	31.4	70.0	n/a
Private property	16,610.6	11.8	26.3	21.4
"Institutional"[d]	9,724.4	6.9	15.4	12.5
Housing tax preferences	4,662.7	3.3	7.4	6.0
"Commercial and industrial" tax preferences	1,479.2	1.1	2.3	1.9
Other partial exemptions[e]	744.4	0.5	1.2	1.0

Source: City of New York, Department of Finance, *Annual Report on the NYC Real Property Tax, Fiscal Year 1999* (October 1998).

n/a = not applicable

[a] "Billable" assessed value is the lower of actual assessed value or "transition value"; increases in the assessed value of business property and multifamily buildings are phased in over a five-year period.

[b] The exempt portion of total value of parcels, in the case of partial exemptions (e. g., for veterans, senior citizens, subsidized housing programs and economic development programs).

[c] All but $940 million consists of city and "public authorities" property. Some of the latter are state agencies and some—like AMTRAK—operate more widely, but nearly all the property is used to provide services to New Yorkers, commuters, and visitors.

[d] Religious, charitable, educational, medical, and cultural organizations.

[e] Veterans, senior citizens, and a state-funded program of school-tax relief (which was in its initial year and will grow much larger in future years).

Table 3-13. *Taxable and Tax-Exempt Property in the District of Columbia, Tax Year 1995*

Type of Property	Assessed Value ($ in millions)	Percent of Total Assessed Value	Percent of All Exempt Assessed Value	Percent of Taxable Assessed Value
Taxable and exempt property	78,269	100.0	n/a	n/a
Fully taxable ("net tax base")	42,169	53.9	n/a	n/a
Exemptions, full or partial	36,100	46.1	n/a	n/a
Fully exempt	31,974	40.9	100.0	n/a
Government property:	22,739	29.1	82.5	n/a
Federal	20,811	26.6	65.1	n/a
Foreign governments and multinational organizations	1,928	2.5	6.0	n/a
D.C. government	3,643	4.7	11.4	n/a
Private property	9,718	12.4	30.4	23.0
Conventional nonprofit	5,146	6.6	16.1	12.2
Special acts of Congress[a]	446	0.6	1.4	1.1
Property-tax relief programs[b]	4,126	5.3	12.9	9.8

Source: Carol O'Cleireacain, *The Orphaned Capital* (Brookings, 1977), Table 3-1, p.58.

n/a = not applicable.

[a] A number of national nonprofit organizations with headquarters in Washington are exempt by special acts of Congress.

[b] Homestead exemption and senior-citizen credit.

nontaxable "sovereigns," or that the worthy services performed by charities deserve to be subsidized by relief from the payment of local taxes. Sovereigns such as the federal and state governments do pay for the goods and services they buy from private providers. This suggests that charities should be paying property taxes that reflect the cost of those local government services they use that otherwise would be purchased from private providers (with some choice in the quantity purchased), but that they should not pay taxes that do not confer benefits on the charitable organizations. But if property-tax exemptions are viewed as subsidies for the worthy things that charities do, then such exemptions should be forth-

Table 3-14. *The Uneven Geographic Concentration of Exemptions within a State: Real Market Value of Exempt Property in Oregon as a Percentage of Real Market Value of Taxable Property, 1998–99*

	Type of Exempt Property (%)			
	"Public"	"Social Welfare"	Business/Housing/ Miscellaneous	All Types
Multnomah County versus the other three reporting counties[a]:				
Multnomah	14.78	6.89	5.91	27.57
Other three counties[b]	7.43	2.61	2.00	12.05
Multnomah versus the rest of the state:[b]				
Multnomah	14.78	6.89	5.91	27.57
28 other counties	11.01	2.05	2.33	15.39

Source: Oregon Department of Revenue, *Oregon Property Tax Statistics, Fiscal Year 1998–99* (1999).

[a] Multnomah County is the central county of Portland Primary Metropolitan Statistical Area (PMSA).

[b] One county in the Portland PMSA and seven other counties did not report data on tax-exempt values.

coming regardless of the value to the charities of the services they consume. The following paragraphs discuss the issue from a standpoint more akin to the sovereignty view than the subsidy view.

If property-tax revenues were used entirely to provide services whose benefits accrue explicitly to identifiable households and businesses and/or increase the value of land within that jurisdiction, then the case for either removal of the nonprofit exemption or fully compensatory PILOTs would be overwhelming: Wherever the beneficiaries of the services produced by the nonprofits are located, services financed with the property tax are in the production function and should be paid for, just as other inputs are purchased. If, on the other hand, property-tax revenues are used entirely to buy redistributive services or other services yielding only collective benefits, then the services will not enter into any rational calculation of the nonprofits' production functions, in which case treating nonprofits as subjects for local taxation requires quite different reasoning.

There is another obvious and relevant dichotomy: Are the services produced by the nonprofits in question consumed locally or beyond the boundaries of the local taxing jurisdiction? If the former, then the nonprofits may be, in part, substituting for services that otherwise would have been provided by the government, requiring increased local or state tax revenue. It might still make sense to tax the property of the nonprofits, in order to make the cross-subsidies more explicit, thereby improving decisionmaking. (But it would make even more sense to require public agencies to make fully tax-equivalent PILOTs, in order to improve their budgetary decisionmaking, since government property is so much more extensive than that of nonprofits.) On the other hand, if the services produced by nonprofits are largely exported from the taxing jurisdiction, then requiring full property taxes or PILOTs is a way of exporting local tax burdens, and invites the same response accorded high local taxes on business enterprises that are exporters: migration to places where the taxes are less onerous. However, the *Camps Newfound/Owatonda* decision makes it clear that the state or local government may not tax charities differently based on whether the beneficiaries are local or not, so that the only way to impose property taxes on service-exporting charities is to impose comparable taxes on charities whose services are consumed locally.

Thus, the local-finance treatment of currently tax-exempt nonprofits ideally might depend on tests of the "facts-and-circumstances" nature. When the local government provides identifiable services directly to the nonprofit organization without payment, the appropriate solution is to render bills for the services, rather than to levy property taxes or require PILOTs based on assessed value. Often, this provision of services without charge is a matter of local government choice. For example, for generations, New York City billed only property-tax payers for water and sewer charges, and it provided trash collection for tax-exempt groups on the same basis as it did for residential properties—that is, without any explicit charges. The city possessed the authority to change its policy at any time, however, and eventually did so. It is more than a bit hypocritical for a mayor to complain about the burden imposed by tax-exempt groups while voluntarily providing municipal services to them without charge.

Consider tax-exempt groups that provide direct services largely to residents of the taxing jurisdiction. Assuming further that these services substitute for services that might have to be provided by the government or purchased from for-profit entities, what if the lifting of the tax exemption so damaged the groups' finances? The "good-government" response calls for making the comparisons explicit rather than implicit. But it is hard to see any argument for taxation.

There are nonprofit organizations whose services are distributed over a wide geographic area, and thus have little impact in the jurisdiction in which their real property is located. If the services have relatively little impact on the economy of that jurisdiction, the case for property-tax exemption seems meager. Even if the groups consume few local public services, they affect the local government's finances by occupying space that could have been used by entities that do pay property taxes. Examples include foundations and museums that own large parcels in exclusively residential suburbs, or self-contained small colleges in rural jurisdictions that house almost none of the college's employees. But if the subsidy principle is the basis for the charities' property-tax exemption, then the solution is for the state or federal government, on behalf of the nonresident beneficiaries of the charities' services, to reimburse the local government for the lost revenue.

Then there are the nonprofit organizations that have substantial roles in the local economy, and for whom the property-tax exemption is functionally similar to economic-development tax incentives granted to for-profit entities. If both types of organizations are large employers (relative to the size of the jurisdiction), it would seem that they should be treated similarly.[20] The assumption that an institution would simply pay the property tax, if required, and behave no differently in any other respect seems unlikely. A more plausible assumption for most large nonprofits is that their payrolls would decline almost immediately by the amount of the tax payment, and that the group would sell some real property, with a negative effect on future employment. It is not obvious that the local government would be better off, even in a narrow fiscal sense. In any case, economic-development tax abatements are zero-sum fiscal games, because the property-tax liabilities abated are then shifted to the remaining taxable property.

There are some "commercial" nonprofits—that is, organizations financed largely by charges imposed for services provided, such as nursing homes and hospitals—that have the authority and economic capacity to pass on property taxes in their charges, especially to third-party payers, such as Medicaid programs. There appear to be no good reasons for property-tax exemption in such cases, since the beneficiaries of the exemptions are the third-party payers, including state and federal governments.

The Future of the Property Tax

The assumption underlying the concern about property-tax exemptions for nonprofits is that the property tax will continue to play a substantial

role in the financing of local government services. There have been periods in which that assumption did not seem valid: in the 1930s, when so
many property owners were simply unable to pay the taxes due, and
between 1965 and 1980, when the local property tax's unpopularity—a
constant phenomenon—was politically effective and spurred movements
to limit increases or even reduce existing levies. However, the sources of
the unpopularity no longer seem great public issues. Americans are not
greatly exercised by the idea that a tax is not progressive, and it is not obvious that the property tax is all that regressive. The most conspicuous types
of alleged hardships, the burden on elderly homeowners and on farmers
on the urban periphery, have been addressed by specific tax-relief measures
in all states. Inequities arising from assessment practices have been
reduced by improved assessment practices in some places, or by classification schemes that formalize what previously had been extralegal and often
capricious policies. The widespread imposition of caps (and the possibility of negative mortgage-interest rates) make a repetition of the experience
of the late 1970s—extremely rapid increases in house prices and property
taxes—almost unimaginable.

The sole remaining serious charge against the property tax stems from
the tax's role in financing public schools.[21] However, the issue here is local
finance—by whatever local tax or taxes—versus state finance. Indeed,
some of the most perceptive school-finance reformers over the years have
promoted the use of statewide property taxes as the solution, and that in
essence was done in Michigan a few years ago. It has been argued, notably
by Fischel (Fischel 1989), that California's *Serrano* decision in 1971 (and
its follow-up rounds) was the primary reason that Proposition 13 was
approved in 1978. Fischel maintains that the decision crippled the
Tiebout system by divorcing local property-tax decisions from school-
spending decisions, thus converting the property tax for schools from a
benefits tax into a deadweight loss. Voters responded by dismantling the
property tax. It is entirely conceivable that other state supreme courts
may cleverly limit differentials among school districts in annual expenditures to no more than $100 per pupil, as the California court did, in
which case rational voters in those states may dismantle their property-
tax systems too.

NOTES

1. In a number of states, the type of property is taxable, with local option to
exempt; a footnote to the Census table that is the source says the option to exempt "is

exercised in most jurisdictions." Note that personal property owned and used by nonprofit organizations exempt from real property taxation is almost always also exempt from personal property taxation.

2. 1957 property-tax revenue data from Netzer (1966), table 2-3, p. 20. Gross product originating data downloaded from U.S. Department of Commerce, Bureau of Economic Analysis (BEA) Web site (http://www.bea.doc.gov/bea/regional/gsp).

3. In 1957, state-assessed property, overwhelmingly TCPU property, was a little over 8 percent of the total assessed value of taxable property. By 1991, that percentage was down to 4.3 percent (U.S. Department of Commerce 1994, xv).

4. The restriction was in Section 306 of the Railroad Reorganization and Regulatory Reform Act of 1976, the so-called 4R Act.

5. Structures and equipment data from the U.S. Department of Commerce, Bureau of Economic Analysis (1999). Gross product by industry data downloaded from BEA Web site.

6. Sometimes this has been accomplished by giving legal sanction to existing practices, as in the 1981 revision of New York state's law on real property tax, which established a classification scheme for New York City and Nassau County that was designed to make the existing inter-class distinctions permanent. However, the distinctions were held unlawful by the state's highest court. Until the late 1960s, formal classification, with the classes effectively taxed at different rates, existed in only three states. By now, some variant of formal classification exists in half the states and the District of Columbia.

7. Data from the 1997 Census of Governments are available only for the count of units of government, at this writing.

8. The inclusion of highways as "not financed from user charges" is valid for local governments in the United States, unlike the state and federal governments. To the extent that motor-vehicle use is subsidized by general taxes, that subsidy arises solely in local government.

9. The correspondence of the data with the theory was most marked in the Chicago North Shore suburbs and an affluent band of suburbs to the west of the city. Tiebout wrote his paper while at his first academic job at Northwestern University, and had been raised in Fairfield County, Connecticut, yet another remarkable example of how perceptive observation of empirical realities can lead to the development of unlikely theoretical abstractions.

10. As with everything in intellectual history, there are precursors to Harberger in this. Especially relevant to the property tax is the work of Harry Gunnison Brown (Brown 1924), a long-time professor at the University of Missouri, an advocate of land-value taxation in part because of his analysis of the incidence of a tax on something whose the supply is fixed. Brown considered the supply of reproducible capital not to be entirely fixed.

11. Another precursor, Earl R. Rolph, emphasized the extent to which excise taxes can be shifted backward to producers of the taxed goods (rather than forward to consumers). He considered the property tax on buildings to be largely an excise tax that was shifted backward to the construction sector of the economy (Rolph and Break 1949; Rolph 1971).

12. In 1973, I noted that a very large share of all capital is not taxed at all, so that the positive excise-tax effects may predominate for most types of capital actually subject to the tax (notably housing) and in most places (Netzer 1973).

13. Examples that come to mind include the offices of some national foundations, whose officers notoriously "do well while doing good."

14. Financial corporations own very little real estate as such. Even office buildings they own and occupy are likely to appear on their balance sheets as financial assets, in the form of ownership interests in subsidiary corporations and mortgage obligations of the subsidiaries.

15. One possible exception is the Wisconsin data. In this case, the state legislature directed the Department of Revenue, which in turn directed local assessors, to make new estimates of the "fair market value" of the privately owned exempt property in their districts and to report these to the Department.

16. Presumably, the percentage would be higher in the major cities within these counties, where the tax-exempt property no doubt is concentrated (except for San Francisco, a combined city-county). The California state Web site provides data only by counties (California State Board of Equalization 1998).

17. Recent (1997) population data for the state capitals located within metropolitan areas show that about half have less than 30 percent of the populations of their own metropolitan areas and that the great majority less than 10 percent of the population of their states (author's calculations from U.S. Department of Commerce 1998, table 307).

18. In the northeastern states, about 40 percent of college enrollment is in private institutions, while in the rest of the country the percentage is 16 (U.S. Department of Commerce 1998, table 307).

19. The Wisconsin, Oregon, and California percentages can be calculated from the tables below. The New York City percentage is from the source used for table 3-12. It appears that "religious" in these places means houses of worship and religiously affiliated schools, hospitals, and other institutions, when the affiliation is explicit. In some other places, data on the value of tax-exempt property may exclude churches as such.

20. The nonprofit entity may be much larger than the typical for-profit beneficiary of tax incentives (e.g., NYU, a larger local employer than any recipient of commercial and industrial property-tax abatements).

21. By 1998, 43 state supreme courts had heard cases challenging school-finance systems on the basis of that state's constitution. The suits were successful in 18 cases, unsuccessful in 20, and yet to be decided in 5 (Federal Reserve Bank of Chicago 1999). The desired remedy has generally been greater state financing of schools, in order to reduce inequalities in school spending.

REFERENCES

Brazer, Harvey E. 1961. "The Value of Industrial Property as a Subject of Taxation." *Canadian Public Administration* 55(1): 137–47.

Brown, Harry Gunnison. 1924. *The Economics of Taxation.* New York: Henry Holt.

California State Board of Equalization. 1998. *1997–98 Annual Report.* Available at http://www.boe.ca.gov/annualreports.htm.

City of New York, Department of Finance. 1998. *Annual Report on the NYC Real Property Tax.* New York: City of New York.

Cragg, John G., Arnold C. Harberger, and Peter Mieszkowski. 1967. "Empirical Evidence on the Incidence of the Corporation Income Tax." *Journal of Political Economy* 75 (6): 811–21.

Federal Reserve Bank of Chicago. 1999. "Resources, Outcomes and Funding of Public Schools." *Chicago Fed Letter* 145b, Special Issue.

Fischel, William A. 1998. "The Ethics of Land Value Taxation Revisited: Has the Millennium Arrived Without Anyone Noticing?" In *Land Value Taxation: Can It and Will It Work?* edited by Dick Netzer (1–23). Cambridge, Mass.: Lincoln Institute of Land Policy.

———. 1992. "Property Taxation and the Tiebout Model: Evidence for the Benefit View from Zoning and Voting." *Journal of Economic Literature* 30 (1): 171–77.

———. 1989. "Did *Serrano* Cause Proposition 13?" *National Tax Journal* 42 (4): 465–73.

Hamilton, Bruce W. 1978. "Zoning and the Exercise of Monopoly Power." *Journal of Urban Economics* 5 (1): 116–30.

———. 1976a. "The Effects of Property Taxes and Local Public Spending on Property Values: A Theoretical Comment." *Journal of Political Economy* 84 (3): 647–50.

———. 1976b. "Capitalization of Intrajurisdictional Differences in Local Tax Prices." *American Economic Review* 66 (5): 743–53.

———. 1975. "Zoning and Property Taxation in a System of Local Governments." *Urban Studies* 12 (2): 206–11.

Harberger, Arnold C. 1962. "The Incidence of the Corporate Income Tax." *Journal of Political Economy* 70 (3): 215–40.

Harberger, Arnold C., and Bruce Neil. 1976. "The Incidence and Efficiency Effects of Taxes on Income from Capital: A Reply." *Journal of Political Economy* 84 (6): 1285–92.

Heilbrun, James. 1983. "Who Bears the Burden of the Property Tax?" In *The Property Tax and Local Finance,* edited by C. Lowell Harriss (57–71). New York: The Academy of Political Science.

Marshall, Alfred. 1899. "Memorandum on Imperial and Local Taxes." Presented to the Royal Commission on Local Taxation and reprinted as Appendix G in Marshall's *Principles of Economics,* 9th edition, 1961, London: Macmillan.

Mieszkowski, Peter M. 1972. "The Property Tax: A Profits Tax or an Excise Tax?" *Journal of Public Economics* 1 (1): 73–96.

Mieszkowski, Peter M., and George R. Zodrow. 1989. "Taxation and the Tiebout Model: The Differential Effects of Head Taxes, Taxes on Land Rents, and Property Taxes." *Journal of Economic Literature* 27 (3): 1098–146.

———. 1986. "The New View of the Property Tax: A Reformulation." *Regional Science and Urban Economics* 16 (3): 309–27.

Netzer, Dick. 1992. "Differences in Reliance on User Charges by American State and Local Governments." *Public Finance Quarterly* 20 (4): 499–511.

———. 1973. "The Incidence of the Property Tax Revisited." *National Tax Journal* 26 (4): 515–35.

———. 1966. *Economics of the Property Tax*. Washington, D.C.: The Brookings Institution.

O'Cleireacain, Carol. 1997. *The Orphaned Capital.* Washington, D.C.: Brookings Institution Press.

Rolph, Earl R. 1971. "The Taxation of Income from Capital." *Journal of Business* 44 (2): 175–79.

Rolph, Earl R., and George F. Break. 1949. "The Welfare Aspects of Excise Taxes." *Journal of Political Economy* 57 (1): 46–54.

Tiebout, Charles M. 1956. "A Pure Theory of Local Expenditures." *Journal of Political Economy* 64 (5): 416–24.

U.S. Department of Commerce, Bureau of Economic Analysis. 1999. *Fixed Reproducible Tangible Wealth of the United States, 1925–1997.* CD-ROM. Washington, D.C.: Government Printing Office.

U.S. Department of Commerce, Bureau of the Census. 1998. *Statistical Abstract of the United States 1998.* Washington, D.C.: Government Printing Office.

———. 1994. *1992 Census of Governments,* Volume 2, *Taxable Property Values,* Number 1, *Assessed Valuations for Local General Property Taxation.* Washington, D.C.: Government Printing Office.

4

What Is the Property-Tax Exemption Worth?

Joseph J. Cordes
Marie Gantz
Thomas Pollak

E xemption from property taxation was the main tax benefit enjoyed
by nonprofit organizations for much of American history, when
local governments were the dominant providers of public goods and services and the local property tax was the principal source of those governments' revenue.[1] As Diamond explains (chapter 5 of this volume), the
historical rationale for the exemption may have been to respect the independence of nonprofit organizations (originally, mainly churches) from
the state, rather than to subsidize the activities of nonprofits. Nonetheless, the economic effect of the exemption is to increase the financial
resources of the nonprofit sector; today, the exemption is increasingly
being viewed, by both supporters and critics, as a subsidy to nonprofit
activities.

Unlike the charitable-contribution deduction under the income tax,
the property-tax exemption has been somewhat controversial politically.
Many local governments view the exemption as a costly drain on their
local tax base, and some scholars argue that it is an unfair and inefficient
subsidy, because it favors nonprofits that own real estate and may encourage some to invest more in real property than they would otherwise.
Some for-profit businesses also worry that the exemption creates an
unfair market advantage for their nonprofit competitors.[2] Nonprofit
organizations are understandably nervous about proposals to curtail the

exemption, either explicitly, by limiting its scope, or implicitly, through political pressure to have nonprofits make "voluntary" payments in lieu of taxes (PILOTs) to local governments.[3]

Much of the debate has occurred in a context almost completely devoid of empirical data. Some jurisdictions provide estimates of how much nonprofit property is currently exempt from taxation, but as noted by Netzer (chapter 3 of this volume), even that information is rather sketchy. There is even less information about the number and identity of nonprofit organizations that benefit from the exemption, how much they benefit, and how the exemption affects nonprofits' investment and locational decisions.[4]

This chapter focuses on how the property-tax exemption affects the finances and operations of nonprofit organizations. The following broad questions will be considered:

- Which nonprofit organizations benefit from the property-tax exemption?
- What is the value of the property-tax exemption?
- Does property-tax exemption affect the financial incentives of nonprofits to own or rent, or nonprofits' choice of location?
- Does the tax exemption encourage nonprofit organizations to engage in commercial activities, and does it give them an "unfair" competitive advantage in conducting those activities?

Distribution and Value of the Tax Exemption among Nonprofits

The value of the property-tax exemption to a nonprofit organization located in community j is given by the equation $E_j = \tau_j \cdot v_j$, where E_j is the value of the property-tax exemption to the nonprofit organization, j; τ_j is the property tax rate in the community in which the organization is located; and v_j is the taxable value of property owned by the organization. In some jurisdictions, the taxable value of property corresponds to current market value, but in many communities only a fraction of market value is taxable. Thus, the taxable value of property, v_j, equals $\alpha_j V_j$, where α_j is the ratio of assessed value to market value in community j, and V_j is the property's market value (Bowman, ed., 1995). Thus, the value of the property-tax exemption to a nonprofit organization is $E_j = \tau_j \cdot \alpha_j \cdot V_j$.

If one knew the property-tax rate, τ_j, and the assessed value, $\alpha_j V_j$, it would be easy to estimate the value of the property-tax exemption for individual nonprofit organizations. These individual estimates could then be compared to other measures, such as an organization's total revenue, in order to gauge the financial importance of the exemption; and individual estimates of property-tax savings could be aggregated to estimate the total value of the subsidy.

There are, however, no comprehensive estimates of the value of the property-tax exemption. One reason is that there is very little information on the market value of property owned by nonprofit organizations. As Dick Netzer notes in chapter 3 of this volume, because nonprofit property is exempt, local assessors have little incentive to devote scarce resources to assess it, so nonprofit property does not undergo the regular valuation process required of taxable property. Moreover, because the property tax is a local tax, there are many different values of the assessment ratio α_j, and the millage or property-tax rate, τ_j. Thus, in principle, one would need to compute many different estimates of the value of the tax exemption in different localities.

Despite these limitations, however, different sources of data can be used to gauge which nonprofit organizations are most likely to benefit from the exemption, and to make "order-of-magnitude" estimates of the value of the property-tax exemption. These data include information compiled by the Federal Reserve Board on the value of real property owned by nonprofit organizations; information from IRS Form 990 returns; estimates compiled by several states of the value of tax-exempt property and/or the revenue impact of the nonprofit property-tax exemption; data compiled by certain cities on the value of tax-exempt properties; and information from financial returns filed by individual nonprofit organizations. Each source has significant limitations, but taken together they can be used to paint a portrait of the economic significance of the property-tax exemption to different types of nonprofit organizations.

Who Benefits?

Ownership of real estate provides a simple index of who benefits from the property-tax exemption. Nonprofit organizations that are required to file the IRS Form 990 tax return must provide balance-sheet information that includes the value of land, buildings, and equipment held by the nonprofit, and the accumulated depreciation on buildings and equipment.[5] Until recently, the only variable that was regularly tabulated was the *depreciated value of land, buildings, and equipment*—that is, the value of land, buildings, and equipment minus accumulated depreciation—as reported in the sample of more than 11,000 nonprofit organizations compiled by the Statistics of Income (SOI) Division of the IRS (hereafter referred to as the SOI sample).

Limitations of the SOI Sample

Although the data in the SOI sample provide some information about which organizations are likely to own tax-exempt property, the information is at best a very rough indicator, for several reasons. First, the amounts reported on the IRS 990 return are based on book values and not market values. Second, the amount tabulated in the SOI sample is the depreciated value, rather than the book value, of buildings and equipment, so the reported amount depends on the cumulative depreciation claimed on these assets. Lastly, the SOI sample is heavily weighted toward large organizations. By design, it includes all nonprofit organizations with assets of $10 million or more, while only sampling from the population of smaller nonprofits. Because the sample weights are based on assets instead of other operating characteristics (such as an organization's activity) the SOI sample will not provide an accurate picture of how ownership of property—as measured by reported (depreciated) amounts of land, buildings, and equipment—is distributed among different types of nonprofit organizations.

NCCS/PRI Database of Digitized Returns

The database of digitized IRS Form 990 returns that has been developed by the National Center on Charitable Statistics (NCCS) overcomes some, though not all, of the limitations posed by the SOI sample. As in the SOI sample, the amounts reported reflect book rather than market values. Unlike those in the SOI sample, however, the digitized data include reported amounts of the *un-depreciated* (book) value of land, buildings, and equipment.[6] Moreover, the digitized data that form the basis for the tabulations presented here comprise about three-quarters of all Form 990 returns filed, and, unlike the SOI sample, are not weighted toward large nonprofits.

Likelihood of Owning Tax-Exempt Property

A measure of whether a nonprofit organization owns property that would benefit from tax exemption is whether the group reports any positive amount for the value of land, buildings, and equipment. Such a measure, however, would overstate the extent of property ownership, because a nonprofit that owned equipment but no real property would still report a positive value for this measure. Thus, a somewhat better indicator would be whether the reported value of land, buildings, and equipment exceeded some minimum.

Table 4-1 shows the percentage of different types of nonprofits that are estimated to own at least some real property, based on three threshold values for the reported value of buildings, land, and equipment: $100,000, $500,000, and $1,000,000. In general, the nonprofit classifications are presented in decreasing order of property ownership. The second column shows the number of nonprofit organizations in each category, and the next three columns show the percentage of nonprofit organizations reporting book values of land, buildings, and equipment of at least $100,000, $500,000, and $1,000,000.

Table 4-1 shows that if the lowest threshold of $100,000 is used, three out of five nonprofits that file the Form 990 return are unlikely to own taxable real property. Using the $500,000 threshold, the fraction of nonprofits with taxable property drops to less than 3 out of 10. Not surprisingly, nonprofits that must use significant inputs of real property to fulfill their primary mission—such as retirement homes, hospitals, and nonprofits involved in providing or supporting higher education—are much more likely to own real property, and hence to benefit from the property-tax exemption, than are others.[7]

Table 4-2 shows how the likelihood of property ownership varies with organization size and age. As might be expected, the results show that the property-tax exemption is more likely to benefit larger organizations and those that are relatively "more established."

How Much Is the Property-Tax Exemption Worth?

Tables 4-1 and 4-2 provide a rough indicator of which types of nonprofits are likely to benefit from the property-tax exemption, but they do not provide information on the value of the tax exemption to

Table 4-1. *Ownership of Real Property by Operating Charitable Organizations, by Type of Charitable Activity (Includes Form 990 Filers Only)*

Type of Charitable Activity	Number of Organizations	Percent of Organizations in Category with Land, Building, Equipment Basis			Percent of Total Organizations with Land, Building, Equipment Basis		
		>= $100,000	>= $500,000	>= $1 Million	>= $100,000	>= $500,000	>= $1 Million
Retirement Homes	4,402	83	78	70	7	11	13
Hospitals	3,931	71	67	64	6	8	11
Higher Education	1,787	66	58	55	2	3	4
Housing/Shelter	6,262	63	50	38	8	10	10
Museums	1,573	54	36	27	2	2	2
Mental Health/Crisis	3,988	53	33	23	4	4	4
Health Treatment/Clinics	1,913	53	34	24	2	2	2
Health Support Services	2,305	50	28	16	2	2	2
Elementary/Secondary Education	5,189	48	33	25	5	5	6
Human Service-Multipurpose	20,734	47	27	18	19	17	16
Employment/Job Related	1,882	46	28	21	2	2	2

Nursing Services	1,790	46	29	21	2	2	2
Animal-Related	1,515	45	20	12	1	1	1
Youth Development	3,262	43	28	20	3	3	3
Other Arts	3,032	37	19	12	2	2	2
Disease/Disorders	2,388	36	18	12	2	1	1
Environmental	1,800	32	18	13	1	1	1
Other	29,765	31	16	10	18	14	12
Religion-Related	4,881	30	16	9	3	2	2
Performing Arts	3,676	29	14	9	2	2	1
Community Improvement	4,472	29	16	11	3	2	2
Medical Research	847	28	14	11	0	0	0
Other Education	8,890	24	14	9	4	4	4
Philanthropy/Grantmaking	127	13	4	3	0	0	0
Total	120,411	42	27	20	100	100	100

Source: NCCS/PRI National Nonprofit Organization Database.

Table 4-2. *Ownership of Real Property by Operating Charitable Organizations, by Organizations' Revenue and Age (Includes Form 990 Filers Only)*

	Number of Organizations	Percent of Organizations in Category with Land, Building, Equipment Basis			Percent of All Organizations with Land, Building, Equipment Basis		
		>= $100,000	>= $500,000	>= $1 Million	>= $100,000	>= $500,000	>= $1 Million
All Organizations	120,411	42	27	20	100	100	100
Total Revenue							
$100,000 or Less[a]	23,526	18	7	2	8	5	2
$100,001–500,000	48,389	28	12	7	27	19	14
$500,001–1,000,000	15,462	51	30	19	16	14	12
$1,000,001–5,000,000	21,470	70	50	39	30	33	35
$5,000,001–10,000,000	5,008	83	74	66	8	11	14
Over $10,000,000	6,556	88	85	82	11	17	23
Organization Age							
Less than Five Years	22,674	25	14	9	11	10	9
Five Years or More	96,337	46	30	22	88	89	90

Source: NCCS/PRI National Nonprofit Organization Database.

Note: In general, organizations with less than $25,000 in revenue do not have to file IRS Form 990.

[a] These data refer to organizations reporting book values of land, buildings, and equipment at or exceeding threshold values.

individual nonprofits. Nonetheless, although the data limitations are serious, several different sources can be pieced together to provide the rough "order of magnitude" of the value of the property-tax exemption.

Aggregate Estimates

At the most aggregate level, as noted by Netzer in chapter 3, the Federal Reserve Board of Governors makes annual estimates of the value of real estate owned by households, corporations, and nonprofit organizations. In 1997, the value of real estate owned by all nonprofit organizations was estimated at $900 billion.

For this number to be made even remotely comparable to the amount of real estate owned by public charities that file the Form 990 return, it must be adjusted downward to remove property owned by churches—which are not required to file the Form 990 return—and by nonprofit organizations that are not charitable Internal Revenue Code section 501(c)(3) organizations, and hence (generally) not property-tax exempt. Although the Federal Reserve estimate does not break out churches from other nonprofit organizations, data from states that attempt to value nonprofit property suggest that roughly one-third of the tax-exempt property is real estate owned by churches. Data from the IRS Statistics of Income Bulletin further indicate that organizations that have legal status as charities own about 84 percent of all assets owned by nonprofits. Applying both of these factors to the $900 billion Federal Reserve Board estimate suggests that charities other than houses of worship held roughly $500 billion in real estate in 1997.

Data compiled by the Minnesota Taxpayers Association (1999) indicate that the average effective property-tax rate that would apply to commercial properties in large metropolitan areas in 1997 would be between 2.0 percent and 2.5 percent, while a recent study by the National Bureau of Economic Research of the value of tax benefits to hospitals puts the national average of the property-tax rate at 1.6 percent (Gentry and Penrod 2000). Multiplying these percentages by $500 billion yields an estimated aggregate value of the property-tax exemption of between $8 and $13 billion nationally, representing between 1.3 percent and 2.1 percent of the total revenue received by the 193,214 nonprofits that filed the IRS Form 990 return in 1997.

Tax-Expenditure Estimates

Alternative estimates of the value of the tax exemption can be obtained from information compiled by the eight states that make an effort to estimate the annual cost, in terms of forgone revenue, of tax-exempt property and/or the property-tax exemption. As table 4-3 shows, the nonprofits located in these states make up approximately one-third of all nonprofit organizations in the United States, accounting for more than one-third of nonprofit revenues. The estimates indicate that the value of the property-tax exemption as a share of total nonprofit revenue, averaged over all nonprofit organizations in each state, ranges from a low of approximately 0.2 percent in Colorado to a high of 3.0 percent in Washington (which also taxes property at the state level).[8]

Estimates from Financial Reports

Table 4-4 provides some additional perspective on the value of the nonprofit tax exemption, based on an examination of the financial statements of 16 nonprofit organizations analyzed in Froelich, Knoepfle, and Pollak (2000). The numbers show there can be considerable variation in the financial importance of the exemption, both within and across taxing jurisdictions.

The Philadelphia Story

Table 4-5 presents estimates of the value of the property-tax exemption to Philadelphia nonprofit organizations.[9] The dollar value of the exemption was calculated directly by applying Philadelphia's commercial property-tax rate to the reported taxable value of real property. Organizations in the Philadelphia database were matched with their IRS Form 990 returns in the digitized database to add information on total revenue. The mean value of the tax savings is just under $60,000, with a median of $10,625; this value represents a mean of just over 6 percent of nonprofit revenue, with a median of roughly 1 percent. These estimates are broadly comparable to, if generally lower than, those reported in table 4-4.

Studies of the Value of Tax Exemption for Hospitals

Studies of nonprofit hospitals provide another source of information about the value of the property-tax exemption to some nonprofits.

Table 4-3. *Estimated Value of the Property-Tax Exemption (State Estimates of Tax-Exempt Property and/or Revenue Losses Attributable to Tax-Exempt Property)* [a]

State	Number of Nonprofits	Revenue[b] ($)	Avg. Effective Commercial Property-Tax Rate (%)	State Rank[c]	Estimated Property-Tax Exemption ($)	Tax Exemption as Share of Revenue (%)
California	22,774	65,462,062,083	1.5	47	724,898,000	1.1
Colorado	3,734	8,423,438,598	2.0	27	17,780,000	0.2
Minnesota	4,607	12,670,172,608	4.7	3	1,770,000,002[d]	1.3
New Jersey	5,327	19,982,864,180	5.0	2	284,000,000	1.4
New York	15,118	84,950,547,645	3.4	7	1,170,000,000	1.4
Oregon	3,086	5,327,548,696	1.5	38	26,811,000	0.5
Washington	4,529	11,758,815,066	1.2	46	396,176,000	3.3
Wisconsin	4,196	11,879,725,127	2.8	15	240,678,000	2.0
State Subtotal	63,371	220,455,174,003	N.A.	N.A.	3,038,123,000	1.4
National Total	193,214	648,168,791,929	N.A.	N.A.	N.A.	N.A.

N.A. = not applicable.

[a] *Sources:* California: http://www.lao.ca.gov/tax_expenditure_299/tep_299_proptax1.html. Colorado: Department of Local Affairs, Division of Property Taxation, 1998, Twenty-Eighth Annual Report for the Governor and the General Assembly. Minnesota: http://www.taxes.state.mn.us/reports/teb/html. Oregon: http://www.dor.state.or.us/statistical/intro.html. New Jersey: http://www.state.nj.us/treasury/taxation/annual98/app_b_98.pdf. New York: http://www.orps.state.ny.us/ref/pubs/exempt/ex96/b43.htm. Washington: http://www.dor.wa.gov/reports/te98/summary.htm. Wisconsin: http://www.badger.state.wi.us/agencies/dor/ra/sum98pro.html.

[b] *Source:* NCCS Core File of Nonprofit Organizations, circa year 1997.

[c] State ranked by the level of the average commercial property-tax rate.

[d] Excludes private colleges and universities.

Table 4-4. *Estimated Value of the Nonprofit Tax Exemption (Selected Financial Statements of Nonprofit Organizations)*

Type of Nonprofit Organization	State	Effective Commercial Property-Tax Rate (%)	Value of Land and Buildings ($)	Estimated Value of Property-Tax Exemption ($)	Total Revenue ($)	Tax Exemption as Share of Revenue (%)
Education and Research	MN	4.7	397,803	18,696	313,453	6.0
Retirement Homes	MN	4.7	42,744,418	2,008,987	37,223,727	5.4
Youth Development	MN	4.7	2,642,016	124,174	2,993,214	4.1
Education and Research	MN	4.7	571,824	26,876	976,684	2.8
Health Care	MN	4.7	13,844,045	650,670	25,554,111	2.8
Community Development	MN	4.7	1,356,129	63,738	2,532,261	2.5
Legal	CA	1.1	9,201,319	96,613	3,980,290	2.5
Human Services	MN	4.7	3,113,520	146,335	7,477,625	2.4
Hospital	MO	2.6	118,313,610	3,093,901	218,426,394	1.5
Job Training	MN	4.7	685,424	32,215	2,586,955	1.4
Religion-Related	NY	2.1	40,884,779	844,679	77,763,083	1.2
Historical Society	MN	4.7	74,547	3,504	345,026	1.1
Animal Protection	NY	2.1	1,161,021	23,987	3,400,066	1.0
Community Clinic	MN	4.7	340,515	16,004	2,446,857	0.7
Religion-Related	IA	2.6	1,161,510	29,619	4,763,186	0.6
Veterans Association	OH	1.8	9,446,332	173,057	80,785,392	0.2

Source: Financial statements used as data in Froelich, Knoepfle, and Pollak (2000).

Table 4-5. *Value of the Property-Tax Exemption to Charitable Organizations in Philadelphia*

Organization Type	Number of Organizations	Tax Savings ($)				Tax Savings as a Percent of Total Revenue			
		Mean	Median	Lower Quartile	Upper Quartile	Mean	Median	Lower Quartile	Upper Quartile
All Organizations	243	59,352	10,625	2,842	51,272	6.2	0.9	0.3	3.1
Cultural Institutions	19	51,224	28,886	3,876	110,500	10.4	1.6	0.5	5.1
Institutions of Learning	35	52,846	26,707	7,140	51,381	3.3	1.1	0.3	2.0
Medical Health Facilities	20	297,246	61,929	10,050	212,481	2.1	0.7	0.4	2.0
Religious Institutions	24	29,782	4,760	2,408	11,356	7.9	3.1	0.8	7.8
Other	145	34,068	8,500	2,482	35,700	6.6	0.9	0.3	3.0

Source: NCCS/PRI National Nonprofit Organization Database and City of Philadelphia Board of Revision of Taxes file of assessed market *value of tax-exempt properties.*
Note: Excludes 45 organizations that reported no land, buildings, or equipment on IRS Form 990.

Using data compiled by the Health Care Financing Administration on property taxes paid by for-profit hospitals, Gentry and Penrod (2000) impute a value for property taxes that would be owed by nonprofit hospitals. Their estimates indicate that the median value of the property-tax exemption nationwide is just under $300,000 in 1995 dollars, and that the median exemption as a percentage of total revenues is 0.7 percent. Gentry and Penrod also use data from three states—New Jersey, Ohio, and Wisconsin—that provided effective tax rates for each municipality to estimate the value of the property-tax exemption. These tabulations yield median values of $649,414 (0.6 percent of revenues) in New Jersey, $429,901 (0.8 percent of revenues) in Ohio, and $277,397 (1.4 percent of revenues) in Wisconsin.

Michigan also undertook a study of the value of the property-tax exemption received by 172 nonprofit hospitals (Michigan Department of Treasury, Office of Revenue and Tax Analysis 1997). The results indicate that the median value of the tax exemption was on the order of $350,000 (1.2 percent of revenues).

Imputing the Property-Tax Exemption to the SOI Sample and the NCCS Core File

The data presented in tables 4-3 through 4-5 suggest the relative importance of the tax exemption to individual organizations. But, in principle, it would be useful to have estimates of the value of the exemption for a broader and more representative group of organizations.

One approach is to use reported information on buildings, land, and equipment in the digitized database of IRS Form 990 returns in order to distribute the (adjusted) Federal Reserve Board estimate of real estate to each nonprofit in the database. This imputed value could then be multiplied by an estimate of the effective property-tax rate faced by each organization in order to arrive at an imputed value of the exemption.

Table 4-6 presents estimates of the imputed values. The imputation was made by the following steps:

1. The estimated market value of real estate held by Internal Revenue Code section 501(c)(3) organizations in the digitized database was computed by multiplying the Federal Reserve Board estimate of real estate held by charities other than religious denominations— $500 billion—by 73 percent. This adjustment was necessary because

Table 4-6. *Estimated Value of the Property-Tax Exemption to Nonprofits with Holdings of Taxable Real Property*[a]
(Property Threshold = $100,000)

	Number of Organizations	Percent with Taxable Real Property	Estimated Tax Savings of Organizations with Taxable Real Property ($)				Estimated Tax Savings as a Percent of Total Revenue of Organizations with Taxable Real Property			
			Mean	Median	Lower Quartile	Upper Quartile	Mean	Median	Lower Quartile	Upper Quartile
All Organizations	151,689	33	203,114	18,259	6,377	65,705	9	2	1	6
Total Revenue										
$100,000 or Less	54,762	7	13,081	7,001	4,087	13,507	54	14	7	28
$100,001–500,000	48,526	28	32,861	8,961	4,289	20,758	11	4	2	9
$500,001–1,000,000	15,435	51	30,546	13,313	5,311	33,517	4	2	1	5
$1,000,001–5,000,000	21,430	70	58,577	24,257	8,516	64,959	3	1	0	3
$5,000,001–10,000,000	4,998	83	147,031	82,281	26,439	188,723	2	1	0	3
Over $10,000,000	6,538	88	1,390,062	427,902	122,786	1,244,655	2	2	1	3
Organization Type										
Performing Arts	5,491	19	79,103	10,079	4,427	29,999	4	2	1	4
Human Service-Multipurpose	24,138	40	49,989	13,443	5,451	39,803	5	2	1	4
Museums	1,904	44	133,682	20,181	6,776	74,993	16	4	2	9
Housing/Shelter	6,613	58	63,526	27,576	10,984	69,427	20	9	4	17
Higher Education	1,898	62	1,477,483	381,507	61,324	1,149,486	4	2	1	4
Retirement Homes	4,393	81	214,039	80,492	30,181	218,013	15	6	3	13
Hospitals	4,000	70	1,736,467	515,603	107,648	1,904,217	4	2	1	3

Source: NCCS/PRI National Nonprofit Organization Database.

Note: The estimated taxable real property attributed to each organization is about 90 percent of the land, building, and equipment basis reported by the organization on its most recent IRS Form 990.

[a] Excludes 1,891 organizations with total revenue less than $0 (263 of which hold property) and 20 organizations with property holdings of more than $1 million and total revenue of less than $5,000.

the organizations currently in the database account for 73 percent of the total number of 501(c)(3) organizations that file Form 990 returns. Making this adjustment resulted in a total value of real estate of roughly $365 billion, which would be distributed to nonprofits in the database.

2. The estimated total was then distributed to each organization in proportion to the organization's estimated share of taxable property. This share was derived by dividing each organization's reported book value of land, buildings, and equipment by the sum of this amount for all organizations in the database. Organizations that reported a book value of land, buildings, and equipment less than or equal to $100,000 were assigned a value of $0 for this calculation. Each organization's share of the total book value of land, buildings, and equipment was used as an estimate of that organization's share of the total value of tax-exempt property; and this estimated share was multiplied by the aggregate total of $365 billion to impute the value of the organization's taxable property.

3. The imputed value of taxable property was then multiplied by the average effective commercial property-tax rate for each state, using data on average commercial property-tax rates compiled by the Minnesota Taxpayers Association (1999). This calculation provided an estimate of the savings from property-tax exemption.

Table 4-6 shows the imputed value of the property-tax exemption, both in dollars and as a percent of total revenues, for nonprofits that are estimated to have taxable property. The results imply that the average imputed value of the property-tax exemption is on the order of $200,000, although about half of nonprofits with taxable property have imputed values of property-tax savings below $18,000, and one-quarter have an imputed tax benefit of less than $6,000. The overall average ratio of the imputed property-tax exemption to total nonprofit revenues is 9 percent, but this average is brought up by the imputed value of the tax exemption among small nonprofits and that of nonprofits in certain "real-estate intensive" sectors, such as retirement homes, housing/shelter, and the arts, where the ratio of imputed property-tax savings to total revenues is relatively high. On balance, the imputations suggest that one out of every two nonprofits benefiting from the property-tax exemption receives savings worth 2 percent of revenues or less.

Some Measurement Issues

Each of the estimates presented above has its own limitations. Using estimates of tax-saving at the state level (table 4-3) involves an implicit reliance on the methods used by state budget analysts to make these calculations. As Netzer notes in chapter 3 of this volume, some of these estimates may reflect serious attempts to assess the taxable value of exempt property, but others may not. The estimates presented in table 4-4 are limited by the fact that organizations generally do not report market values on their financial statements, while the estimates in table 4-5 rely on the accuracy of taxable values developed for the Philadelphia PILOT program.

The dollar figures reported in table 4-6 reflect an attempt to estimate the aggregate market value of real estate owned by nonprofit organizations, but the procedure used to distribute this total to individual nonprofits has several limitations. First, the shares used to distribute the estimated tax savings are themselves proxies for the "true" share of taxable property. In addition, the procedure for imputing the value of the property-tax exemption implicitly assumes that the property-tax rate and the assessment ratios are the same across all jurisdictions within a state. Yet in many states there are apt to be local variations in property-tax rates and assessment practices among jurisdictions. This introduces an element of error in the distributional analysis, with the magnitude of the error depending on whether the localities are required by state governments to adopt uniform assessment practices and tax rates.

Lastly, the magnitude of the imputed values for taxable property is sensitive to the threshold value that is used for land, buildings, and equipment. Table 4-7 shows the results of making the same imputations as those presented in table 4-6, but using a threshold of $500,000 instead of $100,000 as the cutoff for determining whether an organization owns any taxable property. The effect is to reduce the total number of nonprofits that are deemed to own taxable property, increasing, for those that do, the imputed magnitude of both the amount of taxable property per organization and the value of the property-tax exemption per organization.

Painting a Statistical Portrait

For all the reasons listed above, the estimates of tax benefits presented in this chapter are best regarded as indicating the order of magnitude of the tax savings attributable to property-tax exemption, and not as providing exact estimates. Nonetheless, the various sources of data offer a generally

Table 4-7. *Estimated Value of the Property-Tax Exemption to Nonprofits with Holdings of Taxable Real Property*[a]
(Property Threshold = $500,000)

	Number of Organizations	Percent with Taxable Real Property	Estimated Tax Savings of Organizations with Taxable Real Property ($)				Estimated Tax Savings as a Percent of Total Revenue of Organizations with Taxable Real Property			
			Mean	Median	Lower Quartile	Upper Quartile	Mean	Median	Lower Quartile	Upper Quartile
All Organizations	153,599	21	319,091	44,413	20,135	131,454	19	3	1	7
Total Revenue										
$100,000 or Less	56,669	3	49,045	18,246	11,061	32,517	245[a]	26	13	51
$100,001–500,000	48,528	12	66,799	23,072	14,229	39,646	21	9	5	17
$500,001–1,000,000	15,438	30	49,207	28,973	16,597	59,090	7	4	2	8
$1,000,001–5,000,000	21,432	50	80,713	43,103	21,259	92,132	4	2	1	4
$5,000,001–10,000,000	4,996	74	167,718	102,712	42,226	211,169	2	1	1	3
Over $10,000,000	6,536	85	1,453,111	465,404	146,171	1,300,499	2	2	1	3
Organization Type										
Performing Arts	5,545	9	159,161	32,076	17,164	80,663	13	3	1	6
Human Service-Multipurpose	24,330	23	83,203	32,816	17,115	73,435	6	2	1	5
Museums	1,938	29	199,090	44,388	19,860	131,306	10	5	2	9
Housing/Shelter	6,837	46	80,383	39,841	20,046	87,451	64	11	5	19
Higher Education	1,907	54	1,684,948	494,582	150,587	1,335,650	4	3	2	4
Retirement Homes	4,484	76	228,458	90,239	36,127	231,822	45	6	3	14
Hospitals	4,072	64	1,878,101	601,119	159,518	2,076,408	3	2	1	3

Source: NCCS/PRI National Nonprofit Organization Database.

a. Thirteen percent (193) of the 1,533 property-holding organizations with $100,000 or less in total revenue had mean estimated tax savings that exceeded 100 percent of revenue. The estimated taxable real property attributed to each organization is about 90 percent of the land, building, and equipment basis reported by the organization on its most recent IRS Form 990.

plausible picture of the exemption's relative economic importance to individual nonprofits.

First, the results imply that a sizable majority of nonprofit organizations do not own real property and hence do not benefit from the implicit subsidy provided by the property-tax exemption. Indeed, to the extent that competition in rental markets causes the property tax to be shifted forward to tenants, the results in table 4-1 imply that, contrary to popular wisdom, a sizable majority of nonprofit organizations do pay property taxes through their rents.

Second, a nonprofit organization is more apt to own taxable property if it is larger and well-established than if it is small and new. Moreover, nonprofits whose activities make intensive use of real property in fulfilling their primary mission, such as those engaged in housing-related activities (retirement homes and housing/shelter), higher education, health care, and the arts, are more likely to own tax-exempt property, and hence to benefit from the exemption, than are other nonprofits. On the other hand, while smaller organizations are less likely as a group to own taxable property, among those that do, the relative importance of the property-tax exemption is greater.

Finally, while caution needs to be exercised in gauging when the exemption is financially important, the broad implication of the estimates presented in tables 4-3 through 4-6 seems to be that the value of the subsidy is modest for many nonprofits—perhaps on the order of a few percentage points of revenue for most nonprofits that own taxable property. But the results also indicate that there is no truly "typical" nonprofit organization. While a requirement to pay property taxes would have a small to modest impact for many nonprofits, it would significantly affect the operation and financial condition of others.

Property-Tax Exemption and the Choice to Own or Rent

Does the property-tax exemption affect nonprofit organizations' decision to own rather than rent the space in which they are housed? There are two perspectives that can be used in addressing the question.[10]

Case 1: Owning vs. Renting when the Nonprofit Is the Sole Tenant

In the simplest case, the space is to be used entirely to meet the nonprofit organization's primary mission. Suppose that the rental market is competitive and that for-profit landlords must pay both income and property taxes, but are allowed to deduct depreciation.

Under these assumptions, it is easily shown that in a competitive rental market the landlord must earn a profit—after depreciation and taxes—that equals the after-tax rate of return that could be earned by purchasing an alternative investment (e.g., a bond) with the amount of money invested in the property:

(1) $(cq - q\delta) - t(cq - \alpha q\delta) - \tau q(1 - t) = qr(1 - t),$

where c is the gross market rent charged per dollar invested, q is the value of the property, δ is the annual rate of "true" or "economic depreciation," t is the income tax rate, $\alpha q\delta$ is the amount of economic depreciation that can be claimed for tax purposes, τq is the amount of property tax, r is the before-tax return on the alternative investment (e.g., a bond), and $r(1 - t)$ is the after-tax return.[11] Equation 1 assumes that the property tax is deductible as a cost of doing business.

With some rearranging of terms, it can be shown that in a competitive market the gross rent charged by a for-profit landlord will be given by

(2) $c = \dfrac{q[r(1 - t) + \delta(1 - t\alpha) + \tau(1 - t)]}{(1 - t)} \rightarrow \dfrac{c}{q} = r + \delta\dfrac{(1 - t\alpha)}{(1 - t)} + \tau,$

where the term c/q is the so-called rental or user cost per dollar.

A nonprofit organization that owns its building would be its own landlord. The implicit rental cost of owning instead of renting would equal the return the nonprofit could earn if it invested elsewhere the money tied up in the building, or, alternatively, the cost of mortgage payments if the nonprofit had to borrow the funds (qr), plus depreciation ($q\delta$). The cost of owning, c^*, would thus be given by

(3) $c^* = qr + q\delta \rightarrow \dfrac{c^*}{q} = r + \delta.$

From the nonprofit's perspective, the issue of whether it would be better to own or rent would depend on whether the user cost of renting, c/q, was greater than that of owning, c^*/q. It would be financially advantageous to own rather than rent if $c/q > c^*/q$ or if

$$(4) \qquad \frac{c}{q} - \frac{c^*}{q} > 0 \rightarrow \left[r + \delta \frac{(1 - t\alpha)}{(1 - t)} + \tau \right] - [r + \delta] > 0.$$

Collecting and rearranging terms yields

$$(5) \qquad \frac{c}{q} - \frac{c^*}{q} > 0 \rightarrow \tau - \frac{\delta t(\alpha - 1)}{(1 - t)} > 0.$$

Interaction between Property-Tax Exemption and the
Tax Treatment of Depreciation
Equation 5 shows how the property-tax exemption affects the decision to own or rent. The term τ represents the savings in property tax (per dollar invested) that the nonprofit organization receives as an owner (since the nonprofit organization is its own landlord, it does not need to "pass the property tax forward" as a for-profit landlord would); and the term $\delta t(\alpha - 1)/(1 - t)$ shows how tax deductions for depreciation affect the decision to own or rent.

To understand the interaction between the tax treatment of depreciation and the property-tax exemption, it is useful to first consider the case in which $\alpha > 1$, which would be true if the value of depreciation deductions allowed for tax purposes exceeded economic depreciation. As may be seen from equation 5, when $\alpha > 1$, the fact that the nonprofit organization cannot take tax deductions for depreciation may offset the property-tax savings it could receive if it became an owner.

The reason is straightforward. When $\alpha > 1$, the tax system allows deductions that exceed the value of "true economic depreciation." In such cases, tax deductions for depreciation actually provide a tax subsidy to capital. Thus, when $\alpha > 1$ the nonprofit organization in effect gives up the subsidy to capital that the for-profit landlord receives and is forced to pass through to the tenant by market competition. In this case, whether it is financially advantageous to own rather than rent depends on whether the economic gain from the property-tax saving, τ, exceeds the economic loss from the forgone capital subsidy, $\delta t(\alpha - 1)/(1 - t)$.

As may be seen, when $\alpha \leq 1$ a nonprofit would benefit from owning rather than renting. This will occur under one of two depreciation regimes. In the first, the tax system provides the equivalent of true economic depreciation, $\alpha = 1$, and the term $\delta t(\alpha - 1)$ "vanishes." The fact that the nonprofit organization cannot claim tax deductions for depreciation does not affect the organization's decision to own or rent, and the financial benefit from ownership exactly equals the value of the property tax that the nonprofit does not need to pay. This may initially seem counterintuitive, but it follows from the fact that there is no tax subsidy when deductions for economic depreciation are allowed under an income tax, and, hence, there is no implicit capital subsidy that the nonprofit organization loses when it becomes an owner.

Under the second regime, when the tax system allows less than economic depreciation, so that $\alpha < 1$, the incentive to own rather than rent exists whether or not property is exempt from property taxation. When businesses are allowed to claim less than economic depreciation on their assets, the tax system effectively imposes an added tax penalty (instead of a subsidy) on the return to capital, which has to be recovered in the rent. Ownership allows the nonprofit to save this tax penalty along with the property tax.

A Numerical Illustration
These basic points are illustrated in tables 4-8 and 4-9, adapted from Galper and Toder (1981), which show how the property-tax exemption could affect the decision to own versus rent in three different cases. The first is when tax depreciation is equivalent to true economic depreciation. In such an instance, if capital markets equilibrate the after-tax return from investing in a building and the after-tax return from investing in financial assets, then the pre-tax return that a for-profit landlord would need to earn on a building would be the same (on a risk-adjusted basis) as the return on a bond. If the hypothetical nonprofit is assumed to have an endowment sufficient to enable it to purchase either a building or a bond worth, for example, $1 million, then the nonprofit could either invest the endowment in a bond, earn an annual cash income of $100,000, and pay a market rent of $120,000; or it could use the endowment to buy the building, forgo the cash income, and save the market rent of $120,000. In this instance, owning would be the better financial decision: The nonprofit would be better off financially by an amount exactly equal to the property tax it would not have to pay.

In the second case, it is assumed that tax depreciation is more generous than true economic depreciation. Allowing tax depreciation that is more rapid than economic depreciation has the effect of sheltering from taxation a portion of the return that a for-profit investor would earn by investing in the building. In the example, it is assumed that only 60 percent of the return from the building is taxed. If the assumed tax rate is 40 percent,

Table 4-8. *Financial Benefits of Owning versus Renting for a Nonprofit Organization, as a Function of the Tax Treatment of Depreciation and the Property-Tax Rate*

	Tax Depreciation Equivalent to Economic Depreciation; Return to Investment in Building 100 Percent Taxed	Tax Depreciation Exceeds Economic Depreciation; Return to Investment in Building 60 Percent Taxed	Tax Depreciation Less than Economic Depreciation; Return to Investment in Building 130 Percent Taxed
Parameter Values			
Building Value	$1,000,000	$1,000,000	$1,000,000
Pretax Return on Bond	10.0%	10.0%	10.0%
Pretax Return on Building	10.0%	7.89%	12.5%
Property-Tax Rate	2.0%	2.0%	2.0%
Market Rent			
Return to Landlord (building value times the pretax return on the building)	$100,000	$78,900	$125,000
Property Tax (building value times the property-tax rate)	$20,000	$20,000	$20,000
Total Market Rent (return to landlord plus value of the property tax)	$120,000	$98,900	$145,000

Table 4-9. *Cash-Flow Effects of Owning versus Renting for a Nonprofit Organization, as a Function of the Tax Treatment of Depreciation and the Property-Tax Rate*

	Tax Depreciation Equivalent to Economic Depreciation; Return to Investment in Building 100 Percent Taxed		Tax Depreciation Exceeds Economic Depreciation; Return to Investment in Building 60 Percent Taxed		Tax Depreciation Less than Economic Depreciation; Return to Investment in Building 130 Percent Taxed	
	Own	*Rent*	*Own*	*Rent*	*Own*	*Rent*
Building	$1,000,000	$0	$1,000,000	$0	$1,000,000	$0
Bond	0	1,000,000	0	1,000,000	0	1,000,000
Cash Flow						
Rent Saved	120,000	0	98,900	0	145,000	0
Bond Income	0	100,000	0	100,000	0	100,000

then the required pre-tax return a landlord would have to earn would be 7.89 percent.[12]

The implication is that the market rent would equal $98,900, the amount needed to provide the landlord with the competitive pre-tax return of 7.89 percent on the $1 million investment after paying the assumed property-tax bill of $20,000. This is the amount of rent the non-profit would save if it owned the building. In this case, however, renting rather than owning would allow the nonprofit to earn a cash return of $100,000. Thus, owning would save the nonprofit $98,900 in rent, at a cost of $100,000 in forgone cash income from investing in the bond. The nonprofit would have no financial incentive to own rather than rent, since owning would involve incurring a small financial loss.

The third case illustrates what would happen if the tax system allowed investors to deduct less than the value of true depreciation. The economic effect would be to tax more than 100 percent of the return from depreciable assets. In the example, the assumption is that 130 percent of the return would be subject to tax. Because the effect of allowing less than economic depreciation is to make the building more heavily taxed than a bond, a for-profit landlord would also require a somewhat higher pre-tax return to earn the same after-tax return from investing in a building as in a bond. If the assumed tax rate is 40 percent, then the required pre-tax return the landlord would have to earn on the building would be 12.5 percent, compared with a 10 percent return on the bond. The implication is that the market rent would equal $145,000, which is the amount needed to provide the landlord with the competitive return of 12.5 percent on the $1 million investment, and the landlord would also have to pay a tax of $20,000. If the nonprofit owned instead of renting, it would save $145,000 in rent payments while forgoing the opportunity to earn a cash return of $100,000 from investing in the bond. Owning would clearly be more attractive financially, but note that in this case the property-tax exemption is not the deciding factor. Even if the nonprofit were required to pay the property tax of $20,000, it would still earn a "net" return from investing in the "super-taxed" asset of $125,000, which would exceed the cash return from investing in the bond.

One implication of the model is that, other things being equal, non-profit organizations should have a stronger incentive to rent rather than own when the property-tax rate is low and when the depreciation system is relatively generous. The latter condition pertained in the early 1980s, under the Economic Recovery Tax Act of 1981 (ERTA). Indeed, some nonprofit organizations that owned property sought to sell and then lease back such property—most notoriously, Bennington College.[13] In effect, Bennington was willing to pay the property tax (which would be reflected in its lease) in exchange for having the lessor pass through the tax advantages from accelerated-depreciation allowances. Such sale and lease-back provisions were almost immediately disallowed under the Tax Equity and Fiscal Responsibility Act of 1982 (TEFRA), but the incentive to rent rather than to own remained.

These incentives were reversed with the passage of the Tax Reform Act of 1986 (TRA). Basically, TRA scrapped the accelerated-depreciation schedules for buildings, and required that deductions be spread over a fairly long useful life. Many economists believe that the depreciation schedules enacted under TRA effectively allow economic depreciation, so that one might expect the property-tax exemption to provide an unambiguous incentive—which would increase as the property-tax rate rose— to own rather than rent.

Case 2: The Nonprofit Is Not the Sole Tenant

In many cases, a nonprofit organization does not need to occupy the entire building. Modeling the own-versus-rent decision in such situations is more complex, and much depends how the property-tax exemption is applied. For example, suppose that the state grants property-tax exemption for a dual-use building (i.e., part is used by the nonprofit and part is used by other organizations). In that case, if the nonprofit owns the building and rents out part, it saves the property tax, and also acquires a tax-favored source of income. The incentive to own would seem strong. At the other extreme, a state might deny exemption entirely for a dual-use building. In that case, the nonprofit would save no property tax by owning rather than renting.

Effects of Tax-Exempt Financing

In recent years, it has become much easier for nonprofit organizations to issue tax-exempt bonds to finance their activities. Although tax-exempt bond financing is distinct from the property-tax exemption, the ability to issue tax-exempt debt does provide an incentive for nonprofits to borrow in order to own rather than rent (and to increase their use of capital, including buildings generally). If a nonprofit has the ability to borrow in the tax-exempt bond market, it faces a borrowing rate of r_e, which is less than the return, r, that can be earned on an alternative investment. In this case, if the nonprofit organization borrows to finance the cost of acquiring its own building, the implicit rental cost is given by

$$(6) \qquad\qquad c^* = qr_e + q\delta \rightarrow \frac{c^*}{q} = r_e + \delta\,,$$

where r_e is the tax-exempt borrowing rate. From equation 6 it follows that the benefit of owning instead of renting is

$$(7) \qquad\qquad \frac{c}{q} - \frac{c^*}{q} > 0 \rightarrow (r - r_e) + \tau - \frac{\delta t(\alpha - 1)}{(1 - t)} > 0\,,$$

where the term $(r - r_e)$ is the spread between the pre-tax return and the tax-exempt borrowing rate.[14] Thus, the effect of tax-exempt bond financing is to further increase nonprofit organizations' incentive to acquire property; and, like federal changes in depreciation rules, federal tax policy governing the issuance of tax-exempt debt by nonprofits may have a measurable effect on the amount of property that local jurisdictions are able to tax. The main effect of tax-exempt financing, however, would seem to be concentrated in three nonprofit sectors—higher education, hospitals, and nursing homes—that together accounted for three-quarters of the nonprofit organizations that reported having tax-exempt bond liabilities in the 1995 SOI sample.

Property-Tax Exemption and Locational Decisions

How does the exemption affect where nonprofits choose to locate? It might be tempting to conclude that if the property-tax burden tends to be higher in central cities than in suburban areas, then the property-tax exemption may keep some nonprofits from favoring lower-tax suburbs over higher-tax central cities. If correct, this conjecture would imply that policies that weaken or remove the exemption could affect the locational decisions of nonprofits in ways that might disadvantage central cities.

But, as noted above, the evidence indicates that the majority of nonprofits do not own taxable real property; since competition in markets for rental real estate will cause the property tax to be shifted forward to renters, nonprofits that rent will implicitly bear the relatively higher burden of urban property taxes through higher monthly rents. Hence, these nonprofits face the same financial incentives or disincentives to choose an urban location that for-profit businesses would. Thus, the extent to which the property-tax exemption contributes to "locational neutrality" seems limited to nonprofits that are property owners.

Property-Tax Exemption and Commerciality

Does the property-tax exemption encourage nonprofits to undertake commercial ventures and give them an unfair competitive edge in markets in which nonprofits compete with for-profit businesses? As noted by Rose-Ackerman (1982), Schiff and Weisbrod (1991), Cordes and Weisbrod (1998), and Sansing (1998), the property-tax exemption (along with the income-tax exemption) does create a financial incentive for nonprofits to undertake certain types of commercial activity that they might otherwise be inclined to avoid. But the impetus for doing so is not that nonprofits are able to enter a market and undercut the competition. Instead, the existence of property taxes creates a "tax premium" that nontaxed organizations are able to capture. In a world in which for-profit enterprises must pay property and income taxes, the pretax returns to investing in commercial activities will adjust so that the marginal profit per dollar invested is enough to pay a competitive return plus cover property and other taxes. Nonprofits do not have to pay these taxes, and hence are able to pocket the amount of property and other taxes that are embedded in the pretax return. This added return may help overcome any innate aversion a nonprofit might have to earning income from activities that it feels are in conflict with its primary mission.

Hansmann (1987) and Gulley and Santerre (1993) use interstate variations in property- and corporate-tax rates to examine whether the market share of nonprofits in selected industries is higher in states with relatively high tax rates, and find that the size of the nonprofit sector in these industries does increase with the tax rate. Cordes and Weisbrod (1998) find that the share of income that individual nonprofits derive from commercial activities increases with state income- and property-tax rates. These results provide empirical evidence that property-tax exemption can encourage nonprofits to become more commercial than would otherwise be the case.

Conclusion

In the introduction to this volume, Evelyn Brody observes, "Averages mask the widely varying impact of [property-tax] exemptions on particular communities and of taxes or PILOTs on particular nonprofits." The picture this chapter paints of the economic effect of the property-tax exemption on nonprofit organizations illustrates this point in several ways.

The numbers presented in this chapter clearly show that the incidence of the financial benefits provided by the tax exemption falls unevenly throughout the nonprofit sector. The existence of the exemption has little or no direct effect on the financial condition or operations of many nonprofits. But the effects can be quite important for certain types of nonprofits.

The analysis also shows that the exemption has a variety of undesirable, desirable, and mixed effects on how certain nonprofits operate. Given the current tax rules for tax depreciation, the nonprofit exemption provides a financial incentive for nonprofits to own rather than rent property. For nonprofits that own property, the property-tax exemption has the desirable effect of eliminating taxes from the financial calculation of where to locate, although this result does not hold for the many nonprofits that rent rather than own. Lastly, the exemption creates a financial incentive for some nonprofit organizations to engage in commercial ventures they might otherwise avoid; there is empirical evidence that nonprofits respond to this incentive.

Overall, the results in this chapter, along with those presented elsewhere in this volume (especially Netzer, chapter 3), suggest that analysts should take a nuanced view of the property-tax exemption's economic importance to both nonprofits and the communities in which they are located. Netzer points out that, on balance, the exemption does not have a large fiscal impact on many communities, though the effects vary by type of community. In other words, while the overall incidence of the exemption on communities may not be large, it falls more heavily on some communities than others.

The evidence presented in this chapter indicates that the effect of the exemption on nonprofit organizations mirrors its effect on communities. Overall, the economic effects of repealing or reducing the exemption *for the minority of nonprofits that own real property* appear to be roughly equivalent to a drop in revenue of 2 or 3 percentage points.

The importance of this amount should not be discounted, although many nonprofits that would be called on to pay property taxes if the exemption were curtailed could presumably absorb the financial impact of such a cutback with a modest change in operations. But the results also show that the effect of repealing or reducing the property-tax exemption may fall more unevenly on nonprofit organizations *within* communities than *among* communities. For example, the exemption can be financially important to nonprofits engaged in activities that require substantial input of land and buildings and to smaller nonprofits with low cash flows.

Given this perspective, it is worth asking whether the generally modest fiscal benefits to cities from repealing or reducing the exemption would be worth the fiscal costs in terms of the impact of such a change on individual nonprofit organizations.[15] A related question is whether there are ways of crafting more targeted exemptions that reduce the fiscal impact to communities while minimizing the financial effects of limiting the exemption on certain types of nonprofit organizations.

NOTES

1. For an overview, see chapter 3 in this volume and Netzer (1993).

2. For a discussion of the controversies surrounding unfair competition, see Weisbrod (1998) and Steinberg (1991).

3. To the extent that receiving zoning or other regulatory approval is made conditional on the payment of a PILOT, such payments become more and more tax-like in nature. For a recent analysis of the possible effects of requiring PILOTs in Minnesota, see Minnesota Council of Nonprofits (2000).

4. See Steinberg and Bilodeau (1999) for a recent discussion of the policy rationale for providing tax exemptions for nonprofit organizations.

5. Focusing on organizations that file the IRS Form 990 generally limits the analysis to nonprofits that are not churches, which are not required to file an information return (although they may choose to do so).

6. Tabulations of data from the digitized returns in this chapter are based on the version of the NCCS/PRI National Nonprofit Organization Database as of April 13, 2000. For more information about this database, see http://www.nccs.urban.org/digdata.htm.

7. It may be unclear why less than 100 percent of nonprofits classified as retirement homes, hospitals, and higher education are estimated to have less than $100,000 in land, buildings, and equipment. One answer is that these categories include nonprofits that are classified as engaged in a particular activity (e.g., higher education), but that are not directly involved in the provision of the service (e.g., a university foundation).

8. The time periods over which the tax savings from the property-tax exemption are estimated by the state do not coincide exactly with the time frame used to tabulate financial information in the NCSS core file. Hence, the percentages that are presented in the last column of table 4-3 are best seen as rough "order-of-magnitude" estimates of the financial importance of the tax exemption.

9. The authors are grateful to David Glancey for providing these data.

10. The analysis that follows is not intended to apply to houses of worship, where there may be many nonfinancial reasons for owning rather than renting.

11. Economic depreciation is the rate at which a depreciable asset declines in market value. It is related to, but distinct from, the physical rate of wear and tear and/or obsolescence.

12. This return is based on the assumption that capital markets will adjust asset prices and returns until the after-tax return that is earned by investing $1 in a building equals the after-tax return from investing $1 in a bond. If the tax rate is 40 percent, the after-tax bond return is 6 percent. Thus, the building must generate a before-tax return, r, that pays the landlord an after-tax return of 6 percent. This return, r, must satisfy the equation $6.0 = r(1 - .4\alpha)$, where α is the percentage of the return from investing in the building that is taxable. In this example, accelerated depreciation is assumed to shelter 40 percent of the return from taxation, so that $\alpha = .6$. Thus, $r = 6.0/(1 - .24) = (6.0/.76) = 7.89$.

13. For an analysis see Galper and Toder (1981).

14. Readers familiar with the literature on tax shelters will immediately recognize that nonprofits' ability to borrow to finance the cost of owning their own buildings gives nonprofit organizations a convenient form of interest-related tax arbitrage. For a recent analysis of such behavior in the case of hospitals, see Gentry (2000).

15. Minnesota Council of Nonprofits (2000).

REFERENCES

Bowman, John, ed. 1995. *Taxation of Business Property: Is Uniformity Still a Valid Norm?* Westport, Conn.: Praeger Publishers.

Cordes, Joseph J., and Burton A. Weisbrod. 1998. "Differential Taxation of Nonprofits and the Commercialization of Nonprofit Revenues." *Journal of Policy Analysis and Management* 17 (2): 195–214.

Froelich, Karen A., Terry W. Knoepfle, and Thomas H. Pollak. 2000. "Financial Measures in Nonprofit Organization Research: Comparing IRS 990 Return and Audited Financial Statement Data." *Nonprofit and Voluntary Sector Quarterly* 29 (2): 232–54.

Galper, Harvey, and Eric Toder. 1981. "Owning or Leasing: Bennington College and the U.S. Tax System." *National Tax Journal* 36 (2): 257–61.

Gentry, William. 2000. "Endowment Assets, Tax-Exempt Debt and the Capital Structure of Not-for-Profit Hospitals." Unpublished, Columbia University.

Gentry, William, and John R. Penrod. 2000. "The Tax Benefits of Not-for-Profit Hospitals." In *The Changing Hospital Industry: Comparing Not-for-Profit and For-Profit Institutions,* edited by David M. Cutler (285–324). Chicago: The University of Chicago.

Gulley, David O., and Rexford E. Santerre. 1993. "The Effect of Tax Exemption on the Market Share of Nonprofit Hospitals." *National Tax Journal* 46 (4): 477–86.

Hansmann, Henry. 1987. "The Effect of Tax Exemption and Other Factors on the Market Share of Nonprofit versus For-Profit Firms." *National Tax Journal* 40 (1): 71–82.

Michigan Department of Treasury, Office of Revenue and Tax Analysis. 1997. *Non-Profit Hospital Expenditures.* Ann Arbor: Michigan Department of Treasury.

Minnesota Council of Nonprofits. 2000. "Cost Estimate of Payments in Lieu of Taxes on Charitable Institutions and Hospitals." Http://www.mncn.org/bp/pilotcost.htm.

Minnesota Taxpayers Association. 1999. *50-State Property Tax Comparison Study.* St. Paul, Minn.: Minnesota Taxpayers Association.

Netzer, Dick. 1993. "Property Taxes: Their Past, Present, and Future Place in Government Finance." In *Urban Finance Under Siege,* edited by Thomas A. Swartz and Frank J. Bonello (51–78). Armonk, N.Y.: M.E. Sharpe.

Rose-Ackerman, Susan. 1982. "Unfair Competition and Corporate Income Taxation." *Stanford Law Review* 34 (5): 1017–36.

Sansing, Richard. 1998. "The Unrelated Business Income Tax: Cost Allocation, and Productive Efficiency." *National Tax Journal* 51 (2): 291–302.

Schiff, Jerald, and Burton A. Weisbrod. 1991. "Competition between For-Profit and Nonprofit Organizations in Commercial Markets." *Annals of Public and Cooperative Economics* 62 (4): 619–39.

Steinberg, Richard. 1991. "Unfair Competition by Nonprofits and Tax Policy." *National Tax Journal* 44 (3): 351–63.

Steinberg, Richard, and Marc Bilodeau. 1999. *Should Nonprofit Organizations Pay Sales and Property Tax?* Washington, D.C.: National Council of Nonprofit Associations.

Weisbrod, Burton A. 1998. *To Profit or Not to Profit: The Commercial Transformation of the Nonprofit Sector.* Cambridge: Cambridge University Press.

PART II
Contrasting Theories
of Exemption Law

5

Efficiency and Benevolence

Philanthropic Tax Exemptions in 19th-Century America

Stephen Diamond

M odern commentators typically justify the tax exemption for philanthropic organizations by the public services the organizations perform. Sometimes the analogy is made to the exemption of some governmental units: It is inefficient to tax with one hand what would otherwise have to be supported by public expenditures. Exemption is thus ideally revenue neutral, reflecting a calculation that the social value of the services performed by the exempt organization is at least as great as the revenues forgone. Many exemptions, however, do not meet this exacting standard, assuming that it ever could be made operational. Exemption critics continue to use this standard to judge exemptions adversely and to voice fears that the continued use of exemptions is unjust and will in time threaten fiscal solvency. Ever since the Progressive movement and the late 19th century development of budgets, there has been periodic pressure to subject the exemption to a more particularized review and to tailor exemptions—if permitted at all—to the level of public goods and services created and performed by an organization, or to demand that the organization increase its output of goods and services to justify its present exemption.

Critics of exemptions base their criterion for legitimate exemptions on at least loose adherence to a contractual, benefit theory of taxation. Even before Thomas Cooley's 1876 publication of his *Treatise on Taxa-*

tion, taxes were commonly seen as the reciprocal obligation, or price, paid for the protection of persons or property by the state. It has thus been increasingly plausible to see exemptions as state recognition that the institution so rewarded is meeting its obligation to contribute to the state through means other than tax payments.

Commentators armed with this theoretical approach sometimes did claim that history also supported their position, and that such calculations had always—or at least for a long time—been made by governments. This claim, however, was typically asserted rather than demonstrated (Eliot 1875; Adler 1922). Commentators insisted that any exemption must have originated—whether recently or in the dim past—in some such calculation that the benefits provided by the institution outweighed the forgone revenues (Tobin, Hannan, and Tolman 1934; Stimson 1934; Hughes 1935).

Such imaginative recreations of history are not uncommon in modern legal argument. But although history, if we can call it that, was hypothesized to explain the origins of exemptions, there is no particular evidence of these primal cost/benefit calculations. In a sense, this insistence upon the existence of an original policy decision was as ideologically impelled and empirically unconfirmed as the insistence of the common lawyers of the late 16th and early 17th centuries that all common-law rules had existed since the memory of man runneth not to the contrary, and that laws were inherited rather than created, and the insistence of their opponents, with equal absence of evidence, that all customs were the result of an original act of lawmaking (Pocock 1957).

This critique of exemptions reflects a common and deeply held American belief in the possibility of creating a political—or religious or moral—regime on a clean slate, unfettered by outmoded, Old World and feudal—or monarchical—institutions and practices. It posits an America of the newborn or reborn. But there was never such a beginning point, a moment when the social compact was created, or when the primal tax calculations were made. The original colonists brought exemptions with them. Death, taxes, and exemptions run endlessly in our past and will do so in our future.

Specific calculations of the kind advocated by commentators in the 20th century could not have been undertaken or understood by Americans in the early 19th century. Exemptions for educational, philanthropic, and religious organizations (and these three continued to be lumped together by both commentators and legislatures throughout the century) could not have been viewed as subsidies at a time when there was no norm of universal taxation. Exemptions appeared in charters even when there was no norm of general property taxation, but they could not have been given cash values and were not considered a form of expenditure. That there was no pattern of regular taxation meant also that it was impossible to calculate with any accuracy the extent of taxes forgone by any grant of exemption. The question asked—to the extent any question was asked—was not how much a church or university was worth, but whether its continued existence was desirable. The threat of tax liens was a potentially mortal one. The question was thus existential rather than fiscal. Taxation, when there was no capacity to pay, was in a practical sense confiscation. It was also believed that donors wanted reassurance that their bequests would last forever. Accordingly, in 1702, when Connecticut passed a statute that assured donors of the perpetual existence of their bequests, as part of this assurance, it also granted tax-exempt status.

It was not until the growing acceptance of the general property tax in the mid-19th century, with its norm of universal property taxation, that the exemption was challenged. The response was not rejection of exemption but explicit codification of the status. Every outburst of criticism left exemptions strengthened. They did not survive covertly, avoiding public scrutiny. Their reconsideration was intermittent, but intense. Indeed, supporters, as well as detractors, insisted that a clear understanding of the facts would support their particular position. Increasingly, tax exemptions were granted under general rules. Critics complained that such rules, which encouraged extensions by analogy, led to profligate granting of exemptions, and called instead for closer examination of individual entitlements to tax-exempt status. So the demands of equality and uniformity, rather than challenging the legitimacy of exemptions, led to their general extension by category and type. A charter exemption at least had the theoretical virtue of once having been individually considered.

Exemptions only gradually came to be regarded as subsidies, a description employed in particular by the new budget experts, who attacked exemptions as secretive—an evasion of the exercise of legislative choice—but who in fact often hoped to make the budgetary decisions themselves. Although they marched under the banner of disinterested expertise, their critique met with little success. The defense of exemptions was already well developed. From similar postulates, as we shall see, the contestants generated contradictory conclusions. More than a century's additional debate has added little.

What follows is a brief treatment of the history of the issue of exemptions from the property tax in 19th century America, a history that largely shaped the debate for the draftsmen of the federal income tax in the 20th century.

The Early Ad Hoc Period

For several reasons, tax exemptions in the early republic were less controversial than they later became, and were not thought of or criticized as covert public subsidies. There was no formal institutionalized practice of tax exemption at the time of Independence, though there were a variety of institutions that had been given exemptions in their charters of incorporation. Church exemptions simply continued, even as churches were disestablished, with little apparent discussion. As we shall see, the explanations for exemption practices were largely articulated and codified post hoc, only when exemptions were increasingly challenged as violations of the emerging legal norms of equality, universality, and generality. Exemptions may have been suspect as privileges, but when granted by charter or treaty, for instance, they were protected as vested rights.

Chief Justice Marshall was so concerned to protect such privileges that, in *New Jersey v. Wilson*, 7 Cranch 164 (1812), he held that an exemption of land sold by Delaware Indians ran with the land and thus could be claimed by the purchaser. (He noted that one benefit of such a conclusion would be that the Indians would be able to sell at a higher price.) Similarly, in 1819 the Supreme Court held that New Hampshire violated the Contracts Clause of the Constitution by attempting to alter the charter of Dartmouth College. (*Dartmouth College v. Woodward*, 17 U.S. (4 Wheat.) 518 (1819)). These two decisions were subjected to much criticism in the late 19th century, when perpetual grants were being more critically evaluated, even as (or perhaps because) perpetual corporate charters were becoming the norm. Late 19th-century and early 20th-century critics of the *New Jersey v. Wilson* decision worried that the contractualizing of tax exemptions would create a permanent limitation upon government flexibility and authority and enshrine the dead hand of the past. While exemptions granted by charter became relatively rare after the mid-century emphasis upon general legislation,[1] the Contracts Clause was not necessary to protect most existing exemptions. Public opinion, as reflected in law, did so well enough. It was the growth of new exemptions that critics professed to fear.

There was as yet no universal system of taxation, no general property tax that attempted to identify all property within the jurisdiction and tax it at the same ad valorem rate. Thus the very fact of exemption on the one hand incited criticism because, like other charter privileges, it represented feudal or royal favoritism, and on the other hand was less controversial in the abstract, since it did not flout a generally held and codified norm of taxation. In the absence of universal taxation, exemption still functioned, in a sense, expressively rather than instrumentally. Exemption served to demonstrate that an institution was favored by the state, although the extent of the favor was obscure.

In addition, in the early decades of the 19th century, property was often taxed because of its income-producing capacity (Robinson 1902, 85–87; Adams 1900, 28–29). Unoccupied land was commonly not taxed. Not taxing charities and churches, therefore, violated no general prescription that all property was to be taxed, and also reflected a general practice not to seek fiscal blood from a stone. Exempted institutions that received rents did cause controversy. Pew rents were sometimes included in this category. Was exemption to be maintained because the money was used for educational, charitable, or religious purposes, or was exemption to be lost because funds for paying taxes were available?

Finally, routine, annual taxation did not become a feature of American fiscal life until after the economic crisis of 1837. There was thus no way to estimate the dollar value of an exemption, since state taxes typically were imposed only during emergencies. The exemption was thus not a regular subsidy, the equivalent of an annual appropriation of a specific amount. The decision not to tax could never be translated into a dollar figure when there was no settled structure of a regular tax with predictable rates. Taxation in the nation's early years, being neither universal in aspiration nor regular in application, did not compel and, indeed, could not support an understanding of exemptions as specific covert subsidies.

As a matter of legal theory, taxation was always understood to be the quintessential sovereign act. Chief Justice Marshall expressed this in asserting that the power to tax was the power to destroy. Subsequent commentators, both judicial and otherwise, somehow extrapolated from Marshall's apothegm to conclude that the sovereign power to apportion, and consequently to exempt, was absolute (see, e.g., *Griffin v. Mayor of Brooklyn*, 4 N.Y. 419, 426–27 (1851); Burroughs 1877, 6–8). Unless and until the state taxing power was constitutionally constrained—which did not occur until the norms of equality and uniformity began being mandated in the 1830s—the powers to tax, or not to tax, were intermittently used, but were essentially legally uncontestable.

The General Property-Tax Period

In the 1830s, state property taxation became routinized as an annual obligation. It also became regulated, as ascendant Jacksonianism demanded open and equal opportunity and general rules. Individual privileges and special treatments were challenged. For a time, local government laws (as opposed to general legislation for the entire sovereign state), special corporate charters, private divorces, and tax exemptions were among the practices that were unfavorably evaluated and sometimes abandoned. States began either constitutionally or statutorily mandating the general property tax. Taxation was to be equal and universal; exemptions, therefore, became anomalous (Newhouse 1984).

Such criticism obviously did not lead to the end of tax exemptions. California's experience is revealing. Although the original state constitution of 1850, adopted during the period of greatest popularity of the general property tax, mandated equal and uniform taxation, the California legislature initially granted the traditional exemptions that had existed before statehood (Bovard 1900). These enactments survived judicial challenges until the state Supreme Court held, in *People v. McCreery*, 34 Cal. 432 (1878), that the exemption of any but state or federal property was constitutionally prohibited. Typically, however, individual assessors apparently continued their prior practices, by either ignoring church property or minimally assessing it. California's new constitution of 1879 again opted for the general property tax, declaring all but "growing crops" to be taxable property. Churches were at least potentially taxable in California for the rest of the century, the only liberalization of the norm of universality being the exemption of libraries and museums—so long as they charged no fees—in 1894. In 1900, the California Constitution was amended to exempt churches and the sites on which they were located from taxation (see Section 1½, Article 13). The challenge of the general property tax ultimately led, as it had earlier in other states, to explicit constitutional authorization of exemptions.

It was with the critique of exemptions' at least implicit existence in the general property tax that the apologetics of exemption also emerged, and that exemptions became common subjects of explicit constitutional or statutory regulation. Massachusetts did not have church exemption laws until 1837, New Hampshire until 1842, and New Jersey until 1851. Only in Massachusetts did explicit exemption follow relatively closely on disestablishment. Rather, the general property tax was usually the precipitating factor. It was not until 1859 that the first state constitution (that of Kansas) expressly exempted churches from taxation (Zollmann 1916a, 649). By the end of the century, the great majority of states had done so.

Why did the exemption survive? A Pennsylvania court explained the statutory exemption of churches as inspired by "the almost universal, innate promptings of the human heart" (see Zollman 1916a, 649). A New Jersey court in 1853 somewhat less grandly suggested that church tax exemption continued because the practice was "so entirely in accord with the public sentiment that it universally prevailed" (Adler 1922, 77).

The exemptions that emerged from this legislative, constitutional, and judicial tailoring usually included the church and land on which it sat, but not any other property. In particular, church land earning rental income was not exempt, nor typically was any endowment (van Alstyne 1959; *Exemption of Church Property in the Several States of this Union* 1878; Protestant Episcopal Church in the U.S.A. 1875). Educational institutions were also usually taxed on any rent-producing property, although some states exempted their endowments. During the rest of the century, exemptions on endowments were gradually extended (Hannan 1917), perhaps because both tax administrators and reformers increasingly objected to the taxation of intangible personal property, much of which was assumed to be successfully hidden in any event. It thus became possible to create a tax-exempt endowment through the purchase of state or federal bonds (Foote 1877b, 468). Real estate used for commercial purposes, however, continued to be taxed.

Yet churches did not always remain on the sites on which they were established. Urban churches, following their mobile constituencies, relocated, sometimes selling the original site for a large profit. Many people felt it was unfair that no tax would apply to a church that sold its site after the land value had significantly risen, even if the church used the sale proceeds to purchase and build on a new church site. In effect, church or educational missions were being perceived and described as land speculations (Quincy 1872, 583–84). The correlation between exemption and the eternal dedication of property to noncommercially productive use was made explicit when, in 1862, a Pennsylvania judge upheld the exemption of the American Philosophical Society's real estate holdings in Philadelphia's Independence Square, in the absence of any clear statutory requirement that this be done, because the Society could not alter its use of this property in any way (*Philadelphia v. American Philosophical Society*, 42 Pa. St. 9, 19–20 (1862)). Thus, the sale of original sites and the relocation of churches threatened the model supporting their exempt status. Tax exemption in these circumstances increased the force of Henry George's critique of the unearned increment.

This pattern of partial exemption, with the critical criterion being whether the property was being commercially exploited, suggests yet again that exemption was not being thought of as a subsidy. With a subsidy, the critical question is not the use of specific property, but the ultimate dollar value of the exemption. This position was sometimes articulated, but usually to no avail. If the exemption were a subsidy, and the rent earned was used for the support of the institution, then the property should have been at least potentially exempt. Money subsidies are fungible; exemptions, however, were not. It was sometimes feared that exempting rental property would permit unfair competition against fully taxpaying businesses. The argument was often simpler: If income existed, there was something to tax (*State v. Carleton College*, 154 Minn. 280 (1923)). There was also a concern, expressed even by President Grant, that general exemption would lead to vast ecclesiastical holdings, such as those confiscated in England by Henry VIII. This conjured up fears of an establishment of European landlord-tenant relationships, and, with them, the end of political liberty in the United States. The amassing of land, given its finite nature, posed a particular risk of concentrated power and thus may have appeared more dangerous than the amassing of intangible wealth—not that the latter did not also arouse opposition.

The mid-century pattern of exemptions might be described as the summation of a desire to subsidize certain institutions, to maintain a level playing field for economic competition, and to sustain relatively widespread land ownership, but it is more plausible that the practice simply reflected a continuation of the fiscal strategy of taxing only what produced income. Moreover, critics expressed concern about exemption of the land and buildings actually used by churches and charities not because such institutions needed and deserved some public support, but because, if taxed, they might be unable to pay—especially since the property in question was not income-producing—and would, therefore, be seized in tax-foreclosure proceedings. Thus viewed, the question was not whether such institutions deserved of support, and if so, how much, but instead, more starkly, whether or not such institutions should continue to exist. In practice, even with exempt status removed, churches almost never faced such a fate (*Trustees of the First Methodist Episcopal Church, South v. City of Atlanta*, 76 Ga. 181 (1886)).

Cemeteries were a paradigmatic exempt institution. The dedication was, in theory, permanent. Cemeteries continued to remain exempt even when it was generally acknowledged that many were commercially operated for a profit. Nevertheless, throughout the century, cemeteries were exempted because of doubts that anyone would pay taxes on them—it was noted that the dead could not meet fiscal obligations—and fear that the land cemeteries would accordingly be seized and sold (Foote 1877b, 491–92; Zollman 1916b).

The reluctance to exempt income-producing property, whatever the ultimate use of the income, was reflected in statutes that barred exemptions to institutions charging fees. The United States Congress, when imposing an income tax during the Civil War, employed equally formal distinctions and made no general exemption for philanthropic institutions. The tax on institutions, unlike that on individuals, was actually an excise tax rather than an income. Churches and many philanthropies would presumably not have been included within its terms and museums were not taxed if they charged no fees (*Congressional Record* 1869, 1819).

Hospitals, however, apparently were taxed. In 1869, when Representative Morgan, on behalf of the hospital to be established by the terms of James Roosevelt's will, proposed that all hospitals be exempt from the tax so long as they offered free treatment to sick or disabled United States soldiers, Representative Fessenden, the floor manager of the bill, fearing a slippery slope, explained his committee's disagreement:

> The committee on thinking this matter over came to the conclusion that to begin to make exceptions would lead to infinite confusion; the amount would be very large in the end; every effort would be made to bring cases within the principle, if we tried to adopt a principle in reference to it, and we thought it would be entirely unsafe. We therefore objected to introducing anything of this kind into the general bill providing for the raising of revenue. . . . (Ibid. 1869, 2755–56)

The motion to exempt hospitals was overwhelmingly rejected, presumably in part because of wartime demands for revenue. However, in 1863 George Boutwell, the Commissioner of Internal Revenue, determined not to tax the "income of literary, scientific, or other charitable institutions" (Boutwell 1863, 275).

The ambivalent federal tax treatment of hospitals suggests the difficulty the older exemption model had with income-earning property. Property permanently unable to pay taxes—and socially worthy—was most clearly entitled to exemption. There were even challenges to the exemption of churches because they were not, it was argued, commercially unproductive; for instance, Henry Ward Beecher's Plymouth Church in Brooklyn rented out pews for $50,000 a year (Westbrook 1890, 364). Even some church-exemption supporters hoped for a system of free pews in which churches would truly be open to the entire public (Pitzer 1880, 373).

Post–Civil War Debate

As measured by the amount of pamphlet warfare and proposed legislation, the intensity of debate over tax exemptions increased markedly in the 1870s. The focus was on the exemption for churches, but both critics and advocates expected that what was decided with regard to churches would, and should, eventually apply to secular philanthropic and educational institutions as well. In many states, indeed, the tax treatment of religious, educational, and philanthropic institutions was still regulated by a single provision. The conflict may have been triggered by the post–Civil War efforts of evangelical conservatives to amend the United States Constitution to provide for explicit acceptance of religion—and Christianity in particular—in upholding civil order. The Civil War was, to such reformers, God's warning that the American people and their political system were off course. This campaign disturbed the largely unarticulated compromise by which such exemptions had existed, first simply as a matter of custom after formal church support was ended, and then through specific statutory ratification in the decades just before the Civil War. The American Liberal League, in this period led from Boston by Francis Abbot, resisted the evangelical movement and helped initiate a review of Massachusetts tax policy and practices. In its magazine, *The Index*, the League attacked not just the proposed amendment, but the tax exemption as well (Robertson 1968, 71–86; Abbot 1875; Wright 1877). Tax-exemption opponents were also motivated by a fear, shared by much of the evangelical community, of the Catholic Church's growing wealth and power, which they hoped to constrain significantly by ending exemptions. The exemption became a battlefield in the New England elite's confrontation with an increasingly heterogeneous population (Quincy 1872, 653; Hovey 1874, 174).

National leaders supported the elimination of tax exemptions. In 1874, James Garfield called in the House for the end of any ties between church and state (Westbrook 1890, 362). In 1875, President Grant warned of the "evil" of "the accumulation of vast amounts of untaxed church property" (*A Compilation* 1897, 4288). He grimly asserted that failure to deal with this through taxation "may lead to sequestration without constitutional authority and through blood," and proposed "the taxation of all property equally, whether church or corporation, exempting only the last resting place of the dead and possibly, with proper restrictions, church edifices" (ibid., 4289).

Congress enacted a tax statute for the District of Columbia in 1874, under which local authorities imposed property taxes on churches. Churches refused to pay, and some were apparently seized by the government in tax-foreclosure proceedings. For five years, churches requested individual relief, which apparently was often granted, as well as a change in the enabling legislation. In 1879, Congress, with no debate, changed the law to prohibit such taxation in the future and also voted to return the $2,566.68 that had already been collected (*Congressional Record* 1879, 2334; Pitzer 1880, 362–63).

A number of states also considered anti-exemption legislation.[2] The debate in Massachusetts was the most extensive and was influential elsewhere. It rang all the rhetorical changes, appealing to morality and practicality, offering statistical documentation and refuting it. James Parton, for instance, in a pamphlet published in 1873 by the Free Religious Association, presented an argument that was classically liberal, suspicious of all privileges awarded to groups intermediate between the individual and the state: "Whatever property the State protects ought, I think, to contribute its proportion to the State's support" (Parton 1873, 3). He also argued that ending exemptions would aid the Protestant churches, and not just by terminating support for Catholic ones. He suggested that the typical American city had too many underutilized Protestant churches, which were, in addition, not justified by the insignificant doctrinal differences between them, and that taxation would speed up the process by which only the fit survived. Taxation was thus lauded as an aid to evolution in weeding out the inefficient (see also Quincy 1876, 534; Hovey 1874, 173; and Foote 1877b, 487).

Parton was clearly concerned about the growth of the Catholic Church, including himself among those liberal free-thinking Protestants who were "American citizens first, and EVERYTHING ELSE SECOND" (Parton

1873, 7). He praised the confiscations of the French Revolution and related approvingly how Henry VIII destroyed ecclesiastical institutions and secularized monastic property, "that is, *stopped exempting it from taxation!*" (ibid., 7). This narrative, in which Henry VIII slew the demon mortmain, was typical of anti-exemption literature. Reverend Madison Peters insisted, "Indeed, from the earliest days of the church, every chapter in its history teaches the lesson of the danger of its policy as a great property-holder with special privileges" (Peters 1894, 376).

Defenders of the tax exemption regularly noted that such limitless growth in real estate was less than likely, since most states only exempted land on which the church was situated and that Trinity Church in New York City, for instance, paid taxes on its rent-producing property. Critics replied that exemptions posed an eventual threat to the continued power of the sovereign state. Some critics, identifying Protestantism and Republicanism, and personal freedom and individual responsibility, thought the danger demanded a reduction in the size and power of the Catholic Church, particularly its perceived capacity to indoctrinate its own young.[3]

Parton and others criticized ostentatious churches. Some critics simply focused on Catholic opulence—in particular, St. Patrick's Cathedral in New York—and contrasted it to a Protestant esthetic of simplicity. Others, such as Parton, included ostentatious Protestant churches in the condemnation. It was suggested that, for the rich, the church functioned as a social club rather than as a house of God (Parton 1873, 11; *The Nation* 1876, 23–24).[4] The argument against exemption and architectural ostentation was met with an indignant protest that elegance and opulence should not be limited to commercial structures. It was also noted, in an appeal to financial self-interest, that elaborate church edifices increased local land values (Eliot 1875, 377–79). Such grand buildings were a valued element of the conspicuous consumption that defined a desirable neighborhood. This argument was used, in particular, in response to the assertion that the exemption unfairly burdened towns while the benefits of religion, education, and other charitable activities were dispersed over the entire state, or at least over a larger area (Hill 1876, 35; Eliot 1910b, 105–07).

Exemption defenders thought that freedom from taxation allowed churches to concentrate on their spiritual mission. Critics argued that exemption encouraged overbuilding, necessitating the assumption of debt and an obsession with finances (Johnston 1882). There was a difference of opinion over the political as well as the financial consequences of tax exemption. Critics maintained that taxpayers invariably engaged in active and attentive oversight of public spending, and that Boss Tweed, for instance, would never have succeeded in his depredations if the churches had had a financial stake in the matter (Hovey 1874, 4113–14). Others warned—saying the same thing, but casting it in a different light—that the imposition of taxes encouraged political activism, an undesirable consequence if it meant churches meddling in state matters.

The debate over exemptions in Massachusetts divided the Protestant elite, forcing a choice between one's own exemption and one's fear of Roman Catholic expansionism. Charles Eliot, president of Harvard, defended all exemptions in a long letter to the tax commission that was widely quoted thereafter by exemption supporters.[5] Eliot treated the college and the church as equivalent cases. He wrote, "There is a return, both from a church and a college, and from a sewer and a highway, in the benefits secured to the community; but the money which built them is no longer to be counted as property, in the common sense. It can never again be productive, except for the program of the trust for which it was set apart" (Eliot 1875, 369). Here he simultaneously offered two arguments: that churches do provide public services, and that, since churches constitute unproductive property, it was both unjust and impractical to attempt to tax them.[6]

Eliot's response to the subsidy argument—that exemption was an indirect, illegitimate technique to provide grants that would not and should not be directly provided—was in part to confront it head on. He suggested that there had been, at least at one time, a calculated decision to support exempted institutions. "The state believes, or at least believed when the exemption statute was adopted, that the indirect gain to its treasury which resulted from the establishment of the exempted institutions is greater than the loss which the exemption involves" (Eliot 1875, 370). He also suggested that the exemption ideally should include all the property owned by the institution, since universities and churches need the financial support and provide even more valuable services in return. Eliot insisted, "Such is the absolute necessity of the public work which the institutions of religion, education and charity do, that if the work were not done by these private societies, the State would be compelled to carry it on through its own agents, or at its own charge" (ibid., 372). Others, of course, noted that the state could not directly sponsor religion, at least not without constitutional adjustments. Eliot was vague, as he had to be, given his discussion of churches, about whether these were services that the state was traditionally obligated to provide. He magisterially wrote of the needs of civilization as well as of government and simply insisted that "churches, colleges, and hospitals serve the highest public ends" and that "there is no reason for making them contribute to the inferior public charges" such as schools, roads, prisons, and police (ibid., 374). The higher public uses were the ones that shaped the public character. There had been a public decision to provide these exemptions, but there were limits to budgetary precision. Close calculation of benefits, moreover, was not necessary. The exempt institutions fulfilled qualitatively superior functions.

Exemption reflected a recognition of the distinction between benevolence and commerce. Implicitly rejecting the exemptions for infant industries, Eliot argued that the economic calculation that social benefits received offset revenues forgone should not lead to exemptions for socially beneficial private business enterprises, since business would still be pursued, whereas higher education, religion, and philanthropy could never be self-supporting.[7] Moreover, private gain was simply not in the minds of the benefactors of the tax-exempt institutions: "In short, they do not live for themselves and could not if they would" (Eliot 1875, 375). Taxing these institutions would thus not only be illogical (since they provided public services without the vicious tendencies—such as political patronage—of state centralization) and imprudent (since some might disappear under financial pressure), but also mean, because it would tax those of benevolent disposition (ibid., 374). Eliot's description of the withholding of tax-exempt status as "mean" may have been an indirect response to those who argued that people of benevolent or pious disposition would pay whatever was necessary to support their favorite institutions and that, therefore, tax-exempt status was not necessary to keep such institutions afloat. Disagreement as to whether exemptions were necessary for the survival of philanthropic institutions should not surprise us; the issue remains unresolved.

Eliot also declared, with a magisterial comprehensiveness, as he did through decades of intermittent testimony, that the only two ways to pursue the common weal were through grants supported by taxes or through endowments "fostered" by exemptions. The endowment-exemption technique, a New England creation, was the older.[8] The New England institutions of higher education, while successful and famous, were being threatened by competition from the emerging middle-western state universities, which were supported by apparently unlimited tax revenue. Eliot did not ask for equivalent subsidies, but he invoked regional pride and self-interest to argue against weakening the endowment-exemption technique.[9]

Eliot, like others, offered several rhetorical responses to the charge of privilege and favoritism. First, Eliot disaggregated the exempt entity and focused on the benefactors—pious, generous, or both—who paid their taxes and also contributed to endowments. Removing their exemption would, he argued, be tantamount to double taxation.[10] Eliot also hinted that the issue was not the privilege of the exempt entities, but the greed of the assessors (and of other taxpayers). As he asserted in the context of a later debate, the challenge to exemptions was heated by "the fire of ignorance, the fire of jealousy, and the fire of natural desire to get one's own taxes reduced by acquiring the right to tax large masses of visible property which now are exempted. There is also the burning zeal of assessors eager to get hold of new resources for taxation" (Eliot 1910b, 110).

Eliot also looked above the exempt institution to the state itself, arguing, in a 1906 address to a state legislative committee, that a prosperous and successful state should be measured by the number of tax-exempt institutions it could afford. He felt that they brought incalculable benefits: They did not just protect the state, but also improved society and brought the benefits of civilization, the highest purpose of the state. In addition, they did it in ways that the state itself could not. He concluded by observing that Massachusetts had learned within the last 10 years that

> the reservations from taxation are not bad, burdensome, wasteful things, but on the contrary that they are highly profitable and precious things; and that the question really is not how few exemptions they can get along with, but how many they can indulge in. The long and short of it is, gentlemen, the things which make it worthwhile to live in Massachusetts, to live anywhere in the civilized world, are precisely the things which are not taxed; the things exempted are the things which are in the highest degree profitable to the community. Let nobody persuade you for a moment that these invaluable reservations from taxation are a burden on the public; they are what make the common life worth living. (Eliot 1910a, 79–80)

Religious institutions, rather than being anomalous and anachronistic in their exempt status, were paradigmatic. The state was not the best vehicle to pursue all social ends; modernity did not mean the eventual replacement of private with public charity.

Eliot, like others in these debates, called for education and publicity about exemptions:

> The traditional policy of Massachusetts needs, in my opinion, only one defense, and that is, a complete publicity concerning its own workings. If only the whole people of the Commonwealth could be shown just how the endowment and exemption policy has worked, and is working for the highest interest in Massachusetts, the people would not permit that policy to be tampered with. (Eliot 1910b, 110)

Exemption supporters did not believe that its survival depended on secrecy. On the contrary, Nicholas Murray Butler, like Eliot, argued for greater openness, believing that exemptions do not survive in obscurity and that the public must be educated as to what is at stake (New York State Constitutional Convention 1938, 204). Interestingly, this argument directly parallels that used by critics of the exemption of philanthropic and religious organizations. Each side found its position so obvious as not to need any detailed presentation.[11] Eliot and Butler, of course, may just have been demonstrating obeisance to the common political trope that ignorance was dangerous and that the populace always exercised sound judgment when it was put in possession of the facts.

In the 1875 debate, Eliot also maintained that not only did the public understand and value exemptions—when the issue was publicized—but that the process of granting exemptions was preferable to that of granting subsidies. A subsidy generated conflict and accusations of discrimination:

> The exemption method is comprehensive, simple, and automatic; the grant method, as it has been exhibited in this country, requires special legislation of a peculiarly dangerous sort, a legislation which inflames religious quarrels, gives occasion for acrimonious debates, and tempts to jobbery. The exemption method leaves the trustees of the institutions fostered untrammeled in their action; and untempted to unworthy arts and mean compliances. The grant method as practiced here, puts them in the position of importunate suitors for the public bounty, or, worse, converts them into ingenious and unscrupulous assailants of the public treasury. (Eliot 1875, 382)

Subsidies encouraged the mean arts of the lobbyist; fine-tuning invited conflict. Exemptions were preferable to the log-rolling process—which simply emphasized the client-like begging of claimants to government largesse, and the zero-sum nature of the competition between claimants to a share of a fixed pie. At least the exemption proceeded by an ostensibly general rule, and thus not relentlessly reargued. Mugwump and Progressive thought was at least as interested in ending conflict as it was in exposing problems to publicity, although it often expected that the two aims could be pursued simultaneously.

Two of the three Massachusetts Commissioners—Julius Seelye, professor of moral philosophy at Amherst, and James Barker—considered

Eliot's 1875 letter a persuasive defense of church exemptions.[12] They were not, however, particularly swayed by Eliot's argument that exempting benevolent institutions was economically efficient. The benefit theory of taxation was too calculating, and they were not inclined to so contractualize citizenship and so commodify taxation. Rather, the Massachusetts Commissioners, in determining not to alter existing exemption practices, articulated a more traditional and old-fashioned argument. Taxation was coerced by government and, simultaneously, was voluntarily and cheerfully undertaken by citizens, who thereby achieved the highest aim of personal life: the suppression of selfish desires and the subsuming of self-interest into the common good (*Report of the Commissioners* 1875, 154). The suppression of the self and its sublimation into something larger was the goal of the Christian vis-à-vis God and of the citizen vis-à-vis the state. Taxation was thus, in Massachusetts, an act of benevolence, though only incompletely voluntary. Charities and government both existed as vehicles for the perfection of the individual. Exemptions reflected and sustained a merger of government and society.

The Massachusetts Commission of 1875 had thus resisted the commodification of taxation and the effort to treat exemption as legitimate and efficient only when revenue-neutral. Taxation was an act of cheerful self-surrender; so was benevolence. Neither focused on the efficiency of the expenditure. Both emphasized the freedom and voluntary nature of the contribution. It is only when people give without a close tie between payment and return that they are clearly giving rather than purchasing, engaging in self-surrender rather than the pursuit of self-interest. Taxes, as the price of civilization, are both selfless contributions and purchases. There might be budgets for government, but not for society.

With the 1870s came the articulation of nearly all the positions, pro and con, with respect to exemptions that are still asserted today. That the exemption was granted by the state to further its own ends was now clearly stated. Edward Everett Hale conceived of private benevolent institutions as agents of the state (Hale 1881, 256). The allocation between public and private pursuits was just a matter of administrative convenience. Increasingly, exemptions were justified not just as reflecting direct savings to the government, as the work of private organizations supplemented or replaced government services, but also as reflecting governmental support for action that the government did not choose to perform directly.[13] Although the Progressives believed in the need for more government, there was already a powerful fear of bureaucracy and, in particular, of centralization.

A whole new category of exemption was articulated. Church exemptions were better classified as providing services that the government supported, not as providing public services that otherwise would be provided by the government (Killough 1939, 31). Why the government supported these services and why this justified exemptions was not entirely clear. Perhaps these organizations did something that the government could not do directly. Exemptions of commercial ventures that would lead to greater prosperity could pass muster in this way, whereas direct subsidies of such ventures still were not permitted. Sometimes the exempt organization did not reduce the necessary expenditures of the state in its "protective" capacity (i.e., aiding the unfortunate and preventing crime), but the organization did pursue goals that fit within the larger justification and aim of the state itself.

In sum, the tax exemption of churches and philanthropies survived the challenges of the 1870s relatively unscathed. Yet the exemption remained relatively narrow. Defenders of church exemption, in responding to President Grant's attack, noted that income-earning ecclesiastical real estate was often not exempt from property taxation. Moreover, while few churches apparently had endowments, they were taxed in most states (Foote 1877a, 368).

The Emerging Income-Tax Debates

Debate over the merits of exempting religious, philanthropic, and educational institutions might have been expected when Congress deliberated and enacted the 1894 federal income tax. A conception of exemptions as subsidies for services performed might have encouraged a particularized review of exemption, to at least roughly correlate benefits received by the state with tax revenues forgone. Instead, the proposed tax was levied upon certain specified types of business and "all other corporations, companies, or associations doing business for profit in the United States" (Eldridge 1986, section 32, 530). Further language specifically exempted

> Corporations, companies, or associations organized and conducted solely for charitable, religious or educational purposes [the three are still regulated as one], including fraternal beneficiary societies, orders or associations operating upon the lodge system and providing for the payment of life, sick, accident and other benefits to the members of such societies, orders, or associations, and dependents of

such members[;] . . . the stocks, shares, funds, or securities held by any fiduciary or trustee for charitable, religious, or educational purposes; . . . building and loan associations or companies which make loan only to their shareholders; . . . such savings banks, savings institutions, or societies as shall, first, have no stockholders or members except depositors and no capital except deposits. . . . (Ibid., 531–32)

The exemption for philanthropic, educational, and religious organizations was apparently not debated at all in Congress, although the proposed exemption of individual income below $4,000 was challenged as socialist, communist, or whatever other epithet came to critics who argued that all persons should be taxed equally (*Congressional Record* 1894, 6221, 6637 (remarks of Senator Hill), and 6706 (remarks of Senator Platt)).

There was much debate about whether to exempt mutual insurance companies and mutual savings banks, whose exemption was not included in the initial draft.[14] The exemption of the former was apparently limited to those operating on the lodge system, thereby permitting taxation of large Hartford-based mutual insurance companies, whose size was a matter of concern to some congressmen. The argument against taxation was twofold: What such companies were doing was in the public interest and not for profit.

The treatise on the 1894 Act, noting that the exemption of religious, philanthropic, and educational institutions was new, anticipated controversy over whether "charitable" was to be defined as synonymous with "not for profit" (Foster and Abbott 1895, 110–11). Most problematic, presumably, were institutions such as mutual insurance companies or savings banks. In his concurrence with the decision in *Pollock v. Farmers' Loan and Trust Co.* (which held the 1894 tax act unconstitutional), Justice Field sharply criticized the exemption of mutual banks and insurance companies, arguing that they engaged in commercial activity and were of pecuniary value to those who invested in them even though the corporations were themselves not for profit (157 U.S. 429, 597–99 (1895); see Black 1913, 51).

The debate about mutual insurance companies and lodges arose because selflessness and benevolence did not appear to be pure motives here—if they were anywhere. In upholding the property-tax exemption of an Elks Lodge, the Utah Supreme Court applied a "broad and more liberal construction" than for laws exempting property used for profit (*Salt Lake Lodge v. Groesbeck*, 120 P. 192, 194 (1911)). The court did not draw a radical distinction between nonprofit and for-profit institutions, but, instead, argued against any attempt to precisely divide the world into such mutually exclusive spheres. "In earlier times in this state, and in all New England states, the church—commonly called the meeting house— was constantly used for town meetings, lectures, concerts, temperance meetings, political addresses, and for other like special occasions; and no one ever supposed that such use made the meeting house liable to taxation" (ibid., 195). The court ruled that the purpose of the lodge is to "promote good fellowship among its members and for charitable purposes, and in addition thereto inaugurate and conduct a social club for the benefits of its members" (ibid., 195). There was dancing; cigars, liquors, and refreshments were sold at a profit to members only; and profits were used to distribute charity not just to members but to the public at large. The court found that the profitable sale of cigars and liquors and refreshment (available only to members) was "a mere incident" to promoting "good fellowship" among the members of the organization, and in dispensing charity "in the general relief of the distress of the human family, not only to its members and their families, but also to the public at large" (ibid., 196).[15]

The tension between what are, in effect, positive and negative definitions of philanthropy was not resolved by the enactment of the federal income tax. The positive definition looked to the program of the institution: Did it resemble the traditional charitable purposes included in the Statute of Charitable Uses or as subsequently generally accepted? Ostensibly philanthropic ventures became more problematic in this definitional regime the more they diverged from the traditional understanding of charity and the more they pursued purposes that could not easily be described as obligations of the state being administered by the private sector. Such ventures were also vulnerable to challenge when they appeared to be motivated by self-interest—even if not the pursuit of profit—thereby deviating from the strict definition of benevolence articulated, for instance, by Horace Binney in the Girard College case (*Vidal v. Girard's Executors*, 43 U.S. 127 (1844)): "whatever is given for the love of God, or for the love of your neighbor, in the catholic and universal sense—given from these motives, and to these ends—free from the stain or taint of every consideration that is personal, private or selfish" (quoted in *Jackson v. Phillips*, 14 Allen (Mass.) 539, 556 (1867)). The negative definition simply required that the venture not be for profit, that it not resemble an ordinary business activity in methods and aims.

Into the 20th Century

In the 20th century, the criticism of tax exemptions came from tax experts eager to increase control over both the tax and expenditure sides of the budget process and frustrated at islands of autonomy, particularly growing islands (National Tax Association 1915, 13; Plehn 1921; *Report of the Connecticut Tax Commission* 1934; Blodgett 1925; and New York State Constitutional Convention Committee 1938, 209). The exemption had been criticized in the late 19th century by some Protestants who were unhappy with the increasing heterogeneity of American society and reluctant to share their privileges. The new tax administrators, like the earlier critics, generally proposed that existing exemptions be permitted, but that new ones be banned or more strictly confined (Mastick 1927, 83), thereby protecting the budget and also the first entrants.

The tax administrators, usually typical Progressives, often had no great respect for democratic decisionmaking. What offended them was that exemptions removed implicit funding decisions from the budget process, which they hoped to rationalize and to control. Mark Graves, the New York tax commissioner, wrote that he hoped that all exemptions would be abandoned because the result would be more "business-like" (quoted in Mastick 1927, 82). Some critics, recommending that exemptions be replaced by annual subsidies, were confident that the legislature would be unwilling to do in the open that which it had done in secret. The model here is the classic reform one of an aroused public, learning of abuses, imposing reform upon a corrupt log-rolling system in which legislators were more afraid of losing re-election than desirous of pursuing the public good.

This model proved to be flawed. Legislatures were increasingly willing to grant direct subsidies for purposes that once would not have been considered public. Even support of trade, by the 20th century, had become a legislative purpose justifying grants of public funds. By these liberalized standards, exemptions to philanthropic organizations and to churches looked less and less like vestiges of medieval practices.

The groundswell of public opposition that the reformers anticipated never arose. Exemptions survived criticism, often emerging with even more legal protection. When exemptions for churches became problematic, given the growth of the mandate for equal and uniform taxation at mid-century, legislatures actually enacted exemption statutes codifying what had been unarticulated practice. In time, constitutional amendments often mandated such statutes. Tax exemptions were debated, but they survived the debate.

The experts' critique of exemptions did not usually envisage an augmentation of legislative authority. Some thought that requiring subsidies to take the form of direct grants would put a brake on unprincipled legislative largesse. Others thought that subsidies should be granted only through some process of expert analysis in which the costs of taxes forgone were calibrated against the benefits derived from the institution evaluated.[16] Twentieth-century experts opposed general tax exemptions as a silent fiscal drain threatening the stability and predictability of the budget process. It is to be noted that it was the growth of exemptions, and the granting of new ones, that particularly threatened the predictability of the system. In addition, these professionals argued for more control over the expenditure process. As Farwell Knapp told his colleagues at the National Tax Association meetings in 1934, "You who specialize in taxes cannot escape specializing in civics; you cannot escape long and anxious thought on how tax money is spent—that is, on the relative values of governmental functions" (Knapp 1934, 84).[17] They wanted taxes for revenue rather than for regulation. But only if exemptions were intended specifically for institutions that provided services that otherwise would have been paid for by the state could the tax system be described as one which was purely revenue-driven and not also regulatory in structure. This never became the case.

The attempt to limit exemptions to those institutions performing tasks which the state would otherwise have had to undertake or which it already undertook was a technique for making exemptions conform to such a revenue-focused tax system. This attempt was a frequent rallying cry of reformers, since it promised to remove politics from taxation. A neutral, universal tax system permitting exemption only for equivalent private expenditure was, however, never implemented nor even articulated in a way that would elicit general support. In addition, at the other end of the equation, expenditures also became progressively more loosely confined, more discretionary, and, therefore, more susceptible to political pressure (or at least political controversy).

Revenue-neutral exemptions not only assuaged fears of fiscal shortfall, but were also satisfyingly apolitical. Unfortunately, the formula was difficult to apply. What were the benefits provided? How were they to be measured, and by whom? And were these benefits incalculable, as was believed by those who considered benevolent activities undertaken by groups that mediate between the individual and the sovereign state to be not merely interim substitutes for state action? Or, instead, was philanthropy a preferable alternative because private charity benefited both the recipient and the donor?

Paradoxically, this insistence that exemption is justified only by reciprocal benefits provided by the exempt organization, and that efforts should be made to calibrate the exemption to the benefit (or at least to ensure that the taxes forgone not be inappropriately generous), had the effect, in time, of extending the range of exemption. The rhetoric developed to justify existing exemptions proved adaptable to the justification of new ones. Many organizations could claim that they were providing reciprocal benefits. As the limitations of the public-purpose doctrine eroded, and as it was asserted that benefits were undeniable but hard to measure, standards for granting exemption loosened. Exemption granted as a privilege was always vulnerable to the abuse of favoritism, but its ad hoc nature provided a procedure to regulate and resist expansion of the exemption regime. Exemptions granted under general categories and claims of equivalent service were harder to contain. Reciprocal benefits conceded a quasi-contractual conception of exemption that, even if not legally compelled, inevitably invited new claimants and new grantees.

The Committee on Tax Exemption of the National Tax Association complained,

> Exemptions tend to breed rapidly. When one is granted, it is easy to find grounds by analogy for other exemptions. This is especially true of those based on assumed public benefit. . . . Hence many a movement, inaugurated for the assumed or alleged good of all, demands tax exemption as one of its rewards. . . . Many mice nibbling away will destroy a large cheese. There is danger that the whole structure of taxation in the United States will be eaten away unless the mice be checked. (Plehn 1921, 411)[18]

Some judges joined in the critique. In *Matter of Huntington v. New York*, the court first identified the legislature's predicament and then chided it for its weakness:

> The subject of taxation has been a great embarrassment to legislative bodies throughout the history of the world. *Special* interests clash with *general* interests and seek relief, wholly or in part, from the public burden which is essential to the protection of property and the preservation of order. Claims for exemption multiply. When the Legislature yields to the pressure of *special* interests, the precedent breeds a multitude of special statutes and brings confusion into the law. (168 N.Y. 399, 405 (1901))

Other courts read exemption statutes less critically. Newman Baker complained, "Tender-hearted judges often make bad law and the confusion in the tax exemption cases largely is a result of the relaxation of the rule of strict construction" (Baker 1929, 395). The absence of pattern irritated not only academics but also some judges: "There are many judged cases from different states which are not easily reconciled growing out of exemptions somewhat similar to those under consideration here. . . . So much has been written in the textbooks and reports, expressive of divergent views on this subject, that it would be unprofitable to review the cases . . ." (*State v. Fisk University*, 87 Tenn. 233, 242 (1889)).

Critics were frustrated not just by judicial and legislative laxity, but also by the absence of popular support for their reform program. Confounded by the failure of the polity to immediately and enthusiastically heed their warnings and follow their recommendations, they sought an explanation for their relative impotence. The explanation was inertia, a failure by the people to subject old practices to modern reexamination. Farwell Knapp cuttingly commented, "The weight of tradition, which is chiefly another case name for the avoidance of the necessity of thinking, cannot easily be shaken off" (Knapp 1934, 80).[19] In 1921, H.S. Van Alstine, addressing the National Tax Association, poignantly expressed the frustration of the Progressive: "While the theory of equitable taxation has probably never before been more carefully considered, or better understood, the present practice in our federal and state jurisdictions is in many important respects, out of harmony with the ideals and principles upon which our institutions were founded" (Van Alstine 1922, 460). Never had so much been known about the art of government, but apparently never had there been such dissonance between the state of knowledge and actual practice.

Public passivity is not surprising. Taxation looked increasingly complicated. With more than a century of national tax history and a growing variety of taxes, any individual tax practice, rather than being emblematic of American political ideals, could be seen as compensatory or supplementary, part of a larger system which itself was increasingly difficult to comprehend. Exemptions were not covert, but, when considered as subsidies, they were, en masse, increasingly difficult to evaluate. Equal treatment and no favoritism were a mid-19th century rallying cry that could generate enthusiastic support. In the later 19th century, the call for an end to "deadheadism"—the expectation of public handouts—characterized exemptions as symptomatic of the flaws of the paternal state. If exemptions were mere subsidies, the consequences were much less apocalyptic: Citizens were not suffering from discrimination or infantilization; taxpayers were just being overcharged.

The fate of the call for closer calibration of tax exemptions and public benefits represented the fate of much of the Progressive program, which was weakened by several naïve assumptions. Progressives assumed that disagreement was caused by inadequate information and that obtaining facts and publicizing them would lead to action. Yet the debate over exemptions continued, facts remained controversial, differing conclusions were drawn, and politics did not collapse into administration. The rhetoric of facts was adopted by all sides. Each side, in addition, continued to appeal to a world of values, benevolence, or opposition to special privilege that resisted easy quantification.

The tax experts had hoped to be in charge of the process of fine-tuning and eliminating inefficient exemptions. They were not given this role. Their emphasis upon reciprocity and equality between taxes forgone and benefits conferred—a formula that they hoped to apply and expected would result in reduced exemptions and increased tax revenues—instead offered a rhetoric in which new exemptions continued, even as the effort to limit direct subsidies was largely lost.

NOTES

I first looked at the history of tax exemptions for charitable institutions in a paper prepared for the Conference on Tax Exemptions for Philanthropies at the N.Y.U. School of Law; this paper was printed in the *Publications of the Institute of Law and Philanthropy* of that institution in 1991. The present essay, the product of substantial additional research, grew out of that effort.

I would like to thank Peter Dobkin Hall for his helpful comments on earlier drafts of this paper.

1. Moreover, for several decades the Connecticut Supreme Court held that the Contracts Clause protected exemptions granted by statute, even by a general statute (*Connecticut Report* 1925).

2. The Pennsylvania legislature rejected taxation in 1873, Iowa in 1874, Wisconsin in 1880. Missouri apparently taxed churches from 1863 until the mid-1870s, and New Jersey considered and rejected prohibiting tax exemptions at its constitutional convention (Robertson 1968, 78; Wisconsin Senate 1880; Atwater 1874, 340–41). In 1875, the commission appointed to review tax legislation for Massachusetts considered, but rejected, any change in existing exemptions.

3. The effort, led by Senator Blaine, to prohibit constitutionally public aid to sectarian schools reflected the same concern.

4. Parton also offered an argument that combined Jacksonian invocations of self-reliance with a critique of the new wealth which supported the new benevolent institutions. The combination is classic Mugwump—suspicious of charity and hostile to modern commerce. "Hard old money makers, after a long life of hard-dealing, amuse a dreary, childless, friendless, and loveless old age consigning masses of ill-gotten property to the spoliation and mismanagement of trustees" (Parton 1873, 12). Not only were the charitable gifts not in the public interest, they did not even reflect benevolent motives.

5. Eliot's arguments were rejected by 20th-century critics of the exemption (Knapp 1934), as well as by contemporaries like Quincy (1876).

6. We will see that in analyzing income-tax exemptions there was a similar dual response: The institution provided public services and the institutions were simply not for profit—they did not earn income in the ordinary sense.

7. Another university president, Nicholas Murray Butler of Columbia, later told a New York legislative committee that if private bequests were not tax exempt, they would not be given. "The government is attacking public interest and the public service at their very foundation. Neither Communism nor Fascism could do more. It is shutting its eyes to the fact that what is public is infinitely larger and more important than what is official, and that the public interest itself is served through private benefaction in hundreds of ways, which government could not successfully imitate if it would." Butler concluded, again paraphrasing Eliot, "Let moneys retained for personal, for family or for other private uses be taxed if need be, but not those to which the public must look for much that is best in its national life" (New York State Constitutional Conventional Committee 1938, 202–04).

8. New England, as already noted, had used both techniques in the past.

9. Arthur Perry, professor of economics at Williams College and the author of a popular economics textbook in this period, made a similar argument. Perry argued, for instance, that benevolent gifts to philanthropic institutions or to family members should never be taxed as commercial transactions were (Perry 1873, 586–87). His argument was quoted by Representative Andrew Hunter in the *Congressional Record Appendix* (1894). During these debates, Senator Hill disapproved of taxing charities or gifts (*Congressional Record* 1894, 6823). Charles Eliot's contributions to the tax-exemption debate were not limited to his letter to the Massachusetts Commission in 1874. In 1906, he appeared before the Recess Committee on Taxation in Massachusetts, at a time when college dormitories were being threatened with taxation. Here again he distinguished between the tax-subsidy method of supporting higher education, "always effective and far the quickest for a new community," and the method used by the settlers of Massachusetts Bay (Eliot 1910a, 69; see also Hall 1910, 120). The Report of the Joint Committee of the Massachusetts General Court in January 1907 declared, "Our forefathers taxed themselves heavily for the maintenance of schools and colleges. It is in our judgment entirely foreign to the spirit of our whole educational system and to our conception of civic righteousness that we should now tax these institutions for the maintenance of other public activities" (*Exemption from Taxation* 1910, 93)

10. Of course the response was that the recipients of ill-gotten gains were privileged in being able to permanently affect social expenditures through their private endowments (Quincy 1876, 533).

11. In a memorandum filed with the New York Constitutional Convention of 1915, William D. Guthrie declared, "It can readily be demonstrated that the actual cost and value of the services rendered to the public by the private, charitable, and religious institutions, and the saving thereby effected the budget or taxpayers of states and cities, greatly exceed the aggregate of all exemptions granted or other allowances or payments made to them" (New York State Constitutional Convention 1938, 202). Note the confidence that the amounts compared are not even close.

12. Thomas Hills, Boston's tax collector, dissented.

13. The state might not perform certain services because it was constitutionally prohibited from doing so; because many thought that the government could not do as well as private institutions; or because of the specific benefits to the society of having such actions privately undertaken, thus permitting and encouraging benevolent activity.

14. The exemption of fraternal organizations was also the result of lobbying during the course of congressional proceedings (*Congressional Record,* 6697 (remarks of Senator Patton); 4168 (remarks of Senator Cullom); 6623 (remarks of Senator Hill); and 6630 (remarks of Senator Perkins)). See also the discussion of farmer's cooperatives, 6833 (remarks of Senator Frye)). See "Taxation of Church Property" (1892, 178), where the author defended church exemptions in part by noting that "semi-charitable, and semi-commercial" property, such as savings banks and mutual life insurance associations, are partially exempted from taxation.

15. But see *St. Louis Lodge v. Koeln,* 262 Mo. 444, 448 (1914), in which the court rejected an exemption for a similar institution, declaring,

> Charity is not a promiscuous mixer. Here she modestly stands outside or goes her way and waits; waits until the plaintiff [lodge] has finished using the spacious and comfortable rooms for the pleasure of its members. . . until the dancers have tired and gone home; until the billiard rooms have been deserted to the markers; until the plaintiff has paid the cost of its own entertainment and goes out and finds her, and hands her whatever it may have left in its pocket. (Quoted in Baker 1929, 75)

16. Even in the 1870s, Josiah Quincy, a leading critic of exemptions, thought that taxes and thus implicitly exemptions for such institutions should be determined by a disinterested tribunal (Quincy 1876, 530–31).

17. The same experts were also among those who increasingly argued for indirect taxes, on the European model, quoting either Turgot or Colbert in praise of a tax system that plucked the goose while eliciting the fewest squawks.

18. A more intemperate and nativist denunciation of logrolling was delivered by William A. Hough of Indiana (quoted in Baker 1929). Hough told the story of a bill introduced in the Indiana legislature in 1921 to exempt the property, real and personal, of the Young Men's Christian Association. It was then suggested that the property of the Young Women's Christian Association also should be exempted. "'That waked up a contingent in our legislature, which does not need anybody's guardianship in regard to financial matters'" (ibid., 51). So another amendment was introduced exempting the property of the Young Men's Hebrew Association. Hough concluded, "But the exemption of property from taxation once begun is hard to check, and a fourth group got to work and still another amendment was introduced, this time to add to the exemption list the property of the Knights of Columbus" (ibid., 51). This is a paradigmatic example of

Protestant resentment at the demands of an increasingly heterogeneous population for equal treatment.

19. Claude Stimson concluded, with regard to church exemptions, "The retention of this type of exemption, long after the reason for its existence has passed away, suggests that very little progress has been made in this portion of the field of taxation" (1934, 416).

REFERENCES

Abbot, F.E. 1875. Letter to the Massachusetts Tax Commission, *The Index* 6: 145, April 1.

Adams, Thomas S. 1900. "Taxation in Maryland." In *Studies in State Taxation*, edited by J.H. Hollander (28–29). Baltimore, Md.: Johns Hopkins University Press.

Adler, Philip. 1922. "Historical Origin of the Exemption from Taxation of Charitable Institutions." In *Tax Exemptions on Real Estate: An Increasing Menace*, part I (1–84). White Plains, N.Y.: Westchester County Chamber of Commerce.

Atwater, Lyman. 1874. "Taxation of Churches, Colleges and Charitable Institutions." *Presbyterian Quarterly and Princeton Review*: 340–41.

Baker, Newman F. 1929. "Judicial Interpretation of Tax Exemption Statutes." *Texas Law Review* 7: 385–412.

Black, Henry Campbell. 1913. *A Treatise on the Law of Income Taxation under Federal and State Laws*. Kansas City, Mo.: Vernon Law Book Co.

Blodgett, William. 1925. *Proceedings of the National Tax Association*. 18: 352.

Boutwell, George S. 1863. *A Manual of the Direct and Excise Tax System of the United States*. Boston: Little, Brown.

Bovard, F.D. 1900. "Taxing Churches in California." *Overland Monthly* (2d ser.) 36: 332.

Burroughs,W. H. 1877. *A Treatise on the Law of Taxation*. New York City: Baker, Voorhis.

A Compilation of the Messages and Papers of the Presidents. 1897. Washington, D.C.: Government Printing Office.

Connecticut, State of. 1925. *Report of the Commission on Tax Exemptions*. Hartford, Conn.: State of Connecticut.

Cooley, Thomas. 1876. *A Treatise on the Law of Taxation*. Chicago: Callaghan.

Eldridge, Charles W., ed. 1986. *The United States Internal Revenue Tax System*. Buffalo, N.Y.: W.S. Hein.

Eliot, Charles. 1910a. "Remarks before the Recess Committee on Taxation, October 23, 1906." In *Exemption from Taxation* (69–80). Boston: Printed for the colleges and universities of the Commonwealth.

———. 1910b. "Remarks before the Joint Committee on Taxation, Massachusetts Legislature, March 13, 1907." In *Exemption From Taxation* (99–110). Boston: Printed for the colleges and universities of the Commonwealth.

———. 1875. "The Exemption from Taxation of Church Property, and the Property of Educational, Literary and Charitable Institutions." Dec., 1874, Appendix to the *Report of the Commissioners Appointed to Inquire into the Expediency of Revising and Amending the Laws Related to Taxation and Exemption Therefrom*. Boston: Wright & Potter, state printers.

Exemption from Taxation. 1910. Addresses, Reports, Judicial Proceedings, Legislative Bills, Acts and other Documents relating to the Exemption of Massachusetts Colleges and Universities from Taxation. Boston: Printed for the colleges and universities of the Commonwealth.

Exemption of Church Property in the Several States of this Union. 1878. Sacramento, Calif.: H.A. Weaver, book and job printer.

Foote, Henry W. 1877a. "Taxation of Churches." *Unitarian Review and Religious Magazine* 7: 349–68.

———. 1877b. "The Taxation of Churches." *Unitarian Review and Religious Magazine* 7: 465–92.

Foster, Roger, and Everett V. Abbot. 1895. *A Treatise on the Federal Income Tax Under the Act of 1894.* Boston: Boston Book Co.

Hale, Edward Everett. 1881. "Shall Church Property Be Taxed?" *North American Review* 133: 255–56.

Hall, G. Stanley. 1910. "Remarks before the Joint Committee on Taxation." March 1907. In *Exemption from Taxation.* 118–20.

Hannan, William E. 1917. "Property Exempt from Taxation in the Forty-Eight States." *New York State Library Legislative Bulletin* 42.

Hill, Hamilton. 1876. "The Exemption of Church Property from Taxation." Paper read before the American Statistical Association.

Hovey, Alvah. 1874. *Religion and the State.* Boston: Estes and Lauriat.

Hughes, Harold. 1935. "Tax Exemptions." *Tennessee Law Review* 13: 79–88.

Johnston, Rev. George H. 1882. "Church Debts." *Reformed Quarterly Review* 29: 465.

Killough, Lucy. 1939. "Exemptions to Educational, Philanthropic and Religious Organizations." *Tax Exemptions* 23. New York City: Tax Policy League.

Knapp, Farwell. 1934. "Tax Exemptions." *Proceedings of the National Tax Association.* 27: 24–84.

Mastick, Seabury C. 1927. "The Problem of Tax Exemption." *Proceedings of the Eighteenth Annual Meeting of the Conference of Mayors* (76–83). New York City: City Club of New York and the Municipal Government Association of the State of New York.

The Nation. 1876. 22: 2–24. January 13.

National Tax Association. 1915. "Unnecessary Exemptions." *Bulletin of the National Tax Association* 1: 13.

Newhouse, Wade. 1984. *Constitutional Uniformity and Equality in State Taxation,* 2nd ed. Buffalo, N.Y.: W.S. Hein.

New York State Constitutional Convention Committee. 1938. "Tax Exemptions under the General Property Tax." In *Problems Relating to Taxation and Finance* 10: 193–209.

Parton, James. 1873. *Taxation of Church Property.* Free Religious Tracts, No. 1. Boston: Cochrane & Sampson.

Perry, Arthur Latham. 1873. *Political Economy.* New York City: Charles Scribner's Sons.

Peters, Madison. 1894. "Why Church Property Should Be Taxed." *The Forum* 17: 372–79.

Pitzer, A.W. 1880. "The Taxation of Church Property." *North American Review* 131: 362–63.

Plehn, C.C. 1921. "Report of the Committee on Tax Exemptions." *Proceedings of the National Tax Association* 13: 235–411.

Pocock, J. G. A. 1957. *The Ancient Constitution and the Feudal Law.* Cambridge, U.K.: Cambridge University Press.

Protestant Episcopal Church in the U.S.A. 1875? *Laws and Usages in All the States in Relation to the Taxing of Churches.* Utica, N.Y.: Curtiss and Childs.

Quincy, Josiah P. 1876. "The Argument for Tax-Exemption." *Old and New* 11: 529–34.

———. 1872. "The Secularization of Church Lands, A Deacon's Conversion." *Old and New* 7: 580–653.

Report of the Commissioners Appointed to Inquire into the Expediency of Revising and Amending the Laws Relating to Taxation and Exemption Therefrom. 1875. Boston.

Report of the Tax Commissioner. 1934. Hartford, Conn.: State of Connecticut.

Robertson, D.B. 1968. *Should Churches Be Taxed?* Philadelphia: Westminster Press.

Robinson, Maurice. 1902. *A History of Taxation in New Hampshire.* New York City: Macmillan Company.

Stimson, Claude W. 1934. "The Exemption of Property from Taxation in the United States." *Minnesota Law Review* 18: 411–28.

"Taxation of Church Property." 1892. *New England and Yale Review."* 177.

Tobin, Charles J., William E. Hannan, and Leland L. Tolman. 1934. *The Exemption from Taxation of Privately Owned Real Property Used for Religious, Charitable and Educational Purposes in New York State.* Albany, N.Y.

Van Alstine, H.S. 1922. "Federal Subsidies Through Tax Exemption." *Proceedings of the National Tax Association.* 14: 459–60.

van Alstyne, Arvo. 1959. "Tax Exemption of Church Property." *Ohio State Law Journal* 20: 461–507.

Westbrook, R.B. 1890. "Taxation of Church Property." *Current Comment and Legal Miscellany of Philadelphia* 2: 360–64.

Wisconsin Senate. 1880. *Report of the Committee on Charitable and Penal Institutions on the Taxation of Church Property.* Madison, Wisc.

Wright, Elizur. 1877. "Republican Taxation." *The Index* 8: 542–44.

Zollmann, Carl. 1916a. "Tax Exemptions of American Church Property." *Michigan Law Review* 14: 646–57.

———. 1916b. "Church Cemeteries in the American Law." *Michigan Law Review* 14: 391–98.

6

Legal Theories of Tax Exemption

A Sovereignty Perspective

Evelyn Brody

As a threshold matter, to question the nonprofit tax exemption is not to question the value of nonprofits themselves. Vital, independent nonprofit organizations are crucial to American society. Numerous writers have celebrated the benefits of charities' promotion of altruism and volunteerism, collective action free from private profit motive, and pluralistic approach to problems.[1] At the same time, however, Lawrence Stone emphasized the "responsibility on the part of government not to provide tax and other financial benefits that might create an imbalance between [government's] needs for tax revenues and the benefits provided the exempt sector" (Stone 1968, 41). He also worried about the threat to democratic society from an "overcentralization of uncontrolled economic power in any sector. It is ironic . . . that the combination of the federal estate tax, which has as one purpose the prevention of too great concentrations of wealth in private families, and an unlimited deduction for charitable bequests may be resulting in concentrations of uncontrolled wealth in exempt institutions" (ibid.). The focus of this chapter is on the appropriate tax treatment; a reformed tax structure does not preclude desired financial support being provided through direct public subsidies.

In considering the legal issues, this chapter focuses on three sets of relationships: those between government generally and the charitable sector; between a state and both its local governmental units and its charities; and between the federal government and the states. We use the concept of sovereignty to help explain rules that demonstrate different degrees of comity: As we will see, the tax treatment of charities reflects a quasi-sovereign view of the charitable sector, while a true sovereignty battle rages between states and their municipalities. Federal constraints, although less central, operate in important areas, notably with respect to churches.

This chapter describes how the chosen theory of tax treatment can determine what that treatment will look like in the future. Depending on whether the state views exemption as a mechanism for delivering a particular subsidy or, instead, as part of the organic structure of the property-tax scheme, the pressures described in the other chapters in this volume might affect charities' vulnerability to user fees, payments in lieu of taxes, or loss of exemption.

Theories of Exemption: Tax-Base Definition versus Subsidy

Three possible explanations exist, sometimes simultaneously, for property-tax exemption. First, history: We have always done it this way. Second, definition: Our conception of the property-tax base simply does not reach property owned by nonprofit organizations. Third, subsidy: We want to encourage nonprofit organizations.

While inertia and stability clearly explain the current arrangement, we will pass over the first explanation. Even if policymakers did not consciously decide to grant exemption (see Diamond, chapter 5 of this volume), the fact that exemption could be repealed or qualified makes it fair to examine what rationales policymakers would offer were they to design a property-tax system from scratch. Accordingly, we focus on the two theoretical explanations, base definition and subsidy.

Overlying both theories of exemption is a perspective referred to here as the "sovereignty view" of the nonprofit sector (Brody 1998). A sovereignty perspective is easier to recognize in a base-defining approach: Charities go untaxed because Caesar should not tax God (or the modern secular equivalent). But a sovereignty view also explains why a subsidy would take the form of tax exemption rather than the more logical form of direct grants: For all its imprecision, tax exemption keeps government out of the charities' day-to-day business, and keeps charity out of the business of petitioning government for subvention. Moreover, rival sovereigns rarely feel comfortable letting each other grow too powerful (Brody 1997). Thus, a sovereignty perspective also illuminates those rules in the tax scheme that operate to curtail, rather than enhance, the economic strength of the charitable sector.

Base-Defining Theory

The base-defining theory holds that charitable activity does not even rise to the level of taxable activity. Indeed, sectoral distinctions between public and private charitable activities are a modern invention (Hall 1992 and chapter 11 of this volume). Consider, for example, the Connecticut Supreme Court's 1899 description of the "non-taxation of public buildings": "The seats of government, State or municipal, highways, parks, churches, public school-houses, colleges, have never been within the range of taxation; they cannot be exceptions from a rule in which were never included" (*Yale University v. Town of New Haven*, 42 A. 87, 91 (Conn. 1899)).

Charitable activity has enjoyed favorable treatment under a variety of tax regimes. Legal scholars have attempted to cast each exemption in terms that define the tax base (Simon 1987, 73–74). In 1976, Boris Bittker and George Rahdert asserted that the "income" of charities cannot be measured in profit-seeking terms (Bittker and Rahdert 1976, 307–14). Similarly, William Andrews (1972) argued that the charitable-contribution deduction is necessary to properly measure the donor's ability to pay income tax. John Simon (1978) made a similar argument with regard to the estate tax. Thomas Heller (1979) described a normative theory of the charitable property-tax exemption.

Later scholars rejected these base-measuring arguments in favor of subsidy theories (e.g., Hansmann 1981). Nevertheless, some debate remains over which tax-favored rules for charity constitute subsidies rather than being part of the properly measured tax base. In the income-tax context, Stanley Surrey pioneered the theory of "tax expenditures," which recasts tax subsidies as direct-expenditure programs in order to ascertain their equity and efficiency. However, the federal "tax-expenditure budget" includes only the charitable-contribution deduction; despite Surrey's later objection (see Surrey and McDaniel 1985), the income-tax exemption of charities is treated as a normative component of the tax base, and the forgone revenue attributable to income-tax exemption remains unestimated. (The annual federal report does not analyze state taxes.)

A tax-base-defining theory encounters some difficulties describing property-tax exemption for charities. By definition, charities that own property have property in their base. If charities are to be exempt because they do not engage in business activities, then how does the base-defining theory account for the fact that householders form the backbone of any property-tax scheme? If, instead, charities are to be exempt because their property does not benefit from local expenditures funded by the property tax (such as schools), then why should business owners pay property tax? And since certain services—such as police, fire, and trash collection—directly benefit all property owners (Netzer, chapter 3 of this volume), even those opposed to subjecting churches to general municipal tax have no objection to churches having to pay their own way: "They do not need or ask special favors like free water or electricity for which others have to pay" (Kelley 1977, 96).

An alternative argument that imports income-tax notions can support the base theory. Heller suggested that the property tax operates as a complement to the federal personal income tax, which fails to tax the imputed rental value of owner-occupied housing; no such complement would be needed for charities, because they owe no federal income tax (Heller 1979, 216–17). More generally, the property tax, like all tax, is borne by individuals; a property tax imposed on charities would be borne by their beneficiaries, donors, and employees (Swords 1981, 200–26; *Yale University v. City of New Haven*, 42 A. 87, 92 (Conn. 1899)[2]).

Thus, to the extent that beneficiaries of exemptions are low-income, any tax rate other than zero could be viewed as too high (Bittker and Radhert 1976, 314–16). However, the few studies of the distributional effects of charity suggest that most charities do not focus their services on the poor (e.g., Clotfelter, ed., 1992). Indeed, while litigation over the definition of "charitable" has focused on whether the organization must concentrate its services on the poor, most courts have rejected municipal assertions that charging fees for services precludes exemption (see Gallagher, chapter 1 of this volume). Moreover, even contributions can sometimes be viewed as a form of service income, notably where museums or institutions of higher education use donations to support price discrimination. Accordingly, "since the bulk of charitable property is located in urban centers, the overpaying group is likely to be relatively poorer than the proper donor class which benefits from charitable activities" (Heller 1979, 211). As described below, municipalities that challenge exemption or seek payments in lieu of taxes (PILOTs) tend to target charities that have significant income streams, perhaps viewing such charities as better able to pass their costs on to clients. In sum, one could conceive of nonprofits themselves as a proxy for the taxable consumers of the imputed income from owner-occupied property.[3]

Finally, a pure base theory cannot explain why the broad definition of charity occasionally yields when it conflicts with the fundamental public policy against racial discrimination—but not, evidently, other public antidiscrimination policies. (See the section on federal constitutional limitations, below, for a discussion of the Equal Protection Clause of the Constitution.)

Subsidy Theory

The subsidy explanation receives greater credence, from both academics and the U.S. Supreme Court (see the section on federal constitutional limitations, below, regarding exemption for churches). However, the subsidy explanation also raises the most questions: If a subsidy is needed, why is *this* subsidy used? If property-tax exemption is the *quid*, what is the *quo* that charities are providing in return? Why subsidize nonprofit organizations instead of all organizations (or even individuals) that provide the desired public goods? Why grant the most value to the charities that are richest in owned real estate? If nonprofits provide benefits to all state residents, why disproportionately burden the taxpayers in the municipalities where charities tend to cluster?

No court propounding a quid pro quo rationale has quantified whether the public gain equals or exceeds the forgone tax revenue (see Ginsberg 1980, 52;[4] Diamond, chapter 5 of this volume), or whether the forgone taxes match municipal services provided to nonprofit property (e.g., *Walz v. Tax Commission*, 397 U.S. 664, 676 (1970)). However, exemptions have long been used to induce donations. In the early years when states granted individual corporate charters, "The purpose of the tax exemptions was, of course, to bring about the donation of money or property to the institutions" (*People ex rel. County Collector of Cook County v. Northwestern University*, 281 N.E.2d 334 (Ill. 1972)).

Subsidy theory does not focus only on donors; tax exemptions can also be used to induce charities to undertake specific activities or to engage in certain behaviors (Atkinson 1990, 606, n. 292). Under the classic conception of this quid pro quo approach, the state bestows exemption because charities lessen the burdens of government.[5] However, conditioning exempt status on organizations' provision of services that government might otherwise provide would eliminate some important types of entities currently enjoying exemption, including open associational organizations such as the YMCAs and churches (Adler 1922, 80–81; see also Zollmann 1916, 646), and, in some states, closed associations such as fraternal organizations (Baker 1928, 75; Balk 1971, 74–79). Generally, states have not adopted a narrow "essential government function test" (e.g., *American Museum of Fly Fishing, Inc. v. Town of Manchester*, 557 A.2d 900 (Vt. 1989)), adopting instead a "public use" test. In any form, however, the subsidy theory makes charities subordinate to the state, which can decide the parameters of its burdens (e.g., *Camps Newfound/Owatonna, Inc. v. Town of Harrison*, 520 U.S. 564, 598–600 (1997) (Scalia, J., dissenting)). As illustrated above with respect to racial discrimination, if the state is unhappy with—or simply uninterested in subsidizing—certain activities, it can fine-tune the exemption.[6]

It is difficult to defend the continuing practice of property-tax exemption on pure subsidy grounds: Such a crude mechanism does little for labor-intensive charities or those that rent their space (see Gallagher, chapter 1 of this volume). Exemption is most valuable to owners of the most highly taxed assets, thus inducing overinvestment in high-taxed, inner-city real estate (see also Netzer, chapter 3 of this volume, and Cordes, Ganz and Pollak, chapter 4 of this volume). In addition, subsidies delivered through exemptions lack the public-finance virtues of visibility and adjustability:

> Exemptions . . . are contrary to public policy, which requires that all property and all persons should bear a proportionate share of the burdens of society. It is to be regretted that legislatures should ever resort to this indirect mode of conferring favors. It is always much more satisfactory to have their benefactions definite and direct. The other mode is resorted to, to conceal from the public the extent of the donation, for fear of causing dissatisfaction. The consequence, however, often is, that valuable privileges are enjoyed without gratitude and regarded by others with envy and dissatisfaction. (*Brainard v. Town of Colchester*, 31 Conn. 407, 410 (1863))

Exemptions do have the administrative advantage of providing a subsidy at a minimal transaction cost, although this virtue is undercut when municipalities negotiate with individual charities for PILOTs (as described below, in the section on intrastate conflicts).

Finally, exemption can also stimulate needed capital investment that has positive spillover effects. States have long granted exemptions to infant *business* industries, a controversial practice enjoying a resurgence as states deliberately choose to use property-tax exemption to attract businesses. To the extent that charities engage in job-creating "desirable" industries, such an input subsidy could make sense for them as well, but possibly at the expense of other locales.

The Sovereignty Perspective

Some of the deficiencies in either a pure base theory or a pure subsidy theory might be explained by a sovereignty perspective of the nonprofit sector. Early exemptions clearly reflect a sovereign view of the first provider of charity—the church—although poverty relief was always only a part of religion's activities. More generally, the notion of a "private sector" distinct from the "public sector" is relatively recent: When charity was secularized in Tudor England, and private organized philanthropy complemented public poor relief, no one bothered to make fine distinctions between the work of the state and the work of charity (Brody 1996, 1998). The colonial treatment of state-established churches finds similar expression in the long-standing American tax exemption for religious, charitable, and educational institutions. (More precisely, since philanthropy and education arose out of religious activities or impulses, such institutions as Harvard and Yale initially could not be separated from religious institutions.) A sovereignty perspective continues to permeate the American tax treatment of charities.

Of course, no one would argue that the nonprofit sector enjoys true cosovereignty with the public sector, because today even churches lack the compulsory powers inherent in a sovereign (Robertson 1968, 59). However, to test the sovereignty hypothesis, consider a clearer set of examples: the tax treatment of governments. The federal income tax does not reach "income derived from any public utility or the exercise of any essential governmental function and accruing to a State or any political subdivision thereof" (Internal Revenue Service Code § 118). States and municipalities may issue bonds whose interest is tax exempt to bondholders. Payments of state and local income and property taxes are generally deductible. However, user fees paid to governments are treated as nondeductible payments for services. As for the property tax, the largest percentages of untaxed property belongs to federal, state, and local governments; states (and their subdivisions) tax neither federal property nor their own.[7]

Each of these governmental tax treatments has an analogue in the tax treatment of charities. Charities are exempt from the corporate (or trust) income tax. However, income from business activities unrelated to the charity's exempt purpose is subject to tax. Charities may issue tax-exempt bonds, and contributions made to charities are generally deductible from income. However, payments made to a charity for a particular service (such as tuition or for hospital care) are not deductible. States grant property-tax exemption to religious, charitable, and educational institutions.

Moreover, a sovereignty perspective can also explain those state provisions that *limit* the amount or type of property a charity can own tax-free. For centuries, England imposed mortmain proscriptions on charities' ability to hold land, to prevent them from growing into too strong an economic force (Brody 1997, 899–906). As Diamond describes in chapter 5 of this book, similar attempts were urged in this country (see also Youngman, chapter 2 of this volume). Some state exemption laws do include acreage and valuation limits (see Gallagher, chapter 1 of this volume).

A zero rate of tax differs qualitatively, not just quantitatively, from a 1 percent tax. Tax exemption maintains a distance between charities and the state. Similarly, exemption differs in an important political way from an equivalent system of direct grants. In 1874, while defending Harvard's property-tax exemption before the Massachusetts legislature, University President Charles Eliot described how exemption removes charities from the political arena: "The exemption method is comprehensive, simple and automatic; the grant method, as it has been exhibited in this country, requires special legislation of a peculiarly dangerous sort, a legislation which inflames religious quarrels, gives occasion for acrimonious debates, and tempts to jobbery" (Belknap 1954, 2038). Eliot continued by describing how exemption avoids what is now called the "crowding-out" effect of grants:

> The exemption method is emphatically an encouragement to public benefactions. On the contrary, the grant method extinguishes public spirit. No private person thinks of contributing to the support of an institution which has once got firmly saddled on the public treasury. The exemption method fosters the public virtues of self-respect and reliance; the grant method leads straight to an abject dependence upon that superior power—Government. * * * The exemption is wholesome while the direct grant is, in the long run, pernicious. (Belknap 1954, 2038–39)

This view assumes that exempt organizations' goals are in some sense more important, and rest on values that are more enduring, than many regular government concerns (see Swords 1981, 196–99).[8]

Instead of using a blanket tax exemption, the state could determine the type and extent of the services it wants to "purchase," and make direct payments to charities. Such an approach, however, could make it difficult to exclude for-profit providers (Colombo 1993, 864)—as, indeed, we are starting to see in state contracting for services after welfare reform. In self-defense, charity proponents have developed a broader theory, based on organizational form, of how they are providing a public good: They argue that the mere existence of independent charitable institutions provides a community benefit worthy of tax exemption.[9] Peter Swords wrote of "the advantages of pluralism that flow from having a voluntary sector of charitable organizations operating parallel to our governmental system, a sector able to discover new needs and experiment in providing ways of meeting them in a manner that simply is not possible for government agencies" (1981, 18). More abstractly, Rob Atkinson's theory of the "metabenefit of altruistic production" conducted in "communities" of charity comes closest to identifying a sovereign theory of exemption (Atkinson 1990).[10] Skeptics, though, see the quid pro quo as a non sequitur: "If consumers prefer the special ethic in education provided by Harvard, why would they not continue to prefer Harvard even absent exemption? . . . If the major problem with higher education is that the full cost would be prohibitively expensive for most students, a specific form of government subsidy targeted at that particular problem is a far better way to allocate government resources than the scattershot vehicle of exemption" (Colombo 1993, 867). However, a broader conception of the "quo" provided by charities could support the continued exemption of churches, whose religious services the state cannot directly purchase (see the section on federal constitutional limitations, below).

Intrastate Conflicts and the Resulting Pressure on Exemption

Henry Aaron once described the intrastate dynamic of property-tax exemption by saying, "In general, the system by which exemptions are granted and extended in most states seems almost deliberately designed to promote irresponsible legislative behavior" (1975, 84). In the fiscal relationship between a state and its local governments, the property tax has usually operated in three phases: first, the "single-tax era," in which locally administered property tax provided revenue to the states; next, the "separation-of-sources" era, in which states and local governments financed their needs separately, with the states generally ceding the property-tax base to the local governments; and, most recently, the "grants-in-aid" era, in which the states share some of their revenues with local governments (Welch 1972, 275).[11] This transformation helps explain why state-granted tax exemptions linger even as local governments chafe under the consequences of an unevenly distributed burden.[12]

Local governments employ a variety of mechanisms to fight back (see chapters 1 and 2 of this book). First, municipalities commonly charge user fees for specific services. However, user fees cannot recoup the general portion of the forgone tax, notably the amount paid for public schools. Second, a few states allow municipal veto of the exemption, placing certain types of charities in "local option" exemption categories. Third, as nonprofit organizations become more "commercial," property-tax exemptions are sometimes denied on an ad hoc basis, either for an individual charity or for a type of charity. These challenges to the exemption are most likely to succeed when state law requires that charitable organizations provide benefits to the poor and relieve the burdens of government. Fourth, local governments have increased demands for "voluntary" payments in lieu of taxes (see chapters 8, 9, and 12 of this volume).

Currently, governments challenging exemption or seeking PILOTs focus on hospitals, institutions of higher education, nursing homes, and retirement homes. After all, the charities that look most attractive to local governments are those that have "income" (excluding, in general, only donations), and often operate in competition with for-profit businesses; and those whose income comes primarily from patrons (or third parties such as private health insurers and Medicare) outside the taxing jurisdiction. Accordingly, taxing the nonprofit can be viewed as a proxy for taxing the nonresident payors. Under the same theory, municipalities could extend this policy to museums and performing arts organizations—and even to break-even social service nonprofits, thus adding taxes to the costs passed on to the funding state and federal governments. Such a theory might provide a nonconstitutional explanation of why municipalities have not sought to tax churches, which rely primarily on donations and whose benefits are primarily local.

Under this commerciality view, the property tax becomes almost an income tax. But such treatment has a long legacy: Colonial New England's "emphasis on productivity, actual or estimated, distinguishes it from today's 'property tax,' which is levied on capital value" (Warren,

Krattenmaker, and Snyder 1971, 185). In Tudor England, rental income—
including that earned on church property—was taxed (Adler 1922, 44);
and Elizabeth's exemption of private hospitals covered only charities with
small incomes (ibid., 64–65). Similarly, American property-tax regimes
typically require that the property be both owned and occupied by charity in the conduct of its charitable activities, so property rented out to
tenants is taxed. Thus, state property-tax exemption is narrower than
the federal income-tax rules on "unrelated business taxable income" that
allow charities to earn passive income, including rents from real property, free of tax.

The use of PILOTs is controversial. Public finance should not rely on
voluntary, negotiated agreements between the government and individual owners, nor should the public and charities be denied the opportunity
to monitor the arrangements. Since they occur haphazardly and sometimes opportunistically, PILOTs highlight why an ideal tax system is visible, systematic, and evenhanded. Indeed, Leland's findings (see chapter 8
of this volume) reveal that even in cities where PILOTs are made, some
charities or city officials are unaware of them. Moreover, as in any negotiation, either of the two parties could be making the concession: In
some cases, PILOTs represent an erosion of statutory tax exemption; in
others, they forestall the imposition of tax, and so are synonymous with
giveaways.

The drawbacks of PILOTs might encourage states to reform the
property-tax treatment of charities more systemically (although in many
states repeal of exemptions would require a constitutional amendment).
For example, Minnesota recently considered (but abandoned) adopting
uniform standards that would give local governments the option of
assessing fees on nonprofits to cover basic public services (see Salomone's
comment in this volume). If a state systematized PILOTs or even went so
far as to repeal exemption, what might happen next? If nothing else
changed, those residents who do benefit from the activities of local nonprofits would see their costs of charitable services (and donations) rise,
but increases would be offset by a reduction in their share of the property
tax resulting from the broader base. Of course, fees or exemption repeal
might be accompanied by some type of compensating outlay, although
the distribution among benefited charities could differ.

Alternatively, states could leave exemptions in place but compensate
their urban centers by making transfer payments to compensate for
taxes forgone on local charitable property (see Carbone and Brody,

chapter 10 of this volume, for a discussion of Connecticut's state-paid PILOTs for private hospitals and colleges). As a 1977 study observed, "Since state payments would go to the locality rather than to the institution, there would be no interference by the state in the activities of the tax-exempt recipients," thus avoiding "several of the serious pitfalls that have effectively stood in the way of proposals to do away with the tax-exempt device and to replace it with a program of direct state subsidies to the recipient institutions" (Gabbler and Shannon 1977, 2556). In practice, state officials might need to take a more active role in assessing non-profit exempt properties; where no private party makes tax "co-payments," local governments might be tempted to overvalue this base (Welch 1972, 276–77; Rudnick 1993, 340–42; see also Carbone and Brody, chapter 10 of this volume).

Federal Constitutional Limitations

This section considers four provisions in the U.S. Constitution that might affect states' freedom to craft exemptions. As applied today, the Equal Protection Clause, the Contracts Clause, the Commerce Clause, and the First Amendment generally permit states to enact tax schemes that offer exemptions to charities (including churches), so long as the classifications are neutrally designed and administered.

Equal Protection Clause

The courts show great deference to legislatures in tax matters. In 1890 the U.S. Supreme Court wrote, "The provision of the Fourteenth Amendment, that no State shall deny to any person within its jurisdiction the equal protection of the laws, was not intended to prevent a State from adjusting its system of taxation in all proper and reasonable ways. It may, if it chooses, exempt certain classes of property from any taxation at all, such as churches, libraries and the property of charitable institutions" (*Bell's Gap Railroad Co. v. Pennsylvania*, 134 U.S. 232, 237 (1890)). The Equal Protection Clauses proscribe only "palpably arbitrary or invidious classifications" (*Allied Stores of Ohio v. Bowers*, 358 U.S. 522, 530 (1959)).

In one apparently anomalous case, a federal court applied the Equal Protection Clause to strike down Wisconsin's grant of tax exemption to organizations that discriminate on the basis of race, because "a tax exemption constitutes affirmative, significant state action in an equal protection context where racial discrimination fostered by the State is claimed" (*Pitts v. Department of Revenue*, 333 F. Supp. 662, 668 (E.D. Wis. 1971)). In contrast, in *Bob Jones University v. United States*, 461 U.S. 574 (1983), the Supreme Court held, as a matter of statutory interpretation rather than constitutional law, that Congress did not intend the definition of charity in Internal Revenue Code section 501(c)(3) to include educational organizations engaged in racial discrimination.

In the rare litigated cases, courts have rejected challenges to the property-tax exemption of single-sex private schools.[13] A Pennsylvania court held that the Hill School, all-male until recently, qualified as an "institution of purely public charity" under state law because there is no statutory prohibition against single-gender educational institutions (*Pottstown School District v. The Hill School*, 2001 Pa. Commw. LEXIS 796 (Nov. 1, 2001). The high court of Massachusetts never even discussed the merits in dismissing a charge by local assessors that Smith College should be denied exemption because, among other things, the women's college engaged in sex discrimination in violation of the Equal Rights Amendment to the Massachusetts Constitution (*Trustees of Smith College v. Board of Assessors of Whately*, 434 N.E.2d 182 (Mass. 1982)). The court held that the assessors lack the statutory authority to raise such a constitutional challenge, and suggested in dicta that such a challenge would have to be made by the attorney general or, possibly, the commissioner of revenue.

Contracts Clause

The U.S. Constitution provides that "no State shall pass any law impairing the obligation of contracts." In 1812, the U.S. Supreme Court held that a state may make a contract for the permanent tax exemption of particular land, and that the contracts clause prevents future taxation (*New Jersey v. Wilson*, 2 U.S. (7 Cranch) 498 (1812)). In the best-known charities case, an 1819 decision declared a New Hampshire charter granted to a private college to be a contract protected from legislative interference in the appointment of the governing board (*Dartmouth College v. Woodward*, 17 U.S. (4 Wheat.) 518 (1819)). In a pair of 1869 cases, the Supreme Court barred Missouri from imposing real-property tax on a charitable institution and a college whose charters emphasized that the legislature could not unilaterally amend the provisions, which included blanket grants of tax exemption (*Home of the Friendless v. Rouse*, 75 U.S. (8 Wall.) 430 (1869); *Washington University v. Rouse*, 75 U.S. (8 Wall.) 439 (1869)). In *Home of the Friendless*, the Court rejected an argument that the state's grant of exemption lacked the "consideration" required to make a contract binding: "There is no necessity of looking for the consideration for a legislative contract outside of the objects for which the corporation was created. . . .This has been the well settled doctrine of this court on this subject since the case of *Dartmouth College v. Woodward*" (*Home of the Friendless*, 75 U.S., 437). The three-judge dissent asserted the policy counterargument:

> We do not believe that any legislative body . . . has a right to sell, to give, or to bargain away forever the taxing power of the State. This is a power which, in modern political societies, is absolutely necessary to the continued existence of every such society. While under such forms of government, the ancient chiefs or heads of the government might carry it on by revenues owned by them personally, and by the exaction of personal service from their subjects, no civilized government has ever existed that did not depend upon taxation in some form for the continuance of that existence. To hold, then, that any one of the annual legislatures can, by contract, deprive the State forever of the power of taxation, is to hold that they can destroy the government which they are appointed to serve, and that their action in that regard is strictly lawful. (*Washington University*, 75 U.S., 443)[14]

Subsequent court decisions emphasized that a grant of permanent exemption must be stated clearly, because the state's intent to relinquish the prerogative of taxation will not be implied.

In any event, legislatures quickly learned to insert a "reservation clause" in their charters and, later, general nonprofit corporation statutes, ensuring that they could adopt amendments (notably for income-producing property). Thus the problem of blanket exemptions remains confined to a few surviving older institutions.[15]

Commerce Clause

For certain charities, the spillover effect of exemption can extend beyond the state borders, to the states' consternation.[16] In 1997, for example, the U.S. Supreme Court struck down a Maine statute that exempted nonprofit camps only if they primarily served Maine residents (*Camps Newfound/Owatonna, Inc. v. Town of Harrison*, 520 U.S. 564 (1997)). The Court accepted the argument that charitable activity is entitled to protection of the Commerce Clause, which prohibits states from discriminating in interstate commerce. Distinguishing direct governmental grants from tax exemption, though, the Court suggested that it would likely uphold an outright subsidy targeted either to Maine residents or to camps serving residents. However, four justices, who could not conceive of charities as businesses, strenuously objected to the application of the Commerce Clause. Moreover, adopting a subsidy approach but rejecting a constitutional distinction between tax exemption and direct grants, the dissenters would also have permitted Maine to target tax exemption to charities whose services lessen the burdens of state government. Scholars are currently debating whether a constitutional distinction between tax subsidies and direct subsidies can be sustained (Zelinsky 1998). As discussed below, the existence of churches makes this a particularly delicate constitutional issue.

First Amendment: Churches

The First Amendment provides that "Congress shall make no law respecting an establishment of religion, or prohibiting the free exercise thereof. . . ." These Religion Clauses contain a built-in tension. On the one hand, does the Free Exercise Clause require that churches be exempt, regardless of the future treatment of other charities? On the other hand, does the Establishment Clause prohibit special treatment for churches? Although some state constitutions provide greater protection by explicitly exempting churches (note that states cannot provide less protection than offered in the U.S. Constitution), this discussion will focus on the U.S. Constitution (see also Dessingue, chapter 7 in this volume).

Must States Exempt Churches?

No test case exists, because all 50 states and the District of Columbia include churches in their exemption statutes, and the Supreme Court upheld property-tax exemption for churches as part of a neutrally written statute covering a wide range of nonprofit organizations (*Walz v. Tax Commission*, 397 U.S. 664 (1970), discussed below). However, some states limit the amount or value of property that churches may own tax-free. For example, in 1880 the New Hampshire supreme court held that because its state constitution does not mandate exemption for churches, a statutory exemption limited to the first $10,000 worth of property used exclusively as a place of worship was constitutional (*Franklin Street Society v. Manchester*, 60 N.H. 342, 349 (N.H. 1880); the limitation was later repealed). The court reviewed not only the longstanding practice of exempting churches, but also the post-disestablishment change in rationale:

> So long as towns, under the act of 1791, exercised parochial functions, and raised taxes for supporting and maintaining houses of public worship, those places of worship were exempt from taxation as public property by the nature of things, and not by the constitution or by statute. After the act of 1810, when towns were no longer subject to church rates, and the whole management of public worship, including its support, was left to the religious societies authorized and organized for that purpose, the natural reason for exempting this property from taxation ceased. (Ibid.)

Federal income- and employment-tax cases suggest that loss of exemption for churches would "only" be a matter of less funding, and not an interference with the free exercise of religious beliefs (see *Hernandez v. Commissioner*, 490 U.S. 680, 699 (1988), in which the court held that any burden from the nondeductibility of auditing fees paid to the Church of Scientology "derives solely from the fact that . . . adherents have less money available to gain access to such sessions"; see also *United States v. Lee*, 455 U.S. 252, 260 (1982), which held that "Because the broad public interest in maintaining a sound tax system is of such a high order, religious belief in conflict with the payment of taxes affords no basis for resisting the tax").

Closer to the property-tax context, a unanimous Supreme Court ruled that the free exercise clause does not mandate an exemption from a generally applicable sales-and-use tax for religious materials distributed by a religious organization (*Jimmy Swaggart Ministries v. Board of Equalization*, 493 U.S. 378 (1990)). The Court declared that the California "sales and use tax is not a tax on the right to disseminate religious information, ideas, or beliefs per se; rather, it is a tax on the privilege of making retail sales of tangible personal property in California" (ibid., 389). (The Court indicated that exemption for religious publications would be required only in the case of a flat tax that operated as a prior restraint.) Notably, the Court stated,

> The only burden on appellant is the claimed reduction in income resulting from the presumably lower demand for appellant's wares (caused by the marginally higher price) and from the costs associated with administering the tax. As the Court made clear in *Hernandez*, however, to the extent that imposition of a generally applicable tax merely decreases the amount of money appellant has to spend on its religious activities, any such burden is not constitutionally significant. (ibid., 391)[17]

Issues of discrimination against churches have recently arisen in zoning matters. For example, when a municipality adopted a downtown revitalization plan designed to preserve and restore the central business district, the exclusion of churches but not secular nonprofits raised claims of underinclusion and equal protection (*Cornerstone Bible Church v. City of Hastings*, 948 F.2d 464 (8th Cir. 1991)). Applying a rational-basis standard, the circuit court ordered the lower court to "determine whether exclusion of churches from the C-3 zone is justifiable on the ground that a church displaces economic activity to a greater extent than the noncommercial uses the City has allowed in the zone" (ibid., 470–71).[18] Subsequently, Congress unanimously enacted the Religious Land Use and Institutionalized Persons Act of 2000 (Public Law 106-274, 42 United States Code 2000cc, *et seq.*), which bars governments from implementing a zoning or landmark law in a manner that substantially burdens religious exercise, unless it is the least restrictive means to further a compelling governmental interest. In addition, the statute bars governments from totally excluding religious assemblies from a jurisdiction or "unreasonably" limiting religious assemblies, institutions, or structures within a jurisdiction. Court challenges to RLUIPA are expected.

May States Exempt Churches as Part of a Broad, Neutral Statute?
Yes. Indeed, Justice Burger's opinion for the Supreme Court in *Walz v. Tax Commission* emphasized the public benefits that churches provide in common with a broad range of similarly exempted secular institutions:

> The legislative purpose of the property tax exemption is neither the advancement nor the inhibition of religion; it is neither sponsorship nor hostility. New York, in common with the other States, has determined that certain entities that exist in a harmonious relationship to the community at large, and that foster its "moral or mental improvement," should not be inhibited in their activities by property taxation or the hazard of loss of those properties for nonpayment of taxes. It has not singled out one particular church or religious group or even churches as such; rather, it has granted exemption to all houses of religious worship within a broad class of property owned by nonprofit, quasipublic corporations which include hospitals, libraries, playgrounds, scientific, professional, historical, and patriotic groups. The State has an affirmative policy that considers these groups as beneficial and stabilizing influences in community life and finds this classification useful, desirable, and in the public interest. (397 U.S., 672–73)

Moreover, Justice Burger avoided any suggestion that exemption functioned as a quid pro quo for particular services:

> We find it unnecessary to justify the tax exemption on the social welfare ser-
> vices or "good works" that some churches perform for parishioners and oth-
> ers—family counselling, aid to the elderly and the infirm, and to children. . . . To
> give emphasis to so variable an aspect of the work of religious bodies would intro-
> duce an element of government evaluation and standards as to the worth of par-
> ticular social welfare programs, thus producing a kind of continuing day-to-day
> relationship which the policy of neutrality seeks to minimize. (ibid., 674)

The *Walz* majority made clear its view that property-tax exemption constitutionally differs from direct grants: "The grant of a tax exemption is not sponsorship since the government does not transfer part of its revenue to churches but simply abstains from demanding that the church support the state" (397 U.S., 675). Concurring, Justice Brennan agreed: "A subsidy involves the direct transfer of public monies to the subsidized enterprise and uses resources extracted from taxpayers as a whole. An exemption, on the other hand, involves no such transfer. It assists the exempted enterprise only passively, by relieving a privately funded venture of the burden of paying taxes" (ibid., 690 (Brennan, J., concurring), citing Bittker 1969). However, Justice Brennan flatly declared, "General subsidies of religious activities would, of course, constitute impermissible state involvement with religion" (ibid., 690). In dissent, Justice Douglas not only rejected a distinction between exemptions and grants, but also would strike down both: "There is a major difference between churches on the one hand and the rest of the nonprofit organizations on the other. Government could provide or finance operas, hospitals, historical societies, and all the rest because they represent social welfare programs within the reach of the police power. In contrast, government may not provide or finance worship because of the Establishment Clause. . . ." (ibid., 708–09 (Douglas, J., dissenting)).

May States Exempt Churches But Not Other Nonprofits?
Walz suggests not, concluded the North Carolina Supreme Court (*In the Matter of the Appeal of Springmoor, Inc.*, 498 S.E.2d 177, 180 (N. Car. 1998)). In this case, the court struck down a statute granting property-tax exemptions for homes for the aged, sick, or infirm only if those homes were operated by religious or Masonic entities. The court concluded, "Religiously affiliated homes are singled out for a tax benefit denied to others that are similarly capable of carrying out the secular objectives which the State may wish to encourage" (ibid., 183). A three-judge dissent believed that *Walz* supports exemption because the homes at issue were exempted as part of a much broader statute that includes secular institu-

tions, and suggested that to the extent secular homes have a valid complaint it would be under the Equal Protection and Due Process Clauses (an argument not raised).

The North Carolina court in *Springmoor* relied on a U.S. Supreme Court decision voiding a state sales-tax exemption granted to religious but not secular publications (*Texas Monthly, Inc. v. Bullock*, 489 U.S. 1 (1989)). Abandoning the distinction made by *Walz*, the three-judge plurality opinion in *Texas Monthly* declared, "Every tax exemption constitutes a subsidy that affects nonqualifying taxpayers, forcing them to become 'indirect and vicarious "donors" ' " (ibid., 14, quoting *Bob Jones University v. United States*, 461 U.S. 574, 591 (1983), and citing also *Regan v. Taxation with Representation*, 461 U.S. 540, 544 (1983)). Incidental benefit to religious organizations as part of a "wide array of nonsectarian groups" in "pursuit of some legitimate secular end" does not result in establishment of religion, but "when government directs a subsidy exclusively to religious organizations that is not required by the Free Exercise Clause . . . [it] cannot but '[convey] a message of endorsement'. . ." (489 U.S., 14–15). "If the State chose to subsidize, by means of tax exemption, all groups that contributed to the community's cultural, intellectual, and moral betterment, then the exemption for religious publications could be retained, provided that the exemption swept as widely as the property tax exemption we upheld in *Walz*" (ibid., 15–16). Indeed, the Texas legislature subsequently amended the statute to exempt publications of "a religious, philanthropic, charitable, historical, scientific, or other similar organization that is not operated for profit" (Texas Tax Code § 151.312).

The three-Justice dissent in *Texas Monthly* stressed that *Walz* had been an accommodation-of-religion case, which by definition singled out religion for favorable treatment, thus making the breadth of exemption immaterial. In seeking to comply with the Free Exercise Clause, Texas was furthering a secular purpose. The dissent also demonstrated the slipperiness of the slope on which the Court is trying to maintain its balance, by enumerating the sales- and property-tax statutes of 45 states that "provide exemptions for religious groups without analogous exemptions for other types of nonprofit institutions" (ibid., 31–32 and note 12 (Scalia, J., dissenting); see also Weber and Gilbert 1981, 159, table 7-1). Most of these property-tax exemptions relate to parsonages, and several of the sales-tax exemptions related to Bibles. While no recent challenges to parsonage exemptions have yet been reported,[19] states and lower federal courts have begun striking down sales-tax exemptions for Bibles and other religious materials.[20]

Recent Changes in Constitutional Doctrine
As described in this part, the Supreme Court has all but abandoned its position in *Walz* that tax exemption is constitutionally distinguishable from direct grants. However, while the direct-subsidy prohibition on funding churches was never absolute, recent cases call into question what is left of the Establishment Clause. Supreme Court cases had been permitting state funding of services (such as school buses, school lunches, and student loans) to students whose individual choice might incidentally benefit religious schools. In the last few years, the Court has gone further and upheld programs where the funding goes directly to religious schools. States may now provide secular services on parochial school property (*Agostini v. Felton*, 521 U.S. 203 (1997)), and supply educational materials and computers to parochial as well as to secular schools (*Mitchell v. Helms*, 530 U.S. 793 (2000)). The four-Justice plurality opinion in *Helms* would apply only a "neutrality" principle—that is, it would allow funding of religious institutions as part of a general, secularly motivated program—and explicitly repudiated earlier doctrine that applied the Establishment Clause to bar state funding of "pervasively sectarian" institutions.[21] In addition, recent federal "Charitable Choice" legislation permits states to contract with religious organizations for social services, if clients receive protections from coerced participation in religious practices. Several court challenges are proceeding in lower courts. Justice O'Connor's concurring opinion cautions against the plurality's simplistic approach, emphasizing that the state may not provide funds for religious indoctrination.[22] Still, the trend in Supreme Court jurisprudence should reassure those churches worried that they might one day have to prove that the value of their property-tax exemption does not exceed the value of the secular benefits they provide—in *Texas Monthly*'s terms, their contributions to the "community's cultural, intellectual, and moral betterment" (489 U.S., 15).

Conclusion

In probing the base-defining and subsidy rationales, we saw that each carries risks as well as comfort for charities. Under the subsidy theory, critics argue that property-tax exemption lacks fiscal transparency and is both a crude mechanism to match forgone revenue to desired outputs and unacceptably open-ended. Supporters assert that the exemption provides a stable source of needed support, and that lost tax revenue is more than covered by the charitable activity that would otherwise not occur. By contrast, this debate does not take place under the tax-base approach, because exemption is recognized rather than granted, and the inability to target or control the growth of exemptions follows from the organic structure.

Thus, the base-defining rationale appears to offer the higher wall against attack, but charities' unwillingness to debate the fairness and efficiency of exemption has been a source of frustration to municipalities, which might respond by challenging exemptions. Under a subsidy rationale, states might feel more comfortable tinkering with the list of types of activities they wish to subsidize. In practice, certain charities fend off threats embodied in the all-or-nothing exemption regime by making "voluntary" payments in lieu of taxes. Fiscal pressure can also be relieved by having the states compensate municipalities that host exempt charities, as is currently done in Connecticut for nonprofit hospitals and universities. For churches, the constitutional attitude has evolved from a laissez-faire accommodation of religion to a subsidy theory of exemption in which religious organizations merge into the larger universe of exempt organizations, and thus are subject to both neutrally applied tax regimes and neutrally granted exemptions.

NOTES

In preparing this chapter, which is based on and develops Brody (1998), I am grateful for suggestions and comments from David A. Brennen and Richard Schmalbeck.

    1. One of the most complete and eloquent statements was made by Stone:

> The role played by nonprofit organizations is not only desirable but may very well be a prerequisite to the continuation of a democratic society. It is through such institutions that we harness the energies and finances of our private citizens to humane, experimental, creative, and controversial purposes . . . . [Charity] is often a unique pathfinder in social welfare and the sciences to be followed only at a later date by governmental or profit-oriented resources. It affords our citizens the opportunity to participate in public service while maintaining private employment. It organizes parts of our society for social purposes through nongovernmental means where governmental action is inappropriate, would be inconsistent with our way of life or is not possible because the purpose is too controversial. It allows individuals

to voluntarily tax themselves in time and money to advance the good of society according to their individual preferences. In an increasingly complex world, where the individual feels frustrated because of his apparent inability to influence the policies of government, charity affords a clear arena in which an individual can act and make his influence felt for the social good. It provides a unique and flexible form of social organization that counterbalances the vast power of government and the concentrated wealth of the private sector. Therefore, in regulating the conduct of the exempt sector and in its provisions for tax benefits, the purpose of government should be to maintain a maximum of freedom of action and the continued healthy growth and survival of this sector. (1968, 39–40)

2. "The mere stuff of land and buildings is not the subject of taxation, except as it may be the source of profit, present or prospective, to some person bound to contribute to the charges of government" (*Yale University v. City of New Haven*, 42 A. 87, 92 (Conn. 1899)).

3. In a study of the effects of converting to a federal consumption tax, the staff of the Joint Committee on Taxation observed, "One of the most fundamental issues in attempting to measure the value of governmental and nonprofit activities is when should government and nonprofit entities be regarded as producers of goods and services and when should they be treated as consumers?" (Joint Committee on Taxation 1996, ¶ 154).

4. Compare the complaint of Thomas Hare in 1867, regarding the exemption of charitable property from the English poor tax and other taxes: "None of the claimants of such exemption, whether from a national or a local tax, have ever put further any device or pretence to show that the amount fairly chargeable upon their property as its share of the public burden can be saved, so that its collection would be rendered unnecessary in consequence of the benefit derived from the charities" (Hare 1867, 137).

5. A rare declaration of congressional intent appears in the legislative history to Congress' 1938 decision that donations made to foreign charities may not be deducted, with the House Ways and Means Committee stating that charity begins at home: "The exemption from taxation of money or property devoted to charitable and other purposes is based upon the theory that the Government is compensated for the loss of revenue by its relief from financial burden which would otherwise have to be met by appropriations from public funds, and by the benefits resulting from the promotion of the general welfare" (H.R. Rep. No. 1860, 75th Cong., 3d Sess. 19 (1938)). Harvey Dale objects to this declaration as "bad history, because there is no indication that the tax exemption, afforded since the end of the nineteenth century, was predicated on the quid pro quo rationale" (Dale 1995, 660–61 (footnote omitted)). As a technical matter, "lessening the burdens of government" is only one route to federal income tax exemption as a charity under regulations issued under Internal Revenue Code section 501(c)(3). To come within that particular provision, moreover, the organization must demonstrate that the government considers the organization's activities to be its burden.

6. As the Treasury Department testified in 1988, "The role of the quasi-governmental, not-for-profit sector should . . . be restricted to that of supplementing, not supplanting, the activities of for-profit businesses. Thus, tax exemption for public charities should be restricted to those areas where the quality of goods and services that would be produced strictly through market forces is inadequate" (Chapoton 1987, 15).

7. See Jensen (1931), criticizing the maxim that the state should never tax its own property: "The state is regarded as a simple unit, while, as a matter of fact, the state is a

complex organization with many subordinate units, among all of which substantial justice must be maintained" (139). Because distributional problems can be minimized by such methods as enlarging the local taxing jurisdiction (ibid., 145), Jensen advocated taxation of public property only on three grounds: "First, that there is considerable concentration of exempt property; second, that such concentration produces discrimination in tax burdens on local property; and third, that there are no adequate offsets to such discrimination" (ibid., 143).

8. Alfred Balk's 1971 study describes a similar, but modern, skepticism from Yale University's president. In response to a request by the mayor of New Haven for substantial payments in lieu of taxes, "Kingman Brewster declared, 'Offhand I can think of no way in which we would be legally empowered to make a grant to the city government,' and there the matter rested at this writing" (Balk 1971, 122 (footnote omitted)).

9. See, for example, Chauncey Belknap's conception, written in 1954:

> The quid pro quo explanation of tax exemptions, although it has achieved a wide currency and has gained in validity with the broadening of governmental functions, is not adequate as a justification of the privilege [of charity tax exemption] in some of the most important segments of the general area under discussion. It is evident that the tax exemption privilege has much deeper roots than the quid pro quo theory would admit.
>
> The true explanation, and the only principle that affords a complete justification covering the entire field of exemptions. . . , is that government relieves from the tax burden religious, educational, and charitable activities because it wishes to encourage them as representing the highest and noblest achievements of mankind. (2033–34)

See also Ginsberg (1980, 329) (states settled on the nonprofit form as a prerequisite for exemption as an education institution).

10. Atkinson (1990, 617–20) (synthesizing the traditional subsidy view and Bittker and Rahdert's "structural uniqueness" view, by expanding the tax preference to encompass nonprofits' "altruistic provision of goods and services"); Atkinson (1993, 1142–48) (suggesting that the most desirable altruism takes the form of radically independent, self-sustaining communities). A similar theory with more of a subsidy flavor has been offered by John Colombo and Mark Hall (1995), who suggest that tax exemption be limited to organizations receiving at least one-third (or even one-half, for property-tax exemption) of their ongoing support in the form of donations from members of the public. (But see Grimm, chapter 13 of this volume.)

11. In addition, widespread reform of public-school financing has forced states to take greater control of the allocation of property-tax revenue. Economist Steven Sheffrin observes, "As we end this century and begin the next, the property tax technically belongs to local government, but it will effectively be treated by states as part of their own financial resources" (Sheffrin 1998, 143). Even if spending on schoolchildren becomes uniform throughout a state, variations in the concentration of nonprofit property imposes differing burdens on municipalities with respect to their other costs.

12. The dissent in *American Museum of Fly Fishing, Inc. v. Town of Manchester*, 557 A.2d 900, 115–16 (Vt. 1989), describes the state-local relationship in terms echoing the federalism debate over unfunded mandates: "The burden created by local taxes on real

estate is, and for some time now has been, notorious. Every year, almost without exception, those taxes are increased in order that the towns can continue to fulfill their obligations (many of which are required by the legislature)." However, Professor Heller notes that because of legislative logrolling, "Excessive charity costs in property tax ought to be measured against compensating gains from other taxes supporting a variety of programs that may excessively benefit cities" (Heller 1979, 237). As a separate matter, local governmental property as well as state property is exempt; some municipalities own property in other jurisdictions, and some taxing districts overlap.

13. Even before reaching the tax issue, the question has arisen whether the state may prohibit discrimination by private associations. In *Roberts v. United States Jaycees*, 468 U.S. 609 (1984), the Supreme Court held that Minnesota's prohibition against sex discrimination in "public accommodations" does not violate a group's First Amendment rights of free association unless that group is either "intimate" or "expressive"; given that the Jaycees were not such a group, they could be required to admit women as members. More recently, the Court held that the Boy Scouts of America is such an expressive organization, and as such could expel a homosexual troop leader (*Boy Scouts of America v. Dale*, 530 U.S. 640 (2000)).

14. Compare this with Adler, who wrote,

> [A] charter of liberties and immunities was binding only upon the king who granted it. This is shown by the frequent request to confirm old charters. When the King found himself pressed for money, he thought little of disregarding charters of exemption. An early trick of the King was to claim that his great seal was lost and in consequence charters bearing the old seal were void. To regain validity the old charters would have to be sealed by the King's new seal—a process which cost the religious houses much money in fines. (1922, 12–13)

See also Warren, Krattenmaker, and Snyder (1971, 217–21) for arguments against the validity of Contracts Clause doctrine.

15. Other ways around the limitation might exist. For example, Northwestern University's charter exemption provides: "All property, of whatever kind or description, belonging to or owned by said corporation, shall be for ever free from taxation for any and all purposes." The legislature later enacted a statute limiting exemptions to property owned by and *used for* exempt purposes. The Illinois supreme court held that this amendment authorized requiring Northwestern to pay tax on properties it leased out, on the ground that the phrase "property for schools and religious and charitable purposes" in the constitution (as then in effect) must have meant property adapted to and intended to be used directly for education. The U.S. Supreme Court disagreed: "The purposes of the school and the school are not identical. The purpose of a college or university is to give youth an education. The money which comes from the sale or rent of land dedicated to that object aids this purpose. Land so held and leased is held for school purposes, in the fullest and clearest sense" (*University v. People*, 99 U.S. (9 Otto) 309, 324 (1878)). A century later, however, the Cook County collector assessed a tax on the leasehold interests of Northwestern's *tenants*, a maneuver upheld by the Illinois Supreme Court (*Nabisco, Inc. v. Korzen*, 369 N.E.2d 829 (Ill. 1977), *appeal dismissed for want of a substantial federal question*, 435 U.S. 1005 (1978)). Following passage of a nonbinding referendum in the university's home town of Evanston asserting that Northwestern does

not pay its "fair share" for city services, Evanston is now considering imposing a $10-per-employee tax on organizations having more than 1,000 workers—affecting only Northwestern and two tax-exempt hospitals. In addition, Northwestern has sued to enjoin Evanston from declaring an historic district that would put restrictions on dozens of university properties (O'Connor 2000).

16. See, for example, *Yale Club of Chicago v. Department of Revenue*, 574 N.E.2d 31, 37 (Ill. App. 1991):

> The [Yale Club of Chicago] argues that it "is organized and operated to benefit the public by the influence of education" and that it accomplishes this public benefit by "identifying and evaluating applicants to Yale, stimulating interest in Yale among alumni and the public at large, and maintaining a Yale presence in Chicago." An organization designed to benefit Yale exclusively does not appear to dispense its benefits to an indefinite number of people or all those who need and apply for it. The State of Illinois and its taxpayers receive no apparent relief from any economic burden by the YCC's activities. Accordingly, we find it hyperbolic to claim as a "charitable purpose" the benefits reserved exclusively to Yale alumni and students.

17. In addition, the Court rejected the argument that, without exemption, California would become excessively entangled in religious affairs in violation of the Establishment Clause, "because the materials are subject to the tax regardless of content or motive" (*Jimmy Swaggart Ministries v. Board of Equalization*, 493 U.S., 396). "Ironically, appellant's theory . . . would require government to do precisely what appellant asserts the Religion Clauses prohibit: 'determine which expenditures are religious and which are secular'" (ibid., 396–97, quoting *Lemon v. Kurtzman*, 403 U.S. 602, 621–22 (1971)).

18. In *Boerne v. Flores*, 521 U.S. 507 (1997), the Supreme Court held that the federal Religious Freedom Restoration Act of 1993 was unconstitutional as applied to the states. RFRA says, "Government may substantially burden a person's exercise of religion only if it demonstrates that application of the burden to the person—(1) is in furtherance of a compelling governmental interest; and (2) is the least restrictive means of furthering that compelling governmental interest." The city of Boerne denied a waiver to a church that wanted to expand its structure, a historic landmark. In his concurring opinion, Justice Stevens wrote,

> If the historic landmark on the hill in Boerne happened to be a museum or an art gallery owned by an atheist, it would not be eligible for an exemption from the city ordinances that forbid an enlargement of the structure. Because the landmark is owned by the Catholic Church, it is claimed that RFRA gives its owner a federal statutory entitlement to an exemption from a generally applicable, neutral civil law. Whether the Church would actually prevail under the statute or not, the statute has provided the Church with a legal weapon that no atheist or agnostic can obtain. This governmental preference for religion, as opposed to irreligion, is forbidden by the First Amendment. (537)

19. See *Trustees of Griswold College v. Iowa*, 46 Iowa 265 (1877), holding that exemption for church property does not violate a prohibition in the state constitution on levying tithes, taxes, or other rates for church purposes. Some states limit the extent of the parsonage allowance.

20. *Finlator v. Powers,* 902 F.2d 1158 (4th Cir. 1990) (North Carolina); *Thayer v. South Carolina Tax Commission,* 413 S.E.2d 810 (So. Car. 1992); *Haller v. Department of Revenue,* 728 A.2d 351 (Penn.), *cert. denied sub nom. Pennsylvania Department of Revenue v. Newman,* 528 U.S. 929 (1999). Exemptions for sales of religious publications and Bibles remain on the books in Florida, Georgia, and Louisiana, but Tennessee repealed its exemption for the sale of religious publications. In a few states, religious publications are exempted along with publications sold by secular institutions. See generally Gallagher (1999).

21. The "pervasively religious" test came from the plurality opinion in *Roemer v. Board of Public Works of Md.,* 426 U.S. 736 (1976), but has been commonly applied (see, e.g., *Columbia Union College v. Clark,* 159 F.3d 151 (4th Cir. 1998), which upheld Maryland's exclusion of a Seventh Day Adventist college from a State grant program, *cert. denied,* 527 U.S. 1013 (1999); cf. *Bagley v. Raymond School District,* 728 A.2d 127 (Me. 1999), which upheld exclusion of religious schools from Maine's education tuition program). Lower federal courts have applied *Mitchell* narrowly, focusing on O'Connor's refusal to join the plurality opinion's desire to repeal the pervasively sectarian test (see, e.g., *Simmons-Harris v. Zelman,* 234 F.3d 945 (6th Cir. 2000), *cert. granted,* 122 S. Ct. 23 (200), striking down Cleveland's voucher program, which primarily covered religious schools, as advancing religion; *Steele v. Industrial Development Board,* 117 F. Supp. 2d 693 (M.D. Tenn. 2000), which enjoined tax-exempt bond issuance for David Liscomb University and all other pervasively sectarian institutions). The *Steele* court, 117 F. Supp. 2d, 718, observed, "The form of aid provided to Lipscomb was a substantial, affirmative benefit that, unlike property tax exemptions, allowed Lipscomb to dramatically improve its facilities." But the Virginia Supreme Court reads *Mitchell* broadly (compare *Habel v. Industrial Development Authority of the City of Lynchburg,* 400 S.E.2d 516 (Va. 1991), which denied tax-exempt bond issuance for Jerry Falwell's Liberty University, with *Virginia College Building Authority v. Lynn,* 538 S.E.2d 682 (Va. 2000), which denied tax-exempt bond authorization only for the divinity school at Pat Robertson's Regent University, and permitted it for other facilities, on the grounds that First Amendment jurisprudence no longer focuses on the "pervasively sectarian" standard). See generally Crimm 2001.

22. In her concurring opinion in the case, Justice O'Connor explained,

> If, as the plurality contends, a per-capita-aid program is identical in relevant constitutional respects to a true private-choice program, then there is no reason that, under the plurality's reasoning, the government should be precluded from providing direct money payments to religious organizations (including churches) based on the number of persons belonging to each organization. And, because actual diversion is permissible under the plurality's holding, the participating religious organizations (including churches) could use that aid to support religious indoctrination.

REFERENCES

Aaron, Henry J. 1975. *Who Pays the Property Tax? A New View.* Washington, D.C.: Brookings Institution.

Adler, Philip. 1922. "Historical Origin of the Exemption from Taxation of Charitable Institutions." In *Tax Exemptions on Real Estate: An Increasing Menace,* part I (1–84). White Plains, N.Y.: Westchester County Chamber of Commerce.

Andrews, William D. 1972. "Personal Deductions in an Ideal Income Tax." *Harvard Law Review* 86: 309–85.

Atkinson, Rob. 1993. "Reforming Cy Pres Reform." *Hastings Law Review* 44: 1111–58.

———. 1990. "Altruism in Nonprofit Organizations." *Boston College Law Review* 31: 501–639.

Baker, Newman F. 1928. "Tax Exemption Statutes." *Texas Law Review* 7: 50–85.

Balk, Alfred. 1971. *The Free List: Property without Taxes.* New York: Russell Sage Foundation.

Belknap, Chauncey. 1954 (1977). "The Federal Income Tax Exemption of Charitable Organizations: Its History and Underlying Policy." Reprinted as appendix to John P. Persons, John J. Osborne, Jr., and Charles F. Feldman, "Criteria for Exemption Under Section 501(c)(3)," in *Research Papers Sponsored by the Commission on Private Philanthropy and Public Needs* (IV: 2025–43). Washington, D.C.: U.S. Treasury Department.

Bittker, Boris I. 1969. "Churches, Taxes and the Constitution." *Yale Law Journal* 78: 1285–1310.

Bittker, Boris I., and George K. Rahdert. 1976. "The Exemption of Nonprofit Organizations from Federal Income Tax." *Yale Law Journal* 85 (3): 299–358.

Brody, Evelyn. 1998. "Of Sovereignty and Subsidy: Conceptualizing the Charity Tax Exemption." *Journal of Corporation Law* 23 (4): 585–629.

———. 1997. "Charitable Endowments and the Democratization of Dynasty." *Arizona Law Review* 39: 873–948.

———. 1996. "Institutional Dissonance in the Nonprofit Sector." *Villanova Law Review* 41 (2): 433–504.

Chapoton, O. Donaldson. 1987. "Statement of O. Donaldson Chapoton, Deputy Assistant Secretary (Tax Policy), Department of the Treasury, before the Subcommittee on Oversight, House Ways and Means Committee." June 22.

Clotfelter, Charles T., ed. 1992. *Who Benefits from the Nonprofit Sector?* Chicago: University of Chicago Press.

Colombo, John D. 1993. "Why Is Harvard Tax-Exempt? (And Other Mysteries of Tax Exemption for Private Educational Institutions)." *Arizona Law Review* 35: 841–903.

Colombo, John D., and Mark A. Hall. 1995. *The Charitable Tax Exemption.* Boulder, Colo.: Westview Press.

Crimm, Nina J. 2001. "Tax-Exempt Bonds, Religiously Affiliated Institutions and the Establishment Clause." *Tax Notes* 92: 1339–48. September 3.

Dale, Harvey. 1995. "Foreign Charities." *Tax Lawyer* 48: 655–704.

Gabbler, L. Richard, and John F. Shannon. 1977. "The Exemption of Religious, Educational, and Charitable Institutions from Property Tax Exemption." In *Research Papers Sponsored by the Commission on Private Philanthropy and Public Needs* (IV: 2535–72). Washington, D.C.: U.S. Treasury Department.

Gallagher, Janne G. 1999. *Sales Tax Exemptions for Charitable, Educational, and Religious Nonprofit Organizations.* Washington, D.C.: National Council of Nonprofit Associations.

Ginsberg, William R. 1980. "The Real Property Tax Exemption of Nonprofit Organizations: A Perspective." *Temple Law Quarterly* 53: 291–342.

Hall, Peter Dobkin. 1992. *Inventing the Nonprofit Sector*. Baltimore: Johns Hopkins University Press.

Hansmann, Henry. 1981. "The Rationale for Exempting Nonprofit Organizations from Corporate Income Taxation." *Yale Law Journal* 91: 54–100.

Hare, Thomas. 1867. "Charitable Endowments, in Their Relation to the State and to Public Taxation." *Fortnightly Review* II (VIII), New Series: 129–42. Aug. 1.

Heller, Thomas C. 1979. "Is the Charitable Exemption from Property Taxation an Easy Case? General Concerns about Legal Economics and Jurisprudence." In *Law and Economics of Local Governments*, edited by Daniel Rubinfeld (183–251). Washington, D.C.: Urban Institute Press.

Jensen, Jens Peter. 1931. *Property Taxation in the United States*. Chicago: University of Chicago Press.

Joint Committee on Taxation. *See* U.S. Congress.

Kelley, Dean M. 1977. *Why Churches Should Not Pay Taxes*. New York: Harper and Row.

O'Connor, Matt. 2000. "NU Lawsuit Questions Historic Restrictions by Evanston District; Official Says School Target of 'Animosity.'" *Chicago Tribune*. Metro Section, at 3, November 21.

Robertson, D.B. 1968. *Should Churches Be Taxed?* Philadelphia: Westminster Press.

Rudnick, Rebecca S. 1993. "State and Local Taxes on Nonprofit Organizations." *Capital University Law Review* 22: 321–72.

Sheffrin, Steven M. 1998. "The Future of the Property Tax: A Political Economy Perspective." In *The Future of State Taxation*, edited by David Brunori (129–45). Washington, D.C.: Urban Institute Press.

Simon, John G. 1987. "The Tax Treatment of Nonprofit Organizations: A Review of Federal and State Policies." In *The Nonprofit Sector: A Research Handbook*, edited by Walter W. Powell (67–98). New Haven: Yale University Press.

———. 1978. "Charity and Dynasty Under the Federal Tax System." *Probate Lawyer* 5: 1–92.

Stone, Lawrence M. 1968. "Federal Tax Support of Charities and Other Exempt Organizations: The Need for a National Policy." *1968 University of Southern California Tax Institute* 27–78.

Surrey, Stanley S., and Paul R. McDaniel. 1985. *Tax Expenditures*. Cambridge, Mass.: Harvard University Press.

Swords, Peter. 1981. *Charitable Real Property Tax Exemptions in New York State: Menace or Measure of Social Progress?* New York: Association of the Bar of the City of New York and Columbia University Press.

U.S. Congress, Joint Committee on Taxation. 1996. *Impact on State and Local Governments and Tax-Exempt Organizations of Replacing the Income Tax*. JCS-4-96, Apr. 30.

Warren, Alvin C., Thomas G. Krattenmaker, and Lester B. Snyder. 1971. "Property Tax Exemptions for Charitable, Educational, Religious and Governmental Institutions in Connecticut." *Connecticut Law Review* 4: 181–309.

Weber, Paul J., and Dennis A. Gilbert. 1981. *Private Churches and Public Money: Church-Government Fiscal Relations*. Westport, Conn.: Greenwood Press.

Welch, Ronald B. 1972. "The States' Concern over Property Tax Exemptions." *National Tax Association*: 265–82.

Zelinsky, Edward A. 1998. "Are Tax 'Benefits' Constitutionally Equivalent to Direct Expenditures?" *Harvard Law Review* 112: 379–433.

Zollmann, Carl. 1916. "Tax Exemptions on Church Property." *Michigan Law Review* 14: 646–57.

7

The Special Case of Churches

Deirdre Dessingue

A ny discussion of the appropriate tax treatment of nonprofit organizations will inevitably confront the conundrum of churches. By virtue of the religion clauses of the First Amendment, churches present unique but controversial claims to property-tax exemption.

History of the Exemption for Religious Institutions

Church property has been exempt under tax regimes throughout civilized society. In ancient times, Sumeria, Babylon, Egypt, Persia, India, and Israel provided tax exemptions for property of churches or priests or both (Whitehead 1992, 522–45; Pfeffer 1953, 183). Church property-tax exemptions in American colonial times originated from two different traditions under British law (Witte 1991, 372–78): common-law tradition and equity-law tradition. Under common-law tradition, religion was an affair of state, thus justifying exemption of church property on the same basis as other public property. The common-law exemption did not extend to all church property, but, rather, was subject to several significant limitations. Exemption was limited to property owned by established churches and put to religious use (e.g., chapels, parsonages, and religious cemeteries). The exemption extended only to ecclesiastical taxes imposed for church maintenance and use, not to other property taxes, for which established churches frequently were liable. Finally, exemption for church property could be revoked in times of emergency, or eliminated entirely if tax burdens on nonchurch properties proved too onerous (Witte 1991, 372–74; Whitehead 1992, 531–32).

British equity-law tradition, on the other hand, provided property-tax exemption for charitable, as opposed to religious, use. To be sure, religious use constituted a type of charitable use, and was deemed an appropriate means of benefiting an indefinite charitable class.[1] Unlike religious-use exemptions under common law, however, charitable-use exemptions under equity law were available to *all* churches, whether established or dissenting (Witte 1991, 375–78).

Church property-tax exemptions remained in place after the American Revolution, even as disestablishment became the norm (see Diamond, chapter 5 of this volume). With some notable exceptions,[2] tax exemptions for churches have enjoyed wide acceptance throughout U.S. history, a practice "deeply embedded in the fabric of our national life" (*Walz v. Tax Commissioner*, 397 U.S. 664, 676 (1970)). All 50 states and the District of Columbia provide for church tax exemptions through statutory or constitutional provisions, or both (see Gallagher, chapter 1 of this volume; Antineau, Carroll, and Burke 1965). Although history does not suffice as the sole basis for future practice, tradition provides a potent and persuasive rationale for church property-tax exemption.

Subsidy and Quid Pro Quo

The passage of the era of the established churches and consequent loss of public-property rationale required the articulation of replacement theories for property-tax exemption. Through the 19th century, theories of tax exemption focused on the societal benefits provided by exempt entities and their relief of government burdens (Whitehead 1992, 539). This "good works" rationale, with its grounding in acts rather than official status, justified church property-tax exemption solely on the basis of perceived societal benefits flowing from religious practice (Zollmann 1916, 647). These benefits have variously been interpreted to include inculcation of public morality, chastity, modesty, temperance, obedience, and cultivation of public spiritedness, sense of duty, respect, and loyalty to democratic principles.[3] Church property was also believed to enhance neighborhood property values. Finally, churches provided valuable charitable services through their hospitals, parochial schools, and charitable works (Witte 1991, 387–88).

The quid pro quo theory (also known as the subsidy theory) fails, however, when applied to the distinctly *religious* functions performed by churches—the very functions that distinguish churches from the general class of charitable organizations. If tax exemptions are, in fact, forms of subsidy provided by the state in exchange for valuable services, then how can they be offered in exchange for religious services, since the state may not provide, sponsor, or support religious services without violating the Establishment Clause? (See, e.g., *General Conference of Church of God—7th Day v. Carper*, 557 P.2d 832 (Co. 1976); see generally Kelley 1977, 43–44; Pfeffer 1953, 186–87.) As subsidies, exemptions might also be manipulated through a carrot-and-stick approach to reward or discourage particular religious behaviors in accordance with the state's desires, with obvious adverse constitutional implications.

When presented with the issue, the Supreme Court declined to justify church property-tax exemption on the basis of services or "good works" performed. "To give emphasis to so variable an aspect of the work of religious bodies would introduce an element of governmental evaluation and standards . . . which the policy of neutrality seeks to minimize. Hence, use of a social welfare yardstick as a significant element to qualify for tax exemption could conceivably give rise to confrontations that could escalate to constitutional dimensions" (*Walz*, 675). Instead, the Court viewed property-tax exemption for churches, among a broad class of nonprofit organizations, as a permissible accommodation of religion. Acknowledging that both taxing and exempting churches entailed a degree of state involvement with religion, the Court determined that exemption afforded fewer occasions for impermissible entanglement of government with religion (ibid., 674–75).

As conceived in *Walz,* tax exemption did *not* constitute a subsidy, nor did it represent state advancement or sponsorship of religion (ibid., 672). "The grant of a tax exemption is not sponsorship, since the government does not transfer part of its revenue to churches but simply abstains from demanding that the church support the state. No one has ever suggested that tax exemption has converted libraries, art galleries, or hospitals into arms of the state or put employees 'on the public payroll.' There is no genuine nexus between tax exemption and establishment of religion" (ibid., 675).

The underlying premises of *Walz* were questioned, however, when the Supreme Court concluded, in *Regan v. Taxation with Representation*, 461 U.S. 540 (1983), that both tax exemptions and tax deductions *were* subsidies,[4] and as such could be conditioned upon certain behaviors, such as refraining from substantial lobbying, or adopting racially nondiscriminatory policies even when contrary to an educational organization's religious beliefs (see *Bob Jones University v. United States*, 461 U.S. 574 (1983)).[5] In *Texas Monthly, Inc. v. Bullock*, 489 U.S. 1 (1989), a divided Court then concluded that a sales-tax exemption *exclusively* for religious publications violated the Establishment Clause. The three-judge plurality found that a subsidy directed exclusively to religious organizations that is not required by the Free Exercise Clause (as this exemption was not) "cannot be viewed as anything but impermissible state sponsorship of religion" (ibid., 2).

Base Definition and Sovereignty

As an alternative exemption theory, tax-base theory challenges the assumption that government can or should tax everything. The theory is grounded in the notion that wealth forms the appropriate basis for taxation. Nonprofit organizations, to the extent they are not producing wealth, simply do not inhabit the base on which taxation is properly levied. "There is no way to tax *everything*; a legislative body, no matter how avid for revenue, can do no more than pick out from the universe of people, entities, and events over which it has jurisdiction those that, in its view, are appropriate objects of taxation. In specifying the ambit of any tax, the legislature cannot avoid 'exempting' those persons, events, activities, or entities that are outside the territory of the proposed tax" (Bittker 1969, 1288).

Sovereignty theory—under which nonprofits occupy a sphere independent of and equal to that of the state for tax purposes (Brody 1998; Brody, chapter 6 of this volume)—buttresses pure tax-base theory, and is particularly apt when applied to churches, whose unique, constitutionally-based sovereignty claim can be seen as superior to that of other nonprofits. The proper tax treatment of churches is essentially a question of sovereignty (Goodwin 1986, 390). "The issue . . . is not whether the state is *allowed* to grant tax immunities to entities dedicated to fulfilling the role of religion in civil society, but whether the state has any power to tax such entities at all" (Titus 1992, 516, emphasis added). Moreover, if the First Amendment is designed to maintain the zones of sovereignty assigned to church and state, and the Establishment Clause prevents government from supporting religion, then to balance the equation, the Free Exercise Clause must operate to prevent religion from being forced to support the state.

Must States Exempt Churches?

In deciding the constitutional permissibility of church property-tax exemption, *Walz* sidestepped two important questions: Is church property-tax exemption *required*, and if so, when; and is property-tax exemption available exclusively to churches *ever* constitutionally permissible?

Under *Walz,* as reinterpreted by *Texas Monthly,* exemption is permissible, but only because it is "submerged in, and therefore excused by, the exemption of other nonprofits" (Bittker 1969, 1295).[6] Although the plurality opinion in *Texas Monthly* admitted that exemption might in some circumstances be required by the Free Exercise Clause, the small sales tax at issue did not present a burden sufficient to trigger constitutional jeopardy.[7] Significantly, the Court rejected the state's assertion of any compelling governmental interest in avoiding violations of the Religion Clauses as a means of justifying the exemption (ibid., 17–18). Indeed, neither of the Religion Clauses was seen as an obstacle to elimination of the sales-tax exemption for religious publications, if the state elected not to expand the exemption in promotion of some legitimate secular aim (ibid., 21).

The concurring opinion of Justices Blackmun and O'Connor acknowledged the difficulty of reconciling Religion Clause values, with the Free Exercise clause suggesting the necessity of religious exemption and the Establishment Clause militating against it.[8] However, the justices elected to postpone resolution of the issue of when the Free Exercise Clause would *require* a religious exemption by determining that such a case was not before them (ibid., 28).

Nor was such a case presented by imposition of a neutrally applied sales-and-use tax on mail-order sales of religious publications, unanimously upheld by the Court in *Jimmy Swaggart Ministries v. Board of Equalization,* 493 U.S. 378 (1990). Echoing its decision in *Hernandez v. Commissioner,* 490 U.S. 680 (1989), the Court reiterated that taxation merely decreases the amount of money available for religious activities and does not impose a constitutionally significant burden on religious exercise.[9] Responding to the question left open by the Blackmun and O'Connor concurrence in *Texas Monthly*, the Court indicated that only where a flat tax operated as a prior restraint on the free exercise of religious belief would the Free Exercise Clause require tax exemption (*Swaggart*, 388). The Court expressed no view on the question of whether a more onerous tax rate that, even if applied neutrally, would "effectively choke off an adherent's religious practices" violates the Free Exercise Clause (ibid., 392).

Two state courts interpreting state constitutional and statutory provisions have concluded that church property-tax exemption is not mandated. In *Leggett v. Macon Baptist Association*, 204 S.E. 197 (Ga. 1974), the Supreme Court of Georgia, interpreting an exemption for "places of religious worship" in a dispute over the actual use of premises for such purposes, declared that "religious groups do not enjoy a general immunity from the imposition of property taxes under the First Amendment to the United States Constitution." See also *Mordecai F. Ham Evangelistic Association v. Matthews*, 189 S.W.2d 524 (Ky. 1945), which denied exemption to "religious societies" in which a religious corporation was the mere alter ego of an individual minister.

The United States Supreme Court has been clear in its position that the incidental financial burden placed upon religious exercise by neutrally applied taxes, including sales-and-use taxes (*Texas Monthly; Jimmy Swaggart*) and income taxes (*Hernandez*), does not rise to the level of constitutional significance.[10] In each case so far presented to the Court, however, the direct burden of taxation fell on members or adherents, and the level of taxation was deemed insufficient to seriously affect their ability to engage in religious practices. The financial impact of taxing church property cannot be dismissed so easily. Property taxation presents a fixed and substantial burden not present in other forms of taxation. While a church could eliminate income tax by spending contributions and other revenues on religious activities and administrative costs, it could eliminate property tax liability only by disposing of the very sanctuary, temple, mosque, or other house of worship that constitutes the essential, sacred component of most religious practice.

Property tax is imposed on the value of church property, with no regard for the church's ability to pay. Thus, just as property-tax exemption disproportionately benefits organizations that have more real estate, property taxation imposes similarly uneven burdens. This is shown nowhere more clearly than with churches operating in high-value, high-tax, urban areas with declining membership and inadequate resources.[11]

Inherent in the power to tax is the power to control or suppress. "Those who can tax the exercise of . . . religious practice can make its exercise so costly as to deprive it of the resources necessary for its maintenance" (*Murdock v. Pennsylvania*, 319 U.S. 105, 112 (1943)). While the coercive and destructive potential of property taxation is present equally for all charitable organizations,[12] no other groups lay claim to the churches' unique First Amendment status. Investing the state with "potential for the actual destruction of religion cannot be reconciled with the Free Exercise Clause" (Whitehead 1992, 584).

Traditional Free Exercise analysis maintained that facially neutral laws or regulations may nonetheless violate the First Amendment if they unduly burden the free exercise of religion (see *Wisconsin v. Yoder*, 406 U.S. 205, 220 (1972)). The question is "whether government has placed a substantial burden on the observation of a central religious belief or practice and, if so, whether a compelling governmental interest justifies the burden" (*Hernandez*, 699). Under traditional Free Exercise analysis, the burden of a neutrally applied property tax upon a church's exercise of religious worship would be weighed against the government's identified compelling interests in imposing the tax.

However, the traditional compelling-state-interest standard for evaluating Free Exercise cases was dismantled in *Employment Division v. Smith*, 494 U.S. 872 (1990), which virtually eliminated the requirement that government justify burdens on religious exercise by compelling interests. (*Smith* held that the Free Exercise Clause did not relieve an individual of the obligation to comply with a neutral, generally applicable criminal statute against the use of peyote that only incidentally burdened religious exercise.) In the Court's view, only if prohibiting the exercise of religion were the object of a tax would the First Amendment be violated (ibid., 878). The Religious Freedom Restoration Act (RFRA) was enacted in 1993 to restore the least-restrictive-means/compelling-state-interest standard that existed prior to *Smith*.[13] However, RFRA provided little support for Free Exercise claims in the tax area, since the Supreme Court had already endorsed the compelling state interest in a sound tax system (*U.S. v. Lee*, 455 U.S. 252 (1982); see also *Christian Echoes National Ministry, Inc. V. United States*, 470 F.2d 849, 856–57 (10th Cir. 1972), *cert. denied*, 414 U.S. 864 (1973)). Thus, *Lee* presents a more enduring obstacle to any

Free Exercise challenge to church property taxation, one which is not eliminated by RFRA. Also, RFRA was found unconstitutional as applied to the states (*Boerne v. Flores*, 521 U.S. 507 (1997)). Since property-tax exemptions are a matter of state law, the *Smith* rational-basis standard would prevail. In the wake of *Boerne*, however, some states have enacted legislation adopting the pre-*Smith* test for Free Exercise claims that had been included in RFRA.[14] Accordingly, churches may be afforded more protection under state law than under RFRA.

Are constitutional arguments for church tax exemption thus "in tatters" (Thomas 1992, 606)? Does any Free Exercise argument against taxation of churches survive? Or does the strongest argument for exemption arise under the Establishment Clause, on the grounds that property taxation would result in excessive entanglement of government with religion (Thomas 1992, 627)?[15] The issue has never arisen, because states universally provide exemptions, but it is not difficult to imagine a situation in which property taxation imposed on places of worship would impose a substantial, destructive burden on religious practice, resulting in the closure or forced sale of church sanctuaries.[16]

Few religions oppose the payment of taxes as a matter of doctrine or theology, certainly as far as individuals are concerned (see, e.g., Matthew 22:21: "Render therefore unto Caesar that which is Caesar's, and unto God that which is God's"). However, in *Lee,* the claimed exemption from Social Security taxes stemmed from a specific Amish doctrinal obligation not to pay such taxes. No such doctrinal claims were asserted in *Hernandez* or *Jimmy Swaggart.* As enunciated by the Supreme Court, Free Exercise inquiry is not triggered by every burden imposed by government, but rather by those that substantially interfere with the observation of a "central religious belief or practice" (*Hernandez,* 699–700). Does maintenance of a sacred place of worship meet this threshold standard? The Synagogue Council of America, in its amicus curiae brief in *Walz,* argued that "the property used for religious purposes, including the house of worship, the religious sanctuary, and all that is contained therein are . . . intimately connected with religious exercise" (quoted in Kelley 1977, 21). Few would argue this proposition. Ecclesiastical architecture, sanctuary design, and religious art and ornamentation are visible representations of theological self-understanding, doctrine, and liturgical practice, all key matters of church function and autonomy (Carmella 1991, 449–75). Real-property taxation is generally imposed on the ownership of the sanctuary or similar worship space. Does sanctuary *ownership* (as opposed to rental[17]) occupy the same central position under religious tenets, doctrine, or practice?[18] This distinction may be irrelevant, since courts generally will not question "the centrality of particular beliefs or practices to a faith, or the validity of particular litigants' interpretations of those creeds" (ibid., 700).[19] Nonetheless, ownership of a sanctuary or other worship space would undoubtedly provide superior opportunities for religious self-expression, giving the religious organization the ability to control architecture, art, and design.

Imposition of property taxes *solely* on church property would, even under *Smith*, violate the Free Exercise Clause, because such selective taxation evinces hostility toward religion (see, e.g., *Church of Lukumi Babalu Aye, Inc. v. City of Hialeah,* 508 U.S. 520 (1993), in which the court ruled that city ordinances dealing with ritual animal slaughter were not neutral or of general applicability, but rather targeted religious conduct without compelling governmental interest, in violation of the Free Exercise Clause).

On the other hand, in the face of Supreme Court adherence to exemption-as-subsidy theory, any property-tax exemption extended *only* to church property would likely run afoul of the Establishment Clause (see *In the Matter of the Appeal of Springmoor, Inc.,* 498 S.E.2d 177 [N.C. 1998]).[20] The Establishment Clause is likely to prevail even where property-tax exemption would seem to be required under the Free Exercise Clause, although others would argue that, in service of the goal of religious toleration, Free Exercise principles should prevail in conflicts with anti-establishment principles (Tribe 1988, 1201). Consider *Rosenberger v. Rector & Visitors of University of Virginia,* 515 U.S. 819 (1995), in which the Court approved mandatory student fees used to support a variety of student groups, including religious groups, saying that it "recognized special Establishment Clause dangers where the government makes direct money payments to sectarian institutions" (ibid., 842). Does tax exemption, the *non*-taxation of churches, if viewed as subsidy, present the same constitutional difficulties? While the analogy offers some initial attraction, tax exemption does *not* result in the direct transfer of funds to exempt organizations, so the analogy fails.

More likely than property taxation imposed *solely* on churches, however, would be a situation presenting the flip side of *Walz*: the elimination of the church property-tax exemption along with a broad range of other exemptions. Does the Free Exercise Clause have any applicability in this situation? *Smith* suggests not, absent specific targeting of religious

exercise. Although imposition of a mere financial burden is not constitutionally significant, would property taxes so onerous as to result in the
closure or forced sale of church sanctuaries present a *Murdock* situation?
Can the Free Exercise Clause thus be seen as providing churches an enhanced right to property-tax exemption, in the nature of a basic right to
exist, even where the financial wherewithal to otherwise support and
maintain the sanctuary is lacking?

Lyng v. Northwest Indian Cemetery Protective Association, 485 U.S. 439
(1988), an unsuccessful Free Exercise challenge to the Forest Service's
construction of a paved road near sacred Native Americans sites, suggests
not. In that case, the Supreme Court acknowledged the area as "an integral and indispensable part of Indian religious conceptualization and
practice . . . [requiring] privacy, silence and an undisturbed natural setting" (ibid., 442). Nevertheless, the Court concluded that even if the burden of the proposed road were to "virtually destroy the . . . Indians' ability to practice their religion," the Free Exercise Clause afforded no basis
for relief (ibid., 451–52, quoting 795 F.2d 693 (opinion below)). Neither
were Native Americans coerced by government action into violating
their religious beliefs nor did government action "penalize religious
activity by denying any person an equal share of the rights, benefits, and
privileges enjoyed by other citizens" (ibid., 449). If such a threat to the
ability to engage in religious ritual failed to warrant Free Exercise protection, what stronger case could be made for property-tax exemption,
with its subsidy taint?

Further, the exercise of religion, as protected under the Free Exercise
Clause, protects religious beliefs; it does not protect all religious *actions*.
Where does church property fit on the beliefs-acts spectrum? Is there a
valid distinction between the "sacred acts" and "civil acts" of a church?
(See Whitehead 1992, 571–72.) Is church property so intimately connected with and essential to religious practice as to fall within the compass
of protected religious beliefs? Or does church property more appropriately reside among a church's civil acts, such as modes of incorporation or
title to property, which are subject to considerably broader state regulation
and control? (See Witte 1991, 413.)[21]

If church property is deemed essential to religious exercise, and thus
to be accorded enhanced constitutional status, to what property does
this status attach? Any claim to unique First Amendment protection
must perforce be grounded in the exercise of religion *qua* religion, as
distinguished from activities that churches share in common with other

charities. Several functions have historically been associated with churches in the United States, including worship, preaching (including religious education), charitable activities, and administration. Of these, only uniquely religious functions, such as worship, preaching, liturgical rites, doctrine, and selection and supervision of clergy, would appear entitled to enhanced constitutional status. If these functions were translated into property terms, enhanced status would attach to buildings comprising the sanctuary, synagogue, mosque, temple, or other worship space, and property directly and necessarily related to such uses, arguably including a seminary for the training of ministers. General charitable uses, including secular education, health care, and social welfare, would not qualify as core religious uses, no matter how widespread or consistent with church practice or religious tenets. To the extent these represent counterpart charitable uses, they would present no greater claim to exemption than property of non-religious charities.

States, however, provide an array of religious-use exemptions extending beyond those for worship space, including exemption for parsonages, rectories, other dwellings used by clergy,[22] convents, monasteries, church administrative offices, seminaries, cemeteries, youth camps and missions, and retreat houses. California provides two different property-tax exemptions to which a church might lay claim: church exemption (Ca. Rev. & Tax Code § 206), which extends to property used exclusively for religious worship, including churches under construction and parking lots, as well as to cloistered monasteries or convents; and religious exemption (Ca. Rev. & Tax Code § 207), which applies to the entire property of churches that operate schools below college level.

Opponents of elevating uniquely religious use to an enhanced constitutional position argue that such a step would necessitate intrusive government inquiries in order to identify eligible organizations. It is feared that such determinations would lead to divisiveness and excessive government entanglement in religious affairs. Yet these are precisely the sorts of determinations made—without dire consequence—by property-tax administrators across the country in their dealings with current religious property-tax exemption regimes. Administration of existing exemptions, generally requiring both ownership by a church and actual religious use, necessarily involves some degree of government involvement in evaluating entitlement.[23] But not all contact between church and state is constitutionally forbidden. Routine regulatory interaction that involves no doctrinal inquiries, delegations of state power, or "detailed monitoring and close administrative contact" does not offend the Establishment Clause (*Hernandez*, 696–97).

Although both exemption and taxation involve contact between church and state, exemption poses the lesser risk. As the *Walz* court observed in 1970, "Elimination of exemption would tend to expand the involvement of government by giving rise to tax valuation of church property, tax liens, tax foreclosures, and the direct confrontations and conflicts that follow in the train of these legal processes" (397 U.S. 674). These continue to represent the greater constitutional risks today. Absent the demise of subsidy theory, however, support for church property-tax exemption will more likely be garnered in the political and legislative, rather than judicial, arenas. It is there that the weight of historical tradition and the force of popular opinion can most effectively be marshaled to preserve the unbroken practice of exempting church property from taxation.

NOTES

1. The Statute of Charitable Uses (1601) included, for example, "repair of churches" as an enumerated charitable use. This tradition is reflected in the regulations under section 501(c)(3) of the Internal Revenue Code, which define "charitable" in its generally accepted legal sense, including "advancement of religion" (Treas. Reg. §1.501(c)(3)–1(d)(2)).

2. For example, between 1873 and 1876, the National Liberal League attempted to repeal the property-tax exemptions of churches and religious organizations. Indeed, President Grant's final State of the Union address in 1875 proposed an amendment to the Constitution that would have taxed church property (see Robertson 1968, 69–86). Exemption opponents feared, among other things, vast accumulations of ecclesiastical property—ostentatious Catholic churches in particular (see Diamond, chapter 5 of this volume). More recently, as part of the Fair Tax Movement, a 1996 ballot initiative would have removed the Colorado real-property tax exemption for religious purposes, including all churches, synagogues, temples, and mosques. The exemption for *personal* property used in religious worship would have been retained. The initiative, known as Amendment 11, was defeated by an overwhelming margin—83 percent to 17 percent (see Torkelson 1996, 7A).

3. See *Trustees of the First Methodist Episcopal Church, South v. City of Atlanta*, 76 Ga. 181 (1886), regarding property held for religious worship not subject to city paving assessment, which contains a colorful exposition of the contributions religious organizations provide to civic society:

> benevolence, charity, generosity, love of our fellow men, deference to rank, to age and sex, tenderness to the young, active sympathy for those in trouble or

distress, beneficence to the destitute and poor, and all those comely virtues and amiable qualities which clothe life "in decent drapery" and impart a charm to existence, [and which] constitute not only the "cheap defence of nations," but furnish a sure basis on which the fabric of civil society can rest, and without which it could not endure. Take from it these supports, and it would tumble into chaos and ruin. Anarchy would follow order and regularity, and liberty, freed from its restraining influence, would soon degenerate into the wildest license, which would convert the beautiful earth into a howling pandemonium, fit only for the habitation of savage beasts and more savage men. (192–93)

4. Even prior to *Regan v. Taxation with Representation*, some commentators believed that exemption was the equivalent of a direct subsidy, but that there was "nothing undesirable or unconstitutional in direct subsidy as long as it is granted without discrimination" (see Pfeffer 1953, 185; see also dissenting opinion of Justice Douglas in *Walz*: "A tax exemption is a subsidy" (397 U.S. at 705)). Despite the current prevalence of subsidy theory, tax exemption differs from subsidy in several important respects. It conveys no money to the organization. It is open ended; no "amount" of subsidy is determined by the government. Rather, the value of the property-tax exemption is dependent on the value of the property not taxed. Tax exemption does not convert the organization into an agency of "state action" (Kelley 1977, 32–34). Further, subsidies generate political conflict, in contrast to the simple and automatic operation of exemptions (Diamond, chapter 5 of this volume). At least one commentator perceives the distinction to be largely one of perspective, specifically, whether exemption is considered from the viewpoint of the recipient or that of the state. *Walz* implicitly upheld the state's perspective (Zelinsky 1998, 392–399).

5. The organization at issue was a pervasively religious educational institution. The Court specifically reserved application of its holding to "churches or other purely religious institutions" (*Bob Jones University v. United States*, 461 U.S. 574, 604 n. 29).

6. However, Justice Scalia, writing for the dissent in *Texas Monthly*, stated that the *Walz* property-tax exemption was *not* justified by virtue of breadth of coverage, but rather because exemption constituted a reasonable governmental attempt to avoid the "latent dangers" of state hostility toward religion that inhere in property taxes (*Texas Monthly*, 37, Scalia, J., dissenting, quoting *Walz*). Breadth of coverage would be constitutionally required only where the exemption was not specifically or exclusively justified as "an intentional and reasonable accommodation of religion" (ibid., 40).

7. Generally, the free exercise of religion can be burdened in two ways: "by interfering with a believer's ability to observe the commands or practices of his faith, and by encroaching on the ability of a church to manage its internal affairs" (*EEOC v. Catholic University*, 83 F.3d 455, 460 (D.C. Cir. 1996) (citations omitted)).

8. Judge Noonan explained this tension through the principle of double effect: "If a single act has both good and evil effects, the act is good if one intends the good effect and if the good effect is proportionately greater than the evil effect." Thus, religious tax exemptions have "the constitutionally protected effect of permitting the free exercise of religion and the constitutionally prohibited effect of establishing religion" (Noonan 1987, 339).

9. The Court concluded in *Hernandez v. Commissioner*, 490 U.S. 680 (1989), that no special treatment of religious contributions was required in the application of the

federal charitable-contribution deduction. In *Hernandez*, the Court held that "auditing fees" paid to the Church of Scientology could not be deducted as charitable contributions. The Court concluded that the tax code makes "no special preference for payments made in the expectation of gaining religious benefits or access to a religious service" (ibid., 693). Disallowance of deduction on quid pro quo grounds did not violate the Free Exercise Clause. The burden imposed by the fact that Scientology adherents would have less money available to gain access to religious services did not prevail against the government's interest in maintenance of a sound tax system (ibid., 699–700).

10. Nor was the "mere financial burden" of landmarking regulation constitutionally impermissible. See, for example *Rector of St. Bartholomew's Church v. City of New York*, 914 F.2d 348 (2d Cir. 1990), *cert. denied*, 499 U.S. 905 (1991), which rejected a Free Exercise challenge to the city's facially neutral landmark designation law on the grounds that it radically restricted the church's ability to raise revenues and carry out its ministerial programs. Compare that case with *First Covenant Church v. City of Seattle*, 787 P.2d 1352 (Wash. 1990), which found that landmark designation violated the Free Exercise Clause and state constitutional provisions. Specifically, the court found objectionable the effect of the landmarking law "to require a religious organization to seek secular approval of matters potentially affecting the Church's practice of its religion" (ibid., 1359; see generally Carmella 1991, 436–49).

11. As communities of believers, churches are composed of and supported by their members or adherents, typically drawn from the immediate environs. See, for example, Canon 518, Code of Canon Law, which generally defines Roman Catholic parishes as embracing all faithful within certain established territorial boundaries. Exempting churches located in low-income urban areas, which are likely to be populated by low-income members, relieves the derivative burden on these members, since they, through contributions, bear the ultimate burden of maintaining the church. Exempting churches in such localities does nothing, however, to resolve the moral and policy dilemma created by the fact that removing church property from the tax rolls necessarily increases the tax burden on neighboring householders, a group likely to be equally lacking in resources (see Swords's comment in this volume).

12. Tax exemption also presents potential for coercion when exemption is conditioned on undertaking or refraining from certain behaviors. For example, exemption from federal income tax under section 501(c)(3) of the Internal Revenue Code imposes significant limits on an organization's lobbying activities and prohibits political campaign activity entirely. The constitutionality of the political campaign activity prohibition as applied to churches was recently upheld in *Branch Ministries, Inc. v. Rossotti*, 211 F.3d 137 (D.C. Cir. 2000). To the extent that section 501(c)(3) exemption is a prerequisite for state property-tax exemption, these federal restrictions become conditions of the state exemptions.

13. RFRA provides that "government may substantially burden a person's exercise of religion only if it demonstrates that the application of the burden . . . is in furtherance of a compelling governmental interest, and is the least restrictive means of furthering that compelling governmental interest" (42 U.S.C.A. §§2000bb–1(b)).

14. Congress enacted the Religious Land Use and Institutionalized Persons Act of 2000 (RLUIPA), which focuses on two specific issues that had been the subject of extensive Free Exercise litigation. RLUIPA is based on Congress's authority to regulate under the Commerce and Spending Clauses and, in the case of land-use regulation, where an

extensive record of free-exercise problems has developed, under section 5 of the Fourteenth Amendment. RLUIPA applies the same standard to state and local government actions as is applied to the federal government under RFRA. Under RLUIPA, "land use regulation" is defined as "a zoning or landmarking law, or the application of such a law, that limits or restricts a claimant's use or development of land (including a structure affixed to land), if the claimant has an ownership, leasehold, easement, servitude or other property interest in the regulated land or a contact or option to acquire such an interest." Thus, although RLUIPA safeguards the rights of churches with respect to zoning and similar regulations, it adds no protections where property-tax exemption is concerned.

15. "Excessive entanglement" is the third prong of the three-part test for violation of the Establishment Clause set forth in *Lemon v. Kurtzman*, 403 U.S. 602 (1971): "First, the statute must have a secular legislative purpose; second, its principal or primary effect must be one that neither advances nor inhibits religion; finally the statute must not foster 'an excessive governmental entanglement with religion'" (ibid., 612 (citations omitted)). The excessive-entanglement prong originated in *Walz*, which the *Lemon* Court interpreted as confining rather than enlarging "the area of permissible state involvement with religious institutions by calling for close scrutiny of the degree of entanglement involved in the relationship. The objective is to prevent, as far as possible, the intrusion of either into the precincts of the other" (ibid., 614). The Supreme Court modified the *Lemon* test for purposes of evaluating aid to religious schools in *Agostini v. Felton*, 521 U.S. 203 (1997), by recasting the entanglement inquiry as simply one criterion relevant to determining a statute's effect.

16. However, neither the Free Exercise Clause, the Establishment Clause, nor RFRA prevented the forced sale of a church sanctuary for willful *refusal* to pay unemployment taxes (*United States v. Indianapolis Baptist Temple*, 224 F.3d 627 (7th Cir. 2000), *cert. denied*, 121 S.Ct. 857 (2001)).

17. Most church property-tax exemptions apply an "ownership *and* use" standard in determining eligibility. However, California provides an exemption for all churches, whether owned or rented (see Ca. Rev. Tax Code §206.2).

18. For example, the 1917 Code of Canon Law (c. 216) specified three requirements for the constitution of a Catholic parish: distinct territorial limits and part of the population; its own proper church; and its own proper rector and pastor, with "church" understood as a sacred structure devoted to divine worship for the principal purpose of being used by all the faithful for public divine worship (c. 1161) (see Bouscaren and Ellis 1957, 149, 637). The 1983 Code (Canon Law Society of America 1983, c. 515) requires merely a stable community of Christian faithful, without particular reference to a church structure.

19. See, for example, C.R.S.A. §39-3-106(2), whereby Colorado has codified this "non-inquiry" principle in its religious property-tax exemption statute:

> In order to guide members of the public and public law officials alike in the making of their day-to-day decisions, to provide for a consistent application of the laws, and to assist in the avoidance of litigation, the general assembly hereby finds and declares that religious worship has different meaning to different religious organizations; that the constitutional guarantees regarding establishment of religion and the free exercise of religion prevent public officials from inquiring as to whether particular activities of religious organization

constitute religious worship; that many activities of religious organization are in the furtherance of the religious purposes of such organization; that such religious activities are an integral part of the religious worship of religious organizations; and that activities of religious organization which are in furtherance of their religious purposes constitute religious worship for purposes of section 5 of article X of the Colorado constitution. This legislative finding and declaration shall be entitled to great weight in any and every court.

20. To the extent aid to religious schools provides an analogous situation to the "subsidy" of tax exemption, the Supreme Court has emphasized the importance of the principle of neutrality: namely, that "the religious, irreligious, and areligious are all alike eligible for governmental aid . . ." (*Mitchell v. Helms*, 530 U.S. 793, 810 (2000)).

21. The permissibility of church regulation through zoning ordinances, for example, indicates that churches do not have untrammeled discretion regarding location. See, for example, *City of Chicago Heights v. Living Word Outreach Full Gospel Church*, 707 N.E.2d 53 (Ill. App. Ct. 1998), in which the court found that when a church was permitted to locate anywhere in noncommercial zones, it had no Free-Exercise right (or right under the Illinois RFRA) to locate in commercial zones. The city's denial of a special-use permit was appropriate to its compelling interest in enforcing zoning laws designed to reinvigorate the commercial corridor and expand the tax base. See also *Area Plan Commission of Evansville and Vanderburgh County v. Wilson*, 701 N.E.2d 856 (Ind. Ct. App. 1998), in which the court ruled that a zoning ordinance requiring a church to obtain a special use permit did not violate the Free Exercise Clause or constitute a prior restraint on religious speech; and *Korean Buddhist Dae Won Sa Temple of Hawaii v. Naoe*, 953 P.2d 1315 (Haw. 1998), in which the court ruled that building height restrictions did not substantially burden a Buddhist temple's right to free exercise of religion.

22. See also I.R.C. §107, which provides a federal income-tax exclusion for the fair rental value of a parsonage or a parsonage allowance provided to a minister of the gospel.

23. Such analysis could involve determinations regarding the nature of property use (see, e.g., *Maurer v. Young Life*, 779 P.2d 1317 (Co. 1989), in which youth camping activities were ruled to constitute a form of religious worship); or the frequency of religious use (see, e.g., *Pilgrim Rest Baptist Church, Inc. v. Property Tax Administrator*, 971 P.2d 270 (Co. Ct. App. 1998), in which a religious organization's use of vacant lots once a year entitled the property to exemption).

REFERENCES

Antineau, Chester J., Phillip M. Carroll, and Thomas C. Burke. 1965. *Religion Under The State Constitutions.* Brooklyn, NY: Central Book Company.
Bittker, Boris I. 1969. "Churches, Taxes and the Constitution." *Yale Law Journal* 78:1285–1310.
Bouscaren, T. Lincoln, and Adam C. Ellis. 1957. *Canon Law, A Text and Commentary* (Third Revised Edition). Milwaukee: Bruce Publishing Company.
Brody, Evelyn. 1998. "Of Sovereignty and Subsidy: Conceptualizing the Charity Tax Exemption." *Journal of Corporation Law* 23 (4): 585–629.

Canon Law Society of America. 1983. *Code of Canon Law* (English edition). Washington, D.C.

Carmella, Angela C. 1991. "Houses of Worship and Religious Liberty: Constitutional Limits to Landmark Preservation and Architectural Review." *Villanova Law Review* 36 (2): 401–515.

Goodwin, Glenn. 1986. "Would Caesar Tax God? The Constitutionality of Governmental Taxation of Churches." *Drake Law Review* 35: 383–404.

Kelley, Dean M. 1977. *Why Churches Should Not Pay Taxes.* New York: Harper and Row.

Noonan, John T. 1987. *The Believer and The Powers That Are.* New York: Macmillan Publishing Company.

Pfeffer, Leo. 1953. *Church, State and Freedom.* Boston: Beacon Press.

Robertson, D.B. 1968. *Should Churches Be Taxed?* Philadelphia: Westminster Press.

Thomas, Oliver S. 1992. "The Power to Destroy: The Eroding Constitutional Arguments for Church Tax Exemption and the Practical Effect on Churches." *Cumberland Law Review* 22: 605–35.

Titus, Herbert W. 1992. "No Taxation or Subsidization: The Indispensable Principles of Freedom of Religion." *Cumberland Law Review* 22: 505–20.

Torkelson, Jean. 1996. "'God Tax' Goes Down Hard." *Rocky Mountain News.* November 6.

Tribe, Laurence, H. 1988. *American Constitutional Law.* 2d edition. Mineola, N.Y.: Foundation Press.

Whitehead, John W. 1992. "Tax Exemption and Churches: A Historical and Constitutional Analysis." *Cumberland Law Review* 22: 521–94.

Witte, John. 1991. "Tax Exemption of Church Property: Historical Anomaly or Valid Constitutional Practice?" *Southern California Law Review* 64: 363–415.

Zelinsky, Edward A. 1998. "Are Tax 'Benefits' Constitutionally Equivalent to Direct Expenditures?" *Harvard Law Review* 112: 379–433.

Zollmann, Carl. 1916. "Tax Exemption of American Church Property." *Michigan Law Review* 14: 646–57.

PART III
The Economic War within the States: Exemption Battles and PILOTs

8

PILOTs
The Large-City Experience
Pamela Leland

As cities search for new or expanding sources of revenue, anecdo-tal evidence in the early and mid-1990s appeared to suggest that local units of government were beginning to ignore long-established patterns of nonprofit property-tax exemption and increasingly turning to their own nonprofit property owners as a source of municipal revenue. Such efforts to solicit payments in lieu of taxes (PILOTs), municipal-service fees, and/or voluntary contributions from nonprofit organizations were often highly publicized, with city administrators suggesting that these exempt organizations should pay for the municipal services they utilized, and nonprofit executives countering that precious organiza-tional resources would be diverted from critical community needs.

While PILOT activities in some cities (notably Boston and Philadelphia) were widely discussed, no effort was made to document these activities nationally prior to the research reported here. This research attempts to fill the knowledge gap by assessing the extent to which municipal governments were seeking PILOTs from nonprofit organizations in the nation's largest cities, the nature of those attempts, and whether they represented a new trend or simply occurred in a few high-profile cities and states. The project used mail surveys and telephone interviews with public officials and key informants in 73 selected cities to document the nature, extent and impact of such activities. This national study was funded by the National Center for the Revitalization of Central Cities; data collection was completed during spring and summer 1998.

Background on PILOTs

In the early and mid-1990s, the debate over PILOTs had spread throughout the country. By 1997, a number of cities—including Syracuse, Buffalo, Hartford, New Haven, Wilmington, Des Moines, and Baltimore—and states—Kansas, Nebraska, and New Hampshire—had attempted to collect PILOTs from nonprofit organizations (Gallagher 1997). While Utah was the location of some early activity and there was an established program in Boston, in the 1990s it was the commonwealth of Pennsylvania where the most (and the most significant) activity with PILOTs occurred. Pennsylvania is also an excellent example of how legal issues play an important, if not essential, role in the success of PILOT programs.

In 1985, the Pennsylvania Supreme Court articulated five tests for classification as a "purely public charity"—and hence entitlement to property-tax exemption (*Hospitalization Utilization Project [HUP] v. Commonwealth of Pennsylvania*, 487 A.2d 1306, 507 Pa. 1 (1985); see Gallagher, chapter 1 of this volume, and Glancey, chapter 9). This decision cleared the way for successful solicitations of PILOTs—or "voluntary contributions," as they are sometimes called—throughout the state. One of the key elements that allowed for an aggressive (and successful) solicitation strategy arose from the inconsistent application and ambiguous interpretation of the *HUP* criteria by various boards of assessments and lower courts throughout the commonwealth during the early 1990s. As a result, local units of government were able to convince nonprofit organizations that making a PILOT was preferable to an exemption challenge in court. While nonprofit leaders were unwilling to publicly refer to these efforts as municipal "blackmail," research indicated that, for some nonprofits, a choice to "settle" was indeed preferable to the risk of losing exempt status (Leland 1995). By 1994, more than 1,000 nonprofit organizations—including hospitals, colleges, social service and youth-serving organizations, and veterans' groups—had been solicited for such payments in Pennsylvania. Efforts by the city of Philadelphia and other areas after 1994 increased these numbers dramatically in the mid-1990s.

Pennsylvania legislation enacted in 1997 seems to have reduced the ambiguity of the five-point *HUP* test. The legislature and several recent favorable court decisions have led nonprofit leaders to believe that local units of government are in a much weaker position in compelling non-profit organizations to pay PILOTs. Municipal leaders, however, assert that they are still able to raise such monies from nonprofit organizations. Anecdotal information through the late 1990s indicated that some cities continued to seek "voluntary contributions" from local nonprofit organizations.

A larger question is the degree to which the nonprofit sector could provide sizeable new municipal revenue. Research into this potential revenue base has been very limited, and what has been done indicates that "taxing" the property of nonprofit organizations alone would not significantly impact revenues (see Cordes, Gantz, and Pollak, chapter 4 of this volume). In New Orleans, for example, only $440 million of a total assessed property base of $2.5 billion is held by the traditional nonprofit sector (Louisiana Bureau of Governmental Research 1996). And this portion includes the religious sector—typically sacrosanct in any PILOT initiative. In New Orleans (and likely in other cities), it is clear that more revenue is lost because of the exemption of publicly owned property and homestead exemptions for private owners than because of exemptions for property held by charitable organizations.

Parameters of the Research Question

Nonprofit charitable organizations are usually exempted from a host of state and local taxes by state constitution or statute or both (see Gallagher, chapter 1 of this volume). Depending on the type of nonprofit organization and the particular state, nonprofit organizations might not be required to pay locally based property taxes, sales taxes, school taxes, road taxes, business privilege taxes, and/or state income or franchise taxes.

In the research project described here, monies paid by nonprofit organizations to local units of government for charges from which the groups are legally exempt are referred to as "payments in lieu of taxes" or PILOTs. These include "municipal-service fees" for services such as police and fire services, but do *not* include certain types of user or access fees charged to both for-profits and nonprofits (e.g., water, sewer, or cable), unless there is a legal basis for nonprofit exemption from such fees. Nor do PILOTs include fees and charges that nonprofits may pay in one state but not in another if the reason for the payments is a tight or narrow granting of exemption privileges in that state. Remember that state definitions of "charity" vary, as do state designations of exemption privileges and benefits; exemptions must be understood in the specific context of the local or state jurisdiction (Leland 1999a).

In some cases, local units of government, such as the city of Philadelphia, have allowed nonprofit organizations to provide services rather than money. Such payments are referred to as SILOTs (services in lieu of taxes).

Language is a complicating factor in discussing these issues. In Philadelphia, the city agreed to change the name of its "PILOT/SILOT" program after strong reaction from the nonprofit community. Members of the nonprofit sector were adamant that they were *voluntarily* making these payments, and that the phrase "in lieu of taxes" suggested they owed the city something. The program's title was changed to the Voluntary Contribution Program. For those familiar with the city of Philadelphia's program, the irony is evident. The city entered into legal agreements with more than 40 large health and educational institutions that resulted in several million dollars annually in revenue and services. It is widely known that many of these agreements were made after a series of unfavorable or unclear court rulings put many organizations at risk of losing their "charitable" status in the commonwealth if challenged in court (Leland 1995 and 1999b; see also Glancey, chapter 9 of this volume).

Complicating matters even further, some states use the term PILOTs to refer to reimbursements *from the state* to local units of government (typically counties) in which a high percentage of exempt *public* property is located.[1] This is most common in terms of state game and park lands that states (e.g., Pennsylvania) have taken off local tax rolls. In both Connecticut and Rhode Island, moreover, the state partially reimburses local governments for taxes forgone on property held by private educational institutions and hospitals (see Carbone and Brody, chapter 10 of this volume).

Research Methodology

The goal of the project discussed in this chapter was to create a national picture of efforts by local units of government to solicit PILOTs or other tax-like payments from local nonprofit organizations. A key question was whether these activities—whose scope appears to be growing—represent a new trend in the generation of municipal revenue or were merely high-profile activities in a relatively small number of locations. For cities engaged in such activities, specific research questions included the reason for these activities' emergence, the level of revenue being generated, the measure of the success, and any known impact on the nonprofit organizations themselves.

Given the extraordinary number and types of local governments—from school districts to counties, special districts, cities, towns, and townships—this project used a sample of the 50 largest cities in the United States, plus the largest city in each state if the state did not include any of the 50 largest cities. It was assumed either that these kinds of activities would more likely occur in the larger, more-complex units of government, or that respondents from the largest cities would know of such activities in other units of government in their states. A total of 73 cities were included in this sample.[2]

Information regarding PILOT-seeking activities in the sample locations was sought from two sources: municipal finance directors and community leaders/key informants. The primary source was the municipal finance or budget director in each city; their names were purchased from the National League of Cities. The project pursued two strategies to obtain information from the directors. First, a mail survey asked whether these activities were currently taking place, had occurred in the past, or were anticipated for the future; a number of more-detailed questions followed. This survey was fielded in March 1998, and a second mailing to nonresponding finance directors took place in May 1998.

The second strategy entailed a detailed phone interview with the finance director (or his or her designee) in the sample cities. Conducted during the summer of 1998, the phone interview attempted not only to confirm information provided in the mail survey, but also to solicit more specific information about current and future efforts to solicit payments, fees, or user charges from local nonprofit organizations. The interview also verified the treatment of various organizations often considered "nonprofit" but which may, instead, be governmental (e.g., housing authorities and economic development authorities); determined local mechanisms for funding water and sewer expenses; determined the extent of these activities in other local units of government in that area or state; and explored the use of abatements as an economic development strategy.[3]

The second source of information was local community leaders. These key informants received a more limited version of the mail survey sent to municipal finance directors. The local informants were viewed as a source not only for verifying which cities might be engaged in soliciting such payments, but also for providing general information about such activities.

The sample of community leaders was designed to contact approximately half a dozen key informants in each city. We gathered five different national mailing lists representing various constituencies; the lists included state and local United Way representatives, housing and redevelopment officials, community economic development professionals, statewide higher education association executives, and statewide nonprofit association executives. Attempts to gather a mailing list of health care executives proved unsuccessful. Five hundred and eighty-three surveys were mailed in March 1998. While some cities had significantly more potential respondents (given the size of local membership), most cities had four to six; there were only a few cities with fewer than four potential respondents.[4]

Research Results and Findings

Surveys of Municipal Finance Directors

Seventy-three surveys were mailed in March 1998. After the initial mailing and a second mailing to nonrespondents, 49 mail surveys were returned, a response rate of 67 percent. While we attempted phone interviews with all 73 finance directors, contact was successful with only 23; 2 had not responded to the mail survey.

Information came from 51 municipal finance directors by either mail, phone, or both. There was no response from directors in 22 cities. Note that, of the 22 nonresponding cities, key informants indicated that only Portland, Maine, and Little Rock, Arkansas, may have PILOT activities.

Only 7 of the 51 responding cities indicated that they solicited PILOTs, municipal-service fees, or voluntary contributions specifically from nonprofit organizations (tables 8-1 and 8-2). None reported past attempts to collect such fees, and only two cities—Billings and Boise—reported a likelihood that such fees would be collected in the future.

In both Billings and Boise, water and sewer fees are already collected as user fees from all persons and organizations. Billings' proposed PILOT

Table 8-1. *Cities that Currently Solicit PILOTs from Nonprofit Organizations, According to Municipal Finance Directors* ($n = 51$)[a]

Baltimore	Minneapolis
Boston	Philadelphia
Detroit	Pittsburgh
Indianapolis	

[a] A number of other cities in the sample reported receiving payments from federal housing authorities. As payments by governmental agencies, these were not considered to meet the definition of PILOTs used in this research project.

Table 8-2. *Cities that Currently Do Not Solicit PILOTs from Nonprofit Organizations, According to Municipal Finance Directors* ($n = 51$)

Albuquerque	Los Angeles
Anchorage	Manchester
Billings	Memphis
Birmingham	Miami
Boise	Milwaukee
Buffalo	Nashville
Charleston (WV)	New Orleans
Cheyenne	Oakland
Chicago	Ogden
Columbia (SC)	Phoenix
Columbus (OH)	Portland (OR)
Dallas	Sacramento
Denver	San Antonio
Des Moines	San Diego
El Paso	San Francisco
Fort Worth	San Jose
Houston	Seattle
Jackson (MS)	Sioux Falls
Jacksonville (FL)	St. Louis
Kansas City (KS)	Tucson
Kansas City (MO)	Virginia Beach
Las Vegas	Washington (DC)

program would impose an additional "franchise fee" on both for-profit and nonprofit entities. Officials anticipated that this fee might produce approximately $4.5 million a year (compared with a $100-million budget). Although Boise did not report having a specific program in development, respondents indicated that PILOTs were a regular topic of conversation, and that the city was in litigation over the exempt status of one hospital.

In addition to respondents in the seven cities mentioned earlier, two other cities' finance directors reported "possibly" receiving contributions from a single institution (a hospital in one city and a university in another). In both cases, however, the finance director indicated that the city did not "officially" *solicit* these monies, and the director did not know whether a contribution was, in fact, paid. Given the tentativeness of the responses and the indication of no formal PILOT initiative, these two cities were excluded from analysis.

The Key-Informant Survey

Out of 583 questionnaires mailed in March 1998, 159 were returned and usable, for a response rate of 27 percent. An additional 26 surveys were returned "undeliverable" or were filled out incorrectly.[5]

Tables 8-3 and 8-4 report feedback from key informants as to their sample city's current efforts to solicit PILOTs. Key informants reported that 11 of the 73 cities currently received such fees from nonprofit organizations, while 56 cities did not. No surveys were received from key informants in 10 of the 73 sample cities.[6]

However, information from key informants was often incorrect. For example, key informants failed to identify Baltimore and Detroit as cities that solicit PILOTs, and incorrectly identified Boise, Los Angeles, Miami,

Table 8-3. *Cities that Currently Solicit PILOTs from Nonprofit Organizations, According to Key Informants (n = 159)*

Boise*	Milwaukee*
Boston*	Minneapolis*
Indianapolis*	Philadelphia*
Little Rock*	Pittsburgh
Los Angeles	Portland (ME)
Miami	

* Conflicting information was received from key informants in these cities.

Table 8-4. *Cities that Do Not Currently Solicit PILOTs from Nonprofit Organizations, According to Key Informants (n = 159)*

Albuquerque	Des Moines	Newark (NJ)
Anchorage	Detroit	Oakland
Atlanta	El Paso	Oklahoma City
Austin	Fargo	Omaha
Baltimore	Ft. Worth	Philadelphia*
Billings	Honolulu	Phoenix
Birmingham (AL)	Houston	Portland (OR)
Boise*	Jackson (MS)	Providence (RI)
Bridgeport (CT)	Kansas City (KS)	Sacramento
Buffalo	Las Vegas	San Antonio
Charleston (WV)	Lexington (KY)	San Diego
Charlotte	Little Rock*	San Jose
Chicago	Manchester (NH)	Seattle
Cincinnati	Memphis	Sioux Falls
Cleveland	Milwaukee*	Toledo
Columbia (SC)	Minneapolis*	Tucson
Columbus (OH)	Nashville	Virginia Beach
Dallas	New Orleans	Washington (DC)
Denver	New York City	Wilmington (DE)

* Conflicting information was received from key informants in these cities.

and Milwaukee as currently doing so. Moreover, we received conflicting information from key informants in seven cities (see tables 8-3 and 8-4). Some respondents in Boston reported that the city collects PILOTs; other respondents inaccurately said the city did not *currently* collect payments now but will do so in the future. There was similar confusion from respondents in Indianapolis and Philadelphia. We could not verify the activities of Portland, Maine, and Little Rock, Arkansas.

Comparison of Information from Key Informants and Municipal Finance Directors

Of the 45 cities on which information was received from both groups, responses regarding current efforts to solicit PILOTs were generally consistent. In only eight cities did information from finance directors conflict with information from key informants. In four cities (Baltimore, Detroit, Minneapolis, and Philadelphia), key informants indicated that the city did not collect PILOTs when, in fact, it did. In the other four cities (Boise, Los Angeles, Miami, and Milwaukee), key informants indicated the presence of PILOT activities when, in fact, no such activities were in place. As noted earlier, key informants sometimes contradicted one another.

In four cities (Burlington, Fresno, Long Beach, and Tulsa), we received no surveys from either key informants or municipal finance directors.

Overview of PILOT Activities in Large U.S. Cities

The number of large cities participating in PILOT activities and the amount of money raised are reported in table 8-5.

Information from respondents indicated that programs to solicit PILOTs varied widely, with individual explanations for each situation. For example, in several cities, programs had been in existence for more than 25 years (Detroit and Baltimore), while others were only one to two years old at the time of the research. Some programs, such as those in Boston and Philadelphia, covered a variety of organizations, while others targeted specific organizational types (e.g., Detroit solicits PILOTs from group-home and residential programs; Minneapolis, from nursing homes only). A brief description of each of these seven cities (listed in alphabetical order) follows.

Table 8-5. *A Summary of Programs to Solicit PILOTs from Nonprofit Organizations* $(n = 7)$

City	Number of Nonprofit Organizations	Amount Generated ($)	City Budget ($ in millions)	Amount as Percentage of Annual Budget
Baltimore	48	3,400,000	2,200	0.15
Boston	38	19,400,000	1,420	1.4
Detroit	100[a]	4,160,000[b]	2,460	0.17
Indianapolis	1	4,400,000	421	1.05
Minneapolis	6	260,000	936	0.03
Philadelphia	43	6,500,000[c]	1,200	0.54
Pittsburgh	10	2,500,000	323	0.77

[a] This figure is approximate.

[b] 1997 figure; all other figures are for 1998.

[c] This is the amount of cash only. Philadelphia collected a total of $8.75 million in 1997 between PILOTs and SILOTs.

Baltimore

Baltimore initiated its PILOT program in 1974, and has specifically targeted housing facilities, nursing homes, and community development corporations. In 1998, payments from 48 organizations totaled $3.4 million. Payments are based upon an organization's annual operating income, and thus do not change from year to year unless there is a significant change in organizational revenue.

Boston

Boston's current PILOT program was initiated in 1983, although the city has collected PILOTs since the 1930s. The program is broadly based, covering all property-owning nonprofit organizations that wish to add to or alter their property. In 1998, 38 organizations made payments, generating $19.4 million. These payments are separately negotiated between the city and each organization; SILOTs may be included as part of the negotiated payment. The city initiates discussion at 25 percent of the would-be tax amount (measured as the percentage of the city budget spent on police, fire, and snow removal). Agreements have a built-in "inflation clause" and can be in place for anywhere between 10 and 30 years.

Detroit

Detroit's PILOT activities began in 1966 and are directed to housing/residential facilities for the disabled and low-income population. Approximately 100 nonprofit organizations currently make payments, which came to $4.16 million in 1997. All nonprofit organizations are subject to the same formula: 4 percent of the net shelter rent generated.

Indianapolis

The Indianapolis program, initiated by city ordinance in 1994, applies to a single nonprofit organization, a wastewater treatment facility, which pays $4.4 million a year. A third-party consultant determined the assessed property value of the facility and applied the appropriate tax rate to determine the property's tax. The $4.4 million fee is less than half that amount, and was agreed upon after discussions between the city and the facility. This effort, supported by state legislation, allows the city to treat the nonprofit (for PILOT purposes) as if it were a public utility.

Minneapolis

Approved in 1991, the Minneapolis program was implemented in 1992 and has been directed toward only nursing homes that have used tax-exempt bond financing. At the time of this research, six homes were participating, each paying the same percentage (estimated to be about 40 percent) of the would-be tax amount of their properties. These fees are fully reimbursed by the state.

Philadelphia

Philadelphia enacted its Voluntary Contribution Program by executive order in 1994. Fewer than 50 organizations (mostly educational and health care organizations) made payments in 1998, although the program covers all nonprofits other than those found to meet the commonwealth's standards of a "purely public charity" by an independent panel of city employees and two private citizens. Payments were set at 33 percent of the would-be tax amount based on the assessed value of the property. SILOTs could offset up to one-third of the dollar amount. In 1997, nonprofits contributed $6.5 million in cash and services valued at $2.27 million (one-third of $6.75 million) (see also Glancey, chapter 9 of this volume).

Pittsburgh

Pittsburgh's PILOT program is both temporary and informal, and was created through unique agreements between specific nonprofit organizations and the city. These agreements are usually made for periods of 8 to 10 years, although the nonprofit organization can break the agreement by giving six months' notice. While Duquesne University has made payments for approximately 20 years, all other organizations began making payments in the late 1980s. Ten nonprofit organizations—including colleges and universities, hospitals, and recreational facilities—contributed approximately $2.5 million in 1998.

Discussion

Surprisingly, just a few large cities—only 7 among 51 major U.S. cities—solicited PILOTs from nonprofit organizations in 1998. Even more surprisingly, only one city—Boston—solicited a wide range of nonprofit organizations. Philadelphia, Pittsburgh, and Baltimore targeted mainly health care and educational institutions. Detroit and Minneapolis targeted a single type of nonprofit, and Indianapolis received monies from a single organization. Given that only two other cities in our sample saw PILOTs as a "likely" activity in the future, it would seem that the doomsayers have been wrong: There is no massive trend, at least among large cities, to "go after" the nonprofit sector.

However, note a number of caveats. First and most important, these findings are not intended to suggest a similar low level of PILOT activities in small to mid-sized cities. There is some evidence that smaller cities, which have a large percentage of exempt property, do have established, albeit informal, arrangements with particular nonprofit organizations for PILOT-like contributions (e.g., Ithaca and Cornell University; Cambridge and Harvard University). The difficulty of documenting such individualized PILOT activity (Leland 1996) and the sheer number of smaller cities in the United States precluded their inclusion in this research project.

Second, while PILOT programs may not be widespread in large U.S. cities, they can matter enormously to the individual cities or organizations involved. In Minneapolis, 6 organizations contributed an average of $43,000 each; in Pittsburgh, 10 organizations contributed an average of $250,000; in Boston, 38 organizations contributed an average of $510,000. In Indianapolis, one organization contributed $4.4 million.

Consider also the factors that drive certain cities to explore PILOT programs and the degree to which other cities may be affected by these forces. In our survey, the seven finance directors in cities with PILOTs cited both the city's need for revenue and concern over "free" use of public services as the most important factors in implementing PILOT activities. Two respondents cited concern over the nonprofit sector's competition with the for-profit sector as a factor, and one respondent identified concerns over executive compensation and excessive nonprofit organizational revenue as contributing factors. The lesson here is that PILOT programs could become more prevalent if either municipal revenue or public sentiment changes (see also Youngman, chapter 2 of this volume).

Moreover, "user fees" are becoming increasingly attractive for funding municipal services. While some observers see a shift in some costs of government to nonprofit organizations (Gallagher 1997), the shift to user fees for water and sewer has been a growing trend in the delivery of public services for decades, and, for some cities, has been the model of funding from public utilities' inception. It is difficult, therefore, to isolate the shift to user fees as a response to the nonprofit sector. Rather, the mechanism may simply be a more efficient (and equitable) distribution of costs (see Netzer, chapter 3 of this volume).

The goal of this research was to determine whether any city had switched to a user-fee structure specifically to obtain participation from the nonprofit community. Only Buffalo reported switching to the user-fee structure as a response to the tax-exempt status of nonprofit organizations. More than half the cities in the sample already charge for water, sewer, and/or waste disposal through user fees. Indeed, five of the seven cities that solicited PILOTs *also* had a user-fee structure for water and sewer (table 8-6). Clearly, the use of user fees does not preclude the solicitation of PILOTs.

A final caveat concerns the problems of language and definitions raised earlier. Despite efforts to specify definitions and circumstances, there is evidence that some mail-survey respondents may have included certain activities under the category of PILOTs that did not meet our research parameters (e.g., the monies that federal housing authorities pay to local municipalities). This inconsistency in the mail surveys was one reason for the attempts to contact all 73 finance directors by phone. While we remain

Table 8-6. *Cities that Collect User Fees for Water, Sewer, and/or Waste Disposal, According to Phone Interviews with Municipal Finance Directors* ($n = 51$)

Albuquerque	Miami
Anchorage	Milwaukee
Baltimore	Minneapolis
Billings	Nashville
Birmingham	New Orleans
Boise	Ogden
Boston	Phoenix
Buffalo	Pittsburgh
Charleston (WV)	Portland (OR)
Columbia (SC)	San Antonio
Dallas	Seattle
Ft. Worth	St. Louis
Indianapolis	Virginia Beach

Note: We could not verify payment structure for Philadelphia and Detroit.

confident in the results as to the extent of PILOT activities in these major U.S. cities, the issue of terminology will continue to be important in any future research efforts.

Areas for Future Research

As noted, the number of large cities that sought PILOTs from nonprofit organizations in 1998 was unexpectedly low, given anecdotal evidence. This raises an important question for future research: specifically, whether municipal size is a significant and independent variable for finding PILOT activities. This study focused on large cities on the assumption that large cities, whose governments are more complex and more sophisticated, would be more likely to have sufficient resources for pursuing such revenue-generating strategies. It may be, however, that smaller cities, with fewer revenue choices and a more limited economic base, are more likely to engage in PILOT activities. To what extent "size matters" is an important follow-up question.

A number of other related (direct and indirect) questions also emerge from this research:

- Why and how are some cities, such as Boston and Pittsburgh, successful in their attempts to solicit PILOTs when other cities, such as Wilmington, Delaware, and Iowa City, are not? What are the local conditions that result in a successful PILOT program?
- What is the extent of PILOT activity among nonmunicipal units of government, notably special tax districts or school districts?
- In local tax and service-fee treatment, are different nonprofit organizations treated differently across political jurisdictions? Are there patterns by type of nonprofit organization?
- What impact, if any, has the legislation recently adopted in Pennsylvania had on local government efforts to solicit PILOTs?
- What financial and political effects has a PILOT program had on participating and nonparticipating nonprofit organizations?

Summary

As cities continue to struggle with revenue shortfalls and the nonprofit sector faces increased scrutiny, the potential use of PILOTs as a revenue-

generating tool will not likely diminish as a policy issue. Those account-
able for cities' financial needs and revenue shortfalls continue to assert
that local exempt organizations using public services should pay for those
services. Municipal leaders unable or unwilling to further burden local
taxpayers view nonprofit organizations as a legitimate source of revenue.

At the same time, leaders of nonprofit organizations assert that they
cannot afford to pay property taxes, PILOTs, service fees, or voluntary
contributions. They charge that redirecting their resources to local units
of government would hurt clients and limit the organizations' ability to
serve the public good.

Many other stakeholders, however, point to the deep reserves and
endowments held by some large nonprofit organizations, and no longer
accept at face value claims of inability to pay. Furthermore, some observers
assert that modern nonprofit organizations are not the charitable organizations of the past and have simply become another form of "big business."
As has been seen in Pennsylvania, the debate as to a modern definition of
a charity can be fierce and furious. It also appears that the numbers of
those who publicly endorse PILOTs are growing. But advocating such
policies does not translate into implementation: The data from this
research indicate that not only were PILOT activities not widespread in
major U.S. cities in 1998, but they also do not appear likely for the future.

Author's Note

When the results of this research have been shared over the last few years,
people have occasionally asked why a particular city was included (or
excluded) when the person asking claimed to know with certainty that
the city does (or does not, as the case may be) solicit contributions from
its nonprofit community. The response has always been the same: The
information presented here is the information that was given to us by
the chief financial officers in the sample cities, and I am confident we
have accurately portrayed the data that were given to us.

My experience in studying PILOTs since the early 1990s indicates that
much of the lack of comprehensive understanding of PILOT activity is
due to the extensive and different uses of the acronym itself. The term
"PILOT" can mean one thing in Pennsylvania and another in Connecticut; defining the terms and the parameters of the research and ensuring
their consistent application are significant components in the research

task. Great pains were taken to clarify and verify terms and definitions in both the questionnaire and the telephone conversations. I stand by the conclusions that we have drawn from the data shared with us during the data-collection period—although this is not to say that things may not have changed since 1998.

It would be unfortunate if a particular municipal finance director was ill-advised or uninformed as to the revenue-generating strategies within the jurisdiction, but it would not alter the larger conclusion of the research project: that there is no widespread movement toward PILOTs. Such misinformation certainly might affect a particular city's categorization, but the fundamental findings of the research remain the same.

If the primary source of our information—the person entrusted with ensuring the financial health and fiscal accounting of the unit of government—was so uninformed, the appropriate response would not be to challenge the research conclusions presented here; instead, it would be to express condolences to the citizens who will bear the ultimate consequences of the director's lack of knowledge and comprehension.

NOTES

Appreciation is expressed to the National Center for the Revitalization of Central Cities at the University of New Orleans for its financial support of this research. Thanks also go to project assistant William Fishkin for his support and involvement in the data collection and early data analysis. Information in this chapter is drawn from a larger and more comprehensive working paper submitted to the National Center for the Revitalization of Central Cities.

1. The federal government also has a PILOT program.

2. The original research strategy called for a survey of the 50 largest cities. Given the over-representation of some states in such a sample, we decided to broaden the sample to also include the largest city in any state not represented by the 50 largest cities. It was recently discovered that an error was made in determining the largest city in Kansas; Wichita, not Kansas City, is the largest city.

3. Originally the research methodology called for detailed phone interviews for only those cities that indicated PILOT activities. Due to the surprisingly large number of cities that indicated no such activities were taking place, phone interviews with each of the 73 finance directors were attempted. Response to the phone interview was lower than the response to the mail survey (23 phone interviews versus 49 mail surveys). The phone interviews did not reveal incorrect or misleading information in the mail surveys; rather, they allowed us to better understand and expand upon the mail-survey data. In some cases, we decided after the phone interviews that certain activities did not fall under our definition of PILOT activities (e.g., the receipt of monies from federal housing projects).

4. The original research strategy also called for phone interviews with local key informants in each of the sample cities. Given the expanded number of cities in the sample (from 50 to 73), the desire to significantly broaden the pool of key informants, and the benefit of seeking similar information in similar format from both respondent groups, we decided to send a mail survey similar to the survey sent to municipal finance directors.

5. Despite instructions to the contrary, some respondents who communicated no knowledge about the designated sample city instead provided us with information about some city with which they were familiar. This information was, unfortunately, too limited to be useful.

6. These numbers do not add up to 73 because of inconsistent information from key informants in the same cities.

REFERENCES

Gallagher, Janne. 1997. "When Local Governments Come Calling: The Movement to Tax Charities." *Exempt Organization Tax Review* 18 (1): 25–33.

Leland, Pamela. 1999a. "PILOTs: A Comparative Analysis." *Government Finance Review* 15: 33–36.

———. 1999b. "Property Tax Exemption and Municipal Revenue: Philadelphia's Efforts to Solicit Payments in Lieu of Taxes from Charitable Nonprofit Organizations." *International Journal of Nonprofit Law.* Http://www.icnl.org/journal/vol1iss4/pilot.htm

———. 1996. "Exploring Challenges to Nonprofit Status: Issues of Definition and Access in Community-Based Research." *American Behavioral Scientist* 39 (5): 587–601.

———. 1995. "The Extent of the Challenge to Property Tax Exemption in Pennsylvania: A Survey of 67 Counties." In *Nonprofit Organizations as Public Actors: Rising to New Public Policy Challenges* (471–99). Working Papers of the Independent Sector 1995 Spring Research Forum.

Louisiana Bureau of Governmental Research. 1996. *Property Taxes in New Orleans: Who Pays? Who Doesn't? And Why?* New Orleans, La: Bureau of Government Research.

9

PILOTs

Philadelphia and Pennsylvania

David B. Glancey

For Philadelphia's approximately 1.5 million residents, the early months of 1994 truly began to feel like the dawn of a new era. Their extremely popular and energetic mayor, Edward G. Rendell, who had taken the reins of power in January 1992, succeeded in reducing a mountain of debt from prior budgets that left the city near default, and created a sensible revenue and spending plan that resulted in a balanced budget without tax increases or layoffs of municipal workers. Citizens who had felt that the city was soon to be bankrupt both fiscally and socially began to feel cautiously optimistic about their own and the city's future. Local, national, and international entrepreneurs also began to look toward Philadelphia as a place to invest their energy, their expertise, and, most importantly, their money. There was a buzz that the city was on the move again—that Philadelphia, like other urban areas, was going through a renaissance and would soon become an "urban theme park." Life was looking good.

Those who worked for the city in budget or finance or other revenue-analysis positions looked at much more modest horizons. The city had gotten through two budget cycles, paid its vendors and employees, and saved some money through workforce attrition, more-efficient workrules, and employee-benefit packages, all of which were the result of hard bargaining with the municipal unions. There were still questions about the city's fiscal future, however. It was in this context that Philadelphia's Voluntary Contribution Program for nonprofit organizations was born.

Background on Philadelphia and Its Nonprofits

In order to address the city's massive fiscal disorder, the new administration's managers first had to use spending cutbacks to stop the hemorrhaging of dollars. Budget processes were implemented to track every dollar spent by the city on a weekly, monthly, and yearly basis. Department heads had to justify the expenditure of every dollar in their budgets. Each actual departmental budget was reduced by 10 percent each year, reflecting a "target" budget that held spending down even further within the department's allocated budget. A productivity and management-efficiency committee questioned department heads and each department's senior management team in order to find more budget efficiencies, while simultaneously developing and supporting creative management techniques to produce more and better city services. As many corporations were discovering, successful cities needed to do more with less, or risk losing their "customers": businesses, taxpayers, and tourists.

The revenue side of the city's finances also needed reform. Philadelphia's citizens, both individuals and businesses, were taxed to the limit. In the preceding 11 years, the city had increased various taxes 19 times. The city wage tax, a tax of 4.96 percent on wages of residents and 4.31 percent on wages of nonresident employees, was a major factor in population loss and causing businesses to relocate to other areas. Philadelphians had to bear an extraordinary tax burden relative to their suburban neighbors. Robert Inman, professor of finance and economics at the University of Pennsylvania's Wharton School, found that in the two-year period 1994 to 1995, a family in Philadelphia paid a staggering 12.3 percent of its income in local taxes yearly (City of Philadelphia 1998). In fiscal year 1989, the real estate transfer tax was increased to 4.07 percent, the highest tax of its kind in the country. Survey after survey of U.S. cities listed Philadelphia as having one of the top 10 highest per capita and per family tax burdens. While this burden was not the only reason people and jobs left the city, there was no question of some correlation between the city's fiscal policies and the loss of its most important material resource—its people.

In the spending side, no single agency or department was made the target of budget cuts or massive layoffs. Each would feel some pain and, in the aggregate, all would contribute to the well-being of the whole.

The same was true on the revenue side: The city's methods of generating revenue needed reform. Citizens felt they were not being treated fairly compared to their suburban counterparts. Nontax revenues had to be found, and the burden of supporting city services had to be shared more equitably. Every department involved in revenue generation or collection was charged with finding more efficiencies within the existing tax scheme. "No new taxes" and "no tax increases" were the mantras of the new administration. New revenues had to be found within the existing tax structure, and potential revenue sources that were available but had lain fallow for whatever reason, were to be reinvestigated by each agency.

The city's administrators understood that nonprofit organizations played a vital role in Philadelphia's economy and in the lives of its residents and visitors. The city's outstanding medical facilities, colleges, and universities placed Philadelphia among the national leaders in the growing and high-profile fields of health and higher education. High on the list of Philadelphia's strengths were its five medical schools and 15 teaching hospitals, along with 58 four-year colleges and universities in the city's region. Numerous religious, cultural, and human service organizations, most of which are nonprofit institutions, also provide a rich array of services and opportunities to every Philadelphian. However, the very strength of the nonprofit sector was something of a double-edged sword. Tax-exempt nonprofits are no different from taxpaying entities in the service demands they place on local and state governments.

According to the Philadelphia Board of Revision of Taxes (1999), the facts in Philadelphia were as follows: Nongovernmental nonprofits in Philadelphia were exempted from nearly $45.6 million yearly in city property taxes, and from $55.1 million in school-district property taxes. They were further exempt from the city's net-profit tax, business-privilege tax, business use and occupancy tax, and parking tax. Tax-exempt property in the city comprised 25.2 percent of the city's total property-tax assessment, and many nonprofits had physically expanded ownership and development of previously taxable real estate, thereby contributing to the city's declining tax base; the assessed value of nonprofit property in Philadelphia grew from $1.2 billion in 1963 to $2.4 billion in 1979, and to $3.1 billion in 1993.

The Voluntary Contribution Program was an attempt to balance the interests of the nonprofits and the city. The city clearly recognized the valuable contributions many nonprofit organizations made and their importance to Philadelphia's economy, but had to weigh that information against the hard facts showing how the expanding universe of nonprofits was affecting the city's tax base. The Voluntary Contribution Program laid out a reasonable way for nonprofits to return a limited measure of what the city provided in essential tax-supported services. The program called for nonprofits to provide modest payments and services that amounted to far less than what the organizations would owe were they not granted tax-exempt status.

The Voluntary Contribution Program

It is necessary to place the Voluntary Contribution Program in the legal context of early 1994, under the fluctuating law of property-tax exemption in Pennsylvania. In 1985—in what became known as the *HUP* test (named after the court case that established precedent, *Hospitalization Utilization Project [HUP] v. Commonwealth of Pennsylvania*)—the Pennsylvania Supreme Court created a five-prong test to determine whether an institution is a "purely public charity," as required by the state's constitution in order for the institution to qualify as an exempt entity.[1] The court stated that an institution of purely public charity must meet five criteria. It must

- Advance a charitable purpose;
- Donate or render gratuitously a substantial portion of its service;
- Benefit a substantial and indefinite class of persons who are legitimate subjects of charity;
- Relieve the government of some of its burden; and
- Operate entirely free from private profit motive.

The framework delineated by the Pennsylvania Supreme Court set standards that many hospitals, educational institutions, and other nonprofits might not have been able to meet. Indeed, many local governments throughout the commonwealth that were facing growing numbers of tax-exempt properties revoked exemptions, believing that institutions in their jurisdictions did not meet the *HUP* test. In Pennsylvania's 66 counties, local tax boards determine what property is exempt. From 1985 through the mid-1990s, there were as many different interpretations of the *HUP* test as there were counties, and the confusion spread into local and appellate court decisions as well. The subsequent Institutions of Purely Public Charities Act (Act 55 of 1997), an attempt by the Pennsylvania legislature to codify the definition of a "purely public charity," will be discussed later in the chapter. The courts' interpretation of the language of Act 55 will determine the future of Philadelphia's Voluntary Contribution Program.

Thus, in 1994, many organizations in Philadelphia that were treated as exempt might not have been legally entitled to such privileged status. A nonprofit that functioned more as a human service or social welfare organization could meet the standards of the *HUP* test more easily than a group that functioned as a health care provider or an institution of higher education. For example, while a substance-abuse recovery organization and a large teaching hospital could both advance a charitable purpose, it would be much more difficult for the hospital to prove that it donates or renders gratuitously a substantial portion of its services or that it benefits a substantial and indefinite class of persons who are legitimate subjects of charity. Furthermore, some observers found that it would be impossible for a college or university ever to meet the demand that a nonprofit relieve the government of some of its burden, since it can be argued that the government has no obligation to educate its citizens after supporting and funding elementary and secondary public schools. If postsecondary school were not a service that the government had to offer, then a college or university could never relieve a burden of government.

On the other hand, most human service and social welfare organizations seemed to meet the *HUP* test easily, because their funding and spending were much easier to analyze. Charity offered by an AIDS hospice or a halfway house for abused women is simply more tangible than that offered by a hospital or a university, and the filings later supplied to the Voluntary Contribution Board backed up this conventional wisdom. Philadelphia faced a choice: Should it react with the legal baseball bat given to it by the courts, revoking all tax exemptions that might be in doubt and litigating over this issue—bearing in mind that these institutions had helped establish a highly successful and financially robust sector of the city's economy? Or should it collaborate with these institutions and establish a reasonable, uniform program that recognizes their importance and value and asks them to help defray a small portion of the city services they receive? Some jurisdictions responded by pursuing nonprofits with a vengeance, but Philadelphia chose the less confrontational approach.

Creation of the Program

The Voluntary Contribution Program was created and authorized by an executive order in June 1994 (City of Philadelphia 1994). The program was initially called the Payment-in-Lieu-of-Taxes/Services-in-Lieu-of-Taxes (PILOT/SILOT) Program, but Philadelphia's nonprofit community pointed out that the name could be characterized as creating an admission that the participating nonprofits agreed they were taxable entities. Such a characterization could jeopardize the exempt status of the nonprofits and properties they own in other jurisdictions. Recognizing the validity and seriousness of this concern, the city immediately amended the mayor's executive order and changed the name to the Voluntary Contribution Program.

The program contained the following six principal components.

- *Exemptions were provided for those nonprofits that met the test of a "purely public charity."*

The advisory board determined which organizations were "purely public charities" by investigating documents supplied by the nonprofit. Those documents included, but were not limited to, certified financial statements, IRS Forms 990, and mission statements explaining what the institution did and the nature of its charitable acts. This investigation followed face-to-face meetings with chief executives from a multitude of institutions. The city created a telephone hotline for charitable organizations' requests for information. Nonprofit organizations that met the *HUP* test as "purely public charities" were sent letters from the advisory board advising them of the board's decision and encouraging them to continue their good works. The nonprofit community dubbed these notices "home-free" letters.

- *Other nonprofits were asked to make voluntary contributions of 40 percent of the annual property-tax payment they would owe if their property were fully taxable.*

Property-tax assessments were used as a basis for this formula because property ownership was the most common characteristic enjoyed by the majority of the nonprofit organizations. As long as the municipality kept up-to-date, fair, uniform, and accurate property records, property-tax assessments were essential to conducting a fair and uniform program.

The city's research showed that nonprofit institutions benefited from essential services provided to all property owners; the cost of providing such services ranges from a minimum of 49 percent of general fund expenditures to 64 percent or more of local tax expenditures (City of

Philadelphia Finance Department Analyst 1994). Research also found that these institutions are completely exempt from taxes levied on other business entities, and that they benefit from additional charitable discounts (for example, the Philadelphia Water Department discounted $1.8 million in water bills to hospitals and universities in 1992). The requested contribution of 40 percent of nonprofits' forgone property tax was extremely reasonable. As an incentive, nonprofits that entered into Voluntary Contribution Program agreements on or before December 1, 1994, had the option of lowering their voluntary contribution to 33 percent of the annual property tax they would owe if they were taxable.

- *The School District of Philadelphia, and any current or after-created special-services district that also had the power to tax, would be a full participant in the Voluntary Contribution Program.*

Each Voluntary Contribution Program agreement involved not only the city and the nonprofit organization, but also the School District of Philadelphia and, where applicable, the Center City District and any other special-services district that may be created. This ensures that the tax-exempt status of any participating nonprofit would not be challenged by any local government body during the life of the agreement, giving the organization a stable and predictable obligation over the term of the agreement.

- *Nonprofits had the option of substituting up to 33 percent of their monetary contribution with community services.*

Nonprofits were given the option of reducing their cash contributions by performing valuable community services worth up to 33 percent of their cash contribution. The city negotiated with each participating organization to provide the health and educational services that were most needed by the city and school district. Agreements permitted each nonprofit to identify the services it preferred to provide, so long as the city and school district agreed that the services were valuable. One of the rules the city followed during this process was not to attempt to manage the participating nonprofits: When it came to valuing the service component of any voluntary contribution, participants were trusted to value their services fairly, which they seem to have done. It should also be noted that most participants have contributed far more in valuable services than they contracted to provide. Many observers thought that government monitoring of this services option would be obtrusive, but the services offered by the nonprofits were agreed upon relatively easy, and highlighted the many good things an institution can do for its community. In fact, organizations that were deemed to be "purely public charities"—and therefore had not been asked to participate in the Voluntary Contribution Program— offered to perform community services anyway.

- *The entire program was overseen by a Voluntary Contribution Program advisory board that consisted of tax, finance, law, administration, education, and health personnel, along with two citizens appointed by the mayor.*

The board's primary responsibility was to negotiate contracts for cash and services with nonprofits. The board was also responsible for starting and maintaining the program and addressing implementation problems. Not one person was hired by the board to implement this program: Existing personnel supported the board's mission, and all of the board's members volunteered their time and effort to make it successful.

- *The Voluntary Contribution Program agreements were overseen by the advisory board and formalized by contract between the nonprofit and the city, the school district, the Center City District, and any other special-services district that might be created.*

While the Voluntary Contribution Program is, as its name implies, voluntary, each nonprofit that entered the program was required to sign a contract to commit to its contributions. These contracts took the form of settlements in lieu of litigation, and were valid for up to five years. If the board was unable to negotiate an agreement with a nonprofit that it believed did not qualify as a purely public charity, the board referred the matter to the city's Law Department, which attempted to negotiate a settlement. Only when all efforts failed would the city consider a legal challenge to a tax exemption.

The Program in Practice

Immediately after announcing the Voluntary Contribution Program, the city sent letters to all nonprofit institutions that owned real estate in Philadelphia and enjoyed tax-exempt status as institutions of purely public charity. Places of religious worship, cemeteries, public property, and veterans' organizations were not contacted, based on their clearly defined exemption under the Pennsylvania constitution. Approximately 580 institutions representing nearly 2,200 individual property accounts were notified.

As a follow-up to the letter, members of the Voluntary Contribution Program Advisory Board conducted a series of forums for the Philadelphia nonprofit community. Some of the forums were sponsored by local law firms; others were sponsored by various nonprofit associations, such as the United Way and the Greater Philadelphia Cultural Alliance. Other speaking invitations were extended by such organizations as the Delaware Valley Healthcare Council, the State Association of Health Care and Financial Officers, and many individual colleges and universities. At these events, city representatives met with officials of the local nonprofits, described the city's program, and answered questions.

More than 300 nonprofit institutions, including all major nonprofits in the city, submitted materials describing their mission and financial background to the advisory board. Through a working subcommittee, the advisory board thoroughly reviewed each submission and entered into discussions with those institutions deemed eligible for participation in the program. Organizations that the advisory board determined were clearly fulfilling their charitable missions as purely public charities under relevant case law were not asked to make contributions; the vast majority of Philadelphia nonprofits fell into this category.

Some specific examples of institutions categorized as purely public charities are listed below:

- *The Shriners Hospital of Philadelphia.* This is a children's hospital affiliated with the national Shrine Organization. Once a patient is accepted into the hospital, all medical services are free of charge to the child and his or her family.
- *The Navy Mothers Home.* This organization arranges for free temporary living quarters for parents of naval personnel serving in the Philadelphia region.
- *Philabundance.* This organization collects fresh food from commercial and retail establishments and distributes it to people in need throughout the city.

Many other organizations of purely public charity, such as soup kitchens, child welfare shelters, shelters for the homeless and for victims of domestic violence, and workshops for the disabled, constitute the vast majority of Philadelphia's nonprofit community. As stated earlier, how-ever, a number of these institutions indicated a willingness to work with the city to provide some additional services, regardless of the advisory board's determination.

Philadelphia contracted with approximately 50 nonprofits deemed eli-gible for participation in the Voluntary Contribution Program (table 9-1). These institutions made monetary contributions to the city and school district that were equal to 33 percent of what the groups would have paid in property taxes if they were fully taxable. (All these nonprofits took

Table 9-1. *Organizations Participating in Philadelphia's Voluntary Contributions Program, 1995–99*

Albert Einstein Health Care Network	Methodist Hospital
Allegheny Health, Education, and Research Foundation (Bankruptcy filing 1998)	Neumann Medical Center
	North Philadelphia Health System
	Northeastern Hospital
American Law Institute	Our Mother of Good Counsel Center
Chestnut Hill Hospital	Pennsylvania College of Optometry
Children's Hospital of Philadelphia	Pennsylvania College of Osteopathic
Children's Seashore House	Medicine
Commission on Graduates of Foreign Nursing Schools	Pennsylvania College of Podiatric Medicine
	Pennsylvania Hospital
Drexel University	Philadelphia College of Pharmacy and
Episcopal Hospital	Sciences (now known as the University of
Fox Chase Cancer Center	the Sciences in Philadelphia)
Franciscan Health System (includes St. Agnes and Nazareth)	Philadelphia College of Textiles and Science (now known as the Philadelphia University)
Frankford Hospital	
Friends Hospital	Philadelphia County Dental Society
Germantown Hospital and Medical Center	Philadelphia County Medical Society
	Pierce College
Graduate Health System	Presbyterian Medical Center of Philadelphia
Independence Blue Cross	Ralston House
Jeanes Hospital	Roxborough Memorial Hospital
John F. Kennedy Hospital	St. Joseph's University
Kensington Hospital	Thomas Jefferson University Hospital
LaSalle University	University of Pennsylvania
Magee Hospital	Wills Eye Hospital
Mercy Health Corporation	Wistar Institute

advantage of the city's December 1, 1994, incentive and reduced the percentage of their property tax from 40 percent to 33 percent.) Further, participating nonprofits were permitted to offset up to 33 percent of their monetary contribution with services. These services could be services already provided by the nonprofit; they could not, however, be services already required by statute or as a result of litigation.

Some of the more creative solutions negotiated between the city and nonprofit institutions are described below:

- The Frankford Hospital, a medium-sized community hospital, collaborated with the Philadelphia Health Department and the Philadelphia School District to develop a new health center in a Philadelphia public school located in the hospital's community. The center provides medical and mental health services to students, regardless of their ability to pay; links students to doctors in their community; and emphasizes preventive-health practices at an early age.

- Magee Rehabilitation Hospital is a post-acute care rehabilitation hospital for patients with severe rehabilitation needs (e.g., patients who have had strokes, head trauma, or spinal cord injuries). Magee and the city agreed to establish a "Free Care Fund" to assist patients and individuals with disabilities with transportation to and from therapy; payment for prescriptions where no other funding was available; payment for durable medical equipment and orthotics; and clothing, apartment rent, and household expenses to help disabled individuals return to the community.

- The Philadelphia College of Pharmacy and Science, now known as the University of the Sciences in Philadelphia, instituted a program to recruit, retain, and educate Philadelphia-area minority and disadvantaged students to become pharmacists in inner-city health care facilities.

- Peirce College granted tuition scholarships to children, spouses, or members of the Philadelphia Fraternal Order of Police.

These examples include only a few of the creative programs that sprouted from the city's Voluntary Contribution Program. There is no doubt that even more imaginative links between the city and its nonprofit institutions can be created in the future.

As the program evolved, a limited number of institutions were asked to contribute at the "hardship" level of $10,000 a year, instead of making payments based on the value of real estate owned by the institution. This policy recognized the financial condition of these institutions and the mayor's desire not to cause harm through the city's program.

Although the city began with a standard, generic Charitable Contribution Agreement, it was soon discovered that each institution had its own particular needs, which the city sought to accommodate within parameters that preserve the uniformity of the program. All but 1 of the approximately 50 participating institutions elected to enter into an agreement for the maximum term of five years. These agreements were due to be renewed on January 1, 2000.

Table 9-2, below, shows a yearly schedule of the revenue generated by the Voluntary Contribution Program in both monetary and service amounts. The program has been responsible for bringing $28.7 million in cash and $27.3 million in services into the city. Totaling these components, the city and its citizens have received $56 million in revenue and services during the five-year life of the Voluntary Contribution Program (City of Philadelphia 1998).

The Voluntary Contribution Program has helped prevent the strident discord that has characterized other jurisdictions' approaches to dealing with nonprofits. At this stage in the city's program—more than five years after its announcement—not one Philadelphia nonprofit has had its tax exemption revoked or formally challenged. Other cities grappling with this issue, including Washington, D.C.; Albany and Buffalo, New York; and Baltimore, Maryland, have requested information on Philadelphia's program.

It is interesting to note the arc of attitudes and motivations among the various parties throughout this process. Health care institutions and educational institutions started from entirely different viewpoints. The

Table 9-2. *Value of Cash and Service Payments in Lieu of Taxation in Philadelphia, by Year*

Year	Cash Contributions ($ in millions)	Service Amount ($ in millions)
1995	$3.945	$3.3
1996	8.769	6.0
1997	6.512	6.0
1998	4.773	6.0
1999	4.722	6.0

executive and financial officers of health care organizations were practical businesspeople, and were very much aware of the Pennsylvania case law that restricted the granting of real estate tax exemptions. They were also aware of the attitudes that many of Pennsylvania's local governments had toward large, financially secure nonprofits within their jurisdictions. At best, local government officials wanted nonprofits to contribute something to the local tax base; at worst, they wanted to revoke the organizations' real estate tax exemptions entirely. Health care executives in Philadelphia saw the Voluntary Contribution Program as a way to avoid acrimony and litigation. Although these institutions may not have been enamored of the Voluntary Contribution Program, they made a calculated business decision to participate. By so doing, they also enjoyed the public and community relations benefits that flowed to them as part of the Voluntary Contribution Program, and could tout their participation in news and press releases. The mayor and other city and school district officials frequently praised participating institutions at public events, spreading the message to the civic community and the public at large that the participants were good corporate citizens.

The motivations of the educational institutions (i.e., institutions of higher learning) were entirely different. First, educational institutions looked to the University of Pennsylvania for leadership, since the University of Pennsylvania is larger in all ways than any other Philadelphia institution except Temple University.[2] The University of Pennsylvania's executive decisionmaking process seemed to resemble that of executives at the health care institutions—with one significant difference. The University of Pennsylvania had some issues with the city concerning expansion, zoning, security, and licensing fees, the resolution of which became part of an informal agreement that paved the way for the university's participation in the Voluntary Contribution Program.[3] The University of Pennsylvania's agreement to participate in the program encouraged other educational institutions to meet with officials of the Voluntary Program Board and enter into agreements of their own. However, executive and financial officers of these other colleges and universities did not appear to consider the Voluntary Contribution Program a way to forestall potentially difficult litigation. Unlike their counterparts in the health care industry, education executives did not see participating in the Voluntary Contribution Program as a practical business decision. Instead, they seemed to feel put upon, and expressed considerable outrage over the program. Executives who came to academia from other business backgrounds were much less likely to express such attitudes than were those who had risen through the ranks of colleges and universities.

In sum, the Philadelphia experience has shown developing a cooperative agreement between nonprofits and local government is much more productive than creating a confrontational situation and encouraging heated rhetoric. Whether nonprofits wish to admit it or not, the general public has lost confidence in the notion that certain nonprofits, particularly health care organizations and educational institutions, are still charitable. Philadelphia chose not to focus on this perception, but, rather, on the positive economic, social, and cultural impact these institutions have on the city. Starting a dialogue from this position, and probing to find common ground on which to agree, has shed light on how a program modeled on the Voluntary Contribution Program could and should work for both parties. Reasonable negotiations and persuasion were key to the success of the city's program. Mutual respect would never have been reached through litigation and posturing; in other jurisdictions, threats and name-calling have led to a polarized atmosphere.

Philadelphia has benefited in many ways from the Voluntary Contribution Program (City of Philadelphia Mayor's Office 1994):

- *The city is recovering municipal services costs.* Nonprofits operating in Philadelphia receive the full benefit of the city's police, fire, penal, judiciary, and other essential services, which are supported by the taxpaying citizens and businesses of Philadelphia. There is no evidence that nonprofit institutions receive fewer benefits from these services than taxable for-profit entities do. When nonprofit institutions are exempt from paying their share of the cost of these essential services, all other taxpayers must shoulder a heavier tax burden. The Voluntary Contribution Program shifted some of this burden back to the nonprofits by partly recovering the value of essential services provided by the city.
- *The program promotes equity between the private and nonprofit sectors.* When nonprofits produce excess revenue and compete with for-profit businesses, their tax exemption loses its purpose, which is to promote benevolent, rather than self-benefiting, institutions. Some nonprofits may have crossed the line between charity and profit-seeking by directly competing with the private sector for revenues. Tax-exempt status effectively gives nonprofits a subsidy, which creates an unfair competitive advantage. The Voluntary

Contribution Program makes the current system more equitable by having nonprofits contribute a portion of the tax burden that they would have without an exemption.

- *The program helps the city recover lost revenue.* The Voluntary Contribution Program allowed Philadelphia to recoup part of the opportunity costs of allowing a nonprofit to occupy property where a for-profit, tax-paying entity could exist. The program recaptured some of these lost costs in the form of revenue for the general fund. This revenue was applied to alleviate the burden that nonprofits create by using city services.

- *The program increases public awareness of and participation in nonprofit activities.* The citizens of Philadelphia saw a direct benefit from the Voluntary Contribution Program. The opportunity for tax-exempt institutions to contribute services instead of cash benefited the city, increasing the incentive for nonprofits to provide charity services to the community. The interaction between nonprofits and the public increased the accessibility of these services and fostered a greater sense of community around hospitals and schools. Also, the program brought additional educational and medical services to citizens in areas currently underserved by such services.

The Future of the Program, in View of Act 55 (1997)

The world has changed since 1994. The Pennsylvania Supreme Court has broadened its interpretation of the *HUP* test,[4] and the Pennsylvania legislature passed Act 55 of 1997, the Institutions of Purely Public Charity Act (10 P.S. section 371). (See generally Prescott 2000.)

The legislature explains that the intent of Act 55

is to eliminate inconsistent application of eligibility standards for charitable tax exemptions, reduce confusion and confrontation among traditionally tax-exempt institutions and political subdivisions and ensure that charitable and public funds are not unnecessarily diverted from the public good to litigate eligibility for tax-exempt status by providing standards to be applied uniformly in all proceedings throughout the commonwealth for determining eligibility for exemptions from state and local taxation which are consistent with the traditional legislative and judicial applications of the constitutional term. (10 P.S. section 372(B))

While codifying and, according to some interpretations, overruling the *HUP* criteria, the legislature used Philadelphia and a few other Pennsylvania municipalities as examples to encourage charitable institutions to enter into PILOT agreements with the local governments.

During the 12 years between the Pennsylvania Supreme Court's creation of the five-prong *HUP* test and the legislature's passage of Act 55, various court decisions differed on definition of a "purely public charity." Some decisions construed the test strictly, thereby making exempt status very difficult to achieve. Others were liberal, allowing almost any nonprofit to enjoy an exemption, regardless of how little charitable activity actually existed. Throughout this period, however, representatives of the nonprofit community were making a concerted effort to get the legislature to write and define statewide standards for property-tax exemption in Pennsylvania. The legislature started with the five standards enumerated in the *Hospital Utilization Project* case, but it expanded them well beyond what any appellate court had ever decided. In fact, some observers allege that Act 55 specifically overrules *HUP* (Goodman 1999, 328–29). Since the Pennsylvania Supreme Court has always been considered the final arbiter of Pennsylvania's Constitution, it is likely there will be a challenge to the constitutionality of the entire legislative scheme created by Act 55.

Not only did Act 55 change the substantive law of tax exemption, but it also encouraged financially secure nonprofits to enter into voluntary agreements with local governments to help defray some of the costs of local services. Furthermore, the statuted provides a remedy, using mandatory arbitration, for any small business that can prove a nonprofit is using its tax-exempt status to compete unfairly with that small business (see *Dynamic Sports Fitness Corporation of America, Inc. v. Community YMCA of Eastern Delaware County*, 768 A.2d 375 (Pa. Commw. 2001), which upheld the YMCA's exemption as a purely public charity that promotes health, and found that the YMCA's commercial business is not "unrelated" to its charitable purpose).

Development of Act 55

Various iterations of the legislation were introduced in both the Pennsylvania House and Senate in the three years before the act was finally passed. All of them died before final passage. Some observers, including this author, feel that the law exists as it does not because the Pennsylvania legislature's ideological beliefs were expressed in Act 55, but, rather, because certain key members of the House and Senate decided to try to facilitate a peace between nonprofits and municipal governments after more than a decade of legal warfare.

Approximately two months before the final vote on Act 55, the leadership staff of the Senate of Pennsylvania convened a working group that included senior staff of the various committees responsible for Act 55, along with representatives of Pennsylvania hospitals, colleges, and universities and of the Pennsylvania Catholic Conference. Local governments were represented by officials from Philadelphia, Pittsburgh, and the Pennsylvania League of Cities.

The legislative representatives' proposal was relatively simple. First, the definition of the *HUP* standards was off the table, and no further discussions were to take place concerning these provisions: The standards had been fought over for more than three years and the language currently in the draft legislation was final. Second, everything and anything else could be negotiated, but the discussions had to be conducted between the nonprofits and the local governments, in face-to-face meetings with people who had the authority to speak for their principals. Finally, the legislative representatives would not take sides, but would push both sides to reach consensus and avoid an impasse. Philadelphia's agenda was also relatively simple: to preserve all current voluntary agreements and maintain the amount of cash contributions ($5.74 million annually) received by the city and school district.

These meetings began cautiously, with the parties reiterating many of their previously held beliefs rather than presenting any new positions that would move the talks forward. The nonprofits broke the logjam by agreeing to language in the legislative-findings and legislative-intent sections of the act that encouraged nonprofits to enter into voluntary agreements. The local government representatives then agreed to language creating a series of incentives and presumptions deeming an institution a purely public charity. For example, if a nonprofit took part in a voluntary agreement, that organization was presumed to meet the relief-of-government-burden prong of the *HUP* test. Further, a nonprofit could credit up to 350 percent of its actual voluntary contribution to a local government toward meeting the community-service prong of the test. For instance, if an institution's program-service revenue is $500,000 and its voluntary contribution is at least 0.25 percent of the program's revenue ($12,500), then the institution may credit the contribution at

350 percent of its value ($43,750) for purposes of computing "uncompensated goods or services" to prove it has *"donated or rendered gratuitously a substantial portion of its services"* under the community-service criteria of the act. Also, nonprofits could form a community service foundation to defray the costs of public services provided by a local government, so long as any contributions received by the local government were to be used to pay for services that help nonprofit institutions fulfill their charitable mission. Finally, all voluntary agreements that predated passage of Act 55 were not to be affected, impaired, terminated, or superseded by its enactment.

Recent Challenges to Act 55

Act 55 became effective law in the commonwealth on November 27, 1997. But the unanswered question remains: Will this "treaty" keep the peace?

The road to judicial clarification promises to be bumpy. It is only a matter of time before the Commonwealth Court finds that the state legislature has unconstitutionally attempted to define "purely public charity" in contravention of the Pennsylvania Constitution, which grants such authority to the state Supreme Court. The court suggested as much in its recent decision in *Community Options, Inc. v. Board of Property Assessment*, 764 A.2d 645 (Pa. Commw. 2000), in which the court declared that an entity seeking exemption must be defined initially as a "purely public charity" under the terms of the state constitution before being measured by the statutory standards of Act 55. At issue was the exemption of a home for the mentally retarded that received nearly all its funding from government contracts. The trial court had held that the home was not tax exempt under pre–Act 55 standards but became exempt after the effective date of Act 55 because it met the requirements of that legislation, which defined the "relieving the burdens of government" standard in detail. On appeal, the Commonwealth Court agreed that the home was not exempt under pre–Act 55 standards (constitutional standards), but further held that since the home did not meet the strict constitutional definition of "purely public charity," the court need not decide whether the home satisfied Act 55's standards.

The *Community Options, Inc.* case has been criticized by commentators. As Joseph Bright wrote,

> The parties litigating a charitable exemption will now be required to litigate both prior case law and the statutory requirements of the Charities Act [Act 55]. The

result would be particularly inappropriate in the case of the requirement that an institution relieve the government of some of its burden. What constitutes a government burden is best known by the General Assembly, which is the part of the government that assumes such burdens. Therefore, the General Assembly is in the best position to determine what kinds of institutions relieve the government of a burden and what kinds do not. (2000, 1495)

The Pennsylvania Supreme Court granted Community Options, Inc.'s petition for review on September 19, 2001.

Ultimately, it will be up to the Pennsylvania Supreme Court to decide whether the legislature exceeded its constitutional authority by creating standards that enlarge the definition of "purely public charity" (as local governments believe), or whether Act 55 is simply interpreting constitutional standards (as nonprofits believe). Only a court decision that Act 55 improperly redefines "purely public charity" will swing the pendulum back to assist local governments in attempting to create and continue programs like Philadelphia's Voluntary Contribution Program. However, even before Act 55 was passed, the Pennsylvania Supreme Court had been accepting liberal definitions of "purely public charity" (see *City of Washington v. Board of Assessment Appeals*, 550 Pa. 175, 704 A.2d 120 (1997), which upheld the exemption of Washington & Jefferson College; and *Unionville-Chadds Ford School District v. Chester County Board of Assessment Appeals*, 552 Pa. 212, 714 A.2 397 (1998), which upheld the exemption of Longwood Gardens).

The Current Operation of the Voluntary Agreement

In early 2000, Philadelphia began trying to renew the agreements that expired at the end of 1999 with the almost 50 participating nonprofits. In a February 2000 meeting of the Delaware Valley Healthcare Council, a membership organization of all Philadelphia-area health care organizations, and in a March 2000 letter to city of Philadelphia health care institution participants in the 1995–1999 Voluntary Contribution Program, the city reiterated its desire to accommodate change and reach consensus with its health care institutions.

The economic world of the health care industry in Philadelphia has changed dramatically since 1994. The many mergers and acquisitions, the bankruptcy of the Allegheny Health System, the financial hemorrhaging of the University of Pennsylvania health care system, and the closing of stand-alone hospitals, coupled with the drastic change in reimbursement formulas and amounts, have changed a robust economic segment into one that is retrenched and not sure of its future. Accordingly, the city has offered a 50 percent reduction in the annual cash contribution currently being made by health care institutions. These cash contributions had been shared by the city and the Philadelphia School District, with 55 percent of the money going to the school district and 45 percent going to the city's general fund. The city is effectively waiving its share of the cash contribution, and requesting that institutions continue to contribute to the school district in order to assist the children of Philadelphia.

Institutions can choose to renegotiate these agreements for a 10-year term, rather than the standard 5 years. The service contributions due under these agreements would remain unchanged. Furthermore, the city will consider "hardship situations" on a case-by-case basis. While a hardship situation cannot entirely erase a cash contribution, the city and an institution can make an agreement to reduce or minimize a contribution. Such requests may be premised on factors such as operating losses, increases in uncompensated care, major organizational restructuring, reduced reimbursements, and any other circumstances specific to an institution that would show a financial hardship.

No one can predict how Act 55 will affect Philadelphia's Voluntary Contribution Program. The program has successfully distinguished itself from more-aggressive attempts by other Pennsylvania jurisdictions to collect payments in lieu of taxes. By not legally challenging the tax-exempt status of any nonprofit under the auspices of the Voluntary Contribution Program, the city maintains its program is rational, fair, and reasonable. Act 55 specifically encourages programs such as the Voluntary Contribution Program, and establishes certain incentives for nonprofits to enter into them.

On the other hand, with Act 55 expanding the standards of the *HUP* test, thereby making it easier for nonprofits to be deemed tax exempt by the courts, nonprofits may be less likely to follow the collaborative path laid out by the Voluntary Contribution Program. Instead, a nonprofit may be enticed by the more-liberal standards of Act 55 to seek a court determination of its tax-exempt status and opt out of any voluntary program. Such action would once again favor litigation over negotiation, and would replace collaborative and creative thinking about the greater community, in which both taxpayers and tax exempts must coexist, with narrow and insular action that might provoke resentment. Both the city and nonprofits have benefited from Philadelphia's Voluntary Contribution Program. As of early 2001, the program had 22 participants and anticipated annual cash contributions of at least $800,000 a year; the cash equivalent of services provided by the participants remained roughly the same as in prior years. No definite dollar amount is yet available for those service levels, since the law department, health department, and school district have yet to ascertain those numbers.

Obviously, cash contributions have decreased dramatically since 1999, due to significant changes in both the law (judicial interpretations and legislation) and the economic circumstances of the major nonprofit participants. Since the passage of Act 55, there may no longer be a legal reason for any nonprofit to participate in the city's program. Nonprofits evidently believe this. However, 22 have been willing to continue their participation in some scaled-down fashion. Winston Churchill said he stopped trying to predict the future because "it's just one damned thing after the other." The fate of Philadelphia's Voluntary Contribution Program cannot be predicted either, since Act 55 is one thing, but no one knows what the next "other" will be.

NOTES

1. *Hospital Utilization Project v. Commonwealth of Pennsylvania*, 507 Pa. 1, 487 A.2d 1306 (1985).

2. Temple University made a strong case that it was an instrumentality of the commonwealth, and, therefore, not merely exempt from real estate taxes but immune. In fact, most of the real estate on Temple's campus is legally titled to the commonwealth of Pennsylvania. It is also interesting to note that Act 55 of 1997 makes the real property of state-related universities, such as Temple, public property used for public purposes and specifically exempts it from state and local taxation.

3. The mayor and his chief of staff and alumni of the university and its law school closed the deal.

4. *City of Washington v. Washington County Board of Assessment Appeals*, 550 Pa. 175, 704 A.2d 120 (1997); *Unionville-Chadds Ford School District v. Chester County Board of Assessment Appeals*, 562 Pa. 212, 714 A.2d 397 (1998).

REFERENCES

Bright, Joseph C. 2000. "Commonwealth Court: Service Provider to Mentally Retarded Not a Charity." *State Tax Notes* 19 (Dec 4): 1494–95.

City of Philadelphia. 1998. *Seventh Five-Year Financial Plan, Fiscal Year 1999: Fiscal Year 2003*. Including fiscal year 1998. Presented by the mayor, January 27.

————. 1994. *Mayor's Executive Order 94-1*, June 30.

City of Philadelphia Board of Revision of Taxes. 1999. *Annual Budget Message to City Council*. February 16.

City of Philadelphia Finance Department Analyst. 1994. *Memorandum to Deputy Mayor for Policy and Planning re: Estimate of the services provided to nonprofits*, February 17.

City of Philadelphia Mayor's Office on Policy and Planning. 1994. *Report of the Mayor's Advisory Board on Voluntary Contributions*, June 30.

Goodman, Bert M. 1999. *Assessment Law and Procedure in Pennsylvania*. Mechanicsburg, Penn.: Pennsylvania Bar Institute, PBI Press.

Prescott, Jr., Loren D. 2000. "Pennsylvania Charities, Tax Exemption, and the Institutions of Purely Public Charity Act." *Temple Law Review* 73: 951–1030.

10

PILOTs
Hartford and Connecticut

Nicholas R. Carbone
Evelyn Brody

A focus on Hartford, Connecticut, illustrates three features of the state-municipal struggle over the property-tax role and base in a northeastern state. First, the structure and ongoing reform of the property tax in Connecticut—motivated in large part by the school-finance debate—highlights the difficulties of funding state-mandated services at the local level. Second, Connecticut pioneered a program for the state to make payments in lieu of taxes (PILOTs) not only for governmental property but also for private colleges and universities. Third, Hartford's adoption of miscellaneous other approaches typifies the creative and flexible municipal response to the presence of private charitable institutions in struggling cities.[1]

The Geopolitics of the Property Tax and Tax Exemption in Connecticut

Connecticut requires that local governments raise revenue primarily through the property tax. This heavy reliance on the tax is analogous to using a 17th-century workhorse for the 21st century. The boundaries of most Connecticut towns were drawn by 1800, when it made sense for planners to think locally about a range of issues, from types of transportation to which municipal services to provide—police, fire, education, roads, and rubbish removal. Today, with greater citizen mobility, we find cities with high effective tax rates and high poverty. However, an erosion of the property-tax base forces municipalities to either cut services or raise tax rates.[2] Connecticut's property taxes are significantly higher than the national average, although great disparities in tax rates exist among municipalities. Moreover, numerous exemptions to the property tax have an uneven effect on revenues from town to town.

By state law, municipalities may tax only the real (and personal) property not explicitly exempted by statute, and must follow specific statutory procedures for assessing property, including exempt property. Most statutory exemptions apply to classes of property (such as college and university buildings, hospital buildings, and religious facilities), although some apply to individuals (such as veterans, the elderly, or the disabled). As of 1995, municipalities were required to recognize 87 exemptions (29 were local option, 58 were mandated by the state). Many of the exemptions reflect Connecticut's agricultural heritage (e.g., livestock is exempt), but other aspects of base erosion include more-recently favored properties (e.g., manufacturers' inventories, bundled computer software, and airport improvements).

Since many properties owned by federal and state governments, colleges and universities, churches, hospitals, and various charitable and civic organizations are located in the larger cities, the property-tax problems of the urban centers are exacerbated. The tax burden these cities face can accelerate the cycle of urban disinvestment, lead to increased taxes, or force municipalities to cut services—or all three.[3]

Property tax is the sole source of revenue for local government, aside from grants made by the state (see particularly the discussion of state payments in lieu of taxes, below). Connecticut allows no local sales-tax component: All sales-tax—and income-tax—payments go to the state. Nor can municipalities impose fees for services on exempt property owners, such as a charge to a hospital for fire protection services.

Hartford City Council Responses to Fiscal Pressures in the 1970s

Like many other cities, Hartford in the 1970s was a city in crisis. A population of 140,000 lived in 16.8 square miles, one of the highest-density municipalities in the United States. According to a 1974 study by the John C. Lincoln Institute, 54 percent of the tax base was tax exempt. In a three-year period, municipal-owned property, particularly new schools, grew to 20 percent. Low-income housing was concentrated in the city. Only 20 percent of the housing stock was owner-occupied (Wassall 1974).

Municipal strategic action began in 1972, when 12 Connecticut cities, including Hartford, formed a successful alliance to thwart the state's attempt to shift to them the funding of a new regional transit authority, following the bankruptcy of the privately owned bus company. Hartford knew from every analysis that its property-tax base—eroded by the last 10 years' worth of state exemptions—could not sustain the proposed budget. The property tax had already reached its limit, because the state defined how to assess, what to assess, and other aspects of administration. Raising the tax levy would have resulted in diminishing returns: When faced with an increase in taxes and other rising costs of living in the city (such as automobile insurance), compared with the attractiveness of lower suburban taxes and good public schools, residents would simply move out. Using the media to reach the public, the 12-city alliance had each of its mayors, as well as other municipal employees, take turns criticizing the governor during appearances on talk shows and in the newspapers. The governor's popularity plummeted. Homeowners and small business owners, who did not want the property tax expanded to pay for transit services, convinced the state to take over the financing.

After examining all factors that affected Hartford residents' cost of living, the city's leaders also brought several lawsuits based on a perceived mandated overburden, asserting that the municipal property tax had become confiscatory and unconstitutional and amounted to a seizure of property without just compensation. The City Council created class-action lawsuits, and, since every council member belonged to a nonprofit advocacy group, each member filed on behalf of that group. For example, a suit against the state insurance commission complained that Hartford was rated higher than the town next door. A suit against the utilities and the telephone companies complained that they charged higher rates to the poor. The threat of a suit against the assessor, asserting underassessment of utility property, persuaded him to increase the assessment by $50 million. The utility companies objected only to the city's failure to raise this issue *before* the utility sought a rate increase. Of course, with deregulation, it will no longer be so easy for utilities to pass taxes on to their customers, and, for the first time, suburban towns have begun challenging assessments.

Hartford also charged that the way the U.S. Department of Housing and Urban Development (HUD) and the municipalities implemented the community development block grant improperly zoned out low-income housing. When a federal court ruled against the suburbs, HUD sought a settlement. The city hoped that the suburbs would then open up, but they never produced the needed low-income housing.

The Impact of Education Finance

Most of Connecticut's property tax is used to finance education, as in many other states. Over-reliance on the property tax has had an insidious impact on the quality of public education. Local zoning regulations in many municipalities have restricted opportunities for subsidized and/or low- and moderate-income family housing. The restrictions are largely motivated by concerns that such housing will not produce sufficient tax revenues to support the education costs of the families who reside in it. Continued failure to recognize this relationship perpetuates the concentration of low-income families and educational inequities in a relatively small—but growing—number of urban centers and distressed municipalities.

In the early 1970s, a suit brought in the predominantly white town of Canton, Connecticut, charged that the state's reliance on property-tax financing for education was unconstitutional. Hartford filed an amicus curiae ("friend of the court") brief, and helped pay for the experts. In *Horton v. Meskill*, 376 A.2d 359, 172 Conn. 615 (1977) ("Horton I"), the Connecticut Supreme Court declared that, under the Connecticut Constitution, elementary and secondary education is a fundamental right; that children in public schools are entitled to equal enjoyment of that right; and that the current disparities in financing between tax-base rich and tax-base poor municipalities could not withstand strict scrutiny.[4]

In 1979, the Connecticut legislature addressed its obligation to increase funding to education by creating a state-funded "guaranteed tax base," as well as a "minimum expenditure requirement." These changes sought to achieve educational equity by allocating state funding to municipalities based on the town's wealth (as measured by their real and personal property), effort (as measured by the relationship between the town's income and the amount spent on education), and need (as measured by the number of students and their educational status).[5] Hartford's situation improved under the guaranteed tax-base formula. After hiring consultants at city hall to make numerous computer runs on the tax base in order to maximize state support, Hartford was able to qualify for 70 percent state financing of education. The benefits from this formula lasted for years.

Cities' Current School-Finance Situation

Unfortunately, these financing reforms failed to remedy the school-finance problem for Connecticut cities. The debate has continued in the context of overall tax legislation, as well as in the ongoing litigation involving Hartford.

The Connecticut Department of Education was reluctant to evaluate the Hartford education system, even though it was the worst in the state. Finally, Hartford parents and church leaders appeared on the steps of their churches to declare a public emergency in the Hartford school system. Although the city council itself made a similar declaration and ordered the Hartford Board of Education to consult with the State Board of Education, the Hartford Board refused to take any effective action to correct the problems. Meanwhile, the Connecticut Supreme Court issued its opinion in *Sheff v. O'Neil*, 678 A.2d 1267, 238 Conn. 1 (1996), striking down the Hartford school system under the Connecticut Constitution. The state supreme court declared in strong language,

> The public elementary and high school students in Hartford suffer daily from the devastating effects that racial and ethnic isolation, as well as poverty, have had on their education. Federal constitutional law provides no remedy for their plight. The principal issue in this appeal is whether, under the unique provisions of our state constitution, the state, which plays an active role in managing public schools, must take further measures to relieve the severe handicaps that burden these children's education. The issue is as controversial as the stakes are high. We hold today that the needy schoolchildren of Hartford have waited long enough.

The *Sheff* court held that while the state did not intentionally segregate racial and ethnic minorities in the Hartford public school system, "districting" legislation dating back to 1909 was the most important factor in the *de facto* concentration of minorities in Hartford. Because the state mandated that school districts coincide with municipal boundaries, and because the state required all schoolchildren to attend public schools in the school district in which they reside, the court held that the state had an affirmative constitutional obligation to provide a solution, even though there is no *de jure* segregation. When the litigation started in the early 1990s, Hartford public school enrollment was 92 percent minority (primarily black and Hispanic); by the time the case reached the supreme court, minority enrollment was nearly 95 percent. At the same time, most of Hartford's neighboring school districts had minority population percentages in the single digits.

In 1997, Connecticut removed the Hartford Board of Education and appointed state trustees. However, subsequent reforms—such as creating target and magnet schools designed to attract schoolchildren from different districts—are small and insufficient steps, and the governor and the legislature have delayed meaningful reform. The key factor in the litigation is the state's failure to pay 50 percent of the total cost of public education in Connecticut; at the time of the court filing, the state was providing only 33 percent. Nevertheless, a trial court in *Sheff v. O'Neill*, 35 Conn. Supp. 630, 733 A.2d 925 (Conn. Super. Ct. 1999), ruled that litigation was premature. The *Sheff* plaintiffs are monitoring the legislative session to determine when to return to the superior court. Meanwhile, the debate has spread to the older "ring" suburbs: A school-funding complaint not based on race was recently brought on behalf of students in East Hartford and other, older suburbs, as well as students in more urbanized municipalities.[6]

The Real-Property Tax-Reform Context for the School-Finance Debate

In order to prompt public dialogue, the Connecticut Institute of Municipal Studies (CIMS) held a conference in fall 2000 on education and the property tax, an area in which CIMS has long been active. By the end of 1993, its first year, CIMS had convened a Property Tax Revaluation Task Force, and prepared and published the task force's recommendations and findings (CIMS 1994). The report was an important catalyst in the General Assembly's decision to create the Commission on Property Tax Reform. The state statute assigned CIMS to provide staff support and technical assistance to the 32-member commission.

Connecticut had adopted a state income tax in fiscal year 1992–93. But property-tax relief did not pass. In January 1995, CIMS published the commission's first annual report. Although the commission's major recommendations failed to win legislative endorsement,[7] the 1995 session of the General Assembly did adopt recommended legislation to increase the frequency of local revaluation cycles.

Although the Property Tax Reform Commission has been largely dormant since 1995, CIMS has continued working with municipal officials and community leaders across Connecticut to investigate more equitable tax models to support community revitalization efforts. In 1996 CIMS worked closely with the Alternative Tax Policy Task Force of the General Assembly, helping to organize the presentation of community testimony and the participation of expert witnesses at the task force's public hearing in October 1996. CIMS collaborated with Hartford's Fair Tax Committee to analyze and prepare for the anticipated impact of revaluation on different classes of property in various neighborhoods. CIMS also prepared a working paper for a parents' group, Educate Our Children Now, on the connections between property taxes, zoning, and education funding.

CIMS believes that the Property Tax Commission's efforts represent the best opportunity to develop a broad-based consensus to support essential property-tax reform in Connecticut. CIMS believes that the commission's reform effort should be guided by a clear set of policy objectives, and focus on designing and proposing a revenue system of local property taxation that meets several goals (CIMS 1996):

- Link property-tax reform with efforts to reform education and finance.
- Distribute the tax burden among all members of society so that every individual, group, and business bears its fair share of tax responsibility.
- Minimize the influence that taxes have on the general economy, while achieving a predictable, adequate flow of revenue to meet public policy imperatives.
- Equalize the local property-tax burden among municipalities to promote sound land-use development.
- Be a neutral factor in business and residential location decisions.
- Lessen reliance on the local property tax to fund local government and education.
- Reduce the burden of the property tax to bring it in line with other states, to improve Connecticut's competitive posture.
- Revise the administration of the property-revaluation system to ensure timely, accurate revaluation of property that reflects existing market conditions.
- Address the realities of the new economy, which include a shift from a predominantly industrial to a predominantly service base.

The fall 2000 conference convened by CIMS discussed a proposal to shift more responsibility for funding education to the state level, in order to counter individual towns' incentives to protect and expand their tax bases to the detriment of low- and moderate-income residents.

Features of Connecticut Law that Still Constrain Municipal Finance

Early in the 20th century, Hartford's population, like that of other Connecticut cities, was nearly all white. In 1916, local industry started recruiting blacks from the South to work in assembly-line factories—the automobile was invented in Connecticut, and firearms and typewriters were also manufactured in the state. The First Congregational Church decided to house the new workers in Hartford in multifamily housing. Communities were laid out based on how far a person could walk, so the inner cities were compact. Later, the federally subsidized interstate highway system made rural communities more accessible, opening up the suburbs to the educated population and leaving the cities to house the poor.[8]

Hartford cannot improve its inner city until it overcomes three major challenges: reducing the property-tax burden, reducing crime, and providing better education. Unfortunately for Hartford, suburban communities only five minutes' drive away offer all three benefits. Moreover, the problem is as much economic as racial. One of the unintended consequences of the civil rights movement has been the abandonment of the cities by middle-class blacks. Economically integrated cities do not exist.

The rigid borders of Connecticut municipalities argue for a state-level solution to many of the problems of public service financing. The existence of many mature suburbs adds a complicating layer. The old method of expanding the local grand list of taxable property does not work for fully developed towns like East Hartford. Moreover, with most of the development taking place in the lowest-taxed towns, Connecticut is urbanizing its suburbs and suburbanizing its rural areas: The suburbs' gain at the cities' expense is only temporary.[9] Recently, the town of Canaan (Falls Village) unsuccessfully sued its regional school board, complaining that the highly disparate property-tax values in each of the region's six member towns render unconstitutional a requirement that each town pay the same amount per student. The trial court dismissed this suit as raising a non-justiciable, political question.[10]

Property-Tax Exemption for Private Institutions and the State PILOT Program

The Origin of State PILOTs for Nonprofit Hospitals and Universities

Connecticut long made grants and reimbursements to municipalities for a range of exemption classes, and used a PILOT ("payments in lieu of taxes") program for state-owned property. In the 1970s, the cities obtained an expansion of the state-paid PILOTs to reflect exempt property owned by private hospitals and universities.[11] Notably, such an approach leaves out churches, museums, and exempt societies.

The private PILOT issue surfaced in the early 1970s when a large private hospital in Hartford, seeking to expand its facility, requested a zoning change that would, of course, have freed the hospital from paying property tax on the new building as well. In addition, the hospital planned to buy and demolish private homes to make room for its new facility, so the plan came under attack from some neighborhood groups. Many local business leaders sat on the hospital's board and took an active role in its planning and development. Hartford officials met with the hospital to explain the city's reluctance to allow this additional erosion of the tax base. The city pointed out that the percentage of Hartford's grand list that paid no tax had grown by more than 65 percent in eight years. In most cases, the city was powerless to stop nonprofit organizations from acquiring additional property and removing it from the tax rolls. This time, though, the required zoning change provided the city some leverage. Recognizing that approval would not be automatic, business leaders agreed to support expansion of the state-paid PILOT program.

As a political matter, though, the problem of exempt nonprofit property initially appeared to be confined to the big cities—Hartford, New Haven, New London, and Bridgeport—and these municipalities, comprising only about 15 percent of the state's population, elected a small percentage of state legislators. Moreover, Hartford leaders recognized that if the PILOT bill was identified as Hartford's tax proposal, it might jeopardize the bill's chance of being passed by the legislature. After all, Hartford was then struggling to solve a massive revaluation problem between better-off and poorer neighborhoods and between commercial and residential property. Accordingly, Mayor Frank Logue of New Haven agreed to introduce the proposal that the state make PILOTs for nonprofit property.

He led a series of meetings with representatives of tax-exempt institutions from around the state to generate support for the bill. It was clear that many local communities could no longer afford to provide services to those properties and property owners that paid no taxes.

If the PILOT program had not passed, pressure would have grown to levy a direct service charge on tax-exempt institutions to help pay the cost of municipal services they used. In 1972, the Governor's Commission on Tax Reform had echoed other commentators in recommending that tax-exempt institutions be charged a fee for the municipal services they consume.[12] Such an approach, however, was criticized by the institutions as infringing on their operations, and so they threw their support behind the state-paid PILOT proposal.

None of this legislation would have passed without the help of community groups, municipal unions, business leaders, and elected officials, who worked together to develop solutions to the property-tax problem. By demonstrating that Hartford did not waste its tax money—for example, by negotiating hard with city employees—the city won the support of the business community; since many CEOs sat on nonprofit boards, nonprofit organizations also began to support the city. In addition, Hartford was able to form a coalition with labor unions by opening its books to union leaders. Most city workers lived in the suburbs; when the PILOT program was proposed, about one-third of the city employees living in the suburbs contacted their legislators, creating further legislative support for Hartford's efforts. The legislature eventually authorized an annual $10-million fund from which local communities would receive PILOTs for private colleges and hospitals within the municipalities' borders.

The Structure of the PILOT Program for Private Colleges and Hospitals[13]

Like several other state grant programs, payments to municipalities are determined by statutory formulas.[14] When the College and Hospital PILOT program passed in 1978, the state was reimbursing local communities for about 35 percent of the taxes that any state-owned property would pay if it were taxed. The legislature initially set the reimbursement rate for the College and Hospital PILOT program at about 25 percent. (Neither program reimburses for personal property owned.[15]) Over the years, the legislature has increased the reimbursement rate for colleges and hospitals: Rates rose to 40 percent in 1987, 50 percent in 1988, 60 percent in 1991, and 77 percent in 1999. Today, the reimbursement rate for state-owned property is generally 45 percent (but it is 100 percent for any town in which more than 50 percent of all real property is owned by the state, and for certain other property, such as prisons). However, the reimbursement rates are scaled back to the extent the overall amount appropriated would be insufficient.[16] Payments are made once a year, on September 30.

In fiscal year 2001, Connecticut's total PILOT for Private Colleges and General and Free-Standing Chronic Disease Hospitals, as the program is officially called, came to about $97 million, paid to 64 municipalities. Hartford's share was about $18 million, second only to New Haven's approximately $27 million.[17] In general, most of the payment is distributed to communities with the lowest-income residents.[18] In contrast, Connecticut paid only about $66 million in PILOTs on state-owned property. Hartford, as the state capital, received the highest share, about $6.5 million.[19]

Over the years, the percentage of lost tax revenue covered by the PILOT program has increased (since 1999 reaching 77 percent), steadily reducing the "town-gown" tensions that traditionally typify relations in college- and hospital-rich municipalities.[20]

One of the recommendations in the 1995 report of the Property Tax Reform Commission was to increase both the PILOT for state-owned property and the PILOT for college and hospital property to 100 percent. In addition, while it recommended retaining exemptions for federal and religious property ("based on continual and consistent court rulings"), the commission would weigh other exemptions on a needs basis and eliminate categories where possible. The commission also recommended creating new PILOT programs for public housing, business inventories, and state-mandated tax exemptions for personal property owned by colleges, hospitals, and the state. Legislators routinely introduce proposals to increase the PILOT percentage to 100 percent. However, the program remains vulnerable to budgetary pressures. For example, in early 1999, Governor Rowland proposed decreasing the reimbursement percentage for private colleges and hospitals from 77 percent to 60 percent, and the percentage for state property from 40 percent to 20 (see also Jacklin 1999).

Administrative Concern:
Deliberate Overvaluation of Exempt Property

Because neither the exempt college or hospital nor any other party pays any portion of the forgone property tax for which the state makes payments, the state needs to protect itself against municipalities that deliberately overvalue their exempt properties in order to increase the PILOTs.[21] The process requires the municipalities to enter claims on forms provided by the state. Payments are subject to state audit of exempt assessments.[22] (Thus, current PILOTs might reflect prior Grand List adjustments.) If the state wants to challenge a town's claim, it must go to court. For example, if the value all the taxable property in a town increases by 5 percent, and that of tax-exempt property rises by 30 percent, the state Department of Policy and Management might challenge the assessment. In the past, the state effectively addressed this potential problem on a wholesale basis by funding the program with too little money to be worth fighting over.

Other Hartford Approaches to Dealing with Exempt Nonprofits

Zoning Moratorium on Expansion of Nonprofit Service Agencies

Hartford made the news recently when it adopted a zoning moratorium on the expansion of social service agencies in the center city. City leaders explained that they feared the city would never gentrify unless potential homeowners had a downtown that offered restaurants, bookstores, and other business development.

This moratorium, which is still in effect, seems misdirected. If "the protection of and care for human life and happiness, and not its destruction, is the only legitimate objective of good government," as Thomas Jefferson believed, then what is the proper response when the poor are locked into the central city? Until the suburbs open to poor people, the cities must accommodate the delivery of social services near where they live.

Negotiated Services in Lieu of Taxes

There are 13 nondenominational senior centers at various Hartford churches that provide minor health services, physical therapy, education, and other services. These arrangements began when the city negotiated with Hartford churches for services in lieu of taxes (SILOTs), proposing, "We'll supply the director if you'll supply the room." The city appreciated that a parish arrangement makes it easy for seniors to reach the facilities, and the churches saw the benefit of giving elderly parishioners a reason to be at church. The churches' only cost was expense of heating and other utilities. Co-author Carbone is now working with churches to recruit seniors to serve as foster grandparents of schoolchildren.

Nonprofit Community Investment

Nonprofit educational institutions in center cities throughout the United States are beginning to include neighborhood economic investments as part of their missions. For example, North Carolina's Duke University created a $2 million loan program for housing for the poor; Marquette University in Milwaukee invested more than $50 million in neighborhood revival; and Yale offers a homebuyer program that provides up to $25,000 to staff who move to designated areas of New Haven (*Economist* 1999; Yale News Release 1999).[23] Trinity College in Hartford has committed $6 million of its endowment to a $200 million comprehensive, public-private partnership to revitalize schools, recreational facilities, and housing. In a 1999 speech, the president of Trinity College declared, "It would be morally bankrupt for Trinity to teach the liberal arts on our campus and ignore what is happening across the street. . . . Those of us who lead institutions in cities, particularly those of us whose institutions hold sizeable endowments, have a particular obligation to invest in building community and rebuilding cities" (Dobelle 1999).

Future of Local-Government Finance

All state tax systems have, to some extent, been made obsolete by economic and demographic change. States have tended to overlook the need for fundamental tax reform while the national economy has changed. State tax systems have been revised, updated, and reformed to an extent that would be admirable if the American economy were still what it was in 1972. But tax policy has fallen behind the times. It is time to consider more fundamental questions of how well modern state tax systems reflect the modern American economy.

Electronic communication will dramatically change the nature and funding of governments. The nation state's control of knowledge is jeopardized by open communication across borders and global commerce. Moreover, historically property-intensive utilities are vanishing—once every community had a bank, but now banks can be run off a satellite. The profound impact of new information systems on political, economic, social, and even religious systems will be as dramatic as that of the printing press. The entire tax system must be rethought.

Very few people have the luxury to examine overall systems, as did coauthor Carbone in the 1970s. He considered the entire set of economic forces affecting Hartford residents: the insurance industry, the banking industry, the utility bills, and the property tax. As a creative local politician seeking to solve problems, he learned to leverage the responsibility of local government with the authority and resources of the state and federal governments.

NOTES

1. Coauthor Nicholas Carbone's perspective includes his service as majority leader of the Hartford Court of Common Council (city council) in the 1970s, and as director of the Connecticut Institute of Municipal Studies (CIMS) since its founding. Connecticut's General Assembly created CIMS in 1992, in response to Bridgeport's decision to file for bankruptcy. Members of the CIMS Board of Directors, who are appointed by the governor and General Assembly leadership, include the cochairs and ranking members of the General Assembly's Appropriation Committee and its Finance, Revenue, and Bonding Committee; individuals from local and state government; and representatives from the private and nonprofit sectors. CIMS's mission is to play a leadership role in developing strategies to revitalize communities in crisis and to eliminate duplicative public services. CIMS's projects are usually led by a team of stakeholders with relevant experience and expertise. Technical support comes from CIMS staff and selected consultants, who emphasize the practical application of relevant research to develop and promote model strategies.

2. As the City of Hartford wrote in its 1978–79 budget message, citing Judge John F. Dillon's opinion in *City of Clinton v. Cedar Rapids & Missouri Railroad*, 24 Iowa 45-5 (1868), municipal corporations "owe their origin to, and derive their powers and rights wholly from, the legislature":

> [All] city governments, including the City of Hartford, are both legally and financially "creatures" of the state. The legal subjugation to the state is complete and the financial dependence has grown and been forced upon the City by a rural-suburban dominated legislature which historically and collectively since World War II has buried the City with mandates; and, while providing several partial reimbursements, has not significantly expanded revenue-producing authority by permitting wage, taxes, sales tax pass-throughs, excise taxes, income taxes, annexation of the suburbs or any of the normal means allowed in other states. (A-8)

3. Of course, Connecticut did not deliberately set out to burden inner cities with vast sections of untaxed charitable, religious, and educational property. Law professor Richard Pomp testified in a 1977 hearing,

In 1822, [when Connecticut adopted the first such exemption statute,] the city was unchallenged as the center of the region's population, income, industry, and commerce. Property tax rates were low, and the amount of revenue lost because of tax-exempt property was not large in absolute terms, either. . . . The state should not be locked in by history, however; the financial crisis and decay of the cities makes it an appropriate time to reconsider the whole issue of tax-exempt property. (Pomp 1977, 3)

    4. Specifically, the court stated,

The present legislation enacted by the General Assembly to discharge the state's constitutional duty to educate its children, depending, as it does, primarily on a local property tax base without regard to the disparity in the financial ability of the towns to finance an educational program and with no significant equalizing state support, is not "appropriate legislation" (article 8, § 1 [of the Connecticut Constitution]) to implement the requirement that the state provide a substantially equal educational opportunity to its youth in its free public elementary and secondary schools. (376 A.2d at 374–75)

    5. See *Horton v. Meskill,* 195 Conn. 24, 30 & n.2, 486 A.2d 1099 (1985) ("Horton III").

    6. See *Johnson v. Rowland,* Superior Court, Complex Litigation Docket at New Britain, X03 CV 98 0085867S (filed April 21, 1998; first revised complaint filed June 29, 1999).

    7. The Commission's 1995 report reflected a consensus on the following points:

    1. The *property-tax system is the key financial problem facing the municipalities of Connecticut.* The problem arises from the nature of the tax itself; the statutory limitations placed on municipalities in terms of methods of raising revenues; the number and size of the exemptions to the tax; and, for the older and bigger cities and towns, the state's development patterns.

    2. *Connecticut property taxes are significantly higher than the national average.* Also, there exist great disparities in the effective tax rates among Connecticut's municipalities.

    • Per capita property taxes in Connecticut are $471 (or 65 percent) greater than the national average ($1,194 in Connecticut versus $723 in the United States for FY 92).

    • As a percentage of personal income, Connecticut's property taxes are about 24 percent greater than the national average (4.59 percent in Connecticut versus 3.71 percent in the United States).

    • Connecticut places a 22 percent greater reliance on the property tax as a source of tax revenue than the national average (39.1 percent in Connecticut versus 32.1 percent in the United States).

    • 109 municipalities in Connecticut (containing 81 percent of the state's population) have a higher effective tax rate (ETR) than the national median ETR for the largest city in each state.

    • 155 municipalities in Connecticut (containing 94 percent of the state's population) have a higher ETR than the median ETR for all local governments nationwide.

3. *The methods of administering and collecting the property tax in Connecticut are in many cases outdated and inconsistent, and, therefore, in need of significant reform.*

4. *Continuation of Connecticut's current property tax system is likely to result in the blossoming of what is now a very serious problem (and, in some cases, a crisis) into a full-blown, statewide crisis.*

8. The Property Tax Reform Commission summarized the urban/suburban tensions in its 1995 report:

> In summary, with their relatively affordable multi-family housing, proximity to the bulk of employment opportunities, and variety of social service programs (many of which are entitlements for residents), the cities became magnets for more and more lower-income families who cost the city more to support than they (or their landlord) paid in property taxes. When this set of facts is combined with the dispersion of businesses to outlying areas, cities (and some adjoining towns) have found themselves in a continuing downward spiral that they cannot control without help from the state.

9. One commentary in the *Connecticut Law Tribune* observed,

> The real significance of the *Johnson* case, at the outset, is the creation of a political coalition on one public-policy issue that binds communities on a regional basis. It would appear that older, more densely populated suburbs have come to the realization that services expansion and tax base erosion make them look more and more like the central cities that were abandoned in the 1950s–1970s. (Mednick 1998)

10. *Seymour v. Region One Board of Education,* Superior Court, Judicial District of Litchfield (decided January 2, 2001) (unreported case available electronically at 2001 Conn. Super. LEXIS 7).

11. In 1977, Professor Richard Pomp testified at a committee hearing on a variety of options to address the problem of tax-exempt property, including extending the state's PILOT to non-state-owned property, "on the theory that the exemption from the property tax implements state objectives and goals." He continued,

> In order to channel state funds where they are needed most, payments should be made only to jurisdictions having more than the state-wide average of tax-exempt property. Alternatively, jurisdictions might be reimbursed not for all of their tax-exempt property, but only for the amount in excess of the state-wide average. (Pomp 1977, 8)

Such an approach, Professor Pomp testified, would free the charitable institutions and the cities from their adversarial roles: "Both parties are currently on a collision course, as revenue-starved mayors covetously eye the institutions as a source of untapped revenue. By placing the issue in its proper statewide context, a PILOT program for tax-exempts would allow the parties to form a new partnership, to work together harmoniously and constructively at solving more pressing social problems" (ibid., 8).

12. See Pomp (1978, 10). See also Warren, Krattenmaker, and Snyder (1971), quoting a proposal by the Report of the Connecticut State Revenue Task Force that "our localities should be able to impose charges upon eleemosynary institutions related to the direct costs they generate, [including] the costs of fire and police protection, waste disposal services, and the servicing of off-site improvements" (304–05).

13. Rhode Island has a similar program, modeled on the Connecticut statute (Rhode Island Gen. Laws §§ 44-5-11.6 and 45-13-5.1, -5.2). As of 2000, the reimbursement rate is 27 percent (up from 25 percent) of, generally, the taxes certain private and state exempt properties would otherwise have owed; the total is limited to the appropriated amount. The state PILOTs were expected to total $17.6 million in July 2000: $8.7 for private colleges and universities, $6.4 million for private nonprofit hospitals, and $2.5 million for government-owned property (i.e., two state hospitals, a veterans' home, and the sole state prison). While no PILOT covers other state property, such as the capitol, most of the covered property is in Providence, which will receive about $11.8 million of this total (Jerry Marchaud, Rhode Island State Government, Office of Municipal Affairs, telephone conversation with coauthor Evelyn Brody, February 23, 2000).

Maine adopted a constitutional amendment requiring the legislature to reimburse municipalities annually for at least 50 percent of the property-tax revenue they would lose on account of new categories of exempt property enacted after April 1, 1978 (Me. Const. art. IV, pt. 3, § 23). Of course, this leaves municipalities uncompensated for historic categories of exempt property. Moreover, the legislature has on at least one occasion expressed its intent that a category of exempt property (in that case, the re-enactment of a former provision covering telecommunications personal property) is not to "be considered a new property tax exemption requiring state reimbursement under the Constitution of Maine" (Me. Rev. State. Ann. tit. 36, § 458; see Siegel 1997, 430–31).

14. See Conn. Gen. State §12-20a, as amended by Public Act No. 99-1 (June Special Session, June 29, 1999). As described in the *Estimates Book,*

> Payment is made in accordance with §12-20a and §12-20b. In Fiscal Year 2001– 2002, the PILOT to towns and certain lesser taxing districts is calculated at 77 percent of their tax losses due to real property exemptions for eligible private colleges and general and free standing chronic disease hospitals on the 1999 Grand List. In Fiscal Year 2002–2003, the 77 percent PILOT calculation will be based on municipalities' tax losses due to 2000 Grand List exemptions for such properties.
>
> Since payments are subject to state audit of exempt assessments, Fiscal Year 2001–2002 PILOTs may reflect 1998 Grand List adjustments and Fiscal Year 2002–2003 PILOTs may reflect 1999 Grand List adjustments. *Formula-generated totals for Fiscal Years 2001–2002 and 2002–2003 are reduced proportionately to the amount of the appropriation.* [emphasis in original]
>
> *Grant is paid on September 30th.* (State of Connecticut 2001, Introduction, 2).

15. As a separate matter, the original version of the PILOT proposal would have distinguished between old property and new construction, reimbursing first for new

property and then, in later years, reimbursing for previously existing property. However, the distinction was dropped, in part because of concerns about land-use issues (Edward A. Zelinsky, who served as a New Haven alderman during this period; telephone conversation with coauthor Evelyn Brody, October 26, 1998).

16. In 2001, appropriations limited the private PILOT rate to 74 percent, and the state-owned rate to 42.5 percent (Paul LaBella, Connecticut Department of Policy and Management, Intergovernmental Policy Division, telephone conversation with coauthor Evelyn Brody, September 20, 2001).

17. Other grants of more than $1 million were paid to Bridgeport (about $7.8 million), Danbury (about $1.3 million), Derby (about $1.1 million), Fairfield (about $2.8 million), Greenwich (about $1.6 million), Hamden (about $1.7 million), Manchester (about $1.1 million), Meriden (about $1.1 million), Middletown (about $4.4 million), New Britain (about $3.8 million), New London (about $6.1 million), Norwalk (about $1.6 million), Norwich (about $1.1 million), Stamford (about $2.3 million), Waterbury (about $5.6 million), and West Hartford (about $1.3 million) (see August 2001 Estimates Spreadsheet, pp. 9, 13, 17, 21).

18. The Connecticut Property Tax Study Commission, reporting on 1979, the first year of payments under the program, found that,

> Of the total increased expenditure of almost $30 million, 83.6 percent of this would be distributed to communities within the lowest three income deciles. The largest percentage reduction in property tax burden measured relative to income would be experienced by communities in the lowest income group— an average decrease of 10.6 percent. Average percentage reductions generally decrease with increases in community income (Property Tax Study Commission 1981, 169; see also 168, table VI-13).

19. All but a few of Connecticut's 169 municipalities received some payment under this PILOT, 32 of them less than $10,000 (August 2001 Estimates Spreadsheet, pp. 9, 13, 17, and 21).

20. For example, as quoted in the *Yale Daily News*, the spokesman for the mayor of New Haven said: "Traditionally, Yale's tax-exempt status has been a barrier to the City's embracing the expansion of Yale. . . . Tax-exempt property was viewed as an anchor around the municipality's neck." With the increase in the PILOT program to 77 percent, though, a Yale official observed: "taxes are not an issue between the University and the city government" (Forelle 1998).

21. See Conn. Gen. Stat. §12-20b (1999). For a description of the potential problems, see Pomp (1978, 14): "Given that normal assessment techniques may not be suitable for the valuation of tax-exempt property, the state would find it difficult to police the figures supplied by the municipalities." He then discussed proxies, such as the amount of fire insurance carried by the institution, square footage, limiting PILOTs to recently-acquired property and new improvements, and land-only valuations. Less sanguine was Ronald B. Welch, who commented in a 1971 letter: "When no fiscal consequences except higher state payments to local governments flow from high assessments, I see nothing but trouble in state funding of tax losses. . . . The best solution I have thought of is state re-

imbursement based on *future* investments depreciated at a statutory rate" (quoted in Oldman and Schoettle 1974, 344).

22. In a September 20, 2001, telephone conversation with coauthor Evelyn Brody, Paul LaBella of the Intergovernmental Policy Division commented that state auditors do not check every town's claim, but will verify the assessment in a field check if the town claims a large increase over the prior year's valuation, and the state recently entered into a settlement with one town over the valuation of the university.

23. At the end of 1999, Yale's president wrote to the Secretary of the Treasury asking the Clinton administration to support a proposed amendment to the Internal Revenue Code that would exclude up to $25,000 in housing incentives from the taxable income of an employee who purchased and occupied housing in distressed neighborhoods (Levin 1999).

REFERENCES

CIMS. *See* Connecticut Institute for Municipal Studies.

City of Hartford. 1978. *Budget Message for Fiscal Year 1978–1979.*

Connecticut Institute for Municipal Studies. 1996. *Long Term Strategic Plan for Communities in Crisis.* Volumes I and II (text but no charts) are available as "Connecticut Communities in Crisis" at http://www.cimsnet.org/CICrisis/commincrisis.html.

———. 1994. *Property Revaluation Project.* Hartford, Conn.: Connecticut Institute for Municipal Studies.

Connecticut Property Tax Reform Commission. 1995. *Report of the State of Connecticut Property Tax Reform Commission.* Text and tables (but not graphs) are available electronically in LEXIS, Fedtax Library, State Tax Notes File, as 95 STN 34-11, February 21.

Connecticut Property Tax Study Commission. 1981. *Connecticut's Property Tax System: Final Report of Property Tax Study Commission to the General Assembly.* Hartford, Conn.: Connecticut Property Tax Study Commission.

Dobelle, Evan S. 1999. "Stepping Down from the Ivory Tower." Remarks at the National Press Club, Washington, D.C., February 18.

Economist. 1999. "Charity Moves Off Campus." December 4: 31.

Forelle, Charles. 1998. "PILOT Program Sees New, Increased Funding." *Yale Daily News,* October 12, available at http://www.yale.edu/ydn/paper/10.12.98/.

Jacklin, Michele. 1999. "Rowland, Having Giveth, Shouldn't Taketh Away." *Hartford Courant,* March 24. A17.

Levin, Richard C. 1999. Letter to Lawrence H. Summers, Secretary of the Treasury, December 22. Available in *LEXIS, Fedtax Library, Tax Notes Today File,* as 2000 TNT 57-22, "Yale Suggests Linking Urban Homebuyer Programs to New Markets Initiative," March 23, 2000.

Mednick, Steven G. 1998. "You Can't Always Get What You Want: The Legislature's 1998 Session Yielded Mixed Results for Connecticut's Municipalities." *Connecticut Law Tribune,* May 18.

Oldman, Oliver, and Ferdinand P. Schoettle. 1974. *State and Local Taxes and Finance: Text, Problems and Cases.* New York: Foundation Press.

Pomp, Richard D. 1978. "Discussion Draft Prepared for the Greater Hartford Chamber of Commerce's Tax Force on Tax Exempt Property." In *Property Tax Exemptions for Nonprofit Institutions: Problems and Proposals*. Hartford, Conn.: Hartford Chamber of Commerce.

————. 1977. "Testimony Before the State Finance Committee's Subcommittee on Tax-Exempt Property of November 21, 1977." In *Property Tax Exemptions for Nonprofit Institutions: Problems and Proposals*. Hartford, Conn.: Hartford Chamber of Commerce, 1978. Reprinted as "Tax-Exempt Property and the Cities: Striking a Balance," *Journal of Real Estate Taxation* 7, Fall 1979: 50–61.

Siegel, Kirk G. 1997. "Weighing the Costs and Benefits of Property Tax Exemption: Nonprofit Organization Land Conservation." *Maine Law Review* 49: 399–441.

State of Connecticut. Office of Policy and Management, Intergovernmental Policy Division 2001. "Estimates Book—State Formula Aid to Municipalities for Fiscal Year (August 2001)." Published on the Internet, as follows:

The Introduction and Grant Descriptions are available at http://www.opm.state.ct.us/igp/estimat/aug01nar.doc;

Spreadsheets for grants by town (last updated August 16, 2001) are available at http://www.opm.state.ct.us/igp/estimat/estinfo.htm;

Summary information (last modified September 8, 2000) about the "Colleges (Private) and General/Free Standing Chronic Disease Hospitals—Payment in Lieu of Taxes" program, along with contact information, is available at http://www.opm.state.ct.us/igp/grants/c&h.htm.

Warren, Alvin C., Thomas G. Krattenmaker, and Lester B. Snyder. 1971."Property Tax Exemptions for Charitable, Educational, Religious, and Governmental Institutions in Connecticut." *Connecticut Law Review* 4 (2): 181–309.

Wassall, Gregory H. 1974. *Tax-Exempt Property: A Case Study of Hartford, Connecticut*. Hartford, Conn.: John C. Lincoln Institute.

Yale News Release. 1999. "Yale Homebuyer Program Extended Through 2001." Dec. 21. Available at http://www.yale.edu/opa/newsr/99-12-21-01.all.html.

11

Is Tax Exemption Intrinsic or Contingent?

Tax Treatment of Voluntary Associations, Nonprofit Organizations, and Religious Bodies in New Haven, Connecticut, 1750–2000

Peter Dobkin Hall

S cholars of nonprofit organizations have tended to treat tax exemption as a right rather than as a contingent privilege that is subject to the will of courts, legislatures, and public opinion. The historical record suggests that social, political, and economic contingencies have had greater influence on the tax treatment of charities than formal legal status or form of ownership.[1]

This chapter investigates the factors affecting the tax treatment of charitable properties in New Haven, Connecticut, between the mid-1800s and the end of the 20th century.[2] The factors include the following:

- the range of services governments provide and to whom these services are provided;
- the existence of recognized boundaries between public and private action, and the capacity to establish private bodies empowered to hold property;

- the number, density, wealth, and centrality of organizations as they affect public opinion about the organizations' value and trustworthiness;
- the extent to which the public considers tax obligations—or tax exemptions—to impose burdens of corporate citizenship and accountability;
- the extent to which the jurisdiction—state, county, or municipality—extending exemption is also the recipient of services provided by exempt entities; and
- the extent to which differences in wealth and social class affect who benefits from institutions supported through direct subsidy or exemption from taxation or both. Under certain circumstances, this might mean that taxation and tax exemption have redistributional effects, providing support to institutions from which only a small proportion of the community benefits.

Property Taxation and Tax Exemption before 1818

The property of religious bodies and educational institutions was exempted from taxation in New Haven and other Connecticut municipalities during the colonial and early national periods. This was because these entities were regarded as public rather than private institutions and because of the peculiarities of New England tax regime, which levied on polls, on the estimated productivity of land, and on the profitability of certain occupations (Walradt 1912; Warren, Krattenmaker, and Snyder 1971, 185).

Before the American Revolution, tax rates were low because government, although responsible for an extensive range of activities, made families and individuals perform most of the actual tasks of service provision. Public order was maintained by requiring everyone to reside in a household and by giving heads of households responsibility for maintaining order in those households. Rather than constructing almshouses, the government auctioned off the dependent and disabled to households who could provide for their needs at the lowest cost to the public. While towns provided for schools—often by erecting modest structures for the purpose—teachers were paid through fees levied on parents, not through general taxation. Similarly, congregations provided church buildings for the public worship of God, and financed themselves by taxing inhabitants of parishes—or, as they were generally called, "ecclesiastical societies" (Swift 1795, 232–47; Dwight 1822: 385–412).

Colonial Connecticut was home to no private corporations as they are understood today. Religious congregations exemplify the ambiguous character of early corporate entities. They had many of the powers of membership corporations: They could hold property; they were governed by boards of directors—the elders or deacons—and they elected clergy and voted on expenditures. They also had many of the characteristics of public agencies, including the power to levy taxes and appoint tax collectors (Swift 1795).[3] As government bodies, "ecclesiastical societies" were exempt from town and state taxation, as was the clergy.

Although, religious nonconformists were permitted to establish their own congregations after 1708, they remained liable for taxes supporting established bodies.[4] In 1727, the legislature passed a law permitting "sober dissenters" to establish their own ecclesiastical societies, and exempted them from taxation. Conservatives, including jurist Zephaniah Swift, were deeply troubled by this pattern of exemptions. He, like other supporters of the traditional order, believed that "uniformity of religion" was "necessary to the existence of church or state," and viewed the obligation to support this "ecclesiastical order" as part of the social contract. Exempting dissenters from contributing to the support of such religious uniformity altered the nature of the contract. With evident unhappiness (and no small measure of facetiousness), he conceded that the legislature, not the clergy, wielded the power to abrogate the social contract and to make individual rights superior to what he felt were more-fundamental obligations. This concession was a significant point in subsequent debates about exempting charitable, educational, and religious properties from taxation.

Swift's contemporary, Yale President Timothy Dwight, was not so willing to concede the rights of dissenters. In arguing against those who would exempt themselves from what he regarded as the common burdens of citizenship, Dwight wrote,

> I am well aware that . . . there are men, who may, and in all probability will, say, that however good and useful the public worship of God may be, they do not wish to avail themselves of its benefits; and owe, therefore, no contributions to its support. To these men I reply, that he, who has no children, or who does not wish

to send their children to school; and he who does not use the roads, and bridges, of his country, because he is either necessitated, or inclined, to stay at home; may on exactly the same ground claim an exemption from supporting schools, roads, and bridges. . . . The list of individual enjoyments is as much more valuable in a community, where Religion prevails, than where it does not, as the safety, peace, and pleasure of civilized society are more desirable than the exposure, discord, and misery, produced by the furious and malignant passions of uncultivated man. (Dwight 1822, 405–06)

Although the defense of the Congregationalist establishment has been generally treated as a facet of the church-state debate, it also marks the emergence of a new area of controversy regarding tax exemption and tax equity. Public debate over taxation was hardly new: Quarrels between king and parliament over the power to levy taxes had been one of the causes of the Puritan Revolution of the 17th century; "no taxation without representation" had been a motto of the American Revolution a century later; and the high taxes levied by Massachusetts in the 1780s, as it sought to pay down its war debt, had caused an armed insurrection, the Shays Rebellion. But none of those controversies had focused on the issue of exemption.

In fact, the kinds of arguments being advanced regarding tax exemption at the end of the 18th century could not have been advanced earlier.[5] They required a fully articulated and constitutionally embodied conception of individual rights and legislative power—things that were not part of the political culture before the ratification of the federal Constitution. Swift correctly suspected that this codification of taxation would introduce a new order of complexity into debates about the common burdens of citizenship and the grounds upon which individuals or enterprises could be exempted from bearing them.

As the only nonmunicipal and nonecclesiastical corporation in Connecticut, Yale College inevitably became a lightening rod for controversy. Though the college more resembled the kind of eleemosynary corporation with which modern observers are familiar, it nonetheless retained many of the characteristics of a public agency. The original 10-member "corporation" was self-perpetuating and empowered to exercise the familiar powers of corporations. But because membership was restricted to ordained ministers of the established church, and because the legislative grants were far more important as a source of revenue than private donations, the school was generally regarded as a public institution.[6] This public character was reinforced by the 1792 Act of Union, through which the state made a $40,000 donation in exchange for the college's agreement to include the governor, lieutenant governor, and six senior members of the upper house of the legislature as ex officio trustees.

Though established in 1701, Yale did not receive a grant of incorporation until 1745. The 1701 act enabling the "founding and maintenance" of the college contained no provision for tax exemption, nor did the 1723 act, which clarified the powers, duties, and qualifications of the college's trustees. Only in 1745, when the legislature comprehensively redefined the powers and duties of Yale and its trustees, did it also exempt from "all Rates, Taxes, Military Service, Working at Highways, and other such like Duties and services" its "lands and Ratable estate . . . not exceeding the Yearly Value of five Hundred Pounds sterling," as well as "the Persons, Families, and Estates" of the president, professors, tutors, students "and so many of the Servants of said College as give their constant attendance on the Business of it" (quoted in Warren, Krattenmaker, and Snyder 1971, 214).

Even if Connecticut's tax system had levied taxes on the value of real estate (rather than on estimates of its productivity), the number of exempt institutions was so small and the amounts of land those institutions owned so insignificant as to render moot the question of whether their exemption diminished the tax base. The town government owned no real property apart from highway easements. The poll-tax exemption of "constant school masters," ministers, and Yale's officers, faculty, and students, however, may have constituted a significant drain, since Yale's 217 students and faculty—at $60 per capita—represented a revenue loss of more than $13,000, an amount roughly equal to the entire annual budget of the college at the time. Exemption of the real and personal property of faculty and students must have imposed an additional burden.

But the impact of this loss may have been softened by the fact that the municipality needed relatively little revenue to support the minimal services it provided, and also by the fact that the services provided by exempt institutions were shared broadly, equally, and locally. The churches were open to all (indeed, attendance was legally required). For the first century of Yale's existence, the proportion of students from Connecticut ranged between 74 and 94 percent—many from New Haven and surrounding towns (figure 11-1). Though scions of the colonial and revolutionary professional and magisterial elite attended Yale, the college was—compared to Harvard—far more democratic, attracting farmers' sons who, like Noah Webster (Yale College 1778) and Eli Whitney (Yale College 1792), could not expect to inherit family farms.[7] Certainly after 1750, when Yale's grow

Figure 11-1. *Total Enrollments and Enrollments by Connecticut Natives,
Yale University, 1800–1970*

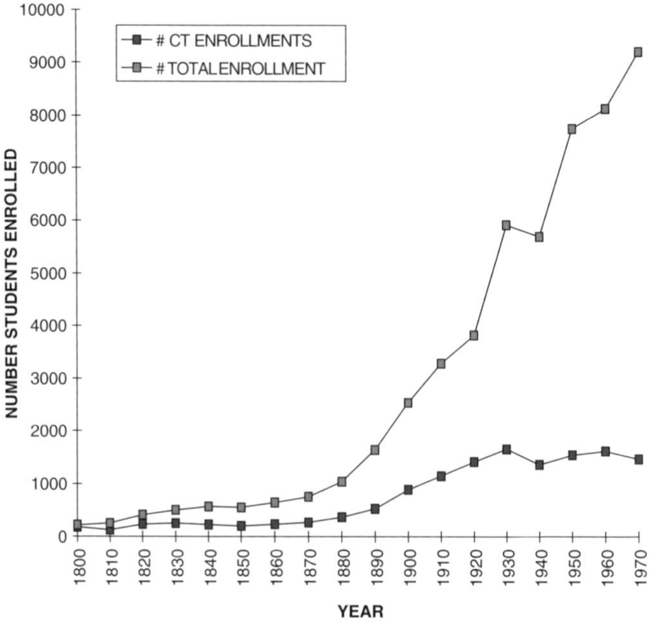

ing enrollment compelled many undergraduates to obtain room and
board in rented quarters in the town, their presence must have been
viewed by local property owners as a distinct blessing.

Changing the Rules: Tax Reform and Privatization, 1818–1873

New Haven's transformation into a commercial, manufacturing, and
transportation center, along with the disestablishment of the Congregational Church, the ratification of a new state constitution, the adoption
and domestication of the English common law, and the reform of Connecticut's tax system, significantly altered the relationship of exempt institutions to the public and to government. In addition, state and local governments not only took on an increasing range of responsibilities, but also
they were more likely to fulfill them directly, rather than contracting with
private providers.[8]

New Haven's economic transformation began after the American Revolution, when a handful of merchants began participating extensively in

trade with Asia, the Caribbean, and the southern United States. The city's Long Wharf, home to the counting houses of its leading entrepreneurs, sent local products to distant markets and received imported goods for distribution throughout the countryside. In 1810, New Haven, with a population of less than 10,000, boasted 29 firms "concerned in foreign trade," as well as nearly 100 stores dealing in dry goods, groceries, ship chandlery, hardware, drugs, crockery, and other commodities (Dwight 1811, 32). Commercial success in trade stimulated other kinds of economic development: In the 1820s, New Haven became a manufacturing center, and by 1860 it boasted railroad and steamship connections to Boston and New York and a population of more than 36,000 (a sevenfold increase over what it had been in 1800; see table 11-1).

The transformation of an agricultural economy into a commercial and manufacturing economy inevitably called attention to the inadequacies and inequities of the existing tax system. As the locus of wealth shifted from real estate to a variety of intangibles—money, stocks, commercial paper, and property located out of state—the existing tax system proved unable to capture benefits from the growing economy. The burden of taxation continued to fall on farmers, while the wealthy and the corporations they controlled were able to pay relatively low taxes, so public sensitivity about the inequity of the system began to emerge.

In May 1817, Governor Wolcott addressed the "ancient" system of taxation in his annual message to the General Assembly, declaring that the system had "ceased to be adapted to the circumstances of the people" (Walradt 1912, 61). Two years later, the legislature enacted major tax reform, with provisions that included levies on dwelling houses ("with due regard to the situation, use or income thereof, whether occupied by the owner or leased"); land (with reference to any and all advantages of soil, situation, and income); "mills, stores, distilleries, buildings, with their improvements, used for manufactories of all kinds . . . valued with respect to situation and present income"; cattle (horses, asses and mules, stallions, and neat cattle); silver plate, turnpike, bank, and insurance stock; and government securities (federal as well as those issued by other states) (State of Connecticut 1819). In addition, the act taxed luxury vehicles at a higher rate than those "generally used on farms or for the transportation of goods, produce, wares and merchandise." Faculty taxes continued to be levied on "attorneys, physicians, surgeons, traders of all kinds, mechanics, taverners, brokers, and distillers." The act continued to exempt "ministers, the president, professors, and students of Yale College, constant school-

Table 11-1. New Haven Human and Organizational Populations, by Year

Year	Human Total Population	Nonproprietary Entities (NPOs)	Total Number of Congregations	Congregations as a Percentage of Total NPOs	Total Number of Fraternal/Sororal Organizations	Fraternal/Sororal Organizations as Percentage of Total NPOs	NPOs per 1,000 Human Population (Density)
1850	20,345	42	21	50	1	2	2.1
1860	36,267	81	35	43	16	20	2.3
1870	50,840	130	53	41	41	32	2.6
1880	62,882	249	57	23	61	32	4.0
1890	86,045	326	72	22	155	48	3.8
1900	108,027	458	65	14	204	45	4.2
1910	133,605	605	90	15	257	43	4.5
1920	162,537	602	111	18	224	37	3.7
1930	162,655	676	102	15	156	23	4.2
1940	160,605	604	98	16	108	18	3.8
1950	164,443	649	118	18	85	13	4.0
1960	152,048	595	136	23	81	14	3.9
1970	137,707	614	120	20	69	11	4.5
1980	126,109	587	190	32	15	3	4.7
1990	130,474	630	183	33	10	2	4.8

masters, and students until the time of taking their second degree" from the poll tax, and also extended the exemption to include all minors (i.e., under 21 years of age) and all persons over 60 years of age.

The 1819 act contained a uniform exemption of "any real estate belonging to the federal or state government, or to any municipality, or to any incorporated academy or college, or to any religious or school society or district, or to any religious or charitable corporation" (Walradt 1912, 65). In exempting those properties, the legislature greatly broadened the impact of real-estate tax exemption, while at the same time removing it from the sometimes nasty political process that required each exemption to proceed from a special legislative act.

Although praising the reformed system, one pamphleteer singled out the tax treatment of Yale for unfavorable comment:

> The exemption from the poll tax of all persons over 60 years of age, and all under 21, is a prominent improvement of the new system, particularly the exemption of minors. The branch of the old law which required a farmer or mechanic, to pay for the polls of his children and apprentices, was calculated in a peculiar manner to bear upon the industry, if not the poverty of the state. The children of the rich, who were sent to college, or educated for either of the learned professions, the sons of the *nobility* as it were, by law were exempt from the poll tax, while the farmer and mechanic were taxed for their children, for no other reason than that they were not rich enough to educate them at Yale College. By the new law, the children of the poor are placed on a level with the rich. (*Judd vs. Trumbull* 1820, 19)

Significantly, this characterization of Yale as an institution patronized by the "nobility," rather than one serving the broader public, anticipated a major theme in criticism of charitable property-tax exemptions—though Yale's transformation into a national institution serving nonlocal constituencies had only begun (figure 11-1). During the 18th century, 80 to 90 percent of Yale students were Connecticut natives. By 1820, this had fallen to 60 percent. By 1850, less than 30 percent would come from Connecticut and less than 15 percent of graduates would reside in the state (Pierson 1983; Hall 1982, 310–11). In other words, over the course of the 19th century, as more students came from out of town and out of state, and were steadily less willing to stay in the state, the public extending the tax subsidy was increasingly less likely to be the public benefiting from it.

Continuing economic growth, urbanization, and rising demand for public services fueled continuing demands for tax reform, many of them tinged with resentment of special privileges extended to corporations and to the rich. In 1834, the legislature acted to restrict Yale's privileges, revoking the real and personal-property tax exemptions enjoyed by faculty and students and limiting the college's real estate tax exemption to an amount yielding annual income of no more than $6,000. This was not a significant limitation at the time, since the college held little real estate other than the land on which it stood. Nonetheless, it indicated that legislators were wary of the potential power of charities to erode the tax base (An Act in Addition to the Act entitled "Concerning the Corporation of Yale College," 1834).[9] In 1850, the state took the final step into the modern era, with a comprehensive tax reform that embodied principles of universal taxation:

> Instead of attempting to name everything which should be taxed, the law was made to read "all real and personal property, except that which is exempt from taxation shall be valued and set in the list." A list of exemptions was thus substituted for the list of taxable property. . . . Personal property was made to include all goods, chattels, money, and effects (except wearing apparel) and all vessels owned by residents of the state in addition to all personal property already taxed. (Walradt 1912, 112–13)

Despite the increasingly translocal character of Yale's student body and the fact that town-gown relations were particularly stormy in the mid-1800s (with local toughs and armed undergraduates fighting periodic pitched battles), a number of factors kept local property owners quiescent. First and foremost, Yale remained physically small, despite steady growth in the size of its student body. Second, growing numbers of students lived in local boarding houses and dined in local restaurants, enriching landlords and business proprietors. Third, virtually all the college's faculty lived in the city, paying taxes on some of its most highly assessed residential properties. Finally, the rapid growth of the city's economy—without significant increases in levels of services—had produced a large and growing tax base (figure 11-2).

In sum, between 1818 and the early 1870s, political, economic, and social situations were aligned in a way that ensured that there would be little discontent with property-tax exemptions extended Yale and other charitable, educational, and religious institutions. In this period, as the tax system was adjusted to capture the benefits of New Haven's shift from an agricultural to a commercial and industrial economy, the city's tax base grew enormously—from $5 million in 1840 to $45 million by 1870. Taxes did increase dramatically at the end of the period (with the mill rate rising from 4 percent in 1860 to 14 percent a decade later), as municipal expenditures nearly doubled. Because these increases occurred during the economic boom associated with the Civil War and involved long-overdue

Figure 11-2. *Total Grand List, City and Town of New Haven, by Tax Year, 1840–1998*

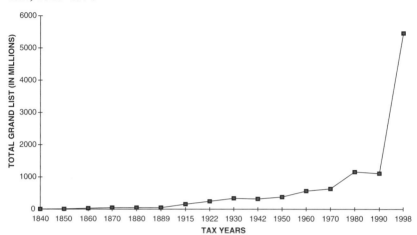

investments in infrastructure—including a new city hall, new schools, and the paving of streets (Benham 1873)—from which the public derived direct and tangible benefits, the increases seem to have aroused no significant opposition. Because the cost of other important additions to infrastructure (most notably the city's water works, which began operations in 1862) were borne by private investors, the increases in taxation were actually considerably lower than they might have been.

The number of churches and secular charitable entities grew impressively between 1820 and 1870, rising from 11 to 130 organizations (table 11-1). These included 53 congregations and 61 fraternal/sororal entities, as well as a host of new social service agencies, including four cemeteries, three old-folks homes, three orphanages, a private library, a dispensary, a historical society, and a Young Men's Christian Association (YMCA). However, because these groups owned little real estate, they did not make a substantial dent in the tax base.

Property-Tax Exemption in an Urbanizing and Industrializing Society, 1873–1940

The decades between the Panic of 1873 and American entry into the Second World War make up a distinct epoch in New Haven's institutional development. During this 70-year period, New Haven's population more than tripled—from 50,840 in 1870 to a peak of 162,655 in 1930, the bulk of the growth consisting of immigrants, who comprised nearly three-quarters of the city's population by 1930 (Dana 1937, 18c). This wave of immigration generated demands for services of every kind: to maintain public order and safety; to provide education, health, and social services; and to create transportation, public utilities, and recreation infrastructures. Some of these services would be provided by private charitable, philanthropic, and religious agencies. Others would be provided by government. The period was marked by a remarkable proliferation of the former and an equally impressive expansion of the latter—both of which developments would have significant impacts on the system of taxation and on the use and public perception of property-tax exemption.

Government required comprehensive reorganization to meet rising demands for services. Since 1784, New Haven had had two governments: a city government, with authority over the commercial center and waterfront, and a town government, with authority over the hundreds of acres of farms and forests that comprised New Haven's substantial periphery. When the city first received its charter, the area had about 9,000 inhabitants, 3,000 of whom lived in the city. A hundred years later, 70,000 people lived within the city and only 3,000 in rural town sections (Baldwin 1884).

Population growth and rising demand for services were initially concentrated in the city, where the immigrants settled close to the factories and commercial establishments in which they found employment; unfortunately, the city's circumscribed area also necessarily limited the size of the tax base. The town, on the other hand, while possessing extensive, potentially taxable real estate, had no desire to shoulder the cost of underwriting services for which its population felt no need. Accordingly, it doggedly fought efforts to consolidate the two governments. Only after a series of scandals—and a decade of lobbying the state legislature by tax- and civil-service-reform groups—was consolidation finally achieved in 1894 (New Haven Taxpayers' Association 1885; *Report of a Committee . . .* 1887 and 1889).[10] The merger of the town and city governments not only greatly enlarged New Haven's tax base, it also further escalated demand for services, as the urban population began to spread into previously undeveloped rural areas. The demand growth was helped along by the rapidly developing network of electric street railways that, by the turn of the century, had begun to stretch beyond the city, first to the suburbs and later to adjacent municipalities.

The role of private firms in creating the utilities infrastructure was mirrored by their role in social service provision. Although the town operated an almshouse on an extensive tract of land in the city's rural Westville section, privately supported social service agencies proliferated after 1860. New Haven boasted the second charity-organization society in the United States. Established in 1880, Associated Charities concerned itself as much with curbing the use of publicly provided poverty relief as a form of patronage as with actually serving the needy.

Between 1870 and 1900, the number of nonproprietary entities had increased from 130 to 458 (350 percent). Of these, 65 were religious bodies and 204 fraternal/sororal organizations. The remaining 189 included old-folks homes, charitable societies, two hospitals, kindergartens, nurseries, four YMCAs, advocacy groups, and a host of athletic organizations, social clubs, and missionary societies—as well as trade associations and labor unions (*New Haven Directory* 1901, 831–52). During this period, organizational density grew to 4.2 organizations per 1,000 population, more than double the density in 1870, indicating that the number of organizations was increasing more rapidly than the human population. More significantly, large organizations like Yale were beginning to expand in size: In 1800, Yale enrolled 217 students; in 1870, 755; in 1900, 2,542 (Pierson 1983, 3–8).

Yale's expanding enrollments in the years before 1870 had little or no effect on the tax base, because, while the number of students increased, the institution did not have the means to significantly expand its real estate holdings or dormitory space. As a result, increasing numbers of students lived and dined in boarding houses—to the considerable financial benefit of property owners. However, with the election of the college's first lay president, railroad economist Arthur Twining Hadley, in 1899, alumni's accumulated wealth began to pour into Yale's coffers. Hadley began the process of physical expansion, with major property acquisitions to the north of the New Haven Green and an intensive building program intended to provide on-campus housing for all undergraduates.[11]

Anticipating the economic impact of this policy, the city's tax assessor challenged the exemption of Yale's dormitory and dining hall properties in 1898. Calling attention to the 1834 legislation that limited the exempt real estate the college could hold to property yielding no more than $6,000 annually, attorneys for the city urged strict construction of the statute, arguing that "the statute does not provide that buildings used for the benefit or promotion of the college, or for the accommodation or benefit of students, or for dining-rooms or sleeping rooms for students, shall be exempt from taxation" (*Yale University v. Town of New Haven,* 71 Conn. 316, 323–24 (1899)). They went on to point out the revenues the college realized from operating these facilities: "The dining-hall is assessed at $8,100. The business carried on in it yields a profit equivalent to the interest upon $10,000, the cost of the equipment, and an additional amount for a sinking fund." Finally, they argued that the dormitories, in raising the cost of attending the college, favored the rich and excluded the poor from the school's benefits (71 Conn., 333). These sentiments doubtless reflected New Haven citizens' accurate perception that Yale had long since ceased to serve the educational needs of New Haven's young men, and was increasingly benefiting the wealthy and privileged from around the nation.

Yale's attorneys began their argument in this case with a selective (but unattributed) excerpt from Harvard President Charles W. Eliot's 1874 report to the Massachusetts legislature on the rationale for exempting real estate owned by charitable, educational, and religious institutions from taxation:

> The reason for treating this institution in an exceptional manner is that it contributes to the welfare of the State. Its function is largely a public function. Its work is done primarily, indeed, for individuals, but ultimately for the public good. Other communities pay large sums to secure the presence of a lunatic asylum, a jail or a state prison; but the assessors of New Haven would strip this venerable seat of learning of an exemption for which it returns, in mere money value, a twenty-fold equivalent. (71 Conn., 317)

Eliot had offered an economic rationale for exemption, based on a variety of arguments about direct and indirect economic benefits accruing to communities from the presence of eleemosynary institutions (see Diamond, chapter 5 of this volume). He clearly recognized, however, that exemption was a subsidy and that, as such, municipalities offering exemption had a right to expect services in return. Eliot acknowledged that "the public burdened" by erosion of its tax base might not be "the same public as is benefited" by the existence of exempt institutions, even though "the whole State, or perhaps the whole country" might reap these benefits. "If abuses have crept in," Eliot concluded,

> let them be reformed. If institutions which are really not of a public character get exempted, cut them off; if greater publicity is desirable in regard to the condition and affairs of the institutions exempted, provide for annual published returns; if there be fear of improper sales of land, long exempted, to the private advantage of the trustees or proprietors of the moment, enact that all sale of such property shall be by order of a court. (Eliot 1874, 393)

Yale's attorneys omitted these points, stressing, instead, the economic benefits the city derived from the college, and going back to the Middle Ages to show that residential and dining facilities had always been considered essential aspects of colleges. Yale's advocates avoided the strict-construction argument by suggesting that exemptions did not erode the tax base because, once property had been devoted to public uses, it could no longer be considered part of the tax base: "The mere stuff of land and buildings is not the subject of taxation, except as it may be the source of profit, present or prospective, to some person bound to contribute to the charges of government" (71 Conn., 330). Persuaded that "students' fees, whether apportioned from room rent or tuition, cannot be treated as income of real estate" and that "land occupied and reasonably necessary for the plant of the College" was not "productive real estate within the meaning of the *proviso* in the Act of 1834," the court upheld Yale's claims (71 Conn., 337). Indeed, the court went further, holding that vacant lots owned by the college, as long as they were not being held for speculative purposes, should also be exempt.

The 1899 case essentially defined Connecticut's rationale for the exemption of charitable properties for the coming century. First, the court decided that property dedicated to a public use is considered intrinsically immune from taxation because Connecticut's property tax derives historically from a set of levies on productivity; and nonproductive property, in this view, is, by its very nature, beyond the reach of tax. Second, the court decided that such property is devoted to services that would otherwise have to be offered by the state (such as public education) or that should be encouraged by the state for humanitarian purposes (Warren, Krattenmaker, and Snyder 1971, 229–30). By rejecting the city's characterization of tax exemption as a subsidy, the court could ignore the whole cost/benefit equation. The court thus aligned itself firmly with the liberal-constructionist view of tax exemption, which held that the intrinsic merit of certain institutions entitled them to less strict construction of pertinent statutes (Zollmann 1924, 464–65; see also Bittker and Rahdert 1976; Simon 1987, 73–76).[12]

Perhaps the most important effect of the 1899 decision was its stimulation of real estate acquisitions by charitable, educational, and religious institutions. The justices, having ruled that real estate owned by such institutions could not be considered revenue-producing, no matter how much income it generated; having permitted charities exemption on undeveloped properties for which a charitable use was contemplated; having ignored the question of whether certain activities carried out by charities competed unfairly with tax-paying enterprises; and having turned a deaf ear to the argument that organizations designated as charitable should operate charitably, had eliminated any possible grounds on which such property acquisitions could be legally discouraged.

As New Haveners became engaged in the Progressive movement that preceded World War I, it was inevitable that Yale's role in the community would become an object of scrutiny and debate. In the autumn of 1911, William Scranton Pardee, a leading local municipal reformer, presented a paper (subsequently printed as a pamphlet), called "The Relations of New Haven and Yale University (The Relation of a Mother and Her Child)," to the Economic Club of New Haven. Pardee pointed out that while Yale had done much for New Haven, "the business men of New Haven citizens (not Yale graduates)" had "given to the university in an amount not fully appreciated" (Pardee 1911, 6). "And when I say that New Haven has been generous to Yale University," Pardee continued, "I include its exemption from taxation because, while it is true that Yale University is exempt by a State law, it is also true that should the time come when the public opinion of New Haven demands that Yale be taxed, Yale will be taxed" (ibid., 6).

Pardee calculated that the total value of exempted real estate and buildings came to $10.4 million—which, taxed at the going rate of 17.5 mills (1.75 percent) would yield $182,731 annually. He added to this the value of Yale's $6.3 million in stocks and bonds, "a very considerable portion" of which, as bonds of companies located outside of Connecticut, would be under the tax laws of the time if owned by private citizens. He then estimated the value of services provided the university by the city at $165,449 (ibid., 8).

The university responded to Pardee's challenge with a pamphlet by University Secretary Anson Phelps Stokes, called *What Yale Does for New Haven—A Study of the Influence of an Endowed University on the Financial Well-Being of Its Home City* (1911). Fifteen of its 21 pages were devoted to financial questions, with the balance engaging the points about Yale's civic role that had been at the center of Pardee's concerns. Holding fast to the "tax base defining" interpretation of the exemption, Stokes refused to concede that Yale constituted any burden on New Haven's taxpayers and ignored the possibility that the city or its citizens contributed anything of value to Yale, instead citing the school's contributions to the city, including university police, general and scholarship aid to local students, university and student purchases of local goods and services, and help in financing local mortgages. He also pointed out that the university had been one of the prime engines of New Haven's growth, rather than an invader that moved in and demanded a tax exemption (ibid., 6). Stokes estimated that these contributions totaled $3.1 million annually.[13]

Besides ignoring Pardee's broader concerns about Yale's potential contributions to civic leadership, particularly as a source of expertise to inform public decisionmaking, Stokes did not mention that the university was embarking on an ambitious program of land acquisition that would nearly double the size of its holdings. This was largely done in secrecy, through third parties and nonrecorded deeds, in order to prevent owners of properties in which the school was interested from artificially inflating their value (Carlson 1998).[14]

In 1920, no doubt responding to a public made especially tax sensitive by wartime levies, Stokes issued a lengthier, albeit more conciliatory, version of *Yale and New Haven* that covered the same ground in much greater financial detail. The pamphlet began with an iteration of Yale's right to tax exemption, quoting from the school's 1745 charter and assorted state statutes and, once again, citing the 1899 court decision, and provided information on other states' exemption of colleges and universities.

Stokes compared the tax rates of college and noncollege towns, concluding that the average tax rates of representative college towns were generally lower than those of non-college towns. He then digressed into a set of historical illustrations of how towns and cities had traditionally competed to secure exempt institutions. He completed discussion of direct and indirect financial benefits with an update of the figures he had given in 1911. This time they totaled $5.4 million, nearly half of which was the fanciful "estimated purchases by students and Yale visitors"—now amounting to $2.7 million. "It is interesting to note," he wrote, "that this total of indirect financial contributions by Yale to New Haven is well above the entire cost of the city administration for the same period" (ibid., 37). Stokes's account of "educational and other benefits" now included activities in public health and medicine, his hopes for the new department of education, and a list of "local public service and civic positions or offices held at present or recently by officers of the University" (ibid., 45), although he did admit that "officers of the University have [not] always been as active in municipal life as is desirable" (ibid., 46).

Modernizing the Tax System, 1900–1930

For a number of reasons, the property-tax exemption became a more salient public issue after the turn of the century. Many progressives questioned private ownership and control of institutions in which the public had a vital interest—especially as charitable, educational, and religious institutions were becoming wealthier and devoting themselves to serving elites.[15] As early as the 1860s, state officials had voiced concern about the need for procedural reform. "So long as individuals and communities are left to adjust for themselves, and practically at their own discretion, the proportion of the public burden which they shall bear," an early special tax commission wrote, "it is the indispensable duty of the state, as the first requisite for a basis of equal taxation, to find a means to ascertain the actual value of all taxable property" (quoted in State of Connecticut 1926). The commission recommended the appointment of a state tax commissioner to have charge of all taxes and assessments, collect all taxes on corporations, and appoint and supervise tax assessors. This proposal was resoundingly rejected by legislators, who jealously guarded traditions of local autonomy.

The reforms suggested in 1868 were finally enacted in 1905, and the early reports of the tax commissioner made it all too clear the extent of the disarray Connecticut's assessment and collection of taxes:

> The tax laws of Connecticut are simply an accumulation of statutory provisions and amendments for a long series of years. There has been no codification of these statutes for over half a century, nor any consideration of them as a whole by any commission since that of 1887. When changes in the tax laws are made there is no particular attempt to correlate the amendments with other provisions of the tax statutes, and neither is the particular section itself re-enacted in most instances. Part of a law often therefore appears to be inconsistent with other provisions of the relating statute. Many of the existing provision are difficult to understand, and some are more or less obsolete (State of Connecticut 1912, 43)

The inevitable result was a casual approach to the basic mechanics of assessment and collection. "The assessment of taxes in a large number of towns in this state is in a deplorable condition," wrote Tax Commissioner Frank Healy in his 1906 report:

> The assessors, who are required under the present law to assess property at its present true and just value, simply copy off the valuations placed on the property the year before, and this practice has continued so long in most towns that any suggestion that the assessors comply with the law, in regard to making a true assessment of the property within their towns, receives no consideration whatsoever (State of Connecticut 1906, 3).

Naturally, a combination of statutory patchwork and bureaucratic lassitude led to assessment lists ("grand lists") that were anything but accurate.

The description of assessment practices written by William H. Corbin, the energetic and reform-minded tax commissioner who served from 1908 to 1920, suggests that tax data compiled before the First World War are of very questionable accuracy (State of Connecticut 1912, 26).[16] The situation began to improve only with the enactment of the federal income and corporation taxes, which brought about codification of state tax statutes and, after a series of highly publicized corruption scandals involving local tax officials, forced standardized practices on the localities (State of Connecticut 1918, 52–54).

Two of the reforms Corbin promoted—annual publication of grand lists and assessments based on fair market value—undoubtedly helped to spark the debate over exemptions in New Haven. Another of his statistical compilations, the quadrennial report of property exempted from taxation (first published in 1914), enabled citizens and municipal officials to compare the impact of exemptions on the tax base of all Connecticut's towns and cities. These bodies of increasingly accurate and comparable data would enable tax reformers to pinpoint abuses and inequities, especially with regard to property-tax exemptions. Very early on, it became apparent that exemptions were being enjoyed by organizations—including fraternal and sororal entities and new manufacturing firms—that were not entitled to them by statute (State of Connecticut 1914b, 218–19). In 1930, the tax commissioner noted that private exempted properties had begun to exceed the value of public ones. By the mid-1930s, as the Depression gutted municipal finances, this imbalance became a matter of state-level concern, especially as the added burden of rising rates of federal taxation affected citizens and businesses alike.

New Haven's Problems: Whither the City? Whither All Cities?

The university's land acquisitions continued during the Depression: Between 1929 and 1940, Yale purchased hundreds of properties in the heart of downtown New Haven and constructed nine residential colleges for undergraduates; a huge research library; a hall of graduate studies; and complexes to house its law, medical, and divinity schools (Pierson 1955, 597–600).

As real estate values collapsed and Yale's expansion removed some of the city's most valuable properties from the tax base, a classic municipal fiscal squeeze developed: a shrinking tax base and rising demand for municipal services. As financial journalist Arnold Guyot Dana recognized in his important study, *New Haven's Problems: Whither the City? All Cities?* (1937), New Haven's problems were not entirely due to the short-term effects of the Depression, but, rather, had structural roots in demographic and economic trends and in the state's defective system of taxation. Contemplating the possibility of the state's floating a $25 million bond, of which the city would receive a share, Dana wrote that unless these structural problems were corrected, the measure would prove not only ineffectual, but harmful (ibid., 2).

Many of the problems Dana identified still exist: the flight of the affluent to the suburbs and the transformation of the inner city into a catchment area for the immigrant poor (by 1930, two-thirds of New Haven's residents were foreign-born); deteriorating transportation infrastructure; and rising taxes and municipal debt that drove out established businesses and discouraged new ones from locating in the city. While New Haven's largest employers, the Winchester Arms Company and Yale, flourished during the 1920s, their prosperity was at the city's expense: Winchester's thousands of employees, most of them low-skilled immigrants, were subject to periodic idleness because of the arms industry's dependence on government contracts. Yale's growth also burdened the municipality as its exempt properties eroded the tax base, increasing numbers of students and faculty drew on municipal services, and more affluent employees moved to the suburbs. Because the tax system was based almost entirely on real estate levies, the city had no way of capturing revenues from institutions and individuals who used its services but paid nothing toward their support.

In addition to documenting the overall growth of tax exemptions in the state between 1913 and 1933, Dana broke them down between governmental and private uses and, within the latter, between types of charitable uses (table 11-2 and figure 11-3). During this period, the value of all types of exempt property rose from $42.1 million to $137.6 million (327 percent); government-owned properties rose from $12.5 million to $34.6 million (276 percent); and properties owned by churches and religious and secular charities rose from $2.8 million to $6.1 million (220 percent), hospital properties from $1.4 million to $6.2 million (450 percent), and Yale properties from $12.3 million to $67.1 million (547 percent) (ibid.,

Table 11-2. *New Haven Public, Private, and Total Exempt Property, by Tax Year, 1915–1998 (in dollars and as percent of total grand list)*

| | Value of Exempt Organizations | | | | | | | |
| | Public Exempt Organizations | | Private Exempt Organizations | | Total Exempt Organizations | | Value of Total Grand List | Mill Rate |
Year	(Millions of $)	(%)	(Millions of $)	(%)	(Millions of $)	(%)	(Millions of $)	
1915	12.5	8	29.6	19	42.1	17	155.7	20.00
1922	9.9	4	33.3	14	43.2	18	247.1	25.00
1930	34.5	10	56.1	17	90.6	27	338.0	25.20
1942	32.3	10	90.4	29	122.7	29	317.0	27.50
1950	37.0	10	102.7	27	139.7	27	376.8	33.75
1960	93.3	17	144.8	26	238.1	43	560.7	39.25
1970	104.9	17	170.8	27	275.7	44	629.0	74.70
1980	371.3	32	275.1	24	646.4	56	1,156.5	71.30
1990	319.7	29	399.0	36	719.0	65	1,106.0	73.50
1998	867.0	26	1,401.0	26	2,268.0	42	5,461.0	34.50

Figure 11-3. *Public, Private, and Total Exempt Property as Percent of Total Grand List, by Tax Year, 1915–1998*

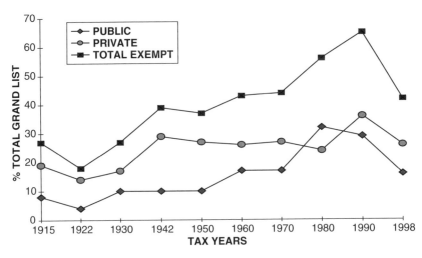

53–54). (These figures are in actual dollars, since costs in 1913 and 1933 were not significantly different.)

Besides their dramatic growth, two things distinguished the impact of Yale's exemptions from those accorded other types of organizations. First, in contrast to most government-owned property, most of Yale's holdings were located either in the central business district (CBD) or between the CBD and the Hamden town line. Both of these areas, if taxed as prime commercial or residential properties, would have yielded among the highest returns available. Second, with only 29 percent of Yale students coming from Connecticut (and a far smaller proportion coming from New Haven), the city was only an indirect beneficiary of the university's educational services. Third, although the institution once attracted wealthy tax-paying homeowners, by the 1930s this was no longer the case. Finally, changing student lifestyles and buying habits had decreased patronage of locally owned businesses. Dana also mentioned taxpayers' complaints that the university was competing unfairly with local businesses by subsidizing housing for visiting athletes and providing other on-campus services for students (ibid., 60–61).

Dana particularly criticized the property-tax exemptions granted to Yale and other eleemosynary entities; the exemptions for such groups, along with government-owed property, had reduced the city's 22.5 square miles of territory to "an effective tax-productive area of [6.25] square miles" (ibid., 66). He pointed approvingly to the 1929 agreement between Harvard and Cambridge—in which the university agreed to limit future acquisitions of exempt property and to make voluntary payments in lieu of taxes—as an example of what could be done, although he believed that the real solutions lay in a shift away from the tax system's reliance on real estate levies and in a reconsideration of tax-exemption policies (ibid., 99).

Urban Redevelopment, the Emerging Nonprofit Sector, and the Tightening Fiscal Squeeze, 1940–1990

Dana's concerns were eclipsed by World War II, which brought huge federal contracts to the city's leading employers and provided a quick fix for the fiscal squeeze New Haven had suffered during the 1930s. The Korean War sustained the boom into the mid-1950s. But once the nation had returned to a peacetime economy, the truth of Dana's observations became evident. He had urged New Haveners to face the fact that industries like Winchester and other arms producers were no substitute for the kinds of enterprises that could maintain steady employment and contribute to long-term economic development. These kinds of industries had begun leaving the city in the 1920s and were not being replaced. The release of pent-up wartime earnings also accelerated the movement of the middle classes to suburbia—a shift already well under way in the 1920s and that accelerated after 1950: Between 1950 and 1980, New Haven's population dropped from 164,443 to 126,109 (table 11-1), while that of contiguous towns doubled and tripled. The early immigrant populations were being replaced by black migrants from the South, attracted to the city by its war industries. Before the war, the black population, which represented less than 10 percent of the city, had been entirely concentrated in the Dixwell-Ashmun Street area. By the 1970s, blacks accounted for nearly half the city's population and occupied three major neighborhoods. Poverty and crime, along with the declining quality of public education, gave additional impetus to the abandonment of the city by white taxpayers. The loss of a resident middle class inevitably affected the city's business population.

As Dana had suggested, New Haven's plight was a manifestation of long-term economic and demographic trends affecting all older cities, especially those of the Northeast. But New Haven was a special case because of the extraordinary extent to which exempt properties had eroded, and would continue to erode, the tax base. When the urban plight became a matter of national concern in the early 1960s, New Haven was one of the cities where federal urban renewal and redevelopment programs were tested.

Fueled by federal and foundation monies, the city launched an ambitious series of initiatives that displaced nearly 20 percent of its population and reconstructed its commercial core (Wolfinger 1974; Humphrey 1992). Residential neighborhoods were paved over by new interstate highways. Office towers, parking lots, and a mall-hotel complex took the place of homes and small businesses. Large nonprofits—Yale, Yale-New Haven Hospital, and St. Raphael's Hospital—took advantage of the flood of new federal funding to expand. Between 1950 and 1990, the proportion of exempt property increased from less than 40 percent of the grand list to nearly 70 percent. While these developments enhanced the range of cultural, educational, health, and human services available and improved the transportation infrastructure, ensuring that suburbanites would continue to work in the city, they made it easier to live outside the city, ensuring that increases in economic activity benefited the suburbs, since the tax system remained narrowly based on real estate. By taking huge amounts of property out of the tax base (exempt property went from 27 percent of the grand list in 1950 to 56 percent by 1980, while the mill rate increased from 34.8 to 71.3), redevelopment drove taxes upward, ensuring the continued flight of taxpaying homeowners and businesses.

New Haven's population of nonproprietary entities underwent a transformation between 1950 and 1990 (tables 11-1, 11-3, and 11-4). Though the number of organizations remained stable, the composition of the organizational population drastically changed: In 1920, over 40 percent of exempt organizations were fraternal/sororal and other mutual-benefit and membership organizations; by 1990 only 2 percent were. Such groups were replaced by human service, health, education, and arts and culture providers, most of which received substantial government subsidies. These trends affected the tax base. The mutual-benefit entities were not tax exempt, and they seldom occupied real estate—when they did, they usually rented commercial space or, as in the case of the city's numerous Masonic lodges, shared a single site. The service-provider nonprofit orga-

Table 11-3. *Percentage of Types of New Haven Nonprofit Entities, by Year*

Year	Arts and Culture	Education	Health Care	Human Services	Mutual Benefit	Religious	Other
1850	5	6	2	11	8	46	22
1900	1	2	1	5	75	14	1
1930	2	5	2	7	53	21	10
1960	1	6	4	7	49	26	7
1990	2	7	10	18	15	33	15

nizations tended to acquire and occupy real estate, because the kinds of services they provided required specially adapted physical plants (e.g., clinics, theaters, classrooms, exhibition spaces).

Finally, there were changes in organizational location. Historically, nonprofits tended to locate near the populations they served. The settlement houses and major social service agencies, as well as a variety of fraternal, labor, and mutual-benefit associations, were concentrated on State Street, adjacent to the industrial and immigrant working-class neighborhoods. Five other such clusters existed: All in all, 20 percent of the city's nonproprietary entities in 1931 met in just six areas.[17] By 1990, the locational relationships between organizations and their constituencies had largely disappeared: There were no clusters of agencies comparable to those of 1931 and, to the extent that they clustered at all, their location was determined by the nature of the services they offered.[18] Most of the major new nonprofit clusters resulted from urban planners' efforts to create centers of

Table 11-4. *Births and Deaths of New Haven Non-Proprietary Entities (NPOs), by 30-Year Period*

Period	Number of NPOs at Start of Period	Number of NPOs at End of Period	Number of NPO Deaths per Period	Percentage of NPOs that Died per Period	Number of New NPOs per Period	Percentage of New NPOs per Period
1870–1899	130	458	85	65	415	91
1900–1929	458	676	256	56	474	70
1930–1959	676	595	427	63	276	6
1960–1989	427	630	310	72	513	81

community activity. Unfortunately, one consequence of the planners' zeal was the destruction of the older clusters' neighborhood-based loci for community life.[19]

Thus, by the 1990s, the city's nonprofits were unlikely to be located in or near communities in need.[20] The most important of them—the hospitals, colleges and universities, and arts organizations—had come to serve largely suburban regional constituencies (and even their employees tended to live in the suburbs). The small to mid-size agencies serving populations at risk appeared to prefer space in the middle-class neighborhoods where their executives and staff lived—or, if suburban, felt less threatened (table 11-5). These data suggest that the new service-provider nonprofits, rather than being community organizations in the sense of being "of, for, and by" the communities in which they were located and which they served, were community-serving organizations run by credentialled professionals, funded by public agencies, foundations, and corporations, and pursuing agendas set by constituencies other than those being served.

Legal Challenges to the Tax Exemption since 1950

As exemptions crept past 40 percent of the total grand list in the late 1940s and postwar demobilization began to affect the city's tax collections, New Haven heeded the warnings of the state tax commissioner and citizen activists like Dana and attempted to challenge the expanding tax-exempt domain. During the war, Yale had filled much of its vacant property with temporary housing for participants in military programs. After the war, it used these structures to house married students and their families. In 1949, the city sent Yale a tax bill for nearly $750,000, claiming that providing housing for married veterans and their families did not constitute an educational use, that the means by which Yale acquired the buildings (from the federal government) did not fall within the definition of donated property in the 1834 statute, and that the income derived from these properties (on which standard rent rates were charged) exceeded the $6,000 statutory limit (*Yale v. New Haven*, 17 Conn. Supp. 155 (1950)).

In the subsequent litigation, the judge, after carefully reviewing the history of Yale's tax exemption, narrowed the issue under consideration to the question of whether "the fact that Yale has undertaken to furnish quarters for married veterans with wives and families divests the prop-

Table 11-5. *Location of Nonprofit Organizations in New Haven Neighborhoods with Largest and Smallest African-American Populations, 1996*

Neighborhood	Population in Neighborhood	Number of NPOs in Neighborhood	African Americans as Percentage of Neighborhood Population	Percentage of Total NPOs in City	Percentage of Total African Americans in City
Newhallville	7,798	14	94	2	17
Dixwell	6,298	28	85	5	13
Long Wharf	1,655	29	60	5	2
Dwight	6,799	19	50	3	7
Hill	17,420	47	50	8	19
TOTAL		137		23	58
CBD	997	74	28	12	*
Yale	5,383	34	14	6	2
East Rock	9,290	93	7	15	1
Westville	6,904	32	10	5	1
Annex	5,362	5	8	0	1
Morris Cove	5,115	12	*	2	*
TOTAL		250		40	5
TOTAL IN CITY	130,550	622		100	63

* = less than 1 percent

erty here involved of the educational nature of its use." Judge Pastore took note of the increasingly expansive definition of what courts were construing as charitable uses—but saw these as justification for continuing to embrace Connecticut courts' historic liberalism in construing grounds for tax exemption. Thus, he ruled that the housing should be treated as exempt:

> The mere fact that there is no precedent here for use by married veteran students and families of college owned and maintained property held and devoted to the use of the university is a circumstance to be considered as to some extent indicative of the general sense of the community that it is not, or is beyond, an educational use, but the essential inquiry is not whether such a use in the past has constituted an educational use, but whether it does under existing conditions.

Interestingly, while giving considerable attention to the financial burdens the properties in question imposed on Yale (which claimed it was losing money on them), the judge gave no attention to the impact exemptions have on the city's tax base. He might, for example, have noted the costs to the city of providing education and other services to the children of the 130 families resident in Yale married-student housing.

The issues raised in 1950 were revisited in 1975, by which time fully half of New Haven's grand list consisted of exempt properties. *Yale v. New Haven*, 169 Conn. 4541 (1975), involved the city's efforts to tax the building housing Yale University Press, a lavish corporate-style structure completed in 1975. Yale had purchased the press's building in 1959, using it to house the press, the Yale Printing Office (which provided general reproduction services to the entire university), and study collections of the Yale Art Gallery. In its decision, the Connecticut Supreme Court took the liberal-construction rationale to its furthest possible length, citing the state's revised charities statute to rule that property held by Connecticut corporations "organized exclusively for Scientific, Educational, Literary, Historical or Charitable Purposes or for two or more such purposes and used exclusively for carrying out" such purposes was *prima faciae* exempt as long as no officer, member, or employee received pecuniary benefit in excess of reasonable compensation. In other words, by the 1970s, charitable exemption no longer hinged on what a corporation did or whom it served, as long as it observed the nondistribution constraint. Yale—and any other nonprofit in Connecticut—was free to provide any good or service for free or for a fee to anyone, regardless of need. Nondistribution had replaced public servingness as the criterion for determining charitableness and, hence, worthiness for exempt status.[21]

Thus liberated from constraints of public responsibility, the exempt portion of New Haven's grand list shot from 44 percent in 1970 to 65 percent in 1990 (table 11-2). Fifty-five percent of this exempt property was held by private nonprofit firms.

Political Challenges to the Tax Exemption since 1950

New Haven pursued a variety of political strategies to relieve the city's fiscal problems; the intensity of its efforts depended on variations in its economic fortunes. During the generally prosperous 1950s and 1960s, little effort was made to seek remedies. But with the election of Richard Nixon in 1968 and the termination of the Great Society programs, of which the city had been a major beneficiary, the fiscal squeeze worsened and public discontent grew. Rising taxes and inflation also served to increase New Haveners' tax sensitivity.

In 1969, Mayor Richard Lee requested that the university make a $9 million payment in lieu of taxes over a three-year period, stating that the total "is less than half the amount it would cost the University were its property not tax exempt" (quoted in Wareck 1985a, 16). Yale President Kingman Brewster expressed doubt about whether the university could legally make such a diversion of its funds. In response, Mayor Lee convened an Exempt Property Study Commission, which, in addition to underwriting an important study of the legal aspects of property tax exemption (later published in the *Connecticut Law Journal*; see Warren, Krattenmaker, and Snyder 1971), made a variety of recommendations, urging both a legislative effort, coordinated with other towns and cities, to change exemption statutes, and a systematic litigation strategy.[22] Yale contributed to the debate over tax exemption by commissioning a group of scholars affiliated with its Institution for Social and Policy Studies to study nonprofits and the financial problems of American cities, but the two-year seminar was the university's sole attempt to address these issues.[23]

Mayor Lee's successor, Bartholomew Guida, did his best to implement the commission's recommendations through litigation (the Yale University Press exemption challenge), through lobbying the legislature to change the exemption statutes and reimburse cities for the cost of exemptions, and through sheer obstinacy. Guida blocked Yale's efforts to construct new buildings by holding up building permits and zoning approvals until the university showed more flexibility on the exemption question. Rather than engaging the city in a productive discussion of alternatives, the university dropped its plans to construct two new residential colleges and, in designing its Center for British Art, put taxpaying commercial storefronts on its first story. The Yale Press moved to less lavish quarters. Ultimately, the university was able to work behind the scenes to have Guida replaced with a more-pliant successor who dropped the exemption issue.

The city's single success with the legislature was a 1978 statute requiring the state to reimburse cities and towns for 25 percent of the taxes they lose due to the real-property exemptions of nonprofit institutions of higher learning and nonprofit general hospital facilities (see Carbone and Brody, chapter 10 of this volume). But the legislature failed to make the necessary appropriations to cover its commitment: In 1982, New Haven was to receive $5.2 million, but it received only $3.2 million (Wareck 1985a, 17).

The Noose Tightens, 1980–1990

The national economic crises of the early 1970s and 1980s accelerated New Haven's downward spiral, reigniting demands for tax reform. In February 1982, the board of aldermen appointed a revenue commission to examine city finances and the impact of tax exemptions (Wareck 1985b). Stephen Wareck, a consultant, provided the commission an unusually thorough analysis of the impact of the property-tax exemption. He recommended that the legislature to review and change exemption laws; that federal and state governments make 100 percent PILOTs to municipalities for tax-exempt educational, medical, and government organizations, or else grant municipalities the power to add exempt properties to their tax rolls; that the city aggressively press the legislature for power to charge tax-exempt groups user fees for city services; and that federal and state governments reimburse hospitals for free medical care to city residents. Wareck devoted particular attention to nonprofits that were competing unfairly with taxpaying businesses.[24]

Yale refused to provide the commission with information about its revenues and properties, so Wareck recommended that the assessor's office "perform aggressive audits" of organizational finances "to determine if properties should be or should have been on the tax rolls" (ibid., 9). He also urged the city to force exempt institutions to file information on the value of their property, and that the list be published annually. Wareck also called for public reporting of exempt properties owned by state and federal agencies, and for an end to the exemptions granted telephone and television cable companies.[25]

The revenue commission's efforts were not successful: New Haven's nonprofits were able to obstruct the work through direct lobbying and use of a corrupt city government. The Speaker of the Connecticut General Assembly, New Haven Democrat Irving Stolberg, proposed legislation to consider the tax-law changes recommended by the commission, but withdrew it because New Haven Mayor Biagio DeLieto was "not supportive" (Dansker 1981).

In 1987, Yale and the city announced that the university would invest $50 million in endowment and other funds in housing, commercial, and industrial development over the next 5 to 10 years ("Yale Plans to Invest" 1987). But the city made no specific promises, and the only product of the plan, a high-tech educational facility called Science Park, was not a success.

The "Yale Deal" and Continuing Decline, 1990–Present

When a coalition of discontented liberals led a revolt against the Democratic machine and captured the mayoralty for black businessman and former Yale public relations officer John Daniels, New Haven felt a brief surge of hope. Yale urbanist Douglas Rae was appointed as the city's chief administrative officer, and many felt that the city's pressing fiscal problems would finally be tackled and the university brought into a working partnership with the city.

Though well-intentioned, Daniels lacked experience, and he inherited a city that had so underfunded its education programs that the state was threatening to take over its school system, and a $38-million budget gap, requiring him to consider massive layoffs of municipal employees and curtailment of vital city services ("City Workers Ask Mayor to Reconsider Layoffs" 1990). Yale's new president, Benno Schmidt, came to the rescue with a controversial proposal that enabled the city to meet its short-term obligations, offering payments and loans to help the city out of its financial problems. In return, however, the university extracted a promise that the city would not in the future challenge the exempt status of Yale properties unless the university changed their use.[26]

Later efforts, notably those of Mayor John DeStefano, called for property-tax reform at the state level, allowing the city government to avoid confrontations with Yale and to blame the inevitable failure of legislative tax-reform initiatives on the suburban representatives who controlled the state's deliberative body. Conspicuously, the issue of the status of property-tax exemptions was not addressed by either DeStefano or the commission; instead, they focused their attention almost entirely on alternatives to the property tax and to regionalization of government service provision. During his first two years in office, DeStefano pursued these efforts energetically, serving on the commission on tax reform appointed by outgoing Governor Lowell Weicker to make recommendations to the legislature (Judson 1994; Condon 1994; Swift and Williams 1994; Williams 1994). The election of Governor John Rowland, as part of the Republican sweep of 1994, put an end to property-tax reform. Very much the candidate of the affluent suburbs, Rowland came into office pledging deep cuts in government spending and elimination of or sharp reductions in the state's unpopular income tax (Ohlemacher 1995; Gladwell 1995).

After 1995, practical politicians could only regard tax reform as a lost cause. Efforts to reform exemptions would alienate New Haven's nonprofit community, which now dominated the city's economy, with four large nonprofits (Yale, Yale-New Haven Hospital, St. Raphael's Hospital, and the Knights of Columbus) employing more people than all other firms in the city combined. Nonprofits' ability to use their immense spending, hiring, construction, and property-acquisitions policies to defend their prerogatives—or to enhance the careers of politicians who served their purposes—meant that tactics used earlier, when the city still possessed a significant commercial and manufacturing sector, were unlikely to succeed. Partnerships with the nonprofits were the only real option.

Mayor DeStefano embraced the nonprofits, advertising New Haven as a resource in the cultural tourism market and considering promoting the city as a headquarters site for large nonprofits such as the Special Olympics.[27] Having abandoned tax reform, he attempted to build the city's tax base through economic development. The centerpiece of this effort was a proposal for a huge regional mall located at the junction of interstates I-91 and I-95. As originally proposed, the mall was to be entirely funded by the developers. But the availability of state economic development bonding turned out to be an opportunity that the city was unwilling to pass up—particularly as it enabled the Democratic machine to steer lucrative contracts to large campaign contributors.

Because the mall promised a short-term fix to the city's fiscal problems, the mayor choose to ignore the long-term problems that it posed. To begin with, every major publicly subsidized economic development initiative in New Haven for the past half-century had ended in dismal failure, in large part because suburbanites preferred to shop in suburban malls. In addition, the mall seemed likely to siphon off business from the city's struggling small businesses (Jones and Haar 2000). Further, because a significant part of the mall funding was to be underwritten by city-issued, tax-anticipation bonds, it would be a financial catastrophe for taxpayers if the mall failed to generate projected revenues. Finally—and most seriously—even if the mall were a success, under the current property-based tax regime, the city had no way of capturing revenues it might generate, except through the highly indirect and problematic route of general increases in property values.[28]

Despite an assortment of well-publicized (and well-subsidized) economic development initiatives, New Haven continued to lose tax-paying businesses. Efforts to promote "sustainable economic growth" proved disappointing, as businesses lured to the city with generous tax breaks failed to fulfill their commitments to the city. Resources were diverted into enterprises that employed few residents and contributed nothing to the tax base, like an annual corporation-sponsored tennis tournament, a minor-league baseball team, and an International Festival of Arts and Ideas. Little went into creating and maintaining the kind of communications, information, and transportation infrastructure needed to attract new businesses.

Early in 1999, an Associated Press story described the city's response to Yale's announcement that it would be spending $5 million in the coming year to acquire 10 centrally located properties: "Unlike in the 1970s, when Yale's plan to build a new dormitory raised a hue and cry that the school was trying to take over New Haven, today city officials see no cause for alarm" ("Yale Plans to Buy More New Haven Property" 1999). The story went on to reveal what lay behind DeStefano's assertion that Yale is "a place-based creature, so that growing it ensures a level of economic activity, diversity, interest, and excitement in the downtown." The school is the city's second-largest taxpayer, through state PILOTs worth about $18.6 million per year (the legislature having increased the percentage reimbursed) and nearly $2 million in taxes paid on non-exempt school property.

The Unanswered Question

In the end, the question posed by Arnold Guyot Dana in 1937—"whither the city? all cities?"—remains unanswered. The fundamental problems he identified remain unaddressed, and New Haven's problems have worsened. The state tax regime continues to favor the suburbs over the cities. The cities remain unable to expand their taxing powers to cover the cost of services provided the suburbs. The amount of taxable property continues to decline, as nonprofits take advantage of depressed real estate values to enlarge their holdings. As malls and inner-city redevelopment activities diminish the number of locally owned businesses, even the prospects of indirect enhancement of the tax base through general increases in the value of real estate seem dim. The current inflows of government economic redevelopment money allow New Haven and cities like it to merely postpone confronting the necessity for tax reform (table 11-6).

Through most of the 20th century, Connecticut tax law and practice have been characterized by two concerns: efficiency and equity. While the tax regime has become more efficient, it has also become steadily more inequitable, as the expansion of government and nonprofit domains has eroded the tax bases of cities, and as the gap between rich and poor increasingly expresses itself in residential patterns. Although the rhetoric of equity was a central feature of the tax commissioners' reports and of the public discourse on taxation during the 1940s, it has largely vanished from both. Today—in Connecticut at least—there is an almost Social Darwinian acceptance of tax inequity and social inequality.

While Connecticut jurists seem determined to adhere to the liberal construction of charities laws as they relate to tax exemption, the precedents set by Pennsylvania, Maine, and other states in recent court decisions and legislation may ultimately make it possible for cities—or even aggrieved citizens—to mount a successful court challenge to the state's tax regime. Such a challenge to Connecticut's system of school financing, which had led to deplorable underfunding of urban schools, succeeded nearly a decade ago—though the state and municipalities have been slow to respond to the court's order to remedy the situation (see Carbone and Brody, chapter 10 of this volume). Still, if a principle as seemingly hallowed as local control of schools can be overturned, there is no reason to believe that laws that produce similar inequities are immune from attack. Indeed, it seems likely that a major economic downturn and the failure of government-funded economic redevelopment schemes like New Haven's

Table 11-6. *Contributions to New Haven's Municipal Revenues, by Category, 1910–1999, in Millions of Current Dollars and as Percent of Total Revenue*

Sources of Revenue	1910 $	1910 %	1920 $	1920 %	1930 $	1930 %	1940 $	1940 %	1950 $	1950 %	1960 $	1960 %	1970 $	1970 %	1980 $	1980 %	1990 $	1990 %	1999 $	1999 %
Property Tax	2.04	80.0	3.60	86.0	7.2	74.0	8.2	80.0	11.2	42.0	N/A		42.4	71.0	66.3	52.0	120.5	38.0	137.3	31.0
Licenses, Permits, and Fees	0.04	1.6	0.015	1.5	0.9	1.0	0.5	5.0	0.4	4.0	N/A		4.4	7.0	1.3	1.0	5.1	2.0	7.9	2.0
Federal, State, and Local Governments	0.13	5.2	0.19	1.0	0.3	3.0	0.4	4.0	13.6	53.0	N/A		9.8	17.0	41.3	33.0	162.8	51.0	269.7	62.0
Program Income	N/A	N/A	N/A	N/A	N/A	N/A	N/A	N/A	N/A	N/A	N/A		N/A	N/A	0.6	0.4	1.3	0.2	4.7	1.0
Investment Income	0.03	1.2	0.04	1.0	0.2	2.0	0.1	1.0	0.3	1.0	N/A		1.2	3.0	4.8	1.0	2.8	0.8	3.9	1.0
Other Revenue	0.30	12.0	0.30	7.0	1.1	11.0	0.9	2.0	N/A	N/A	N/A		1.1	2.0	11.4	9.0	29.6	8.0	13.4	3.0
Total Revenues	2.50	100.0	4.20	100.0	9.7	100.0	10.1	100.0	25.5	100.0	N/A		58.9	100.0	125.7	100.0	322.1	100.0	436.9	100.0

N/A = data not available.

mall may again make exemption and equity issues salient to citizens and politicians. In light of this, nonprofits would do well to prepare themselves for increasing skepticism about the legitimacy of their exemptions.

NOTES

Reliable quantitative data on municipal taxation and tax exemptions in Connecticut are remarkably easy to find for years between 1900 and 1970, thanks to the biennial and quadrennial reports issued by the Connecticut Tax Commissioner. However, it is difficult to find this information for years after 1970: The reports are no longer published, and municipal tax officials, citing record-retention policies that allow them to dispose of certain kinds of records after 10 years, have thrown away invaluable assessment and grand-list information. In addition, political distortion of the assessment process—evident in New Haven's 1990 reassessment, which grossly undervalued exempt properties in the city—constitutes a significant obstacle to both scholarship and policymaking.

Nonetheless, I am grateful to the staff of New Haven's tax assessor, who gave me free rein to rummage through what remained of old records, and to the librarians at the New Haven Colony Historical Society, who called my attention to materials I would have otherwise overlooked and who cheerfully acceded to my often-outrageous duplicating requests. Michael Morand and Cynthia Farrar, from Yale's Office of Community Affairs, were unfailingly helpful in providing contemporary university publications on tax and economic issues. I am especially grateful to my colleague Harry S. Stout for giving me a copy of Arnold Guyot Dana's *New Haven's Problems: Whither the City? All Cities?* (1937)—the critique of municipal finance and tax exemption that inspired my own work in this area.

1. Property-tax exemptions have never, for example, been exclusively a charitable prerogative: Property belonging to government itself has always been exempted from property levies; and, over time, governments have extended exemptions to virtually any kind of activity or enterprise they wished to encourage, from early industrial enterprises to contemporary shopping malls.

2. New Haven has been chosen as the locus of this study for a number of reasons. First, because its political culture has been studied perhaps more exhaustively than any other city of its size (Dahl 1961; Miller 1966; Wolfinger 1974; Domhoff 1978; Polsby 1980; Humphrey 1992), there is an unusually extensive body of information about how the city and its institutions—public and private—operate. Second, its organizational population—particularly its nonproprietary entities—have been studied with unusual thoroughness (King and Huntley 1928; Dreis 1936; Hall 1999). Third, the city has been the subject of major studies on the role of charitable tax exemptions in municipal finance (Dana 1937; Meyer and Quigley 1977a; Heller 1979). Fourth, New Haven's situation is a good example of the fiscal dilemmas faced by municipalities whose commercial and manufacturing enterprises have been replaced by a nonprofit service economy.

3. Connecticut jurist Zephaniah Swift wrote,

> The state is divided into certain districts, called societies, which have the power of assembling, of holding annual meetings, of appointing a clerk, treasurer and

committee, of laying taxes, and appointing a collector to collect them. The major part of the inhabitants of a society have the power to call and settle a minister, and make agreements with him respecting his salary, which shall be binding on the whole, and their successors. They are to lay taxes annually for the support of the gospel ministry, and can appoint collectors, and enforce the collection. If the allowance for the maintenance of a minister, be too scanty, on application, the general assembly may grant relief, and where the preaching of the gospel is neglected for a year or years, the general assembly may grant a tax, and when collected, the county court may dispose of it for the use of the ministry in the society. Such are the powers vested in located societies (Swift 1795).

4. Like most of England's North American colonies—and, indeed, all European nations—Connecticut had an established church.

5. As Stephen Diamond suggests, tax exemptions—like most laws and legal practices—were customary, rather than being based on systematic rationales. The economic concepts underlying modern rationales for tax exemption required norms of universal taxation that did not exist in early America (Diamond, chapter 5 of this volume). Further, such concepts required a money-based economy, which did not exist in the colonies until the end of the 18th century. In rural Connecticut in the 18th century, although taxes were calculated as sums of money, they were likely to be collected in the form of levies of labor on town roads and other public works.

6. Of the $118,459 in donations and grants received by the college between 1701 and 1800, 72 percent came from government (Sears 1919, 24; Pierson 1983, 518–23).

7. For information on the democratic character of higher education in the late 18th and early 19th centuries, see David F. Allmendinger's *Paupers and Scholars: The Transformation of Student Life in Nineteenth-Century New England* (1975).

8. As noted, colonial towns had a wide range of responsibilities for health, education, religion, and infrastructure—but provided services through contracting. This pattern continued in the early 19th century, though chartered corporations were increasingly likely to participate in contracting agreements for services ranging from operating almshouses and asylums for the insane, blind, and deaf to building bridges and turnpikes. Although Massachusetts moved toward direct government provision of services in the 1830s, this shift did not occur in Connecticut until the 1860s.

9. In the 1820s and '30s, Jacksonian legislators and jurists throughout the country acted to restrict charities' capacity to hold property. New York's legislature restricted the testators' charitable bequests, and limited the size of endowments. The concerns that led to such legislation were voiced by Virginia Supreme Court Justice Henry St. George Tucker, who, in an 1832 decision, denounced the "wretched policy of permitting the whole property of society to be swallowed up in the insatiable gulph of public charities" (*Gallego's Executors v. the Attorney General*, 30 Va. (3 Leigh) 450 (1832)). These concerns did not rise from public unhappiness with tax exemptions, but from more general fear of mortmain.

10. The consequences of this divergence in preferences can be seen as early as the 1840s, when city residents, having suffered several disastrous fires and epidemics, began agitating for the creation of a public water supply. Over the course of nearly two decades, these efforts were thwarted by townsmen, who refused to be burdened with the cost of

services from which they were unlikely to benefit directly. The system was finally built by a private company headed by industrialist Eli Whitney, Jr., who justified his investment in part by the fact that his gun factory would be able to use the power generated by the water company's excess capacity (Hall 1993). Similar disagreements developed over the paving of streets, fire protection, schools, poor relief, and other public services.

11. An anecdotal tribute to Hadley's land-aggressive property acquisition involves the president standing in conversation with a member of the Yale Corporation near the formidable gateway to Grove Street Cemetery, which bears the motto, "The Dead Shall Be Raised." Hadley is said to have glanced at the motto and remarked, "If Yale wants the land, they will be."

12. The decision was perhaps unsurprising, considering the Connecticut Supreme Court composition. Four of the five justices had significant connections to Yale: David Torrance, Frederic B. Hall, and Charles B. Andrews had been awarded honorary degrees, and Simeon E. Baldwin was a member of the Yale College class of 1861. Torrance and Baldwin were members of the Yale Law School faculty. The justices had the good political sense to turn the task of writing the decision over to Justice Hamersley, the only one of their number with no Yale connections.

13. These figures were questionable at best: Since Yale police confined their attention to Yale properties, the benefit to the community as a whole was minimal; the calculation of "general aid to local students," based on endowment income divided by the number of current students from New Haven, was fanciful; the $200,000 in annual purchases of goods and services was the total of what Yale had purchased the previous year from *all* suppliers, many of whom were not based in New Haven; and the $1.3 million "estimated purchases by students and Yale visitors" was entirely guesswork. (It is difficult even today, with sales-tax receipts and survey techniques, to estimate this kind of figure accurately.)

14. To his credit, Stokes was not entirely disingenuous about increasing Yale's potency as a "factor for the good of the community." An Episcopal priest himself, he was instrumental in recruiting a leading social preacher, Charles R. Brown, as dean of the divinity school. Brown made Yale the national leader in training young men for alternative ministries in "practical philanthropy." Using New Haven as a laboratory, divinity school faculty and students conducted surveys of the city's social problems, and actively engaged in community service through the Yale Hope Mission and other settlement houses. Stokes also helped obtain foundation funding for transforming Yale's medical school into a modern research faculty with close ties to New Haven (now Yale-New Haven) Hospital. The medical school's program in public health, led by Charles-Edward Amory Winslow, made important contributions to the community. But these were exceptions to the rule. While Yale's counterparts among private research universities invested in schools of business management and public administration, which could have made contributions to New Haven's public life comparable to those made by the schools of divinity and public health, Yale made the humanities a higher priority than public service. Although President Angell tried to turn Yale toward the community through interdisciplinary enterprises like the Institute for Human Relations, the largesse of John W. Sterling, Edward Harkness, and Payne Whitney drew it in other directions.

15. See, for example, clergyman Washington Gladden's 1895 attack on the eagerness with which churches and colleges solicited "tainted money" from plutocrats like John D. Rockefeller (Gladden 1895); exposures of New York's wealthiest Episcopal parish as the

city's biggest slumlord (Russell 1909a, 1909b, 1909c; Baker 1909); and Thorstein Veblen's 1916 critique of business control of higher education (Veblen 1918). The period was also marked by intense struggles over municipal control of public utilities—a perennial issue in New Haven.

16. During his long tenure, Corbin used every means at his disposal to codify and standardize assessment practices. He attended national and regional meetings of tax officials, and held an annual conference for assessors and members of boards of relief (which reviewed assessments and granted relief to aggrieved taxpayers) that featured tax experts from Connecticut and surrounding states. He created a library of reference materials on taxation and assessment that he invited local officials to use. And he used his published *Biennial Reports* to educate local officials and to keep them abreast of statutory and judicial issues. Despite these efforts, on the eve of the war he was still complaining that

> in all but a handful of towns, too little time is given to the work required by the statutes; the compensation in general is inadequate; the property is not viewed and valued by at least two members of the board; valuations on previous lists are followed too closely; there is too little effort to equalize valuations between continuous and similar property, as explicitly required by the statutes, and, in too many instances, the property owner continues to be the co-assessor in determining and agreeing absolutely on the valuation which shall be placed on his property (State of Connecticut 1914a, 13).

17. In 1930, 40 organizations listed the Swedish Fraternal Building at the corner of Elm and State Streets as their meeting place; 22 others met at 117 Court Street, around the corner; and another 16 convened at 28 Crown, just off State Street. This was one of several similar clusters: 20 black voluntary associations met at 76 Webster or 139 Goffe; Catholic organizations were concentrated in the 400 block of Orange Street; 28 labor unions and fraternal/sororal organizations listed 210 Meadow Street as their address; and 16 Masonic organizations listed 285 Whitney Avenue as their meeting place.

18. Thus, for example, the major funders of social services and some of the key service providers (United Way, the New Haven Foundation, the Visiting Nurses Association, the Girl Scouts, and Family Counseling of Greater New Haven) were located in the Community Services Building at 1 State Street; health care agencies tended to cluster in the vicinity of the city's two major hospitals; social service agencies serving the African-American community were concentrated in and around Dixwell Plaza at 200-226 Dixwell Avenue; arts agencies clustered on Audubon Street, in or around the Greater New Haven Community Foundation building; the surviving Masonic lodges had made the Masonic Temple at 285 Whitney their headquarters; and the rest of New Haven's nonprofits occupied a variety of usually rented offices around the city—primarily in the Central Business District and the East Rock, Prospect Hill, and Yale neighborhoods (which together contained 35 percent of the city's nonprofits).

19. During renewal, the old Elm-Court-State-Crown area, which had once housed nearly 100 nonprofit associations, was razed and turned into subsidized housing and parking lots; the Meadow Street cluster, once home to 30 labor and fraternal/sororal entities, vanished under the Oak Street Connector, the major approach to I-95; 76 Webster Street, which provided shelter to a dozen African-American associations, was destroyed during

the renewal of the Dixwell area. Other clusters, like the concentrations of fraternal/sororal entities in Westville (at the Masonic Temple on Whalley Avenue) and Fair Haven (126 Grand) had fallen prey to the Depression, white flight, and aging membership.

20. The inverse relationship between the location of nonprofits and the location of the populations they served was evident: Only 23 percent of New Haven's nonprofits were located in the city's five predominantly black neighborhoods, which together contain 58 percent of the city's African-American population; in contrast, 40 percent of New Haven's nonprofits were located in the six neighborhoods with the lowest proportion of black residents (totaling a mere 5 percent of the city's African Americans). The locations of nonprofits most likely to serve the needs of low-income African Americans—civil rights, employment, health, and housing groups—reveal this pattern even more clearly: The four neighborhoods that were more than 50 percent African American were home to only two of the city's six civil rights organizations, 11 of 69 employment-related organizations, 13 of 56 health care agencies, and 7 of 32 housing agencies.

21. The court's nod to nonprofit commercialism and entrepreneurialism was affirmed when the legislature adopted the American Bar Association's Model Nonprofit Corporation Act, which shifted the fiduciary standards applying to charitable corporations, permitting these organizations to behave little differently than business corporations with regard to conflicts of interest, management of assets, and accountability to members, donors, and the public. In effect, the act meant that the only remaining differences between nonprofit and for-profit firms had to do with how they distributed their surpluses.

22. See City of New Haven Exempt Property Commission (1970) for full details on the proposals for possible legislative action.

23. Yale responded to continuing political pressure on the property-tax exemption by empanelling the Joint Study Group on Legal and Economic Relationships between Universities and Their Host Municipalities, a group of researchers from the law school and the Institution for Social and Policy Studies (ISPS), an entity established to bring the social sciences to bear on "real world" problems. The group commissioned scholarly research, which was presented during a two-year seminar of faculty and students from Yale and nearby institutions, as well as representatives from local business and governments (Meyer and Quigley 1977a, xv; see also Wareck 1985a, 17). Although the group was of extraordinarily high caliber, including such eminences as political scientist Charles E. Lindblom, economist John R. Meyer, and legal scholar John G. Simon (who later founded Yale's Program on Non-Profit Organizations), its findings tended to favor continuing exemptions for the university. Despite identifying trends that pointed to continuing deterioration of the city's economy (Meyer and Quigley 1977b), contributors to the seminar suggested that the city seek to increase its revenue base through economic development (Getz and Leone 1977a), alternative forms of taxation (especially income, payroll, and sales taxes) (Leone and Meyer 1977; Gadsden and Schmenner 1977), and user fees on city services (Kemper and Quigley 1977; Getz and Leone 1977b; Kemper and Schmenner 1977). The study determined that the university provided more services to New Haven than New Haven provided to the university.

The researchers have approached the exemption issue with a focus on whether the university had any equitable obligation to make tax payments or PILOTs to the city. They did not assess the extent to which New Haven citizens benefited from Yale's educational services, nor did they consider the potential impact of the city's continuing decline on the university. Overall, the group's conclusions enabled Yale to decline any responsibility to the community, and shifted the burden of improving New Haven's lot to the legislature—for only the legislature could empower the city to levy alternative taxes. Dominated as it was by representatives of suburban communities that benefited from avoiding the costs of the urban-based services they used and from ghettoization that kept the poor and African Americans sequestered, the legislature was unlikely to provide cities like New Haven significant relief.

The 1972–73 seminar was the last serious effort Yale or Yale scholars would make to study either local tax exemption or the city's problems. Although the seminar gave rise to the first university-based center for the study of nonprofit organizations—the Program on Non-Profit Organizations (PONPO)—few of the program's more than 250 working papers have addressed local property-tax issues. Efforts to convene a similar roundtable in the early 1970s ran into serious opposition. Although ISPS maintained a Center for the Study of the City for a few years, the program terminated when its urban specialist, Douglas Yates, was denied tenure. Without faculty interested in such programs, the urban-studies major briefly offered in the late 1960s and early 1970s passed from the scene. While its American studies, architecture, and sociology programs have from time to time offered courses focusing on urban issues, Yale has steadfastly resisted creating a formal urban-studies program or department, most recently in fall 1999, claiming that such specialized majors violated its commitment to liberal arts education ("Reject Urban Studies Major" 1999).

24. As Wareck wrote,

> Renting real estate to a bank is not a hospital function. Dispensing estate planning advice is not a healing art. Operating a pharmacy that competes with local taxpaying pharmacies, as does operating a film society, a repertory theater, and a golf course, open through various "guest" devices to the public at large. Operating a profit-making faculty medical practice, whose receipts have doubled to more than $47 million in the four years 1979–1983, raises the question whether legitimate teaching and research boundaries have been exceeded. Is teaching and research a camouflage for a medical business? Even though the proceeds of the business are devoted to the medical school, isn't the University practice of medicine nonetheless a business? If the University were devoting the profits from the operation of a supermarket to teaching and research, the supermarket would nonetheless be taxed. Private physicians pay taxes on their offices and equipment while keeping current in the latest medical and clinical practice, why shouldn't the University which is practicing medicine? (1985a, 7)

25. Wareck's observations were mild compared to those of Revenue Commissioners Richard Wolfe and Anthony Gambardella, who wrote a minority report attached to the revenue commission's final recommendations (Wolfe and Gambardella 1985). They declared: "New Haven, the seventh poorest city in the US, subsidizes the second richest university in America. New Haven delivers millions of dollars of costly public services free of charge to the university: a kind of reverse Robin Hood arrangement. Simple justice as well as New Haven's urgent revenue needs demand changing this situation now" (ibid., D1).

Gambardella and Wolfe were critical of the PILOT program enacted in the late 1970s, since it only compounded the inequities of the state tax regime, while allowing wealthy institutions a free ride (ibid., D4). The minority report concluded by expressing skepticism about New Haven's continuing—and continuously failing—efforts to promote economic development.

26. Not everyone was pleased with the "Yale Deal." "It's disgraceful opportunism on the university's part," said Alderman Jonathan J. Einhorn. "Yale should already be making payments in lieu of taxes for the services it uses, and the university has other taxable properties it refuses to place on the city's tax list. The agreement is an absolute home run for Yale and a disgrace for New Haven" ("Officials in New Haven" 1990). Many saw Yale's closing off Wall and High Streets as further indications of the university's fortress mentality toward the city. Shortly after the agreement was announced, protesters covered street signs in the area with stickers saying "Benno Boulevard: Property of Yale University," and throughout the city signs appeared with the motto, "Tax Yale, Not Us."

27. The mayor was able to ignore the tax-exemption question in part because of a peculiarity of the 1991 reassessment, in which the exempt proportion of the grand list dropped from 65 to 42 percent of assessed properties, despite significant increases in the amount of property acquired by nonprofits in the previous decade. This had the effect of diminishing the visibility of property-tax exemptions as a political issue.

Still, not everyone was willing to accept the situation. Some civic activists complained about the increasing concentration of human service providers in their neighborhoods, and sought to have the city impose a moratorium on the location of additional facilities—akin to Hartford's efforts to limit the number of nonprofits in the city (Martson 1996; Bass 1996). But this proved to be a losing proposition.

28. The mayor's understanding of New Haven's fiscal issues was clearly stated in an article that appeared in the June 1999 *Government Finance Review* (DeStefano 1999). DeStefano's extended description of his economic strategies mentioned privatization, renegotiation of union contracts, and other cost-cutting initiatives. Not a word was said about either tax reform or property-tax exemption.

REFERENCES

Allmendinger, David F. 1975. *Paupers and Scholars: The Transformation of Student Life in Nineteenth Century New England.* New York: St. Martin's Press.

Baker, R.S. 1909. "The Case against Trinity." *American Magazine* 68: 2–16.

Baldwin, Simeon E. 1884. An *Address upon the Expediency of Consolidating the Town and City Governments in New Haven.* New Haven: Published by the New Haven Civil Service Reform Association.

Bass, P. 1996. "A Little Dwight Lie." Column. *New Haven Advocate*, August 15.

Benham, J.H. 1873. *Benham's New Haven Directory and Annual Advertiser.* New Haven: Printed and published by J.H. Benham.

Bittker, B.I., and G.K. Rahdert. 1976. "The Exemption of Nonprofit Organizations from Federal Income Taxation." *Yale Law Journal* 85 (3): 299–358.

Carlson, M.F. 1998. "A Tale of Two Blocks: Institutional Land Assembly in New Haven, 1911–1928." *Journal of the New Haven County Historical Society* 45 (1): 2–30.

City of New Haven, Exempt Property Tax Commission. 1970. *Recommendations.* Unpublished manuscript. New Haven Colony Historical Society.

"City Workers Ask Mayor to Reconsider Layoffs." 1990. UPI, February 25.

Condon, T. 1994. "Cities Beset by Fallout from Property Tax." *Hartford Courant,* January 13, B1.

Connecticut General Assembly. 1834. "An Act in Addition to the Act Concerning Yale College." May Session. Chapter XXV, 510.

Dahl, R.M. 1961. *Who Governs? Democracy and Power in an American City.* New Haven: Yale University Press.

Dana, Arnold Guyot. 1937. *New Haven's Problems: Whither the City? All Cities?* New Haven: Privately printed for the author.

Dansker, B. 1981. "University Aid to New Haven Questioned." *New York Times,* May 3, 20.

DeStefano, J. 1999. "Strategies for Financial Recovery: The City of New Haven Experience." *Government Finance Review* 15 (3): 21–32.

Domhoff, G. William. 1978. *Who Really Rules?: New Haven and Community Power Reexamined.* New Brunswick, N.J.: Transaction Books.

Dreis, T.A. 1936. *A Handbook of Social Statistics of New Haven, Connecticut.* New Haven: Institute of Human Relations, Yale University.

Dwight, T. 1822. *Travels in New England and New York.* New Haven: S. Converse, Printer.

———. 1811. *Statistical Account of the City of New Haven.* New Haven: Walter and Steele, Printers.

Eliot, C.W. 1874. "To the Commissioners of the Commonwealth, appointed to inquire into the expediency of revising and amending the laws of the State relation to taxation and the exemptions therefrom." In *Report of the President and Treasurer,* 1874. Harvard University, Cambridge, Mass.: Printed by the University.

Gadsden, C.H., and R.W. Schmenner. 1977. "Municipal Income Taxation." In *Local Public Finance and the Fiscal Squeeze: A Case Study,* edited by J.R. Meyer and J.M. Quigley (69–100). Cambridge: Ballinger Publishing Company.

Getz, M., and R.A. Leone. 1977a. "Prospects for Economic Development: The New Haven Case." In *Local Public Finance and the Fiscal Squeeze: A Case Study,* edited by J.R. Meyer and J.M. Quigley (21–40). Cambridge: Ballinger Publishing Company.

———. 1977b. "Fire Fighting Benefits." In *Local Public Finance and the Fiscal Squeeze: A Case Study,* edited by J.R. Meyer and J.M. Quigley (121–142). Cambridge: Ballinger Publishing Company.

Gladden, W. 1895. "Tainted Money." *Outlook* LII (November 30): 886–87.

Gladwell, M. 1995. "Era of Cuts Misses Property Taxes; States Target Income Instead." *Washington Post,* March 2, A1.

Hall, Peter D. 1999. "Law, Politics, and Charities." Paper presented to the National Society of Fund-Raising Executives (NSFRE) conference, "Public Trust/Public Policy: Issues for Fund Raising Research," Alexandria, VA, June 17–19.

———. 1993. "Organization as Artifact: A Study of Technical Innovation and Management Reform, 1983–1906." In the *Mythmaking Frame of Mind: Social Imagination and American Culture,* edited by James Gilbert (178–208). Belmont: Wadsworth Publishing Company.

———. 1982. *The Organization of American Culture, 1700–1900: Organizations, Elites, and the Origins of American Nationality.* New York: New York University Press.

Heller, T.C. 1979. "Is the Charitable Exemption from Property Taxation an Easy Case? General Concerns about Legal Economics and Jurisprudence." In *Essays on the Law and Economics of Local Governments*, edited by D.L. Rubinfeld (183–251). Washington, D.C.: The Urban Institute.

Humphrey, D.C. 1992. "Teach Them Not to Be Poor: Philanthropy and New Haven School Reform in the 1960s." Doctoral Dissertation, Teachers College, Columbia University. Ann Arbor: UMI Dissertation Services.

Jones, D.P., and D. Haar. 2000. "'Cannibal' Effect Predicted for Mall; Report Reverses 1999 Findings." *Hartford Courant*, February 22, A3.

Judd vs. Trumbull, or Plain Truths: addressed to the real friends of the state of Connecticut of every sect, denomination, and party, whatever. 1820. New Haven: Printed by J. Barber.

Judson, G. 1994. "New Haven Mayor Pushes Property Tax Issue." *New York Times*, January 4, B5.

Kemper, P., and J.R. Quigley. 1977. "Refuse Collection Policy." In *Local Public Finance and the Fiscal Squeeze: A Case Study*, edited by J.R. Meyer and J.M. Quigley (101–20). Cambridge: Ballinger Publishing Company.

Kemper, P., and R.W. Schmenner. 1977. "Police Services—Their Costs and Financing." In *Local Public Finance and the Fiscal Squeeze: A Case Study*, edited by J.R. Meyer and J.M. Quigley (143–86). Cambridge: Ballinger Publishing Company.

King, W.I., and K.E. Huntley. 1928. *Trends in Philanthropy: A Study of a Typical American City*. New York: National Bureau of Economic Research.

Leone, R.A., and J.R. Meyer. 1977. "Tax Exemption and the Local Property Tax." In *Local Public Finance and the Fiscal Squeeze: A Case Study*, edited by J.R. Meyer and J.M. Quigley (41–68). Cambridge: Ballinger Publishing Company.

Martson, Olivia. 1996. "The Rights of City Dwellers." Letter to the Editor. *New Haven Advocate*, August 29.

Meyer, J.R., and J.M. Quigley. 1977a. *Local Public Finance and the Fiscal Squeeze: A Case Study*. Cambridge: Ballinger Publishing Company.

———. 1977b. "Fiscal Influences upon Location Patterns." In *Local Public Finance and the Fiscal Squeeze: A Case Study*, edited by J.R. Meyer and J.M. Quigley (1–20). Cambridge: Ballinger Publishing Company.

Miller, W.L. 1966. *The Fifteenth Ward and the Great Society: An Encounter with the Modern City*. Boston: Houghton-Mifflin Company.

New Haven Directory, Including West Haven. 1901. New Haven: The Price and Lee Company, Publishers.

New Haven Taxpayers' Association. 1885. *Second Annual Report of the Executive Committee to the Members of the Taxpayers' Association*. New Haven: New Haven Taxpayers' Association.

"Officials in New Haven Clash on Yale Tax Deal." 1990. *New York Times*, October 7, B3.

Ohlemacher, S. 1995. "Ways to Save Sought as Rowland's Budget Takes Shape: Will It Help Residents More to Cut Property Than Income Tax?" *Hartford Courant*, March 13, A3.

Pardee, W.S. 1911. *The Relations of New Haven and Yale University (The Relation of a Mother and Her Child)*. New Haven: The Tuttle, Moorehouse and Taylor Company.

Pierson, G.W. 1983. *A Yale Book of Numbers: Historical Statistices of the College and University, 1701–1976*. New Haven: Yale University.

———. 1955. *Yale: The University College, 1921–1937*. New Haven: Yale University Press.

Polsby, Nelson. 1980. *Community Power and Political Theory: A Further Look at Problems of Evidence and Inference*. New Haven: Yale University Press.

"Reject Urban Studies Major." 1999. Editorial. *Yale Daily News*, November 30.

Report of a Committee Appointed to Enquire into the Advisabililty of Establishing a Town Workhouse and into Methods of Supporting the Town Poor. 1887. New Haven: Tuttle, Morehouse and Taylor, Printers.

Report of the Committee to Investigate the Affairs of the Government of the Town of New Haven Appointed by a Special Act of the General Assembly Passed June 22, 1889. Hartford, Conn.: State of Connecticut.

Russell, C.E. 1909a. "Trinity's Tenements—The Public's Business." *Everybody's Magazine*, February: 279–80.

———. 1909b. "Trinity: Church of Mystery." *Broadway Magazine*, April/May. .

———. 1909c. "The Tenements of Trinity Church." *Everybody's Magazine*, July: 47–57.

Sears, Jesse B. 1919. *Philanthropy in the History of American Higher Education*. Washington, D.C.: Office of Education.

Simon, J.G. 1987. "The Tax Treatment of Nonprofit Organizations: A Review of Federal and State Policies." In *The Nonprofit Sector: A Research Handbook*, edited by W.W. Powell (67–98). New Haven: Yale University Press.

State of Connecticut. 1926. *Report of the Tax Commissioner 1925 and 1926 to His Excellency the Governor*. Public Document, No. 48. Taxation - Document No. 220. Hartford: Printed by the state.

———. 1918. "Administration of the Income Tax." *Report of the Tax Commissioner 1918*. Public Document, No. 48. Hartford: Printed by the state.

———. 1914a. *Report of the Tax Commissioner 1914*. Public Document, No. 48. Hartford: Case, Lockwood and Brainard Company.

———. 1914b. *Quadrennial Statement to the General Assembly of Property Exempted from Taxation*. Public Document No. 52. Hartford: Printed by the state.

———. 1912? *Report of the Tax Commissioner for the Biennial Period 1911 and 1912 to His Excellency the Governor*. Public Document, No. 48. Hartford: Published by the State.

———. 1906. *Report of the Tax Commissioner 1906*. Public Document, No. 48. Hartford: Case, Lockwood and Brainard Company.

———. 1819. *Public Statute Laws*, Chapter 2. Hartford: Printed by John Russell.

Stokes, A.P., Jr. 1920. *Yale and New Haven: A Study of the Taxation Question and of the Benefits Derived Locally from an Endowed University*. New Haven: Published for the university.

———. 1911. *What Yale Does for New Haven: A Study of the Influence of an Endowed University on the Financial Well-Being of its Home City*. New Haven: The Tuttle, Moorehouse and Taylor Company.

Swift, M., and L. Williams. 1994. "Regional Cure for Urban Tax Dilemma; Regional Cure Urged for Urban Property Tax Woes." *Hartford Courant*, February 8. B1.

Swift, Zephaniah. 1795. *A System of the Laws of the State of Connecticut*. Windham, Conn.: Printed by John Byrne for the author.

Veblen, T. 1918. *The Higher Learning in America. A Memorandum on the Conduct of Universities by Businessmen*. New York: B.W. Huebsch, Inc.

Walradt, H.F. 1912. "The Financial History of Connecticut from 1789 to 1861." In *Transactions of the Connecticut Academy of Arts and Sciences* (March 17): 1–139.

Wareck, S. 1985a. "Consultant's Conclusions, Comments, and Recommendations." New Haven Revenue Commission, 1981–1985. Unpublished manuscript. New Haven Colony Historical Society.

———. 1985b. "New Haven Board of Aldermen Revenue Commission. Report on Tax Exemptions. Partial Preliminary Draft Report." Unpublished manuscript. New Haven Colony Historical Society.

Warren, A.C., Jr., T.G Krattenmaker, and L.B. Snyder. 1971. "Property Tax Exemptions for Charitable, Educational, Religious, and Governmental Institutions in Connecticut." *Connecticut Law Review* 4 (2): 181–309.

Williams, L. 1994. "Task Force Backs Plan to Cut Local Property Taxes; Panel Backs off Rise in State Levies." *Hartford Courant,* December 23, A3.

Wolfe, R.D., and A. Gambardella. 1985. "Minority Report." New Haven Revenue Commission Final Report. Unpublished manuscript. New Haven Colony Historical Society.

Wolfinger, R.E. 1974. *The Politics of Progress*. Englewood Cliffs: Prentice-Hall, Inc.

"Yale Plans to Invest $50 Million in Endowment and Other Funds in New Haven." 1987. *New York Times,* May 21, A1.

"Yale Plans to Buy More New Haven Property; The Ivy League University Already Owns about 6.4 Percent of the City's Acreage." 1999. *Providence Journal-Bulletin,* January 3, 2B.

Zollmann, Carl. 1924. *American Law of Charities*. Milwaukee: The Bruce Publishing Company.

PART IV
Exploring Future Directions

12

Impact Fees

An Alternative to PILOTs

Woods Bowman

The charitable property-tax exemption is here to stay, although, as Weisbrod (1988) points out, it distorts input prices and gives exempt entities an incentive to hoard scarce urban land.[1] Municipal officials will be quick to add that the exemption also erodes the local property-tax base. They see the charitable tax exemption as an unfunded mandate, which troubles them because the property tax is the most reliable, stable, and predictable revenue source that most of them have. According to the New York Conference of Mayors and Municipal Officials, "More and more the state government uses the local property tax as a means of funding statewide social and economic policy. . . . State officials take the credit, and local officials and taxpayers pay the bills" (Baynes 1996, 9).[2] New York officials' attitude hardly seems unique, although in most municipalities in New York and elsewhere the charitable exemption is overshadowed by exempt government property and partial exemptions granted to individuals and for-profit businesses (Netzer, chapter 3 of this volume).

Evidence is fragmentary, but the value of charitable exemptions has probably lagged growth in other exemptions. Nevertheless, tax exemptions can cause distortions in land prices, leading in turn to perverse incentives that provide sufficient justification for a corrective policy. Because the economic effects of an exemption are the same regardless of the identity of the property owner, such a correction should also include the larger category of tax-exempt government property, particularly state-owned property. This chapter refers to "exempt entities" instead of "charities" to emphasize this point.

When property is removed from the tax roll, tax bills on remaining property will rise, public services will decline, or both. Depending on how the exempt property is subsequently developed, demand for services may rise, pushing tax rates still higher or causing current services to be spread more thinly. This chapter proposes a new form of community impact compensation (CIC, pronounced "kick") analogous to a development-impact fee, to relieve the burden on a community's taxpayers caused by rising tax bills or declining public service levels. But because every dollar taken from a nonprofit organization or government is one that cannot be used to further that group's mission, it is imperative that economic principles inform the discussion of the relationship between exempt property owners and their host communities.

The only current alternatives are PILOTs (payments in lieu of taxes) and SILOTs (services in lieu of taxes), which are unsatisfactory for several reasons: They increase the annual fixed cost to the property owner; their amounts are arbitrarily established, inviting periodic haggling with municipal officials; PILOTs in particular are secretively and unevenly administered (Leland, chapter 7 of this volume); and, perhaps most of all, even where PILOTs are pursued aggressively, they appear to raise a surprisingly small amount of cash (Glancey, chapter 9 of this volume). Needless to say, the philanthropic community is not pleased with PILOTs. According to the National Society of Fundraising Executives (NSFRE), "requiring payments from not-for-profit organizations in lieu of taxes would require [them] to increase fees for services provided, eliminate programs, and force them to raise additional philanthropic funds from the community to cover the payments" (1997, 2).

Trustees of tax-exempt entities, who accept a moral obligation to their host community in principle, nevertheless value the quasi-sovereignty that tax exemption confers (Brody, chapter 6 of this volume). Even trustees of wealthy tax-exempt entities are rightfully concerned about violating their "duty of care" by giving away money in the absence of a legal obligation,[3] increasing their organization's fixed costs—even by a small amount—and setting a precedent that could invite other, larger, demands in the future. Trustees would be expected to prefer SILOTs, which are mission-related, since the organization would incur the associated overhead costs in any event. Because overhead costs are quasi-fixed costs, the value of a SILOT to a host community often exceeds the real resource cost to the tax-exempt entity—a win-win situation. (Curiously—and perhaps pointedly—the NSFRE position paper cited above is silent on the subject of SILOTs.)

Trustees might be more amenable to making cash payments, however, if there were an economically acceptable theoretical framework that fixed boundaries for appropriate compensation. The trick is to use economic principles to develop a payment methodology that provides such a framework, is transparent and easy to administer, does not require annual haggling with elected municipal leaders, and preferably does not increase the fixed cost of operations. Of course, trustees and municipal officials would both be happy if the state stepped in and offered to pay PILOTs for tax-exempt entities equal to the property taxes that those groups would owe if their properties were taxed. Connecticut has had a program to reimburse a portion of the forgone tax (now at 77 percent) since the early 1970s (Carbone and Brody, chapter 10 this volume), but so far only Rhode Island has followed Connecticut's example (Rhode Island's reimbursement rate is now 27 percent), and state payments do not address the problem of distorted land prices rated by categorical property-tax exemptions.

An Alternative Proposal

The Theory behind the Property Tax

Before an alternative is introduced, a brief discussion of the mechanics of the property tax is in order, because the property tax differs from all other taxes. For every tax except the property tax, a legislative body establishes the rate by law, and revenue then rises or falls as the size of the tax base increases or decreases. An exemption for one group merely decreases the government's income; it does not increase the amount of tax paid by others. In the case of a property tax, however, the levy (the amount of money a city council or school board wants to raise) is established in law annually by the budget ordinance. The property-tax rate is then derived anew each year by dividing the levy by the tax base, which is the taxable value of real property. The fraction of all taxable property owned by an individual taxpayer determines his or her share of the levy.

Therefore, if one property owner, or class of owner, is relieved of the obligation to pay a share of the property tax, the taxable value of real property falls, and the tax burden shifts onto other property owners, who must pay more. Unlike other taxes, the property tax is zero-sum.

If the demand for public services decreased whenever property was removed from the tax roll, a shift in the tax burden might not be much of a problem, because the levy might fall, depending upon how the property was used after reclassification. The worst-case scenario from a local government's perspective would be that demand did not decline, so the levy would remain the same and tax rates on the remaining property would rise. New sources of revenue could, in principle, offset the shift by reducing the levy, but property levies are rarely observed to fall.

Theoretically, property tax differentials between communities should be capitalized into property values, meaning that property values will change by an amount equal to the present value of expected future differences in property-tax payments discounted over an infinite time horizon. The evidence bears this out. After reviewing the literature, Fischel (2000) concludes that the "persistent property tax differences among homes within the same housing market will be fully [100 percent] capitalized" (60). (See also Netzer, chapter 3 of this volume.)

Thus, property values are discounted whenever a community's tax-exempt sector expands. Persons or firms buying into the community would be able to acquire property there at a price lower than would have prevailed if the tax-exempt sector had not expanded. Assuming that the tax-exempt sector subsequently neither expanded nor shrank, the market value of the property would be the same when it was later sold, and its owner would realize neither capital loss nor gain.[4] As long as taxpayers live in the community, they will experience no tax disadvantage from the presence of exempt neighbors, *no matter how large*, unless those exempt neighbors acquire or develop additional property during the taxpayers' residency.

The only persons who would experience a capital loss are those who own property in a community when its tax-exempt sector expands. Such capital effects are realized only when property is sold *and* the proceeds are withdrawn from the community. If the seller buys property within the same community, he or she is buying at a similarly discounted price, and therefore experiences no capital loss. In effect, property-tax exemption imposes a lump-sum tax on owners of nonexempt property who take their capital *out* of a community, so this effect is referred to here as an "exit tax." Even though the exemption is in the form of a capital loss instead of a cash payment, it is a tax in every other respect: It is an involuntary payment and it need not bear any relation to the value of services received. (Of course, should the tax-exempt sector shrink, capitalization would increase the value of taxable property, creating an exit subsidy instead.)

It was on this basis that Quigley and Schmenner (1975) argued that "an old exemption is a good exemption," because people will adjust their behavior to accommodate existing tax structures, avoiding those that impose excessive costs. Quigley and Schmenner's research showed that exempt property was becoming more concentrated in central cities, and they expressed concern that taxpayers were taking increasing capital losses on their homes. The authors suggested replacing property tax with an income tax, or supplementing it with federal and state subsidies—proposals that did not get off the ground.

Instead, this chapter discusses the merits of a proposal to require that tax-exempt entities removing property from the tax roll, or developing property that is already off the roll, to pay compensation to taxing bodies *equal* to the aggregate amount of exit taxes imposed on all taxpayers. (A compensation payment neutralizes the sum of all exit taxes the exempt entity imposes on its host community, but is not an exit tax itself.) This proposal has all the advantages being sought: It improves the efficiency of property-tax exemption by pricing land closer to full resource cost; it does not increase the annual fixed cost to the exempt property owner; as a lump-sum payment, it forestalls periodic haggling with municipal officials; and it is transparent and easy to administer uniformly.

Before calculating CIC, let us first calculate the exit tax arising from an expanding tax-exempt sector as it falls on a single taxpayer, beginning with the equation defining the ith property-tax bill, x_i. The following derivation assumes only one class of property, but it is easily generalized to multiple classes assessed or taxed at different rates. It also assumes that tax-exempt property generates no offsetting external benefits to the host community. Thus,

$$x_i = Ra_i,$$

where a_i is the taxable (assessed) value of the ith taxpayer's property, $R \equiv (L/A)$ is the tax rate, L is the real property levy, A is the value of all *taxable* property within the community (i.e., the tax base), and $A > L > 0$. These inequalities simply ensure that the levy, while not zero, will not be literally confiscatory.

The total differential below shows the relationship among incremental changes in the system variables.[5] Since the rate may vary, we substitute L/A for R:

$$dx_i = (a_i/A) \, dL - (a_i \, L/A^2) \, dA + (L/A) \, da_i.$$

In equilibrium, $dx_i = 0$. The change in capital asset value, the exit tax, is da_i, thus

$$Exit \; tax \equiv da_i = - a_i[(dL/L) - (dA/A)].$$

Notice the negative sign indicating that, when the quantity in brackets is positive, residents experience an economic cost. (A benefit would carry a plus sign.) As expected, a shrinking tax base ($dA < 0$) or an increasing levy ($dL < 0$) raises the exit tax.

To calculate the community impact, we sum over all taxpayers (all i). Since the expression in brackets is constant and $\Sigma a_i = A$,

$$Community \; Impact = -A[(dL/L) - (dA/A)]$$
$$= -(dL/R) + dA$$

In the first equation, community impact is expressed in terms of a difference between percent changes. In the second, it is expressed as the difference between the capitalized change in the levy and the dollar change in the tax base.

So if a tax-exempt entity removes property from the tax roll but does not change the property's use, there will be no impact on the levy ($dL = 0$), and the community impact is simply dA. However, if the tax-exempt entity develops its property in such a way that it increases the levy (e.g., erecting buildings that require municipal water and sewer services), then $dA = 0$, and the community impact is $-dL/R$. Notice the signs in the second equation: Although dA carries a plus sign, dA itself is negative when property is removed from the tax roll, and dL carries a negative sign, indicating that the community receives a benefit when the levy falls and experiences a cost when it rises. CIC, then, is equal in magnitude to the community impact, but of the opposite sign, indicating that wealth is flowing in the opposite direction.

If a community is subject to a binding rate-limit constraint, the key variables A and L cannot vary independently, so

$$dL/L = dA/A.$$

The levy change effectively neutralizes the change in taxable property, causing the exit tax and community impact to be zero.

An example may help clarify these concepts. Evanston, a suburb of 70,000, bordered by Chicago on the south and Lake Michigan on the east, is home to Northwestern University, which had an annual budget in 1999 of $750 million—six times the budget of its host city. Northwestern's endowment is already larger than the market capitalization of United Airlines, and its capital campaign is expected to raise $1.4 billion. Northwestern occupies 263 acres of prime lakefront real estate, or 5 percent of the land area of the city—more than all other nongovernmental tax-exempt property in the area combined. It is little wonder that Evanston sees Northwestern as a deep pocket—in 1990, the city council, flexing its home-rule powers, enacted a tax on college tuition.[6]

However, the city itself owns 228 acres (not counting streets and alleys), and all governmental entities combined own more than twice as much as the university. Private individuals claim partial property-tax exemptions totaling 5 percent of all taxable property—about the same as the proportion of land owned by Northwestern. If Northwestern began paying property taxes, the average residential tax bill might fall by between 5 and 20 percent. The cumulative effect of various assumptions is responsible for such a wide range.[7] The change would probably be in the lower half of the range, between 5 and 10 percent.

Now assume that the university acquires $1 million in residential property for classrooms and laboratories from a tax-paying owner. The assessed valuation, on which the property tax is based, averages about 20 percent of fair market value for residential property.[8] Thus, the tax base would shrink by $200,000 and, if levies and service levels did not change, the dollar value of the community impact due to the university's purchase would likewise be $200,000, divided among overlapping taxing bodies in proportion to their tax share on the affected parcels. Further, assuming site-acquisition cost would be 10 to 15 percent of project costs, community-impact compensation would add 2 or 3 percent to the cost of the project—a manageable amount for the university and, best of all from the school's perspective, a one-time payment that could be rolled into a capital campaign to cover construction costs.

Community-impact compensation represents the capitalized value of the effect of exemption on tax bills. But because capitalization may not be 100 percent, CIC is not the same as the present value of forgone tax receipts (the *capitalized* value of a perpetual stream of tax receipts). In equilibrium systems, where all costs and benefits are internalized and actors have perfect foresight, full capitalization and convergence between capitalization of the exemption and capitalization of the current tax bill could be expected. In this example, using tax rates prevailing in 1999, Evanston would lose approximately $22,000 annually. The discount rate equating a perpetual annuity of $22,000 with a lump-sum payment of $200,000 is 11 percent. Thus, a municipality receiving a CIC could invest the lump sum, and in effect create an endowment equal to the value of property removed from its tax roll. It could replace about 45 percent of lost tax revenue by investing in virtually risk-free U.S. Treasury bills at the 5 percent rates prevailing in mid-2000, and might actually generate more than enough to replace lost revenue by accepting greater risk. Of course, the municipality could also spend its CIC at one time, but this would not be prudent unless the city were to use the one-time payment to increase its capital stock.

Should compensation be made to all overlapping taxing bodies? The model used here would indicate that all taxing bodies should receive CIC. People move in or out of a community in response to the entire package of public services and tax rates. If a particular service (e.g., the quality of the school system) is a factor for many people in deciding where to live, movers who value that service will set the price for others bidding against them (e.g., those with school-age children will set the price, even though other bidders do not have families involved in the school system). In other words, even if a taxing body does not provide service to property per se, its budget is still relevant, and changes in its budget will be reflected in property values.[9]

CIC penalizes tax-exempt entities that hoard land and improves economic efficiency, transferring resources to local taxing bodies to balance out the negative effect that removing property from the tax roll has on the localities' budgets. An exemption for any *class* of property, regardless of ownership, should give rise to CIC. CIC should apply to public and private colleges and universities, as well as to both public and private nonprofit hospitals.

To be logically consistent, communities should compensate tax-exempt entities whenever property held by those entities is returned to the tax roll, enlarging the tax base and generating a capital gain to tax-payers. Whether this assumption is logical or not, however, it is safe to anticipate that communities will resist doing so. Consider what happens as property values rise over time: As long as the value of tax-exempt property rises at the same average rate for the community as a whole, the perpetual annuity generated by CIC will be the same as the revenue a host community would receive if it taxed exempt entities as it does other property owners. This result occurs because the property tax is zero-sum; as long as all property values rise or fall at the same rate, individual properties will continue to pay the same relative share of the levy. The only circumstance in which a community experiences an opportunity loss is if the value of tax-exempt property rises *faster* than the average value of taxable property. Then and only then does the difference between CIC and forgone taxes represent a continuing subsidy to the charitable sector.

Differences in the growth of property values between the taxable and tax-exempt sectors are hard to measure because in most places tax-exempt property is not assessed (Netzer, chapter 3 of this volume). In any event, future taxpayers will not be harmed because they will incur no cost, having bought into the community at a discounted price. Therefore, a policy swap may be proposed: Tax-exempt entities forgo recapture rights, and the local community accepts the fact that it *may be* providing a continuing, albeit smaller, subsidy.

The story is not over, however. A CIC payment will overcompensate a host community if the community's charitable sector produces localized positive externalities—benefits that are distributed free to the community at large—that are not taken into account when the CIC is calculated. The most commonly cited positive externality associated with higher education is the benefit that comes from having well-educated neighbors, as might be the case in an area near a university or hospital. Many externalities, like this one, spill over the boundaries of a host community. There is no reason a tax-exempt entity would confer positive externalities on its host community in an amount equal to the property tax the community loses, except by chance. The swap proposed here implicitly assumes that the tax-exempt sector creates zero positive externalities to host communities. Any error this assumption introduces is a second-order problem compared with those created by the status-quo exemption of certain property, so positive externalities do not seriously compromise the proposed policy swap.[10]

Development-Impact Fee Analogy

A lump-sum payment associated with real estate development is not novel, but it has not been applied in this way before. This proposal extends the concept of "development-impact fee," an accepted urban planning tool.

> Development-impact fees aim to require new development to account for its fiscal impact on the community by accounting for its proportionate share of the cost of new or expanded capital facilities. . . . One of the major advantages of impact fees over other alternatives is the relative ease with which they can be designed, adopted, implemented, and changed. They have the very significant advantage of being administratively efficient. . . . Because of their many practicalities and acceptance by the courts, impact fees are becoming institutionalized. (Nicholas, Nelson, and Juergensmeyer 1991, xix)

Development-impact fees developed after the nationwide tax revolt of the late 1970s and early 1980s, inspired by California's Proposition 13, that raised the bar for passing bond issues for capital projects through public referenda. Although only 11 states have statutorily authorized development-impact fees, local governments elsewhere have used their police powers over land use to enact the fees. Some scholars (e.g., Bauman and Ethier 1987) argue that development-impact fees now exist in some form in all 50 states. CIC would be easily recognizable by planning professionals, state legislatures, and the courts. However, there is an important difference:

> [Development-impact fees] generally fall within the general system of land development regulation as contrasted with revenue-raising (taxation) programs. The objective of development-impact fees is not to raise money. Rather, the objective is to ensure adequate capital facilities. (Nicholas et al. 1991, 3)

Local governments wishing to raise money for operations, in addition to ensuring "adequate capital facilities," could not enact CIC without explicit statutory authority.

Local governments might obtain half their objectives without changing state law, by adopting development-impact fees linked to expansion of exempt entities solely to upgrade public infrastructure. While legal advice is beyond the scope of this chapter, it seems clear that, in the absence of statutory approval, courts would insist that several criteria be met before development-impact fees encompassing charitable real estate development were authorized:

- Fees may be no greater than necessary to compensate for capital costs.
- Capital costs cannot be calculated on an ad hoc basis; there must be a comprehensive, community-wide capital improvement plan (CIP) to support cost estimates.
- Fees cannot be linked to ownership status (e.g., charitable, proprietary, government). Thus, fees would have to apply to all hospitals, not just nonprofit hospitals. Fees must apply to all institutions of higher education: nonprofit, state-sponsored, and public community colleges.
- Fees cannot be a property tax in disguise, so those linked to improvements must take account of different property purposes and uses.

If development-impact fees as presently interpreted by the courts were applied without explicitly permissive statutory language, they could not compensate for reclassification of property into the tax-exempt sector, and they would compensate for only capital costs, not all costs. In the language of the equations used above, development-impact fees compensate neither for dA/A nor for the portion of dL/L attributable to operating costs. An authorizing statute must recognize that raising revenue is a legitimate purpose before lump-sum fees can be used to compensate communities for expansion of their tax-exempt sectors.

This proposal gives policymakers a new tool for balancing local government's need to raise resources against exempt entities' need for public support. State legislatures enacting CIC may want to limit the laws' application to communities where exempt entities hold a large fraction of the area's land.[11] A threshold is a crude but effective way for lawmakers to recognize an increasing rate of marginal dissatisfaction with *new* tax exemptions as a function of tax-exempt property already in the community. Legislatures may also limit CIC to certain kinds of property within a class (e.g., parsonages and parking lots), while leaving other kinds of property untouched (e.g., places of worship).

State legislatures enacting CIC laws may want to include a waiver provision to allow each separate unit of local government or school district to instead negotiate a services in lieu of taxes (SILOT) agreement with individual property owners. Requiring CICs would encourage tax-exempt entities to think of creative ways they could help their host communities, since they know the default option would be to pay compensation. Both parties win if the present value of the service is *more valuable* to the local community than the projected CIC, and if the present value of the marginal cost to the exempt entity is *less* than the projected CIC.

In order to minimize problems of asymmetric information, SILOT agreements should be renegotiated after a fixed term, such as 10 years.[12] At the beginning of the agreement's term the exempt entity seeking a waiver should file a capital development plan that describes property acquisitions and development planned over the course of the term. Substantial deviations from the plan, except unanticipated gifts of real estate, would void the agreement. Such a requirement would not create an unreasonable burden, since large, well-run organizations have capital plans anyway. Tax-exempt entities in particular need such plans to support their fund-raising campaigns. SILOT agreements may be configured to provide an explicit quid pro quo. For example, the property-tax exemption for nonprofit hospitals is criticized on the grounds that hospitals do not provide enough charity care to their host communities (Hyman 1990); some research (e.g., Bowman 1999) shows how hospitals can be given an incentive to provide charity care by taxing them but offering offsetting tax credits.

State governments would probably find CIC payments more acceptable than PILOTs as a way of helping the governments' own host communities. Seventeen state governments already recognize an obligation and have enacted statutes that purportedly bind them to provide financial support for host communities in which their facilities are located. But even within this well-meaning group, enforcement is incomplete and haphazard. Minert (1997) has found, for example, that

> Payments cover 90 percent or more for services in Connecticut, 84 percent in Wisconsin, about 17 percent in Michigan, and only a token amount in New York. Payment programs in Delaware, Kentucky, New York, Vermont, and Virginia apply only in their capital cities. . . . Colorado, Maryland, Minnesota, Missouri, Nevada, and Pennsylvania make payments in lieu of property taxes to local government, but only for state-owned forest, wildlife, park, and recreational lands. (1)

Baynes (1996) reports that, in New York,

> Not all state-owned land is exempt from property taxation. . . . The full-value of state-owned property in New York is $45.6 billion, upon only 6 percent of which the state voluntarily pays property taxes. The state's property tax payments amount to $79 million, with the state also making $3.4 million in PILOT payments. . . . (16)

States that do not currently make payments would probably be less resistant to making a lump-sum CIC than an ongoing annual payment. Moreover, CIC would be part of development costs, which state governments usually finance by issuing bonds, a relatively painless method of paying for long-term projects. Local governments would also have the necessary tools to enforce compliance, such as refusing to record a transfer of deed or withholding a building permit until the state meets its CIC obligation.

The proposal presented here addresses the concerns charitable organizations have, as laid out in the introduction. It requires legislative action, thereby solving the duty-of-care problem. The theoretical framework described in this chapter sets parameters for legislative action and subsequent implementation, including possible negotiations over SILOT offsets. Because compensation is paid only when real estate is developed, the proposal neither exposes an organization to continually escalating demands through periodic negotiations with local officials nor increases fixed costs.

The proposal has some shortcomings, of course: A cash-poor tax-exempt entity might receive a gift of land that it is not allowed to incorporate into its inventory until the group (or the donor) pays a CIC. But this is not fatal, because the organization could use the property as collateral for a loan to pay the CIC until its fortunes improved, or could sell the property (unless the gift were restricted).

The proposal might also be affected by barriers to entry into nonprofit (tax-exempt) industries. Would the additional costs the proposal imposes on start-ups discourage the founding of new churches, schools, low-income housing for special populations, and health care facilities (the most land-intense nonprofit organizations)? It seems unlikely that that would be the case. The vast majority of new organizations start off in leased quarters, where they pay property tax as part of their rent. The real barrier to property ownership is attracting donors of sufficient means to finance acquisition. Despite the inducement of the property-tax exemption, many storefront churches will never graduate from leasing to ownership. The proposal discussed here may *delay*, but probably will not prevent, start-ups from acquiring real property. But the proposal may mean that when an exempt entity finally acquires the property, it will not buy as much. Still, a 10-percent increase in acquisition cost is unlikely to put much of a crimp in acquisition plans, or to significantly hamper the tax-exempt sector as a whole. The change in consumption patterns would not be entirely unwelcome: The point of this proposal is to discourage mindless acquisition of property and hoarding of scarce urban land.

The problem, if there is one, is not about entry; it is about exit. Property-tax exemption creates a barrier to exit. By lowering exempt nonprofits' fixed costs, the property-tax exemption makes it less likely that such groups will be forced out of business by economic hardship. Although CIC does not raise the fixed costs of operations, it is still a cost and, as such, would lower the exit barrier by a modest amount, encouraging the departure of nonprofits that were not providing services efficiently.

Consider the following three situations: Tax-exempt entities swap property; a tax-exempt entity actually creates land, as Northwestern did when it filled in the Lake Michigan shoreline; and an entity enjoys its tax-exempt status as a result of a legislatively granted charter, which can be amended only by mutual consent. CIC is essentially a tax on the privilege of taking property off of the tax roll, so if tax-exempt entities swapped property, there would be no change in the amount of exempt property (even if the parcels were located in different tax jurisdictions), and hence no CIC would be required. Likewise, if an entity owned waterfront property and had the ability to create land, it would not be removing property from the tax roll when it created land, and should not be liable for a CIC payment. The last question would undoubtedly be litigated, but if CIC were imposed on the seller (or donor) when real property was removed from the tax roll, a strong argument could be raised in defense of a fee. Subsequent improvements probably could not be subjected to CIC obligations.

Conclusions

What would Evanston's public finances look like today if CICs had been used since Northwestern University's founding, 150 years ago? (This question is hypothetical—especially because Evanston did not incorporate until 13 years after the university's founding.[13]) According to the exit-tax model, it is doubtful that the lack of CICs has had any great adverse impact on residential property values. But it is helpful to use some basic calculations to estimate the size of the current community endowment that could have been generated by 150 years of CIC payments.

John Evans, after whom Evanston is named, paid $25,000 for the 360 acres he gave to establish the university. Assuming the property was assessed at 11 percent of full value, the current rate for vacant land, the initial CIC would have been $2,750. Had this small sum been invested in the stock market for a return of 8 percent per year (an average risk-free return of 4 percent, plus an average risk premium of 4 percent), it would be worth $283 million today.[14] However, local officials would not have been likely to wait patiently until 2001 to use this resource. If they had spent the risk premium during the past 150 years, while the principal grew at the risk-free average of 4 percent, the community endowment would now be nearly $1 million. (This is not a misprint. A few percentage points, when compounded over 150 years, make a big difference.) Assuming a 6 percent risk premium, which is more typical of the recent past, the amount available for appropriation would be $60,000.

No doubt local officials would scorn this petty amount, but it is just the tip of the iceberg. The CIC proposal calls for an impact fee on property improvements. Under the more conservative assumption that *all* earnings are spent (not just the risk premium), then the base for calculating the community's endowment is the un-depreciated book value of improvements to the university's Evanston campus, or about $650 million.[15] This actually understates the gross value of improvements, on which CICs are calculated, because old buildings are taken off of the books when they are destroyed to make room for new buildings. Using these very conservative assumptions, a CIC equal to 2 percent of estimated improvement costs could have generated an endowment of $13 million, and, given a 6 percent risk premium, $780,000 a year available for appropriation. A 3 percent CIC could have provided nearly $1.2 million a year.

In this example, CIC payments generate less than Evanston and its school districts might raise if they could tax the university directly. The difference serves to emphasize that CICs are not simply a property tax by another name, but rather are fees that compensate a host community for additional costs—whether they arise from a need to expand infrastructure, from new service demands, or from capital losses on residential property. Furthermore, the amount of money is significant. Keep in mind that the calculations above assume that CICs had been in place for a long time. In the beginning, CIC would raise modest amounts, but for large cities (and probably Evanston) it would be a steady source of revenue.

The idea of endowing a municipal government is somewhat fanciful, and by itself should not be taken too seriously.[16] It is merely an analytical device that provides a contemporary value for revenue streams occurring over long periods of time. Nevertheless, it also serves to highlight the choices that municipalities and school districts have about using CIC windfalls. Unlike annual PILOTs, which are swallowed up as merely another source of revenue for operating budgets, CICs are episodic. Those generated by improvements to property are linked to the costs imposed on the municipality by those improvements. CICs force communities to think carefully about the nature and scale of their costs— a beneficial exercise in its own right.

Perhaps the best feature of this proposal is that it aligns the interests of the community with those of its tax-exempt sector, turning adversaries into allies. Some communities embrace their tax-exempt sector, while others are loath to see it expand and grow. However, if communities received compensation when, and only when, land is acquired or improved, they might be more willing to accept growth and expansion, and might even come to embrace it. It is worth a try.

NOTES

1. This essay is based on a paper presented at the 26th Annual Conference of the Association for Research on Nonprofit Organizations and Voluntary Associations (ARNOVA) on December 6, 1997, in Indianapolis. The principle articulated here is the same whether the exemption is awarded to charitable organizations or to governments, and is based on what economists call partial-equilibrium analysis. The theory of the second best ("The General Theory of the Second Best," by R.G. Lipsey and K. Lancaster, 1956), which takes a general equilibrium point of view, cautions analysts to look at all other distortions caused by the tax system. It is possible that distortions in market prices caused by exempting certain property from taxation are a useful correction of distortions caused by other tax policies. To the author's knowledge, there is no research on the question as it applies to the charitable property-tax exemption, so this chapter leaves the issue open.

2. Mullen (1990) studied the total tax burden arising from all overlapping governments in a sample of New York towns and villages, and concluded that property-tax exemption does indeed limit local fiscal capacity. Note, however, that municipal officials are just as hard on the state: "Unfortunately for the large majority of municipalities and property taxpayers in New York, the state has no equitable statewide policy on property tax or PILOT payments to all of the local governments providing essential services to state properties" (Baynes 1996, 16).

3. It seems probable that a decision to make a PILOT would be covered by the nonprofit version of the "business judgment rule."

4. Of course, there would be general property inflation, or possibly deflation, but as long as the value of all property changed at the same rate, the share of property taxes paid by any taxpayer would remain unchanged, just as if the value of property had remained constant. For simplicity's sake, this discussion generally assumes that price changes affect all properties more or less equally.

5. In the notation of calculus, dx_i represents an incremental change in the ith property owner's tax bill, dL represents an incremental change in the levy, dA represents an incremental change in the tax base, and da_i represents an incremental change in the taxable (assessed) value of the ith taxpayer's property.

6. The mayor vetoed the council's action, and the council could not muster the majority to override the veto. Subsequently, the state barred all local governments, even those with home-rule authority, from taxing tuition.

7. Land-use data are from the city of Evanston. Data on the value of exemptions are from the Cook County Clerk's office. Both are 1996 figures. Cook County classifies property; if the Cook County Assessor were to assess Northwestern University for tax purposes, the property would likely fall into the commercial category, which has an effective tax rate about three times that of residential property. Commercial property is notoriously hard to assess, and most large commercial property owners persuade the assessor to lower the "full value" below market value. Assuming that Northwestern could persuade the assessor to figure the property's full value at two-thirds of its market value; that the school owns 5 percent of all land, or 8 percent of *taxable* land, in the county; and that the market value per square foot of the school's property is about the same as the market value per square foot of residential property, then Northwestern would pay about 15 percent of total property taxes. If we further assume that tax levies would rise to capture some of this new taxing capacity, and that lakefront property is on average 25 percent more valuable per square foot than landlocked property, then residential tax bills might fall by 10 to 20 percent. The results are very sensitive to how the assessor would value the property. If, as expected, the assessor were to calculate a lower full-value figure, the reduction in residential tax bills might be half as much—between 5 and 10 percent.

8. The "assessed valuation on which the property tax is based" is called the "equalized assessed valuation." It is adjusted by the state Department of Revenue to compensate for different average assessment rates among counties. Sales-assessment ratio studies show that the Cook County Assessor assesses residential property at 10 percent of full value. The adjustment factor applied by the state Department of Revenue is about 2, so the equalized assessed valuation is about 20 percent of full value.

9. However, taxing bodies that cover all or most of a metropolitan area should not be compensated, because they do not influence where people choose to live. In Evanston's case, this criterion rules out Cook County, the Forest Preserve District, and the Metropolitan Water Reclamation District.

10. Theoretically, a tax-exempt entity's economic impact on its host community, in terms of employment and increased taxable business activity, is irrelevant to tax policy. Were it not so, every commercial and industrial business enterprise would be entitled to exemption from the property tax. However, at a practical level it is relevant. We observe communities competing to entice for-profit companies to locate within their borders by offering tax breaks. If Northwestern were to move to a new location, there would probably be a long list of communities vying for its favor.

11. Of course, states cannot compel the federal government to pay taxes, but this proposal can give guidance to Congress for appropriately compensating local governments. Land area is used instead of value to simplify the calculation and to avoid the need to assess nonprofit-owned property in states that do not now do so.

12. "Asymmetric information" is an economist's way of saying that one party to a transaction (in this case the exempt entity) has more knowledge of the facts essential to striking a fair bargain.

13. The founding grant was 360 acres. With additional purchases, the university eventually owned 630 acres, but it then divested itself of most of its holdings. For the last 40 years, the school has owned 240 to 260 acres, including 84 acres that were reclaimed from Lake Michigan at a cost of $9 million.

14. Estimates for total returns over the 150 years between 1850 and 2000 are inferred by averaging data for two periods: 1802–1990 and 1871–1990 (reported by Siegel 1992). For stock returns prior to 1870, Siegel used bank and railroad stocks only; after that date, he used the average returns of all stocks traded on the New York Stock Exchange. He constructed the risk-free rate by subtracting the risk premium from the commercial-paper rate. He also estimated that the CPI (if such had existed in the 19th century) would have averaged just below 2 percent since 1802. To obtain an estimate of the currently prevailing risk premium, I use data for 1966 through 1990. All estimates are conservative, inasmuch as they do not take account of the bull market of the 1990s. All rates have been rounded to the nearest one-half percentage point.

15. The figure reported as undepreciated book value of land, buildings, and equipment on Northwestern's financial statements has been adjusted to exclude the book value of the medical school's campus in downtown Chicago, assuming that it represents about 25 percent of the total. However, the figure includes the cost of equipment, although equipment is not normally defined as an improvement to property. This adjustment allows capture of different kinds of structures with their different implications for municipal services. Laboratories are equipment-intensive and pose special problems for firefighters, so including equipment in these calculations gives laboratories appropriately disproportionate weight.

16. Fanciful, perhaps, but not out of the question, as Alaska's Permanent Fund demonstrates.

REFERENCES

Bauman, Gus, and William H. Ethier. 1987. "Development Exactions and Impact Fees: A Survey Of American Practices." *Law and Contemporary Problems* 50 (1): 51–68.

Baynes, Peter A. 1996. *The Eroding Tax Base: New York's Property Tax at a Crossroads.* Albany, New York: The New York State Conference of Mayors and Municipal Officials.

Bowman, Woods. 1999. "Buying Charity Care With Property Tax Expenditures." *Journal of Policy Analysis and Management* 18 (1): 120–25.

Fischel, William A. 2000. "Municipal Corporations, Homeowners and the Benefit View of the Property Tax." In *Property Taxation and Local Government Finance*, edited by Wallace Oates (33–78). Cambridge, Mass.: Lincoln Institute of Land Policy.

Hyman, David A. 1990. "The Conundrum of Charitability: Reassessing Tax Exemption for Hospitals." *American Journal of Hospital Law and Medicine* 16 (3): 327–80.

Minert, Charles L. 1997. Research Response to the Illinois General Assembly. Springfield, Ill.: Legislative Research Unit.

Mullen, John K. 1990. "Property Tax Exemptions and Local Fiscal Stress." *National Tax Journal* 43 (4): 467–79.

National Society of Fund Raising Executives. 1997. "Payments in Lieu of Taxes: A Position Paper." Alexandria, Va.: National Society of Fund Raising Executives.

Nicholas, James C., Arthur C. Nelson, and Julian C. Juergensmeyer. 1991. *A Practitioner's Guide to Development Impact Fees.* Chicago: Planners Press, American Planning Association.

NSFRE. *See* National Society of Fund Raising Executives.

Quigley, John M., and Roger W. Schmenner. 1975. "Property Tax Exemption and Public Policy." *Public Policy* 23 (3): 259–97.

Siegel, Jeremy. 1992. "Equity vs. Fixed-Income: Return Patterns since 1802." *AAII Journal* 14 (5). Accessed July 5, 2000, at the American Association of Individual Investors Web site, http://www.aaii.org.

Weisbrod, Burton A. 1988. *The Nonprofit Economy.* Cambridge: Harvard University Press.

13

Targeting the Charitable Property-Tax Exemption to Collective Goods

Robert T. Grimm, Jr.

Nonprofits, Property-Tax Exemptions, and Escalating Scrutiny

The nonprofit sector is currently in the throes of a major debate over the future of its property-tax benefits. Local governments around the United States are increasingly turning to nonprofit organizations to help alleviate their growing deficits and to finance the municipal services nonprofits use. All types of nonprofits currently face challenges to their traditional property-tax exemptions, and numerous other public charities already make partial payments in lieu of taxes (PILOTs) or pay the full amount of property tax they would owe as a for-profit entity.

The current debate over the property-tax exempt status of nonprofits stems largely from the recognition that some exempt organizations engage in primarily commercial (e.g., retail sales and fees for services) rather than philanthropic activities. The growing number of groups involved in such activities is galvanizing many citizens to view nonprofit organizations as for-profit enterprises in disguise, or as organizations that actually exploit the public good. The nonprofit sector's lack of a sophisticated response to this criticism is contributing to the perception: Few in the nonprofit world seem willing to examine the sources of public ire.

The "donative theory" recently constructed by legal scholars John Colombo and Mark Hall (1995), although accorded minor attention by the research and nonprofit community (Grimm 1999; Kingsman 1997;

Scrivner 1998; Steinberg and Bilodeau 1999), provides a detailed policy approach to the current controversy by proposing to tie the receipt of tax benefits to the production of substantial collective goods. This chapter analyzes the feasibility of the donative theory, and then implements and evaluates the theory in relation to property-tax exemptions, using a case study of 129 Indianapolis nonprofits. This chapter does not, however, advocate the donative theory or provide a detailed examination of the numerous rationales for nonprofits' tax exemptions (see Brody 1998; Brody, chapter 6 of this volume). Instead, this chapter examines the impact of a new proposal for defining the parameters of the charitable property-tax exemption, providing a brief review of the historical context of the nonprofit property-tax debate, and then examining one prospect for making sense out of the current property-tax deliberations.

Lester Salamon argues that the American political focus on the government's responsibility to serve the needs of its citizenry largely overshadowed public debate or scrutiny of the nonprofit sector and its role in society from the 1950s to the 1980s. He believes the situation changed when the Reagan administration began espousing the virtues of the philanthropic tradition and increasingly promoted nonprofits as major service providers. The nonprofit sector responded to this policy shift "not by becoming more charitable," however, "but by becoming more commercial" (Salamon 1995a, 195). Henry Hansmann asserts that a large portion of the nonprofit sector currently encompasses "'commercial' nonprofits": organizations that "receive virtually all of their income from the sale of services rather than from donations and that frequently compete directly with for-profit firms" (1989, 91). Hansmann also identifies other reasons for the emergence of numerous commercial nonprofits. He cites the changing function of health care in America as an example of nonprofits whose original philanthropic mission became obsolete or lost over time. In the past, hospitals primarily served as charity health providers, but the emergence of public and private insurance in the 20th century transformed health institutions into commercial corporations providing private goods (one good per individual), and raised questions about the legitimacy of their charitable tax-exempt status. Estelle James concurs, writing that hospitals' "rationale for remaining nonprofit appears to be disappearing . . . and we are currently seeing a wave of conversions, assets sales, and contracting-out arrangements, from nonprofits and for-profits, among the Blues, HMOs, and hospitals" (1998, 275). James further notes that many studies demonstrate that there is little difference, except in the case of teaching hospitals, between the behavior of for-profit and non-profit hospitals in such areas as uncompensated care (which is minimal in both organizational forms). Hansmann also argues that the nonprofit sector contains organizations that founded themselves as nonprofits because they felt that that status would help them achieve financial success, assuring their clients of the groups' goodwill toward society and creating a "halo effect" that could be used in marketing sales and services. The groups would, of course, also benefit from valuable federal and state tax breaks. Indeed, Salamon writes that commercial nonprofits currently create "60 percent of the expenditures of the nonprofit sector" (1995b, 10).

A recent collection of essays edited by Burton Weisbrod (1998) finds empirical evidence for this commercial behavior, which has been initiated by declines in governmental funding of nonprofits, as well as by nonprofits that have taken advantage of situations in which legal and institutional constraints on commercial behavior were lifted. Economists often assume that nonprofits reluctantly engage in commercial behavior to cross-subsidize their preferred production of collective goods (see Cordes, Pollack, and Gantz, chapter 4 of this volume). In fact, recent evidence (Anheier and Toepler 1998; Young 1998) shows that nonprofit industries such as social services and arts and humanities organizations (which are experiencing declining government funds) often take on commercial ventures to cross-subsidize their public-serving mission. This group of institutions undertakes these ventures slowly and cautiously because commercial ventures often "crowd out" donations: Donors observe an institution charging a price for services formerly provided for free, and see no need to subsidize endeavors that now appear to be self-supporting. In contrast, the major growth of commercialism stems from the decisions of nonprofits in health and higher education (particularly in life sciences and technology) to pursue commercial ventures without much concern for declines in donations (Powell and Owen-Smith 1998; Sloan 1998). Once public policy and institutional changes occurred—including the advent of Medicare, Medicaid, and private insurance to pay health care costs, and the Bayh-Dole Act (1980) that allowed nonprofit universities and small business to retain the property rights to inventions produced through federally funded research—these organizations responded opportunistically by generating and charging for private goods.

The growing chasm between the popular view of the nonprofit sector as privately supported philanthropy and the increasingly commercial nature of the nonprofit sector has provoked criticism from the business sector and the media (see Youngman, chapter 2 of this volume). Still, Richard Steinberg (1991) observed that most of the current work on nonprofit tax preferences fails to examine the extent and negative impact of nonprofit tax benefits in markets in which for-profits and nonprofits compete. Nonetheless, the gap has attracted public attention because, in the competition between nonprofits and for-profits, nonprofits' tax benefits could influence prices of goods or services. Nonprofits that rely upon user fees may also price needy individuals—sometimes the very people they hope to serve—out of the market. Salamon concluded that the persistence of negative press coverage and public scrutiny of nonprofits' commercial activity have created a "profound moral and political crisis, a fundamental questioning of the whole concept of the nonprofit sector" (1995b, 6).

Challenges to Nonprofits' Property-Tax Exemption: Recent Events in Pennsylvania and Colorado

The nonprofit world has experienced public scrutiny before (Hall 1987), but objections to nonprofits' property-tax benefits reached new heights in the late 1980s. Pennsylvania and Colorado provide examples of this growing lack of public confidence in nonprofits. A 1985 Pennsylvania supreme court case, *Hospitalization Utilization Project (HUP) v. Commonwealth of Pennsylvania*, 487 A.2d 1306, 507 Pa. 1, redefined a "purely public charity" as possessing all of the following characteristics:

- Advancing a charitable purpose;
- Donating or rendering gratuitously a substantial portion of its services;
- Benefiting a substantial and indefinite class of persons who are legitimate subjects of charity;
- Relieving government of some of its burden; and
- Operating entirely free from private profit motive.

Property-tax exemption challenges to Pennsylvania nonprofits multiplied tremendously in the decade after this case (see Gallagher, chapter 1 of this volume; Leland 1996). However, as Glancey (chapter 10 of this volume) describes, 1997 legislation in Pennsylvania may have stemmed these threats.

In Colorado, a group successfully petitioned to have Amendment XI added to the November 1996 ballot (Youngman, chapter 2 of this volume). The referendum proposed stripping property-tax exemptions from all nonprofits except those described as providing essential services: schools (including colleges and universities); orphanages; community corrections facilities; and housing facilities for poor, elderly, homeless, or abused people. Colorado nonprofits responded by forming Citizen Action for Colorado Nonprofits and spending $750,000 on a campaign driven by the slogan "Don't Hurt the Helpers." Colorado nonprofit leaders presented the public with a compressed view of the varieties of organizations that make up the charitable tax-exempt sector, with commercial nonprofits conspicuously but understandably absent. The measure failed by a significant margin.

Even with this election result, the nonprofit sector is increasingly perceived as more than a collection of food banks or activities that most people commonly associate with charitable "helpers." Many nonprofit commentators see the public furor increasing (Gallagher 1995 and Leland 1994) and recommend replacing it with "deliberate debate" (Leland 1994, 1372). Hansmann wrote that "wherever this line is ultimately drawn between exempt and nonexempt nonprofits, in the end there is likely to be a large portion of the sector that is nonexempt," but the alternative may be the eventual loss of preferential treatment for the entire sector (1989, 96).

Formulating the Donative Theory

The donative theory developed by Colombo and Hall provides a revised foundation for reconfiguring the tax-exempt sector. Colombo and Hall would tie nonprofits' tax-exempt status to the reception of a substantial level of donor support, because basing tax-favored treatment upon donations has strong historical roots. In the early part of the 20th century, state courts justified their liberal granting of exemptions to hospitals, for example, by using the evidence of a strong donor base. Despite the belief that giving is far from purely altruistic (e.g., Burlingame 1993 and Margolis 1982), Colombo and Hall further argued that "a donation rather than a purchase means that a sacrifice was made" (1995, 124). Colombo and Hall wished to circumvent discussions concerning the motives for giving, a task they viewed as peripheral to whether a nonprofit deserves a subsidy. The donative theory places great faith in donors' evaluations of nonprofits, and questions the worth of organizations that lack significant donor support. The donative theory also implies the possibility of trading an increase in property-tax rates for an expansion of the tax base; homeowners would clearly prefer a base expansion, which would force nonprofits to pay property taxes, rather than a rate increase, which might affect homeowners themselves.

Hall and Colombo posited a "twin failure explanation for why donative nonprofits exist" and deserve tax benefits: market failure and governmental failure (1995, 100). As to the former, economists argued that capitalism works well for answering individual needs (private goods) but not collective needs, such as a safe neighborhood, because of free-riders: In other words, people will often want to have others volunteer time or money for collective goods, rather than doing so themselves. Individuals may enjoy living in a safe neighborhood but, hoping that others will pick up the slack, they may not donate to its maintenance. If the government's power to tax could erase all free-rider problems, the need for private donations would also be eliminated. However, Burton Weisbrod's classic public-goods theory explains why the government will always undersupply public or collective goods (i.e., a governmental failure). Weisbrod pointed out that many groups do not possess the ability to lobby the government to enact or supply enough of a collective good (Weisbrod 1972; Weisbrod 1977; Weisbrod 1988). Since American democracy ties itself to the wishes of the median voter, Weisbrod concluded, nonprofits must serve as private producers of collective goods not undertaken by the government or market. The income- and property-tax exemptions and charitable deductions granted by the government serve as what Colombo and Hall call a shadow or matching subsidy "by amplifying the effect of private donations" (Colombo and Hall 1995, 107). They pointed out that although citizens may oppose paying for a collective good directly, they remain more open to a partial subsidy, even if they do not actively want it, because it represents a cost significantly lower than direct support and implies more political "give and take." Colombo and Hall hypothesized that because all members of society support a special interest or directly benefit from one, tax exemptions are the government's way of aiding its entire citizenry by providing collective goods and services that experience market and (apparent) governmental failure.

To implement the donative model, Colombo and Hall proposed creating a donative threshold or index based on the percentage of gross revenue an organization receives from donations. They gauged this index according to Weisbrod's collectiveness index (Weisbrod 1980), which demonstrated that "traditional 'charitable' institutions—religious, cultural and social welfare organizations—all receive more than one-third of their revenues in the form of donations" (Colombo and Hall 1995, 198). They further noted that the *1992–93 Nonprofit Almanac* largely confirmed Weisbrod's observation in major nonprofit industry groups (Hodgkinson et al. 1996). Colombo and Hall also cited the one-third threshold for nonprofit foundation status found in Internal Revenue Code Section 170. Nevertheless, Colombo and Hall suggested that some flexibility in the donative threshold could be created for historically exempt organizations—such as educational institutions—that may require less assurance of worth or need. The resulting theory Colombo and Hall proposed works upon a three-tiered, donative-threshold system: A nonprofit would become exempt from income tax when donations amount to 10 percent of total support; would be entitled to donation deductibility and all other charitable income-tax benefits at 33 percent; and would become exempt from paying property taxes at 50 percent. This higher threshold for property-tax exemption was designed to avoid double-counting: "A rather large percentage of non-donative revenue is necessary to create a significant subsidy effect under the income tax exemption because of the fact that donations do not count as taxable revenues, but this is not the case for property tax exemption since donated property counts as property" (1995, 200).

Colombo and Hall devoted the last portion of their book to predicting, without nonprofit financial data, the 10 percent and 33 percent thresholds' impact on the nonprofit sector, but they neglected to provide an account of the effects of the 50 percent threshold for property-tax exemptions. To create a realistic sample of the nonprofit world in a major city and test the donative model's potential impact on the city's nonprofit sector, this chapter uses a data sample that was drawn predominantly from available 1993 Internal Revenue Service Forms 990 filed under Internal Revenue Code section 501(c)(3) by 129 Indianapolis nonprofits. These 129 nonprofits, chosen from the Guidestar System (http://www.guidestar.org) and a report prepared by the National Center for Charitable Statistics (1997), do not include nonprofits with revenues under $25,000 or any religious organizations (which do not need to file IRS 990 tax forms). The sample, therefore, presents a limited view of the city's entire nonprofit sector.

The 129 nonprofits were classified according to the National Taxonomy of Exempt Entities (NTEE) advanced by the National Center for Charitable Statistics (http://nccs.urban.org/ntee-cc/index.htm), and grouped into major industry categories: arts, culture, and humanities; education; environmental, animal-related, and public-benefit; health; and human services. Religious nonprofits were excluded for reasons previously noted, and international affairs organizations were omitted because no data existed on this minor segment of the Indianapolis nonprofit sector. The normally separate public-benefit, environmental, and animal-related categories were also combined because of their small numbers in the sample. The delineation resulted in the following breakdown of organizational types: 9 percent of the groups were categorized as arts, culture, and humanities; 12 percent as education; 9 percent as environmental, animal-related, and public-benefit; 38 percent as health; and 33 percent as human services organizations.[1] This breakdown is a fairly reasonable depiction of nonprofit filers nationally and in Indiana (Hodgkinson et al. 1996, 246; Stevenson et al. 1997, 125–28)—except for the oversampling of health organizations, justified by health nonprofits' close ties to large amounts of fixed capital and high number of property-tax exemption challenges (Leland 1994).

We turn now to the revenue and expense streams related to the donative theory. To avoid promoting excessive fund-raising costs, Colombo and Hall proposed counting only net contributions: the amount of gross contributions minus the organization's cost of fund-raising. They asserted that an organization's fund-raising expenses should be subtracted from contributions because "a system that keys tax exemption to a specific level of donative support encourages aggressive fund-raising campaigns," and could create fund-raising abuses such as "a charitable entity that spends a very small portion of a donation on delivery of charitable services and the lion's share covering the costs of fund-raising itself" (1995, 212). This argument resonates with scholars who feel that efficiency is not measured as well with fund-raising cost ratios—fund-raising expenditures divided by donations received—as it would be if the measure were the numerical difference between donations and fund-raising costs (Steinberg 1995; 1997). Many nonprofits, however, fulfill part of their educational and advocacy mission by fund-raising, and research has yet to determine an accurate method to account for the reported fund-raising costs that actually represent the production of collective goods (Steinberg 1997). Note too that the current validity of nonprofits' reported fund-raising costs remains more questionable than any other financial category used in this study (Froelich and Knoepfle 1996), and that the donative theory would require stricter accountancy oversight.

My analysis compares donative thresholds that subtract reported fund-raising costs (thereby controlling excessive fund-raising); that do not subtract reported fund-raising costs (as a crude way to compensate for fund-raising's collective-goods production); and that subtract reported fund-raising and administrative costs (because many nonprofit corporations assign their fund-raising expenses to administrative costs[2]). Colombo and Hall wavered on whether government grant income should be considered part of a nonprofit's gross revenue. They asserted that since government grants represent only half of their twin-failure basis for the donative theory (i.e., market failure but not governmental failure), grants should not be considered donations. The authors believed that the presence of government grants signals the democratic approval of direct funding and negates the need for an extra subsidization in the tax code. Colombo and Hall stated that government grants should be counted in gross revenue, because government grants expand output. Later in their book, they revised this assertion because "it makes little sense for the government to tax the very money it pays out" (Colombo and Hall 1995, 204). Colombo and Hall posited that "a combination of the donative theory and the theory that the government should not tax its own money" could exclude government grants from the process of creating a donative threshold—that is, from both the numerator and denominator (ibid., 205). However, there are numerous examples in which the government does indeed tax itself or entities that receive some government funds, including Social Security and unemployment insurance benefits. This study provides donative thresholds both ways: those that include government grants in and those that exempt government grants from an organization's gross revenue.

Colombo and Hall also proposed including volunteer labor—in addition to monetary contributions—in an organization's donative revenue, but they did not provide a thorough analysis of how to formulate a feasible quantitative measure. Indeed, donated labor should be included in any measure of a nonprofit's output of public or collective goods, but the authors also recognized that an "obvious difficulty is how to place a monetary value on donated time" (Colombo and Hall 1995, 203). Independent Sector's *Giving and Volunteering* used a $12.13 hourly rate for volunteers, as determined by the 1993 average hourly wage for nonagricultural workers, but it seems unlikely that this crude valuation would serve as an acceptable governmental measure (Hodgkinson and Weitzman 1996, 30). A more accurate valuation would base volunteer labor's cost on how much an organization would be willing to pay to get that service. Further research could create an administratively determined value for volunteer labor, broken down by industry or subindustry groups, using volunteer hours in that industry multiplied by a set value per hour to that nonprofit.

Recognizing that data on volunteers' worth to a nonprofit could be improved, this chapter provides an estimated valuation for volunteer labor that is derived from Independent Sector's *Portrait of the Independent Sector: The Activities and Finances of Charitable Organizations*, which provides data to determine a ratio of donation dollars (D) to volunteer dollars (V) received by major industry groups (Hodgkinson et al. 1993, 33, 59). This ratio appears plausible given research suggesting a correlation between donating and volunteering (Hodgkinson and Weitzman 1996, 4–5). The arts, culture, and humanities industry group, for example, has a ratio of $1.64 to $1.00, or $1.64 in donations received for every dollar of value created by volunteers (see table 13-1 for all industry ratios). These industry ratios of D:V have been used here to create a monetary value for each Indianapolis organization's volunteer labor. Use of an administratively determined value for volunteers circumvents a problem Colombo and Hall foresaw: Volunteers provide a loophole for nonprofits needing to augment their donative thresholds. "An entity straddling the donative threshold would be tempted to call for far more volunteers than it actually

Table 13-1. *Value Ratios of Donations to Volunteers, by Nonprofit Industry*

Nonprofit Industry Group	D:V[a]
Arts, Culture, and Humanities	$1.64:$1.00
Education	$0.91:$1.00
Environment and Animal-Related[b]	$0.46:$1.00
Health	$0.49:$1.00
Human-Services	$0.50:$1.00
Public-Benefit[b]	$0.30:$1.00

Source: Author's calculations based on Hodgkinson et al. (1993).

[a] Equals amount of donations received for each dollar earned through volunteers. These ratios are determined by the total amount of private contributions in each nonprofit industry (from total revenues of nonprofit industries in Hodgkinson et al. 1993, figure 33 and percentages of total revenue from private contributions in figure 34) and compared to value of full-time equivalent volunteers in nonprofit industry groups (ibid., figure 68).

[b] Although this study combines public-benefit nonprofits with environment and animal-related nonprofits into one group, the Independent Sector data made a distinction between the two groups, so two volunteer ratios are used here for the environment, animal-related and public-benefit group.

needs to staff" an activity because "all volunteers' time could be counted" (Colombo and Hall 1995, 204). Note, however, that such a ratio methodology means that nonprofits that receive zero dollars in donations also receive zero dollars in volunteer labor, but this study assumes that organizations that receive no contributions probably obtain little volunteer support. The following section reports the results of donative thresholds that include this ratio methodology for determining the value for volunteers and of those that do not include a value for volunteers.

Implementing the Donative Theory: A Case Study of 129 Indianapolis Nonprofits

The alternative constructions of the donative theory include the six variables described in table 13-2 and the 12 formula variations detailed in table 13-3. The donative-index score of the 129 Indianapolis nonprofits was then determined by applying the 12 formulas to each nonprofit. In summary, formulas that subtracted fund-raising costs[3] only slightly lowered an organization's donative index, with an overall mean

Table 13-2. *Definitions of Variables Used in Calculations of Nonprofits' Income*

Variable	Definition
Administrative Costs (A)	Management expenses not allocated in the cost of fund-raising or program services
Donations (D)	Amount of private contributions given to a nonprofit in one fiscal year
Fund-raising Costs (F)	Expenses allocated to a nonprofit's fund-raising efforts in one fiscal year
Government Grants (G)	Dollar amount of government grants given to a nonprofit in one fiscal year
Total Revenue (TR)	Gross revenue earned by a nonprofit in one fiscal year (including private contributions, government grants, fees for services, and investment income)
Volunteer Labor Value (V^*)	Estimated monetary value of volunteer labor during the fiscal year of a nonprofit, calculated by using industry donation to volunteer labor ratios outlined in table 13-1

Table 13-3. *Donative-Theory Formulas*

Description of Formula	Basic Formula	Formula Including Fund-Raising Costs	Formula Including Fundraising and Administrative Costs
Variations with donations (D) that also include governmental grants (G) in total revenue (TR)	$\dfrac{D}{TR}$	$\dfrac{D - F}{TR}$	$\dfrac{D - F - A}{TR}$
Variations with donations (D) that exclude government grants (G) from total revenue (TR)	$\dfrac{D}{TR - G}$	$\dfrac{D - F}{TR - G}$	$\dfrac{D - F - A}{TR - G}$
Variations with donations (D) and estimated volunteer labor (V*) that also include governmental grants (G) in total revenue (TR)	$\dfrac{D + V^*}{TR + V^*}$	$\dfrac{D + V^* - F}{TR + V^*}$	$\dfrac{D + V^* - F - A}{TR + V^*}$
Variations with donations (D) and estimated volunteer labor (V*) that also exclude governmental grants (G) from total revenue (TR)	$\dfrac{D + V^*}{TR + V^* - G}$	$\dfrac{D + V^* - F}{TR + V^* - G}$	$\dfrac{D + V^* - F - A}{TR + V^* - G}$

Notes: A = administrative costs, D = donations, F = fund-raising costs, G = government grants, TR = total gross revenue and V^* = volunteers (estimated monetary worth).

loss of -2.71 percent ($N = 516$). By industry, the mean loss ranged from a low of -1.29 percent for environmental, animal-related, and public-benefit nonprofits ($N = 44$) to a high of -6.25 percent in arts, culture, and humanities nonprofits ($N = 48$). By contrast, formulas that excluded administrative costs[4] created a much larger decline in the donative index, with an overall mean loss of 16.97 percent ($N = 516$), a low mean score of -9.04 percent in health nonprofits ($N = 196$), and a high mean score of -29.90 percent for arts, culture, and humanities nonprofits ($N = 44$).

For variables that augment an organization's donative score, subtracting governmental grants from each organization's total revenue[5] created a small mean increase—2.58 percent ($N = 774$)—in donative score. By industry, the mean increase in formulas that excluded government grants from total revenue ranged from a low of 0.00 percent ($N = 72$) in arts, culture, and humanities nonprofits to a high of 6.12 percent ($N = 66$) in environment, animal-related, and public-benefit nonprofits. Equations that included the estimated value of an organization's volunteer labor created a much higher increase than formulas subtracting governmental grants. Indeed, formulas that included estimated volunteer labor[6] showed an overall mean donative-index increase of 13.85 percent ($N = 774$), ranging from a low of 5.72 percent ($N = 90$) in education nonprofits to a high of 27.90 percent ($N = 66$) in environmental, animal-related, and public-benefit nonprofits (table 13-4). Overall, it appears that fund-raising costs and government grants make little difference in a nonprofit's donative-index score, but that administrative costs significantly decrease, and estimated volunteer labor significantly increases, an organization's donative-index score.

Table 13-4. *Mean Change That Variables Cause in Donative-Index Scores, by Industry and Total Sample*

Nonprofit Industry	Fund-Raising Costs (F)	Administrative Costs (A)	Government Grants (G)	Volunteers (V*)
Arts, Culture, and	−6.25%	−29.90%	+0.00%[a]	+11.42%
Humanities	($N = 48$)	($N = 48$)	($N = 72$)	($N = 72$)
Education	−1.32%	−12.25%	+0.24%	+5.72
	($N = 60$)	($N = 60$)	($N = 90$)	($N = 90$)
Environment,	−1.29%	−19.52%	+6.12%	+27.20%
Animal Related,	($N = 44$)	($N = 44$)	($N = 66$)	($N = 66$)
and Public				
Benefit				
Health	−2.21%	−9.04%	+2.78%	+10.13%
	($N = 196$)	($N = 196$)	($N = 294$)	($N = 294$)
Human Services	−2.46%	−14.08%	+3.75%	+14.78%
	($N = 164$)	($N = 164$)	($N = 246$)	($N = 246$)
Total	−2.71%	−16.96%	+2.58%	+13.85%
	($N = 516$)	($N = 516$)	($N = 774$)	($N = 774$)

Source: Author's calculations based on NCCS (1997) and GuideStar (1997).
N = number of samples calculated for the mean score.
[a] This zero score for the arts, culture, and humanities group does not indicate that subtracting G from TR never increased an organization's donative index, but rather that subtracting G from an organization that has a negative total in its numerator (resulting from subtracting F or subtracting F and A) will only cause a more-negative score when TR becomes smaller.

Property-Tax Exemptions at the 50 Percent Threshold

The study now turns to how many organizations, by industry, would remain exempt from the property tax if Colombo and Hall's proposed threshold, receipt of a donative-index score of 50 percent or higher, were used (table 13-5). The education group would experience the greatest change, with only 13 to 20 percent of education nonprofits remaining property tax-exempt in all 12 formula variations.[7] Further, not one university, college, private school, or educational loan corporation could keep property tax-exempt status under any of the equations.

The arts, culture, and humanities group had the lowest percentage of organizations that would be exempt under four formulas subtracting administrative costs:[8] Only one (8 percent) small arts organization that sponsors concerts and competitions, Cathedral Arts, remained exempt. Under six formulas,[9] 33 percent of arts, culture, and humanities nonprofits would not have to pay property taxes, but the majority of museums and theaters, a public radio station, and the state historical society received too little in contributions to remain exempt. The exempt organizations in this group included two small arts corporations, the Eiteljorge Museum and the Indiana State Symphony Society. Under two formulas that add estimated volunteer labor,[10] half the organizations would continue to be exempt, including the four just noted as well as the Indiana Repertory Theater and Indianapolis Public Radio.

Among health nonprofits, between 20 and 29 percent passed the donative threshold for property-tax exemption under six formulas.[11] As with the previous two groups, many organizations frequently recognized as health nonprofits—hospitals, clinics, and rehabilitation centers—would pay property taxes. However, the American Lung Association of Indiana, the Indiana Children's Wish Fund, the Marion County Cancer Society, and the Muscular Dystrophy Foundation of Indiana would retain their property-tax exemption. Under the other six formulas,[12] between 35 and 41 percent of health nonprofits would retain property-tax exemption, including the organizations just mentioned as well as the Indiana Chapter of the Multiple Sclerosis Society, the National Kidney Foundation of Indiana, a nursing-services organization known as Midland House, and a chemical-dependency treatment center, Fairbanks TLC; no additional hospitals or clinics would be exempt.

As for human service nonprofits, 32 to 51 percent would be exempt under eight formulas.[13] Unlike health and arts, culture, and humanities nonprofits, more commonly recognized human service nonprofits would

Table 13-5. *Nonprofits Passing the 50 Percent Property-Tax Exemption Tier of the Donative Theory, by Industry Group and Total Sample (detailed by percentage and organizational number)*

Donative-Theory Formulas	Arts, Culture, and Humanities (TN = 12)		Education (TN = 15)		Environment, Animal-Related, and Public-Benefit (TN = 11)		Health (TN = 49)		Human Services (TN = 42)		Total Exempt Nonprofits (TN = 129)	
$\dfrac{D}{TR}$	33%	(N = 4)	20%	(N = 3)	55%	(N = 6)	22%	(N = 11)	48%	(N = 20)	34%	(N = 44)
$\dfrac{D-F}{TR}$	33%	(N = 4)	20%	(N = 3)	55%	(N = 6)	20%	(N = 10)	45%	(N = 19)	33%	(N = 42)
$\dfrac{D-F-A}{TR}$	8%	(N = 1)	13%	(N = 2)	18%	(N = 2)	20%	(N = 10)	32%	(N = 13)	22%	(N = 28)
$\dfrac{D}{TR-G}$	33%	(N = 4)	20%	(N = 3)	64%	(N = 7)	29%	(N = 14)	50%	(N = 21)	38%	(N = 49)
$\dfrac{D-F}{TR-G}$	33%	(N = 4)	20%	(N = 3)	64%	(N = 7)	27%	(N = 13)	48%	(N = 20)	36%	(N = 47)
$\dfrac{D-F-A}{TR-G}$	8%	(N = 1)	13%	(N = 2)	18%	(N = 2)	20%	(N = 10)	34%	(N = 14)	23%	(N = 29)
$\dfrac{D+V^\star}{TR+V^\star}$	50%	(N = 6)	20%	(N = 3)	82%	(N = 9)	39%	(N = 19)	55%	(N = 23)	47%	(N = 60)
$\dfrac{D+V^\star-F}{TR+V^\star}$	33%	(N = 4)	20%	(N = 3)	82%	(N = 9)	39%	(N = 19)	55%	(N = 23)	45%	(N = 58)

(Continued)

Table 13-5. Nonprofits Passing the 50 Percent Property-Tax Exemption Tier of the Donative Theory, by Industry Group and Total Sample (detailed by percentage and organizational number) (Continued)

Donative-Theory Formulas	Arts, Culture, and Humanities (TN = 12)	Education (TN = 15)	Environment, Animal-Related, and Public-Benefit (TN = 11)	Health (TN = 49)	Human Services (TN = 42)	Total Exempt Nonprofits (TN = 129)
$\dfrac{D + V^\star - F - A}{TR + V^\star}$	8% (N=1)	20% (N=3)	82% (N=9)	35% (N=17)	46% (N=19)	42% (N=54)
$\dfrac{D + V^\star}{TR + V^\star - G}$	50% (N=6)	20% (N=3)	100% (N=11)	41% (N=20)	62% (N=26)	51% (N=66)
$\dfrac{D + V^\star - F}{TR + V^\star - G}$	33% (N=4)	20% (N=3)	100% (N=11)	41% (N=20)	60% (N=25)	49% (N=63)
$\dfrac{D + V^\star - F - A}{TR + V^\star - G}$	8% (N=1)	20% (N=3)	82% (N=9)	39% (N=19)	50% (N=21)	41% (N=53)

Source: Author's calculations based on NCCS (1997) and GuideStar (1997).
N = number of nonprofit organizations that are exempt from the property tax.
TN = total nonprofit organizations in each industry sample.

remain exempt: Big Brothers of Indianapolis, Habitat for Humanity of Greater Indianapolis,[14] the Indiana Association of United Ways, the Jewish Federation of Greater Indianapolis, and the Indiana Special Olympics. The human service organizations that would not be exempt also comprised some well-known and surprising nonprofits: the Castleton Volunteer Fire Department, the Franklin Volunteer Fire Department, Goodwill Industries of Central Indiana, and the Central Indiana Council on Aging. The fact that the two volunteer fire departments—organizations providing collective goods—failed the donative threshold (both received between 70 and 80 percent of their revenue from program services) illustrates the need for the provisos or exceptions implied by Colombo and Hall: There may be cases in which collective goods cannot be provided unless a significant share of a nonprofit's costs are covered by sales of services. It should be noted that lowering these volunteer departments' donative threshold to 10 percent, and in some cases to 33 percent, would allow both departments to receive a property-tax exemption, and that merely adding estimated volunteer labor[15] would push the Franklin Volunteer Fire Department over the 50 percent threshold. In addition, 55 to 62 percent of the human service organizations, such as the Boy Scouts of America Council, Coleman Adoption Services, Habitat for Humanity of Greater Indianapolis, the Indiana Crime Prevention Coalition, and Pleasant Run Children's Home (as well as other organizations already noted as exempt above), would not pay property taxes under four formulas,[16] but the Central Indiana Council on Aging and Goodwill Industries would not be exempt.

The environment, animal-related, and public-benefit group would experience the least amount of alteration. Seven (64 percent)[17] and six (55 percent)[18] of its nonprofits would retain property-tax exemptions in formulas including or excluding fund-raising costs and government grants. The Indianapolis Humane Society, the Indianapolis Urban League and the Indiana Environmental Institute, for example, maintained their exempt status, while nonexempt organizations included only public-benefit organizations (except for the Indianapolis Zoological Society) such as the Hudson Institute. In addition, use of equations that subtract administrative costs but do not include estimated volunteer labor[19] resulted in two organizations—the Indianapolis Humane Society and the Indianapolis Urban League—securing property-tax exemption. Conversely, by adding estimated volunteer labor, 82 percent[20] to 100 percent[21] of this group's organizations acquired property-tax exemptions: Two (18 percent) community economic development organizations—the Indiana Economic Development Council and East-side Community Investment—were taxable under three formulas subtracting government grants from total revenue[22] and under one formula not subtracting government grants from gross revenue but including administrative costs.[23]

Property-Tax Exemptions at the 33 Percent Threshold

Although Colombo and Hall's recent book "gingerly" suggested a tiered tax-exemption system (Colombo and Hall 1995, 201), much of their earlier works centered on a single 33 percent threshold for all tax exemptions and deductions (Colombo 1993). Therefore, it makes sense to provide a brief description of which nonprofits would be exempt from property taxes under a 33 percent donative threshold (table 13-6). The education industry would see little, if any, change, under six formulas[24] that result in no increase in the number of exempt organizations; the other six formulas would allow one more organization (7 percent increase) to receive property-tax exemption: Two would grant exemption to Junior Achievement[25] and four to Park Tudor Foundation (a private school).[26]

Up to two more arts, culture, and humanities nonprofits would be exempt under four formulas that include fund-raising costs or fund-raising and administrative costs but not estimated volunteer labor.[27] The other formulas, however, caused a 25 to 50 percent increase in the number of exempt organizations. In the four formulas that created a 50 percent increase,[28] only two organizations fell short of the threshold: the Indiana Historical Society and the Phoenix Theater.

Between one and seven more health organizations (a 2 to 14 percent increase) became exempt, the major changes occurring in six formulas.[29] This change mainly helped organizations already noted as exempt under five formulas[30] for the 50 percent threshold (such as the Dyslexia Institute and Midland House) to be exempt under some formulas excluding estimated volunteer labor. Six formulas[31] provided an even smaller increase, as two nonprofits (representing a 4 percent increase) became exempt: the Indiana Family Health Council and the Greater Indianapolis Council on Alcoholism.

Overall, the number of tax-exempt human-service nonprofits also slightly expanded, with up to five more organizations (a 12 percent increase) becoming exempt. The highest augmentation occurred in formulas that included an organization's estimated volunteer labor.[32] In

Table 13-6. *Nonprofits Passing the 33 Percent Property-Tax Exemption Tier of the Donative Theory, by Industry Group and Total Sample (detailed by percentage and number reported)*

Donative-Theory Formulas	Arts, Culture, and Humanities (TN = 12)	Education (TN = 15)	Environment, Animal-Related, and Public-Benefit (TN = 11)	Health (TN = 49)	Human Services (TN = 42)	Total Exempt Nonprofits (TN = 129)
$\dfrac{D}{TR}$	83% (N = 10)	20% (N = 3)	64% (N = 7)	36% (N = 18)	48% (N = 20)	45% (N = 58)
$\dfrac{D-F}{TR}$	50% (N = 6)	20% (N = 3)	55% (N = 6)	33% (N = 16)	48% (N = 20)	40% (N = 51)
$\dfrac{D-F-A}{TR}$	8% (N = 1)	20% (N = 3)	46% (N = 5)	22% (N = 11)	37% (N = 15)	27% (N = 35)
$\dfrac{D}{TR-G}$	83% (N = 10)	20% (N = 3)	82% (N = 7)	39% (N = 19)	50% (N = 21)	47% (N = 60)
$\dfrac{D-F}{TR-G}$	50% (N = 6)	20% (N = 3)	73% (N = 6)	35% (N = 17)	50% (N = 21)	41% (N = 53)
$\dfrac{D-F-A}{TR-G}$	8% (N = 1)	20% (N = 3)	46% (N = 5)	27% (N = 13)	42% (N = 17)	30% (N = 39)
$\dfrac{D+V^\star}{TR+V^\star}$	83% (N = 10)	27% (N = 4)	91% (N = 10)	43% (N = 21)	62% (N = 26)	55% (N = 71)
$\dfrac{D+V^\star-F}{TR+V^\star}$	83% (N = 10)	27% (N = 4)	91% (N = 10)	43% (N = 21)	57% (N = 24)	54% (N = 69)

(Continued)

Table 13-6. *Nonprofits Passing the 33 Percent Property-Tax Exemption Tier of the Donative Theory, by Industry Group and Total Sample (detailed by percentage and number reported) (Continued)*

Donative-Theory Formulas	Arts, Culture, and Humanities (TN = 12)	Education (TN = 15)	Environment, Animal-Related, and Public-Benefit (TN = 11)	Health (TN = 49)	Human Services (TN = 42)	Total Exempt Nonprofits (TN = 129)
$\dfrac{D + V^\star - F - A}{TR + V^\star}$	33% (N = 4)	20% (N = 3)	82% (N = 9)	41% (N = 20)	54% (N = 22)	45% (N = 58)
$\dfrac{D + V^\star}{TR + V^\star - G}$	83% (N = 10)	27% (N = 4)	100% (N = 11)	45% (N = 22)	71% (N = 30)	60% (N = 77)
$\dfrac{D + V^\star - F}{TR + V^\star - G}$	83% (N = 10)	27% (N = 4)	100% (N = 11)	45% (N = 22)	69% (N = 29)	59% (N = 76)
$\dfrac{D + V^\star - F - A}{TR + V^\star - G}$	33% (N = 4)	20% (N = 3)	91% (N = 10)	43% (N = 21)	63% (N = 26)	50% (N = 64)

Source: Author's calculations based on NCCS (1997) and GuideStar (1997).
N = number of nonprofit organizations that are exempt from the property tax.
TN = total nonprofit organizations in sample.

these formulas, organizations newly exempt from tax rolls included the Indiana Black Expo, Pleasant Run Children's Home, and the Indiana Chapter of the Committee for the Prevention of Child Abuse.[33]

The environment, animal-related, and public-benefit group experienced only a minor increase of up to three organizations per formula, but this is understandable given that 80 to 100 percent of the group was exempt under the 50 percent threshold. The nonprofits that would join the property-tax rolls were again only public-benefit organizations (except the zoo): East Side Community Investments,[34] the Hudson Institute,[35] the Indiana Association for Community Economic Development,[36] the Indiana Economic Development Council,[37] the Indianapolis Zoological Society,[38] and the National Committee on Planned Giving.[39]

Nonprofit Behavior in a Donative-Theory Tax World

Given that the 12 variations under a 50 percent or 33 percent threshold would cause between 40 percent and 78 percent of all the nonprofits in this sample to lose their property-tax exemption, implementation of a mechanism based on the donative theory would cause nonprofits to attempt to minimize the impact of new property taxes. In two recent works, Brody and Cordes (1999) and Cordes, Gantz, and Pollak (chapter 4 of this volume) found that the loss of nonprofit property-tax exemptions would not produce the dramatic results intimated by such nonprofit associations as the National Society of Fund Raising Executives (NSFRE 1997). Most taxable nonprofit property owners would need to make up, on average, approximately 1 to 3 percent in gross revenue lost, but some nonprofits could face significant cutbacks. Many nonprofits, such as hospitals and universities, could try to finance an extra 1 to 3 percent revenue growth through increased fees and minor reductions in costs or activities, or through seeking property-tax exemptions—as do for-profit groups—on the basis of the economic boost such groups provide to the local community. This new property-tax regime would also need to determine whether some fee-for-service income derived from government funds (such as Medicare payments), arrangements particularly prominent in health and human service nonprofits (Smith and Lipsky 1993), should be counted as collective goods instead of private goods. Numerous human service and health nonprofits would argue that such government-nonprofit partnerships constitute the production of collective goods.

Nonetheless, some nonprofits would probably face significant cutbacks, particularly land-intensive nonprofits (such as nursing homes) and small or young nonprofits with little cash flow.

Moreover, this property-tax exemption system should allow newly taxable nonprofits to request and reestablish their property-tax exemptions if the groups can prove that their commercial ventures cross-subsidize collective goods or that their commercial activities represent an explicit accomplishment of their public-serving mission. Throughout American history, charities have often used commercial ventures or social entrepreneurship to subsidize their production of collective goods (see, e.g., Sander 1998). Furthermore, Dennis Young's 1998 study of commercialism in social service nonprofits illustrated how commercial activity can further a nonprofit's public-benefit mission. He observed, for example, that the Girl Scouts sell cookies not only to increase their revenue base but also to foster leadership skills.

It is also important to stress that only a small number of nonprofit organizations would face major financial cutbacks under a tax mechanism that targeted the property-tax exemption to collective goods. The revenue losses reported in the Brody and Cordes study (1999) and in Cordes, Gantz, and Pollak, Chapter 4 of this volume, probably represent an upper limit, because of reasons noted above and because taxable nonprofits would no doubt lower their land use and, if possible, move to an area with lower tax rates. The donative theory might also spur commercially oriented nonprofits to use their land more efficiently, as well as remove the current incentive to locate in high-tax areas. Indeed, a recent study by Cordes and Weisbrod (1998) found that nonprofits disproportionately undertake commercial ventures in states with high property-tax rates, which can give nonprofits a comparative advantage over for-profits.

Finally, 29 organizations (22 percent) in this sample of 129 Indianapolis nonprofits reported a property value of $0. This percentage remained consistent within each nonprofit industry group, except for the arts, culture, and humanities group (8 percent), and included many nonprofits that would fall short of a 50 percent or 33 percent donative threshold under any formula. Consequently, even if all nonprofits become part of the property-tax rolls, many nonprofits would never experience any financial impact. Moreover, while this chapter neglected religious organizations and the typically landless nonprofits earning under $25,000 in total revenue, one could conservatively estimate—using the California Data Base as a guide (Orend, O'Neill, and Mitchell 1997, 448)—that between one-quarter to more than half of 501(c)(3) nonprofits would not experience any revenue loss if the laws regarding nonprofits and property taxes changed.[40] Many nonprofits operate without occupying any property and thus have no need for the municipal services paid for through property taxes. Numerous other nonprofit organizations already "are paying market-rate rent on office or program space, thus paying taxes through rents to landlords" (Leland 1994, 1372), but this is certainly not true in a depressed rental market. One other possibility, however, is that nonprofits also rent from other nonprofits, but these arrangements are occasionally taxed too (Gallagher, chapter 1 of this volume).

Conclusion: Future Property-Tax Exemption Policy for the Nonprofit Sector

The nonprofit sector increasingly contains organizations that predominantly focus or depend upon commercial ventures, produce private goods, and thus operate much like for-profit firms. For example, 18 percent of the nonprofits in this data set obtained none of their revenue from donations; 28 percent of the nonprofits obtained less than 1 percent from donations. The donative theory examined in this chapter questions the policy of allowing property-tax benefits to such commercial nonprofits. As illustrated by the debates in Pennsylvania and Colorado, the American public and government are aware of this profound change within the nonprofit sector. The increasing recognition of commercial nonprofit behavior can logically be connected to the rise in scrutiny and criticism of the privileges of organizations formed as 501(c)(3) charities (see Youngman, chapter 2 of this volume). Furthermore, there are no signs that nonprofits will stop erratically paying property taxes in the future.

Efforts to target the property-tax exemption to collective goods provide one method for defining the boundaries of nonprofits' tax privileges. This approach—which is based upon the belief that a substantial amount of donations given by the public represent worthiness and an acknowledgment of citizens' willingness to allow a nonprofit to receive governmental subsidies—represents one alternative for reconfiguring the tax treatment of the nonprofit sector. This chapter critiqued and advanced the development of the donative theory, and connected it to the current debate over nonprofits and their property-tax exemptions.

The findings from the Indianapolis study indicate that, given any donative-threshold modification, a significant number of organizations within the nonprofit sector (40 to 78 percent) and most nonprofit industry groups would lose their property-tax exemption. More than other industry groups, education (73 to 87 percent) and health (55 to 80 percent) nonprofits failed donative thresholds for exempting taxes on real estate holdings—a predictable finding, given current studies on commercialism and nonprofits. Still, the donative theory would also significantly affect the other three nonprofit industry groups, with arts, culture, and humanities (17 to 92 percent), human services (29 to 68 percent), and environmental, animal-related, and public-benefit (0 to 82 percent) nonprofits being added to property-tax rolls. Well-known nonprofit corporations, such as universities, hospitals, and museums, would find themselves paying property taxes. These changes would probably bring about nonprofit organizational behaviors and legal exceptions that would minimize the impact of new property-tax bills. Further, the current debate neglects to note that between 25 percent and more than 50 percent of nonprofits either do not occupy any property, and thus do not need the services property-taxes pay for, or already pay for municipal services by renting operating space from landlords that pay property tax. Targeting the property-tax exemption to collective goods would not cause financial hardships for many nonprofits.

The erratic attempts to regulate nonprofits currently being undertaken in Pennsylvania (see Glancey, chapter 9 of this volume) could very well represent the future property-tax treatment of the nonprofit sector. Would the tax mechanism described here, or a modification of it, provide a way to systematically explain and define the future property-tax privileges of the nonprofit sector? If so, how could it be implemented? A preliminary discussion of such an endeavor has been provided in this chapter, but further refinements and dialogue are needed. If developments in the donative theory prove inadequate, what other approaches could delineate the sector in the 21st century and solve the present conflict? The climate is ripe for a systematic reform and definition of the charitable property-tax exemption, but the direction for that reform is less clear.

NOTES

The author thanks Evelyn Brody, Dwight F. Burlingame, Joseph Cordes, Richard Steinberg, and Dennis R. Young for helpful comments.

1. Totals do not sum to 100 percent due to rounding.

2. Indeed, many nonprofit executives devote a large portion of their time to raising funds (see, for example, Cook 1994).

3. $(D/TR$ and $D - F/TR)$, $(D/TR - G$ and $D - F/TR - G)$, $(D + V^*/TR + V^*$ and $D + V^* - F/TR + V^*)$, and $(D + V^*/TR + V^* - G$ and $D + V^* - F/TR + V^* - G)$, excluding outliers.

4. $(D - F/TR$ and $D - F - A/TR)$, $(D - F/TR - G$ and $D - F - A/TR - G)$, $(D + V^* - F/TR + V^*$ and $D + V^* - F - A/TR + V^*)$, and $(D + V^* - F/TR + V^* - G$ and $D + V^* - F - A/TR + V^* - G)$, excluding outliers.

5. $(D/TR - G$ and $D/TR)$, $(D - F/TR - G$ and $D - F/TR)$, $(D - F - A/TR - G$ and $D - F - A/TR)$, $(D + V^*/TR + V^* - G$ and $D + V^*/TR + V^*)$, $(D + V^* - F/TR - G$ and $D + V^* - F/TR)$, and $(D + V^* - F - A/TR + V^* - G$ and $D + V^* - F - A/TR + V^*)$, excluding outliers.

6. $(D + V^*/TR + V$ and $D/TR)$, $(D + V^* - F/TR + V^*$ and $D - F/TR)$, $(D + V^* - F - A/TR + V^*$ and $D - F - A/TR)$, $(D + V^*/TR + V^* - G$ and $D/TR - G)$, $(D + V^* - F/TR + V^* - G$ and $D - F/TR - G)$, and $(D + V^* - F - A/TR + V^* - G$ and $D - F - A/TR - G)$ excluding outliers.

7. $(D - F - A/TR)$, $(D - F - A/TR - G)$, $(D + V^* - F - A/TR + V^*)$, and $(D + V^* - F - A/TR + V^* - G)$.

8. All formulas except $(D - F - A/TR)$, $(D - F - A/TR - G)$, $(D + V^* - F - A/TR + V^*)$, and $(D + V^* - F - A/TR + V^* - G)$.

9. The formulas included two that did not subtract any expenses from donations, four subtracting fund-raising costs, and two with and without government grants: (D/TR), $(D - F/TR)$, $(D/TR - G)$, $(D - F/TR - G)$, $(D + V^* - F/TR + V^*)$, and $(D + V^* - F/TR + V^* - G)$.

10. $(D + V^*/TR)$ and $(D + V^*/TR + V^* - G)$.

11. (D/TR), $(D - F/TR)$, $(D - F - A/TR)$, $(D/TR - G)$, $(D - F/TR - G)$, and $(D - F - A/TR - G)$.

12. $(D + V^*/TR + V^*)$, $(D + V^* - F/TR + V^*)$, $(D + V^* - F - A/TR + V^*)$, $(D + V^*/TR + V^* - G)$, $(D + V^* - F/TR + V^* - G)$, and $(D + V^* - F - A/TR + V^* - G)$.

13. (D/TR), $(D - F/TR)$, $(D - F - A/TR)$, $(D/TR - G)$, $(D - F/TR - G)$, $(D - F - A/TR - G)$, $(D + V^* - F - A/TR + V^*)$, and $(D + V^* - F - A/TR + V^* - G)$.

14. Except under formulas $(D - F - A/TR)$ and $(D - F - A/TR - G)$.

15. Formulas $(D + V^*/TR + V^*)$, $(D + V^* - F/TR + V^*)$, $(D + V^*/TR + V^* - G)$, and $(D + V^* - F/TR + V^* - G)$.

16. $(D + V^*/TR + V^*)$, $(D + V^* - F/TR + V^*)$, $(D + V^*/TR + V^* - G)$, and $(D + V^* - F/TR + V^* - G)$.

17. (D/TR) and $(D - F/TR)$.

18. $(D/TR - G)$ and $(D - F/TR - G)$.

19. Formulas $(D - F - A/TR)$ and $(D - F - A/TR - G)$.

20. Using formulas $(D + V^*/TR + V^*)$, $(D + V^* - F/TR + V^*)$, $(D + V^* - F - A/TR + V^*)$, and $(D + V^* - F - A/TR + V^* - G)$.

21. Using formulas $(D + V^*/TR + V^* - G)$ and $(D + V^* - F/TR + V^* - G)$.

22. $(D + V^*/TR + V^*)$, $(D + V^* - F/TR + V^*)$, and $(D + V^* - F - A/TR + V^*)$.

23. $(D + V^* - F - A/TR + V^* - G)$.

24. (D/TR), $(D - F/TR)$, $(D/TR - G)$, $(D - F/TR - G)$, $(D + V^* - F - A/TR + V^*)$, and $(D + V^* - F - A/TR + V^* - G)$.

25. $(D - F - A/TR)$ and $(D - F - A/TR - G)$.

26. $(D + V^*/TR + V^*)$, $(D + V^* - F/TR + V^*)$, $(D + V^*/TR + V^* - G)$, and $(D + V^* - F/TR + V^* - G)$.

27. $(D - F/TR)$, $(D - F - A/TR)$, $(D - F/TR - G)$, and $(D - F - A/TR - G)$.

28. (D/TR), $(D/TR - G)$, $(D + V^* - F/TR + V^*)$, and $(D + V^* - F/TR + V^* - G)$.

29. (D/TR), $(D - F/TR)$, $(D - F - A/TR)$, $(D/TR - G)$, $(D - F/TR - G)$, and $(D - F - A/TR - G)$.

30. $(D + V^*/TR + V^*)$, $(D + V^* - F/TR + V^*)$, $(D + V^* - F - A/TR + V^*)$, $(D + V^*/TR + V^* - G)$, and $(D + V^* - F - A/TR + V^* - G)$.

31. $(D + V^*/TR + V^*)$, $(D + V^* - F/TR + V^*)$, $(D + V^* - F - A/TR + V^*)$, $(D + V^*/TR + V^* - G)$, $(D + V^* - F/TR + V^* - G)$, and $(D + V^* - F - A/TR + V^* - G)$.

32. $(D + V^*/TR + V^*)$, $(D + V^* - F/TR + V^*)$, $(D + V^* - F - A/TR + V^*)$, $(D + V^*/TR + V^* - G)$, $(D + V^* - F/TR + V^* - G)$, and $(D + V^* - F - A/TR + V^* - G)$.

33. Except formulas $(D + V^* - F/TR + V^*)$ and $(D + V^* - F - A/TR + V^*)$.

34. (D/TR), $(D - F/TR)$ $(D - F - A/TR)$, $(D - F - A/TR - G)$, and $(D + V^* - F - A/TR + V^*)$.

35. (D/TR), $(D - F/TR)$, $(D - F - A/TR)$, $(D/TR - G)$, $(D - F/TR - G)$, and $(D - F - A/TR - G)$.

36. $[(D - F - A/TR)$ and $(D - F - A/TR - G)$.

37. (D/TR), $(D - F/TR)$, $(D - F - A/TR)$, $(D - F - A/TR - G)$, $(D + V^*/TR + V^*)$, $(D + V^* - F/TR + V^*)$, $(D + V^* - F - A/TR + V^*)$, and $(D + V^* - F - A/TR + V^* - G)$.

38. $(D - F/TR)$, $(D - F - A/TR)$, $(D - F/TR - G)$, and $(D - F - A/TR - G)$.

39. (D/TR), $(D - F/TR)$, $(D - F - A/TR)$, $(D/TR - G)$, $(D - F/TR - G)$, and $(D - F - A/TR - G)$.

40. Historically, religious nonprofits have owned more property than other charities (in fact an extensive amount of property) but—as mentioned earlier in the chapter—religious nonprofits are not required to file IRS Form 990 returns, so we do not have good data on these organizations.

REFERENCES

Anheier, Helmut K., and Stefan S. Toepler. 1998. "Commerce and the Muse: Are Art Museums Becoming Commercial?" In *To Profit or Not to Profit: The Commercial Transformation of the Nonprofit Sector*, edited by Burton A. Weisbrod (233–48). Cambridge, UK: Cambridge University Press.

Brody, Evelyn. 1998. "Of Sovereignty and Subsidy: Conceptualizing the Charity Tax-exemption." *Journal of Corporation Law* 23 (4): 585–629.

Brody, Evelyn, and Joseph J. Cordes. 1999. "Tax Treatment of Nonprofit Organizations: A Two-Edged Sword." In *Nonprofits and Government: Conflict and Collaboration*, edited by Elizabeth T. Boris and C. Eugene Steuerle (141–75). Washington, D.C.: Urban Institute Press.

Burlingame, Dwight. 1993. "Altruism and Philanthropy: Definitional Issues." *Essays on Philanthropy* 10. Indianapolis: Indiana University Center on Philanthropy.

Colombo, John D. 1993. "Why is Harvard Tax-Exempt? (And Other Mysteries of Tax Exemption for Private Educational Institutions)." *Arizona Law Review* 35: 841–903.

Colombo, John D., and Mark A. Hall. 1995. *The Charitable Tax Exemption*. Boulder, Colo.: Westview Press.

Cook, Weaver B. 1994. "Courting Philanthropy: The Role of University Presidents and Chancellors in Fund Raising." Ph.D. diss., The University of Texas at Austin.

Cordes, Joseph J., and Burton A. Weisbrod. 1998. "Differential Taxation of Nonprofits and the Commercialization of Nonprofit Revenues." In *To Profit or Not to Profit: The Commercial Transformation of the Nonprofit Sector*, edited by Burton A. Weisbrod (83–104). Cambridge, U.K.: Cambridge University Press.

Froelich, Karin A., and Terry W. Knoepfle. 1996. "Internal Revenue Service 990 Data: Fact or Fiction?" *Nonprofit and Voluntary Sector Quarterly* 25 (1): 40–52.

Gallagher, Jane. 1995. "Taxing Nonprofits: Is There A Trend?" *The Exempt Organization Tax Review* 11: 1276.

Grimm, Jr., Robert T. 1999. "Reforming Property Tax Exemption Policy in the Nonprofit Sector: Commercialism, Collective Goods, and the Donative Theory." *Nonprofit Management & Leadership* 9 (3): 241–59.

Hall, Peter D. 1987. "A Historical Overview of the Private Nonprofit Sector." In *The Nonprofit Sector: A Research Handbook*, edited by Walter W. Powell (3–21). New Haven: Yale University Press.

Hansmann, Henry. 1989. "The Two Nonprofit Sectors: Fee for Services versus Donative Organizations." In *The Future of the Nonprofit Sector: Challenges, Changes, and Policy Considerations*, edited by Virginia A. Hodgkinson, Richard W. Lyman and Associates (91–102). San Francisco: Jossey-Bass Publishers.

Hodgkinson, Virginia A., and Murray S. Weitzman. 1996. *Giving and Volunteering in the United States*. Washington, D.C.: Independent Sector.

Hodgkinson, Virginia A., Murray S. Weitzman, and John A. Abrahams, with Eric A. Crutchfield and David R. Stevenson. 1996. *Nonprofit Almanac: Dimensions of the Independent Sector, 1996–1997*. San Francisco: Jossey-Bass Publishers.

Hodgkinson, Virginia A., Murray S. Weitzman, Stephen M. Noga, and Heather A. Gorski. 1993. *A Portrait of the Independent Sector: The Activities and Finances of Charitable Organizations*. Washington, D.C.: Independent Sector.

James, Estelle. 1998. "Commercialism among Nonprofits: Objectives, Opportunities, and Constraints." In *To Profit or Not to Profit: The Commercial Transformation of the Nonprofit Sector*, edited by Burton A. Weisbrod (271–86). Cambridge, UK: Cambridge University Press.

Kingsman, Bruce. 1997. "Public Goods Theories of the Nonprofit Sector: Weisbrod Revisited." *Voluntas* 8 (2): 135–48.

Leland, Pam J. 1996. "Exploring Challenges to Nonprofit Status: Issues of Definition and Access in Community-Based Research." *American Behavioral Scientist* 39 (5): 587–601.

———. 1994. "Responding to a Property Tax Challenge: Lessons Learned in Pennsylvania." *The Exempt Organization Tax Review* 6: 1359–73.

Margolis, Howard. 1982. *Selfishness, Altruism, and Rationality: A Theory of Social Change*. Chicago: University of Chicago Press.

National Center for Charitable Statistics. 1997. Http://nccs.urban.org/.

National Society of Fund Raising Executives. 1997. "Payments in Lieu of Taxes: A Position Paper." Alexandria, VA: National Society of Fund Raising Executives.

NSFRE. *See* National Society of Fund Raising Executives.

Orend, Richard J., Michael O'Neill, and Connie S. Mitchell. 1997. "State Nonprofit Databases: Lessons from the California Experience." *Nonprofit Management & Leadership* 7 (4): 447–54.

Philanthropic Research. 1997. GuideStar Directory of American Charities. Http://www.guidestar.org/.

Powell, Walter W., and Jason Owen-Smith. 1998. "Universities as Creators of Intellectual Property: Life-Science Research and Commercial Development." In *To Profit or Not to Profit: The Commercial Transformation of the Nonprofit Sector*, edited by Burton A. Weisbrod (169–94). Cambridge, U.K.: Cambridge University Press.

Salamon, Lester. 1995a. *Partners In Public Service: Government-Nonprofit Relations in the Modern Welfare State.* Baltimore: Johns Hopkins University Press.

———. 1995b. "The Crisis of the Nonprofit Sector." Paper presented at the Annual Conference of Independent Sector. October 24.

Sander, Kathleen S. 1998. *The Business of Charity: The Women's Exchange Movement, 1832–1900.* Urbana: University of Illinois Press.

Scrivner, Gary N. 1998. "Review of *The Charitable Tax Exemption, Federal Taxation in America: A Short History, and Dimensions of Law in the Service of Order: Origins of the Federal Income Tax, 1861–1913.*" *Nonprofit and Voluntary Sector Quarterly* 27 (1): 107–18.

Sloan, Frank A. 1998. "Commercialism in Nonprofit Hospitals." In *To Profit or Not to Profit: The Commercial Transformation of the Nonprofit Sector*, edited by Burton A. Weisbrod (151–68). Cambridge, UK: Cambridge University Press.

Smith, Steven R., and Michael Lipsky. 1993. *Nonprofits for Hire: The Welfare State in the Age of Contracting.* Cambridge: Harvard University Press.

Steinberg, Richard. 1997. "On the Regulation of Fundraising." In *Critical Issues in Fundraising*, edited by Dwight Burlingame (234–44). New York: John Wiley & Son.

———. 1995. "United Cancer Council v. Commissioner of the IRS and the Indirect Regulation of Fundraising." Indiana University Center on Philanthropy Working Paper #95-21. Indianapolis: Indiana University Center on Philanthropy.

———. 1991. "'Unfair' Competition by Nonprofits and Tax Policy." *National Tax Journal* 44 (3): 351–64.

Steinberg, Richard, and Marc Bilodeau. 1999. "Should Nonprofit Organizations Pay Sales and Property Taxes?" White Paper. Washington, D.C.: National Council of Nonprofit Associations.

Stevenson, David R., Tom H. Pollak, and Linda M. Lampkin, with Kathryn L.S. Pettit and Nicholas A. Stengel. 1997. *State Nonprofit Almanac 1997: Profiles of Charitable Organizations.* Washington, D.C.: Urban Institute Press.

Weisbrod, Burton, ed. 1998. *To Profit or Not to Profit: The Commercial Transformation of the Nonprofit Sector.* Cambridge, UK: Cambridge University Press.

———. 1988. *The Nonprofit Economy.* Cambridge: Harvard University.

———. 1980. "Private Goods, Collective Goods: The Role of the Nonprofit Sector." In *Research in Law and Economics, Supplement 1*, edited by Kenneth W. Clarkson and Donald L. Martin (139–77). Greenwich: JAI Press.

———. 1977. *The Voluntary Nonprofit Sector: An Economic Analysis.* Lexington, Mass.: Lexington Books.

————. 1972. *Toward a Theory of the Voluntary Non-Profit Sector in a Three-Sector Economy.* Madison, Wisc.: University of Wisconsin.

Young, Dennis R. 1998. "Commercialism in Nonprofit Social Services Associations: Its Character, Significance, and Rationale." In *To Profit or Not to Profit: The Commercial Transformation of the Nonprofit Sector,* edited by Burton A. Weisbrod (195–216). Cambridge, U.K.: Cambridge University Press.

COMMENTARIES

Property-Tax Exemption for Charities

The Minnesota Experience

Daniel Salomone

In setting out the legal and political framework of the property-tax exemption enjoyed by charities, Janne Gallagher (chapter 1 of this volume) and Joan Youngman (chapter 2 of this volume) reach the same conclusion in their chapters: that scrutiny of public charities will increase. Experience in the state of Minnesota demonstrates that each element of the exemption has been, and will continue to be, strongly contested.

Legal and Societal Trends

Gallagher's review of the legal standards of public charities provides important distinctions and generalizations. First, charitable exemptions stem from both state constitutions and legislative authority. In Minnesota, for example, the state constitution guarantees property-tax exemptions for churches and houses of worship; property used solely for educational purposes by academies, colleges, universities, and seminaries of learning; and property exempt by federal law, such as U.S. government property, Indian lands, and certain public housing.[1] These exemptions cannot be altered by legislation. However, the Minnesota constitution empowers the legislature to define or limit exemptions for property owned by churches (other than houses of worship), institutions of purely public charity, property owned by a governmental entity and used solely for public purposes, public hospitals, and public burial grounds (Minnesota House of Representatives 1994).

Second, Gallagher reminds us that possession of Internal Revenue Code section 501(c)(3) status does not bear much relation to state property-tax exemptions. Though 501(c)(3) status may be necessary to secure the exemption, it certainly is not sufficient. This is contrary to the common perception that 501(c)(3) entities are truly tax free.

Third, Gallagher notes the variety of state approaches to exempting charities, as well as the increasing trend toward more scrutiny, testing, and denial, based on two important 1985 state supreme court cases—*Intermountain Health Care* (Utah) and *Health Utilization Project* (Pennsylvania)—and the evolving application of multipart tests. Litigation in Minnesota, mostly involving public charities, centers on the application of a six-part test found in the 1975 Minnesota Supreme Court case *North Star Research Institute v. County of Hennepin*, 306 Minn. 1, 236 N.W.2d 754 (1975). *North Star's* six factors relate to whether, in helping others, charities expect material reward; are supported by gifts and donations; provide assistance without requiring recipients to pay; use all income from property and gifts to advance their charitable purpose; restrict benefits to certain classes of beneficiaries; and, when dissolved, make income available to private interests.

Because no statutory rules exist for what is or is not a pure charity, and since *North Star* and subsequent cases have ruled that all six factors need not be satisfied to qualify for the exemption, the Minnesota Department of Revenue is developing "guidelines" for local assessors. Draft guidelines for assisted-living facilities, for example, provide examples of activities that might satisfy each factor, and how compliance could conceivably be documented (Minnesota Department of Revenue 2000). In the draft, assessors are reminded that taxation is the rule, and the burden of proof is on those seeking exemptions, and that tax exemptions are based on the accomplishment of public purposes.

Finally, Gallagher notes that although ownership of charitable property is necessary to the exemption, use of charitable property is equally necessary. In general, charitable property must be used for charitable purposes. Excessive amounts of property, investment holdings, budget reserves, and competition with for-profit organizations jeopardize property-exempt status. For example, Minnesota assessors are advised

that assisted-living facilities with more land or larger structures than reasonably needed to accomplish their charitable purpose should be split
into taxable and exempt parts.

The Property-Tax Exemption in the Political Context

Joan Youngman covers social and cultural factors that change the public's perception of nonprofits and charities. She notes that such groups'
growing size, business demeanor, involvement in for-profit activities,
and political involvement with controversial issues have increased
their visibility. Increased attention from the press—particularly when
scandals come to light—has made the public, and hence politicians,
more willing to question exempt organizations' preferential tax treatment. Youngman asserts that the political aspects of the charity-
exemption debate are the most lively and unpredictable, and she
appropriately ascribes much of the conflict to the unique character of
the property tax.

First, the property tax lacks a clear rationale. Under what theory is it
supposed to distribute the burden of the government? As an "ability-to-
pay" tax, it taxes only real-property wealth (and some personal-property
wealth), but not other forms of wealth. Many property owners—such as
cabin owners in Minnesota and seniors everywhere—argue that wealth
has little to do with ability to pay tax bills. Although the property tax has
some characteristics of a benefits tax, it fails to correlate payments with
benefits received, since it is based on value alone. In Minnesota, until
recent reforms, only about 20 percent of an average property-tax bill was
for city services, where the benefits test might be the strongest. The
biggest part of the property tax bill—the school portion—diffuses benefits broadly over a wide set of taxpayers, including those outside the
taxing jurisdiction.[2] But rationale and politics aside, Minnesota's local
property tax raises $4.7 billion annually, about as much as the state per-
sonal income tax; it is unlikely to be revoked.

The most troublesome aspect of the property tax—one that will continue to threaten charitable exemptions—is its zero-sum nature. Unlike
other state or local taxes, local property-tax levies and taxable values are
usually fixed in advance, and tax rates are determined mathematically,
not statutorily. So exemptions automatically shift taxes to non-exempt
property, absent offsetting levy adjustments or increases in local revenue

from other sources, such as fees or intergovernmental aid. This shift is highly publicized in Minnesota, where the effects of annual tinkering with statutory classification rates (class-specific exemption rates) are closely monitored and reported by the press. When exemptions are proposed, legislators, the press, and the public ask proponents how they propose to offset the local revenue loss so that taxes do not shift to other properties.

Charity exemptions have the same effect. Though most exemptions have been on the books for a long time, taxpayers in Minnesota know that repealing or restricting them would increase the tax base, decrease local tax rates, and provide tax relief to other property owners. Tax shifts from most charitable-exemption changes might be of little consequence, but there is an overwhelming desire to protect homeowners, farmers, and seniors, all of whom vote in local elections. Owners of cabins, businesses, and apartment buildings are less likely to live and vote where their property is located, so it is not surprising that they bear a disproportionately large share of local levies.

Youngman notes that property-tax expenditures—the granting of preferences through exemptions instead of direct appropriations—often are not the best way to provide assistance to favored properties, but they are sometimes seen as the only way. Charities account for nearly 5 percent ($57 million) of all property-tax exemptions in Minnesota.[3] Exemptions for public property, schools, and hospitals are much more significant, at $538 million, $405 million, and $135 million, respectively. The preference for tax expenditures over appropriations is part of a bigger theme in state and local taxation. Popular resistance to spending and tax increases makes tax expenditures, indirect taxation (business taxation), and progressive tax increases more attractive.

Confusion about the purpose and guiding principles for the local property tax makes it easy for advocates to lobby for exemptions, particularly if the dollar value of proposed exemptions is relatively small. Youngman notes that the absence of norms for what should be taxable makes the property tax seem arbitrary, and encourages a steady erosion of the base. This is especially true in highly classified states, such as Minnesota, where state law arbitrarily redistributes tax burdens among many classes of property. Proliferation of exemptions and class-specific tax rates, in effect, cheapen the status of long-standing charity exemptions. In a sense, charities might ask, "What good are tax exemptions if everyone is getting them?"

Both authors note that pressure for local governments to find more sources of local, own-source revenues will keep tensions high between public charities and taxing jurisdictions. Factors such as loss of federal funds, taxpayer resistance, tax limitations, the fear of losing local sales-tax revenue from electronic commerce, the aging of the politically powerful baby boomers, and new personal-property exemptions associated with utility deregulation make it more likely that charitable exemptions will be attacked, and more likely that payments in lieu of taxes (PILOTs) and other compensating payments will need to accompany future base exemptions.

Minnesota may be ahead of the curve on this. Virtually all significant base exemptions are coordinated with increased state aid or local expenditure reductions or with state takeovers of local functions. Even changes in classification rates are neutralized with state aid to offset tax shifts.

Postscript on Governor Ventura's Tax Proposals for Nonprofits

In January 2001, after nearly two years of study and discussion, Minnesota Governor Jesse Ventura unveiled a "Big Plan" for state tax reform, with proposals in nearly all areas of taxation, including taxes on nonprofit organizations.

The focus of the plan was a $1.3 billion reduction of school property taxes, financed by extending the state sales tax to business and personal services, and by creating a new state property tax on nonresidential properties, such as businesses, resorts, and golf courses. The plan would have increased the state's share of school funding from 65 percent to 85 percent, while providing a third round of sales tax rebates and significant reductions in the personal income tax.

The plan's goal for school levies had strong public and legislative support. But opposition to the idea of taxing services, and subsequent reductions in projected state revenues, forced the governor to revise his proposal to focus mainly on the property-tax reforms. One large block of opposition to the Big Plan was removed when the administration, under heavy fire from the nonprofit sector, withdrew its sales tax and property-tax proposals affecting exempt entities.

The Big Plan would have repealed sales tax exemptions for YMCA, YWCA, and JCC membership dues, and for tickets or admissions to events sponsored by nonprofit groups. Offsetting the tax increase from these changes were proposals to raise the annual limit on other exempt sales made by senior and youth groups (from $10,000 to $25,000) and to extend it to all exempt organizations, and to fully exempt all purchases made by section 501(c)(3) entities having federal determination letters and state tax-identification numbers. Currently, only certain purchases by selected nonprofit groups are exempt. Although these sales tax proposals would have provided nearly $12 million in net tax relief to the nonprofit sector, a firestorm of opposition against taxing membership dues and ticket sales led to their withdrawal. Those who would have benefited from expansion of exemptions were relatively silent.

Also withdrawn from the plan was a controversial proposal to allow cities to impose a fee on "institutions of purely public charity" to cover public safety expenditures. Under this proposal, the estimated market value of exempt property would have been subject to the same classification rates (assessment ratios) applied to higher-valued homes and lower-valued businesses (1.5 percent of value); the resulting taxable value would have been subject to only a portion of city tax rates, determined by dividing each city's public safety expenditures by its taxable property base. Public property was excluded because certain state-aid payments already compensate cities for the public-property exemption. Hospitals and nursing homes were also excluded because the tax increase would likely have required Medicaid rate increases. So the proposal was effectively limited to about 5 percent of all tax-exempt property. Though of relatively minor fiscal significance ($3.2 million a year if all cities adopted it), even this limited provision was viewed by opponents as being the proverbial camel's nose under the exempt-entity tent.

Conclusion

The Gallagher and Youngman chapters make it clear that we need more clarity on the definition of public charity. While few bright-line tests can be found, principles are evolving that will guide decisions on taxability. In any event, considerable ambiguity will likely remain as to what is needed specifically to protect the charitable exemption. Determinations will continue to be made on a case-by-case basis.

Further, rationalization of most local property-tax systems would create additional predictability and stability for exempt, and potentially exempt, taxpayers. For example, the Minnesota Taxpayers Association has argued for a realignment of state aid, increasing support for state mandates and other state interests (such as K–12 spending), and decreasing subsidies for municipal functions that have the character of services to property. If property-tax levies are more closely tied to benefits and services to property owners, then they take on the character of user fees, making the tax more understandable and fair, and exemptions—even those for charities—harder to defend. The growing use of PILOTs, special assessments, and special taxing districts could lead to the same outcome, but only if they are applied consistently.

Until such reforms occur, the debate over nonprofit and charity exemptions will continue, and, as always, policy will be determined in the political arena. Gallagher suggests charities need to sell the public on the virtue of their exemption. Youngman sees a rough ride for charities, but predicts that they will likely win out in a popularity contest against businesses and governmental agencies, which, she suggests, may have even bigger public relations problems.

NOTES

1. Minnesota Constitution Article X, § 1.

2. Reforms enacted by the 2001 Legislature include a substantial portion of the property-tax reforms proposed by Governor Jesse Ventura. A notable result of those reforms is that the school share most property-tax bills will fall from 45 percent to 25 percent.

3. The 5 percent figure excludes tax expenditures associated with value limitations and classification.

REFERENCES

Minnesota Department of Revenue, Property Tax Division. 2000. *Assisted Living Care Facility Bulletin* (Draft Copy, March 23).

Minnesota House of Representatives, House Research Information Brief. 1994. *Tax Exempt Property: An Overview of Minnesota Law* (September).

A Public-Choice Approach to Explaining Exemptions and PILOTs

David L. Sjoquist

There are three broad questions associated with the issue of the taxation of nonprofits. First, how should nonprofits be treated with regard to taxation? This normative question is the one on which most of the writing on the taxation of nonprofits seems to have focused (Young 1999; Brody and Cordes 1999; and Simon 1987 provide discussions).

Second, what effect does the current tax treatment have on the behavior of nonprofits? For example, research has been conducted on the effect of property-tax exemption on the charity's decision to own or rent (e.g., Cordes, Gantz, and Pollak, chapter 4 of this volume), on an organization's choice of nonprofit or for-profit status (e.g., Goddeeris and Weisbrod 1999), and on the relative market share of nonprofit and for-profits hospitals (e.g., Gulley and Santerre 1993).

Third, why are nonprofits treated the way they are? This is the question that is most relevant to the four chapters in part III, "The Economic War within the States." And while the authors do not base their chapters on it, this is still the question common to all four. They represent descriptive case studies of changes in attitudes toward, or treatment of, payments in lieu of taxes (PILOTs) and property-tax exemptions for nonprofits. These chapters comprise some of the first research on this question. My purpose is not to provide a critique of the chapters, but rather to suggest a simple unifying framework for their findings.

The decision to provide or remove a property-tax exemption (or to adopt a PILOT) can be put in a public-choice framework, in which competing groups lobby (or otherwise bring pressure on) elected officials in order to obtain a certain policy.[1] We might consider taxpayers, perhaps organized by the local government, on one side of this issue, and non-profits and their supporters on the other. Within such a lobbying model, the pressure a group is able to exert depends on the number of individuals or organizations that lobby and on the resources that each side brings to bear. The amount of lobbying for or against a property-tax exemption or PILOT will depend on the benefits and costs that individuals or groups expect to receive from successfully implementing their preferred alternative.

In this model, we assume that a property-tax exemption for nonprofits exists, and focus on the efforts to remove and retain it or to impose or prevent a surrogate such as a PILOT. It is helpful to think of just two groups, those who oppose the exemption and those who support it (in reality, of course, individuals range from strongly supporting to strongly opposing such programs). An individual's choice of group will depend on whether the net benefits for the individual are larger for imposing a PILOT (or removing the exemption) or for preventing a PILOT (or retaining the exemption).

Within the framework of a lobbying model, and based in large part on the material contained in the four chapters in part III, the following are thoughts about which specific factors might influence the pressure for eliminating a property-tax exemption or imposing a PILOT. Essentially, the discussion focuses on which conditions would lead to higher net benefits. In discussing each factor, we assume that other factors are given. The discussion could apply to a single nonprofit, a type of nonprofit, or nonprofits in general.

Consider first those who oppose the exemption:

- The larger the potential reduction in an individual's property taxes, or increase in public services, the greater the incentive to try to bar exemptions. Thus, the larger the amount of revenue per capita that would be obtained from eliminating the property-tax exemption or adopting a PILOT, the larger the incentive to try to implement such a policy. This suggests that the more important property taxes are relative to other sources of revenue in a jurisdiction, the greater the incentive to remove the exemption. Likewise, the larger the ratio of the total value of the exempt property to the property-tax base, the larger the incentive to remove the exemption. In New Haven and Hartford, Connecticut, exempt properties (including government-owned as well as nonprofit) were nearly 70 percent and 54 percent, respectively, of the total value of real property. Such situations provide a strong incentive for attempting to collect property taxes from the nonprofits.

- In jurisdictions that are fiscally strapped, either the property-tax rate is already so high that resistance to a further increase will be strong, or the increase in property-tax rate necessary to finance government services is very large. In either case, residents are likely to look for other sources of revenue, such as nonprofits' exempt property. As noted in part III, Philadelphia, New Haven, and Hartford were experiencing fiscal stress when they tried to implement PILOTs.

- The less residents of the taxing jurisdiction directly benefit from the nonprofits' services, or the less widespread the benefits, the greater the incentive to eliminate the exemption. In the case of a private university such as Yale, for example, the direct beneficiaries (i.e., the students) are mostly not from the local community. However, residents who work for or supply goods and services to a nonprofit are likely to support maintaining the exemption.

- The likelihood that someone will lobby in support of or in opposition to a nonprofit's exemption may depend upon whom the nonprofit serves, the nature of the services provided, and the nature of the nonprofit. First, the more that benefits go to groups with a higher profile or to those with greater lobbying strength (e.g., the nonpoor), the smaller the expected effort to remove the exemption or to adopt PILOTs. Second, many nonprofits are a source of non-pecuniary benefits (e.g., the satisfaction residents receive from a nonprofit's work in reducing teen pregnancy, or the prestige that comes from living near a world-famous museum or university). The greater the extent of such benefits, the less inclined individuals are likely to be to lobby to eliminate the exemption. Third, if the nonprofit's services are similar to those provided by for-profit organizations, residents may question the benefit from the property-tax exemption. This may help explain the frequent challenges to the exemption for hospitals by many communities (McDermott and Cornia 1989). Likewise, nonprofits that provide free services and commercial nonprofits may be treated differently. Fourth, if the nonprofit could easily move, concerns over the possible loss of jobs may curtail efforts to eliminate the exemption or impose a PILOT.

- Assuming that the exemption is authorized at the state level, the uniformity of nonprofits' distribution across the state will affect lobbying efforts. For example, if most of the nonprofits are in one central city, then city residents may lobby for a change in the exemption policy, but non-city residents are not likely to. Alternatively, if the nonprofits are widely distributed, then there should be lobbying from throughout the state. It is an empirical question whether the more-intensive lobbying by the central city in the former case is more effective than the less-intensive lobbying by a larger population in the latter. The attempt, described by Carbone and Brody (chapter 10 of this volume), to involve citizens throughout Connecticut in lobbying to change the exemption policy can be seen as an effort to overcome the problem of having just one city involved. The Connecticut case also illustrated nonprofits' ability to shift their local problem to the state.

The mere existence of benefits from eliminating the property-tax exemption may not necessarily result in any lobbying. For example, each member of the general public would likely reap a small benefit from eliminating the property-tax exemption for nonprofits, and thus free-riding is likely. If this is the case, we would expect little effort by individuals to eliminate the exemption. This result often appears in public-choice models, and suggests that a change in policy toward nonprofits requires either a major change in incentives to lobby or the existence of an organization (e.g., a municipal government) that forestalls free-riding.

Similarly, public attitudes toward nonprofits can also affect the likelihood of lobbying for removal of exemptions. If nonprofits are viewed as extensions of government, as Hall (chapter 11 of this volume) points out they were in the early days of the country, then voters are probably less inclined to tax them. However, if the public's view of nonprofits changes, as Hall notes it has, then the inclination to tax nonprofits is also likely to change.

The likelihood of lobbying will also depend on whether it is expected to be effective. If individuals do not believe they will succeed, then they will probably be less inclined to lobby.

Now consider the factors that might affect the likelihood that nonprofits, and those who are inclined to support them, will work to keep the exemption or resist adoption of a PILOT.

- The larger the cost to the nonprofit of losing the exemption or the adoption of a PILOT relative to the nonprofit's ability to pay, the more likely it is that the nonprofit will oppose such a change. Thus, a large nonprofit (e.g., a hospital or university) would probably be very resistant to a PILOT and the loss of the exemption. But if a PILOT requires a nonprofit simply to document that it is serving local residents or to hold a bake sale, then there is not likely to be much opposition, since the cost would be low relative to nonprofits' ability to pay.
- Nonprofits that rent are less likely to oppose the elimination of the exemption than those that own. However, a nonprofit may expect to own property in the future, and thus still oppose a change. There are also cases in which nonprofits rent from another nonprofit; in states that exempt property leased between nonprofits, presumably the rent would increase if the exemption were eliminated. Nonprofits in that situation would likely oppose the elimination of the exemption or the imposition of a PILOT.
- Nonprofits may believe that the elimination of the property-tax exemption will open the door to changes in other aspects of their tax treatment. Thus, nonprofits might see the costs of eliminating the property-tax exemption as being greater than simply the property taxes they would then have to pay, and might cause them to oppose the elimination more strenuously. This, it was suggested, was the logic behind reluctance of nonprofits in Philadelphia to agree to any language in the PILOT that implied they should pay property taxes (Glancey, chapter 9 of this volume).
- A nonprofit might benefit in various ways from agreeing to a PILOT, or even from elimination of the property-tax exemption. The greater these benefits, the less likely the nonprofit will oppose such policies. For example, there might be public relations value to a university from making contributions to assist the local community, if the university can present such payments as an enhancement of the university's community-engagement mission. There might be also be more-direct benefits. For example, it might be easier for a nonprofit to pay the local government to clean up an adja-

cent neighborhood than for the nonprofit to do the cleanup. The imposition of a PILOT might help spark a successful fund-raising campaign. And, as noted in several of the chapters, a nonprofit might have to agree to a PILOT as a quid pro quo for getting a zoning change or a building permit.

- A nonprofit may agree to a PILOT if it means avoiding the risk of having to make even bigger payments. When the PILOT program was introduced in Philadelphia, for example, there was the distinct possibility that the city had the authority to eliminate a property-tax exemption. As Glancey (chapter 9 of this volume) suggests, nonprofits may have agreed to the PILOT program out of fear the city would eliminate the exemption all together. Given that it is now clear that the city does not have that authority, it will be interesting to see if the nonprofits are as willing to renew their PILOT agreements.

- The smaller the nonprofit or the nonprofit sector, in relative terms, the less lobbying force it presents, and hence the less effective the sector will be at fighting an effort to eliminate the exemption. Of course, the smaller the sector, the less likely there will be an effort to eliminate the exemption or impose a PILOT.

The effectiveness of lobbying, of course, will depend on the effort each side exerts; strong lobbying from one side will offset strong lobbying from the other. In addition, the institutional setting will affect the likelihood that a given level of lobbying will be effective. For example, if the exemption is provided by the state's constitution, as opposed to a general law, then changing it will be more difficult. On the other hand, if, as was the case in Philadelphia, a city has more leeway to challenge an exemption, then the outcome is likely to be different.

The chapters in this section present evidence that is consistent with the simple framework I have outlined. And thus, perhaps, it is a framework that helps explain when nonprofits will face increased pressures to adopt PILOTs and when they will be unsuccessful in resisting them.

NOTE

1. See Becker (1983) for the seminal presentation of the formal lobbying model.

REFERENCES

Becker, Gary S. 1983. "A Theory of Competition Among Pressure Groups for Political Influence." *The Quarterly Journal of Economics* 98 (3): 371–400.

Brody, Evelyn, and Joseph Cordes. 1999. "Tax Treatment of Nonprofit Organizations: A Two-Edged Sword?" In *Nonprofits and Government: Collaboration and Conflict,* edited by Elizabeth T. Boris and C. Eugene Steuerle (141–75). Washington, D.C.: The Urban Institute Press.

Goddeeris, John H., and Burton A. Weisbrod. 1999. "Why Not For-Profit? Conversions and Public Policy." In *Nonprofits and Government: Collaboration and Conflict,* edited by Elizabeth T. Boris and C. Eugene Steuerle (235–65). Washington, D.C.: The Urban Institute Press.

Gulley, O. David., and Rexford E. Santerre. 1993. "The Effect of Tax Exemption on the Market Share of Nonprofit Hospitals." *National Tax Journal* 46 (4): 477–86.

McDermott, Richard E., and Gary C. Cornia. 1989. "Property Tax Exemption for Nonprofit Hospitals." *Hospital and Health Services Administration* 34 (4): 493–506.

Simon, John. 1987. "The Tax Treatment of Nonprofit Organizations: A Review of Federal and State Policies." In *The Nonprofit Sector: A Research Handbook,* edited by Walter W. Powell (67–98). New Haven: Yale University Press.

Young, Dennis R. 1999. "Complementary, Supplementary, or Adversarial? A Theoretical and Historical examination of Nonprofit-Government Relations in the United States." In *Nonprofits and Government: Collaboration and Conflict,* edited by Elizabeth T. Boris and C. Eugene Steuerle (31–67). Washington, D.C.: The Urban Institute Press.

Reform as Preservation

Edward A. Zelinsky

The property-tax exemption for charities is today best understood in the context of other policies, programs, and exemptions that, by alleviating the most politically compelling pressures from taxpayers, have perpetuated the property-tax's existence. Indeed, it is difficult to assess the exemption for charitable properties without considering the plethora of devices that bestow tax relief on a wide array of noncharitable property owners.

While academics and policy analysts were debating the merits of the property tax during the latter half of the 20th century, legislators and voters were responding to taxpayers' loudest complaints about the local property levy. The result has been a nationwide expansion of devices that answer some of the most politically urgent outcries about the tax. These devices fall into three categories: provisions that abate the local property taxes of particular kinds of taxpayers (e.g., homeowners, the elderly, farmers); general limitations that cap the taxes local governments can impose; and increased financial assistance to municipal treasuries to offset the need for local property-tax revenues.[1]

Among the best-known devices in the first category is the classic homestead exemption, which immunizes from taxation a portion of the value of each taxpayer's principal residence (e.g., the first $10,000 of the taxpayer's primary home).[2] Since commercial and industrial real estate does not receive equivalent exemption, the burden of the tax shifts toward such nonexempted property.

Equally well known are devices—variously denoted as homestead provisions,[3] "circuitbreakers,"[4] or income tax credits[5]—which provide relief for an individual's property-tax obligation on the basis of the person's age (typically, 65 or older), income level,[6] or disability. Despite the arguments that belie the image of the fixed-income retiree squeezed by property taxes—the putative fixed-income retiree has substantial imputed income from his or her home; the community may have educated the retiree's children at considerable cost; given the inflation-adjusted nature of Social Security and many private pensions, the retiree's income is not so fixed—the image of the cash-poor elderly property taxpayer packs significant political wallop. Legislatures have, unsurprisingly, responded.

Particularly noteworthy has been the increasing use of state income-tax systems to bestow property-tax relief. Such use allows legislators and governors to make clear to the public that they (rather than municipal officeholders) are abating the property-tax burden, since, on an annual basis, the credit is reflected on taxpayers' state income-tax returns (rather than their local property-tax bills). One need not accept the premises of public-choice theory in their starkest form to see the resulting political advantage to state officials, in contrast to alternative forms of reducing property-tax obligations (e.g., state assistance to municipal treasuries) that channel relief through the municipality and thus fail to alert taxpayers that that their relief ultimately emanates from the statehouse, not city hall.

As an administrative matter, such credits have much to commend them. The annual return for state income taxes is a particularly efficient means of channeling income-based property-tax relief, since the return must be filed anyway, and thus constitutes a preexisting device for communicating, at low marginal cost, the availability of property-tax relief (Zelinsky 1986, 1010). Taxpayers who file state income-tax returns are reminded to take the credit for property taxes. Moreover, taxpayers who disclose income on their returns automatically reveal their income levels for the purpose of the property-tax credit, allowing the credit to be calibrated to the appropriate level.

Many critics of the property tax would view the profusion of circuitbreakers, homestead exemptions, and income-tax credits for property taxes paid as important steps in the demise of the property tax. In practice, though, these devices have undergirded a different political dynamic: By addressing some of the most politically compelling complaints about the property tax, such mechanisms "fix" the tax, inoculating it against more radical surgery.

One could imagine scenarios where progressively higher homestead levels or more-generous circuitbreakers so decimate the property-tax base that it effectively ceases to exist. So far, however, the dynamic has been to ameliorate: By alleviating the burdens of homeowners, these devices have tended to preserve the tax from more radical assault, allowing the property tax to play a reduced, but still important, role in financing local government.

Yet another approach has been the classification of different types of properties for the purpose of taxing the various classes at different rates. At one level, homestead exemptions, tax credits, and circuitbreakers—usually available only to homeowners—implicitly serve as classification devices, since they target relief to one kind of real estate (i.e., principal residences). However, classification schemes in their prototypical form explicitly divide all taxed properties into a variety of different categories, each with its own effective tax rate.[7] Not surprisingly, the politically sensitive categories—owner-occupied homes, the homes of the disabled, farms—tend to receive the most lenient treatment under such schemes.

As an administrative matter, classification schemes raise important issues of workability. As the number of categories multiplies, the problems of pigeonholing particular properties become more pronounced. Moreover, under such arrangements, political pressure mounts, both to create more categories and to manipulate the categorization of specific properties. At a more theoretical level, broad classification schemes (even more so than narrowly focused circuitbreakers, homestead exemptions, and property-tax credits) violate the basic premise of ad valorem property taxation (i.e., that tax burdens should be allocated in accordance with fair market value). Under the prototypical classification scheme,[8] two adjacent properties with identical fair market values may have significantly different tax obligations because they are classified differently.[9]

Even in states without general classification schemes, one form of property is often singled out generically for more lenient taxation: farm land, frequently taxed on less than its fair market value.[10] The defense of such favorable treatment typically invokes the image of the family farm on the cusp of suburban development. If that farm is appraised and taxed at fair market value (i.e., as land subdivided for housing) the family will be forced to sell the farm to pay property taxes. If the farm is taxed more lightly, the argument goes, the family can continue its agricultural lifestyle. Special tax treatment for farm land appeals to the most basic cultural iconography of American life, as well as to contemporary concerns about suburban sprawl. For present purposes, however, classifying farm land for more favorable property-tax treatment reconciles a distinct, well-organized group—farmers—to the continuance of real-property taxation.

In contrast to devices that abate the taxes of particular taxpayers and properties, a second type of provision imposes general limitations on localities' ability to tax. The best known of these is California's Proposition 13, which generally precludes municipalities from taxing more than 1 percent of assessed value. Proposition 13 spawned a host of similar property-tax limitations throughout the country.[11] Even in states that did not adopt such limitations, Proposition 13 created a climate that increased the (already great) sensitivity of municipal officials to the political perils of raising property-tax rates.

Some observers viewed Proposition 13 as validating the belief that the property tax was doomed to extinction. In retrospect, the reality has, again, been more complex: By capping locally derived property-tax revenues, Proposition 13 and its progeny have generally provided sufficient relief from property taxation to preempt further efforts to abolish the tax.

A third practical reason that local property taxation has survived into the 21st century has been the growth of alternative revenues for municipal treasuries, revenues that have mitigated the need to raise funds from the property tax and have correspondingly reduced localities' reliance on property-tax dollars. In part, the growth of alternative revenues has taken the form of increased state aid to localities, filling the financial gaps left by Proposition 13 and its progeny. In response to state judicial determinations that educational funding overly reliant on local property-tax revenues is constitutionally defective, states have provided more aid to public school systems (Sokolow 1998). Municipally imposed user fees constitute yet another expanding revenue source for localities in the wake of property-tax limitations (Sheffrin 1998, 135).

In the context of this volume, a particularly notable revenue source for localities has been expanded payments in lieu of taxes (PILOTs). PILOTs come in a variety of configurations. In one, a higher level of government that owns property uses its general revenues to reimburse the lower-level jurisdictions in which the property is located for some or all of the taxes the property would yield if it were taxable. Thus, for example, the federal government in a variety of instances reimburses states and localities for taxes such jurisdictions would otherwise receive from federally owned land.[12] Similarly, many states compensate municipalities for state-owned (i.e., tax-exempt) properties within the municipalities' borders.[13] In the case of other PILOTs, states reimburse localities for properties owned by governmental instrumentalities (e.g., publicly owned utilities, housing authorities, airport commissions).[14] In still other variations of PILOT programs, such instrumentalities are directed or authorized to use their own operating revenues to make payments to localities in lieu of taxes.[15] At least two states (Connecticut and Rhode Island) make PILOTs from general revenues to reimburse municipalities for the presence of certain private, nonprofit institutions within the municipalities' respective boundaries.[16]

In another version, PILOTs come to the locality by agreement between the locality and a private tax-exempt entity, which sends a check to the municipal treasury while the entity retains its exempt status. While these PILOTs are nominally voluntary, the political reality is usually more complicated, since the municipality brandishes any number of potential sanctions to induce the payments.[17] These sanctions range from marshaling public opinion against the exempt entity if it declines to make PILOTs, to denial of zoning relief or building permits desired by the tax-exempt entity, to, in extreme cases, threats to seek political or judicial revocation of the entity's tax-exempt status.

In practice, it is typically in everyone's interest to compromise on a "voluntary" PILOT, which is often less than the full tax that would be paid on loss of exempt status, but which, from the municipality's perspective, provides immediate financial succor.

In short, a variety of measures have, over time, alleviated many of the most burdensome features of the property tax. By responding to the most pressing political imperatives, these measures have immunized the local property tax from outright abolition—a classic case of reform as preservation.

NOTES

1. In theory, there is a fourth category of devices that has abated the pinch of the real property tax: market-based arrangements, such as so-called "reverse mortgages," that permit older persons to borrow incrementally against the unrealized appreciation of their homes. However, in practice, such market-based devices have not played a significant role in alleviating discontent with the property tax.

2. See, for example, Texas Tax Code Sections 11.13(a) and 11.13(b), which provide all adults with a basic "exemption from taxation" for county and school district property taxes for the adult's "residence homestead"; Florida Statutes Section 196.031(1), which grants "every person" an "exemption from all taxation" of the first $5,000 of "his or her permanent residence"; and West Virginia Constitution Article X, Section 1b, Subsection C, which authorizes the legislature to adopt an exemption up to $20,000 for real property "used exclusively for residential purposes" by nonelderly, nondisabled homeowners.

3. Typically, states with general exemptions supplement them with additional or more generous exemptions for elderly, disabled, and/or low-income homeowners. See, for example, Florida Statutes Section 196.031(3), which increases homestead exemptions for homeowners aged 65 and older and for disabled persons; 35 Illinois Compiled Statutes Section 200/15-170, which establishes a "Senior Citizens Homestead Exemption"; Kentucky Revised Statutes Section 132.810(2)(a), which provides a homestead exemption for persons 65 and older and for disabled homeowners; South Carolina Code Section 12-37-250, which provides a homestead exemption for taxpayers age 65 and older, "totally and permanently disabled," or "legally blind"; Texas Tax Code Section 11.13(c), which provides additional exemption from school district taxation for residences of the disabled and those age 65 and older; and West Virginia Constitution Article X, Section 1b, Subsection C, which requires homestead exemption for taxpayers who are 65 or older or who are disabled.

4. See, for example, 68 Oklahoma Statutes Section 2802(9), which designates Oklahoma's property-tax relief provisions as a circuitbreaker for low-income, elderly, and disabled homeowners); and District of Columbia Code Sections 47-1806.6(a)(2) and 47-1806(a)(3), which labels income tax credits for property taxes paid as circuitbreakers.

5. See, for example, Rhode Island General Laws Section 44-33-5, which establishes an income tax credit for "property taxes accrued"; and Michigan Statutes Section 7.557(1522), which credits "property taxes on the homestead" against state income taxes.

6. Maryland limits its credit for property taxes by wealth as well as by income. See Maryland Property Tax Code Section 9-104(i)(1): "A property tax credit under this section may not be granted to a homeowner whose combined net worth exceeds $200,000...."

7. See, for example, Minnesota Statutes Section 273.13. See also Bowman (1991, 426–29).

8. California's Proposition 13 can be understood, in part, as a classification scheme that categorizes property by the year in which it was acquired by the taxpayer. As has been widely noted, this frequently results in substantially similar properties being taxed at radically different levels, because the earlier acquired property is essentially assessed at its historical acquisition cost, while the more recently purchased property is assessed more closely to its fair market value (Sexton, Sheffrin, and O'Sullivan 1999).

9. Municipalities frequently engage in a form of classification by abating, permanently or temporarily, the property-tax liabilities of newly constructed projects. See, for example, Youngman (1998), for a discussion of "widespread use of tax incentives for business location and expansion" (123).

Such abatements are designed to attract economic development that would not otherwise occur within the locality. While these kinds of development-attracting property-tax abatements raise important issues, they are not central to the current analysis, which focuses on property-tax devices aimed at mollifying popular objection to such taxation. Indeed, economic development abatements are often politically contentious, since homeowners and small business people may resent the perception that they are paying higher taxes than large (often out-of-town) developers and corporations.

10. See, for example, Alaska Statutes Section 29.45.060(a), which provides that municipal property taxes on farm land "shall be assessed on the basis of full and true value for farm use and may not be assessed as if subdivided or used for some other non-farm purpose"; and Oregon Revised Statutes Section 308.370(1), which provides that farm land shall "be valued at its value for farm use and not at the assessed value it would have if applied to other than farm use."

11. See, for example, Sokolow (1998); McGuire (1999); Sheffrin (1998); and Shadbegian (1999).

12. See, for example, 31 U.S. Code Section 6902(a)(1): "[T]he Secretary of the Interior shall make a payment for each fiscal year to each unit of general local government in which entitlement land is located. . . ."

13. See, for example, California Public Resources Code Section 4654, which provides that "there shall be paid to each county in which lands acquired for state forest purposes are situated . . . an amount equivalent to taxes levied by the county on similar land similarly situated in the county. . . ."); Colorado Constitution Article XXVII, Section 10, which mandates that state land acquired pursuant to Great Outdoors Colorado Program "shall be subject to payments in lieu of taxes to counties in which said acquisitions are made"); and Massachusetts Annotated Laws Chapter 58, Section 17, which dictates that payments in lieu of taxes shall be made to towns in which certain state-owned institutions are located.

14. See, for example, Iowa Code Section 463A.4: "The state shall make payments in lieu of taxes to compensate for the loss of tax revenues occasioned by the fact that property is owned by the upper Mississippi riverway commission, and thereby exempt from taxation by subdivisions of this state."

15. See, for example, Burns Indiana Code Section 36-3-2-10, which provides for PILOTs from "public entities" such as airport authorities and wastewater treatment facilities; Kentucky Revised Statutes Section 58.580, which requires the Churchill Downs Authority to make PILOTs in "an amount equal to the local property taxes Churchill Downs would have paid under private ownership"; and Maryland Transportation Code Section 6-411, under which the Administration of the Port of Baltimore is required to make PILOTs "to the Mayor and City Council of Baltimore" for certain properties.

16. Connecticut General Statutes Section 12-20a; Rhode Island General Laws Section 45-13-5.1. See generally Carbone and Brody, chapter 10 of this volume.

17. See, for example, Goldberg (1999): "Not that the city would say, exactly, that it has been blocking Harvard since the land-buying ruckus began," . . . but Boston "wants

to complete the deal on the [PILOT] payments, and it is 'first things first from the city's perspective' " (A11). See, also Youngman (1998): "At the local level, cities have exerted increased pressure on exempt institutions to initiate or increase payments in lieu of taxes" (120), and Youngman, chapter 2 of this volume.

REFERENCES

Bowman, John H. 1991. "Real Property Classification." In *State and Local Finance for the 1990s: A Case Study of Arizona*, edited by Therese J. McGuire and Dana Wolfe Naimark. Tempe, Ariz.: School of Public Affairs, Arizona State University.

Goldberg, Carey. 1999. "Harvard Deal With Boston Hints at Era Of Harmony." *New York Times*, August 26.

McGuire, Therese J. 1999. "Proposition 13 and Its Offspring: For Good or for Evil?" *National Tax Journal* 52 (1):129–38.

Sexton, Terri A., Steven M. Sheffrin, and Arthur O'Sullivan. 1999. "Proposition 13: Unintended Effects and Feasible Reforms." *National Tax Journal* 52 (1): 99–111.

Shadbegian, Ronald J. 1999. "The Effect of Tax and Expenditure Limitations on the Revenue Structure of Local Government, 1962–87." *National Tax Journal* 52 (2): 221–37.

Sheffrin, Steven M. 1998. "The Future of the Property Tax: A Political Economy Perspective." In *The Future of State Taxation*, edited by David Brunori (129–45). Washington, D.C.: Urban Institute Press

Sokolow, Alvin D. 1998. "The Changing Property Tax and State-Local Relations." *Publius: The Journal of Federalism* 28 (1): 165–87.

Youngman, Joan M. 1998. "Property, Taxes, and the Future of Property Taxes." In *The Future of State Taxation*, edited by David Brunori (111–27). Washington, D.C.: Urban Institute Press.

Zelinsky, Edward A. 1986. "Efficiency and Income Taxes: The Rehabilitation of Tax Incentives." *Texas Law Review* 64: 973–1037.

The Charitable
Real Property-Tax Exemption
as a Tax Base–Defining Provision

Peter Swords

Some tax code provisions that give relief from taxation may be regarded as a means of defining the tax base.[1] It may be assumed that not everything is subject to tax. As Boris Bittker conceptualized tax policy,

> There is no way to tax *everything:* a legislative body, no matter how avid for revenue, can do no more than pick out from the universe of people, entities, and events over which it has jurisdiction those that, in its view, are appropriate objects of taxation. In specifying the ambit of any tax, the legislature cannot avoid "exempting" those persons, events, activities, or entities that are outside the territory of the proposed tax. (Bittker 1968, 1288)

In contrast to tax code provisions that give relief from taxes for nontax reasons, such as encouraging industry,[2] tax base-defining provisions usually are grounded in tax policy. Decisions not to tax something are made because, given the intrinsic logic of the tax system, it does not make sense to do so. It is argued here that the charitable real property-tax exemption is a provision that defines the tax base and not, by contrast, a provision introduced into the tax code for nontax reasons such as encouraging the provision of charitable services. We do not mean to tax all property, and one type we never meant to tax is property held by charities and used for charitable purposes.

In deciding whether we have charitable exemptions for reasons of normative tax logic, we are led back to the origins of tax policy. Why do we have taxes? Many reasons have been offered, but the simplest and most immediate is that we have taxes to raise funds to support government activities and services. Very few people, if any, like to pay taxes; they would rather keep the money and use it for their own purposes. They are willing to pay taxes, however, because they recognize the need for government. But if manna regularly rained from heaven with funds specified solely for support of government in amounts more than sufficient to finance all government activities, it is very unlikely that we would have any taxes.[3]

The tax-base explanation of the charitable exemption offered here is very simple. What we include in the tax base is money and wealth that we otherwise would use for ourselves. By taxing, we reduce private use of money and wealth to provide funds to support the government.[4] On the other hand, we choose not to tax money and wealth that we have turned over to entities that will use it to benefit the public only and not us individually (except as we are members of the public).[5] We do not mean to include such money or wealth in the tax base in the first place.[6] Such entities are what we define as charities: public-serving nonprofits that are proscribed from advancing private interests improperly and that are established for the sole purpose of benefiting the community as a whole.[7]

When we apply this general theory to the property tax, the argument is that property transferred completely and forever from private use such that it can only be used to provide community-wide benefits (and not to benefit any individuals improperly) is not in the tax base. We tax only property that is used to benefit individuals in their private, individual capacity, such as residences and industrial and commercial property (where individual owners are benefited privately as a result of the property's use).

The argument may be made more persuasive when we consider that only people, not (inert) property, pay taxes. In other words, property taxes are paid out of the pocketbooks of property owners. Setting aside the fact that in some sense charitable nonprofits do not have owners,[8] the persons who would pay a property tax imposed on charities in most cases are those who have already contributed to the charities' support (this is somewhat oversimplified, but still a useful view of property taxes[9]). Thus, such a tax would be similar to a sales tax on contributions to charities. As in the general tax-base argument for charitable exemptions, we choose not to tax money that we have given up entirely for the public benefit and that we cannot apply to our personal benefit.[10]

In developing the tax-base argument for the charitable exemption, we have divided wealth into two categories: wealth used and available for private, personal ends, and wealth used solely for public ends. We have argued that the tax base comprises only the first category. Notice that if the tax base were expanded to include all or part of the second,[11] and the amount needed from taxes for government support remained the same, the tax rate could presumably be reduced.[12] We have suggested that the decision of what we want in the tax base is grounded in tax policy, and, further, that the tax policy question asks what part of private wealth ought to be reduced by taxation to support the government. Do we believe that wealth available for private personal ends should not be reduced because money and wealth turned over to charities to advance public ends has been exempted?[13] Or do we believe people should be taxed on the wealth they have transferred to charities and have consequently given up the ability to use for their own ends, in order to avoid reducing the tax burden on assets that would otherwise be used solely for private ends?[14] There is no final answer. Ultimately, it is a matter of moral choice: Upon whom and what is it fair to lay the burden of tax?

NOTES

1. Much of the analysis in this section was first assayed in Swords (1981).

2. "Tax expenditure" provisions are examples of such provisions. Individuals who regard charitable tax exemptions as tax expenditures usually argue that these provisions were put into tax codes to encourage the provision of charitable goods and services. This is a reason that has little, if anything, to do with tax policy.

3. Those who believe that one function of taxes is to redistribute income and wealth more equitably might still want taxes to effect this redistribution. It seems highly unlikely, however, that such a tax bill would be passed today. In any event, tax exemptions, properly viewed, are for the most part redistributive. In a narrow sense, nonprofits' efforts to aid the poor are redistributive; more broadly, nearly every charitable effort is redistributive. By definition, charitable purposes aim to benefit the whole public. Those who give up assets to establish and maintain nonprofits are usually at the higher end of the income/wealth ladder (this is certainly the case for large transfers); and, as there are many more people at the lower end of the ladder, and as charities are organized to benefit everyone on the ladder, it follows that these transfers may be viewed as redistributive. This covers transfers of property to charitable purposes.

But not everyone may accept that charitable purposes aim to benefit everyone in the community, not just a certain class (however large—e.g., the poor). Take an organization designed to eradicate homophobia. The organization would expect that lesbians and gays will benefit from its efforts, but it might also suppose that the rest of the community will benefit as well. The organization's logic might run as follows: "As a result of our efforts, homophobes will be led to confront their prejudices and may become more thoughtful and informed on the issues raised by these feelings. Consequently, they may emerge as better citizens in the community, as well as become liberated from dark and bothersome feelings. Those who are not infected by this prejudice will also likely receive benefit from the community's becoming more informed and reflective about this divisive issue." An organization devoted to the opposite side might also believe that it was helping the public better understand the issue. Similarly, even though charitable efforts to benefit the poor may be thought of as redistributive, they can be expected to help not only the poor but also the rest of the community, who presumably will be comforted to know that there will be a safety net to catch them if they stumble, and gratified to live in a society that takes care of those who are less well off. Note that this argument is supported if the intent and thrust of a charitable effort are meant to benefit everyone in the community, not that the effort does so in fact. The claim here is that virtually all charitable purposes are aimed at providing what the economists call public goods.

4. In developing a similar tax-base theory to justify the deduction from personal federal income taxes for charitable contributions, William Andrews expresses the kernel of the argument when he observes, "Income should ultimately be defined and differentiated for personal taxes by its uses, not its sources. The intended primary effect of a direct personal tax is to curtail private consumption of economic resources needed for public use" (Andrews 1972, 375).

5. In addition, such wealth cannot be used improperly to advance the private interests of individuals. Improperly advancing the private interest of individuals occurs when a nonprofit organization pays more money to an individual than the worth of what it receives back from the individual. An example would be paying an excessive salary—one that was far higher than salaries paid for comparable positions in the same geographic area—to an organization's executive director. Improperly transferring a nonprofit's money or wealth constitutes a violation of what has been called the nondistribution constraint, the heart of the definition of charity. Here is how the originator of the concept describes the nondistribution constraint:

> As noted . . . , nonprofit firms are not barred from earning profits. Indeed, many nonprofit firms consistently show an annual accounting surplus. Rather, the critical characteristic of a nonprofit firm is that it is barred from distributing any profits it earns to persons who exercise control over the firm, such as members, officers, directors, or trustees. This does not mean that a nonprofit cannot pay reasonable compensation to anyone who supplies labor or capital to the organization; it is only that residual earnings cannot be distributed. All residual earnings must, instead, be retained and devoted to financing the services that the organization was formed to provide. As a result of this "nondistribution constraint," a nonprofit firm by definition has no owners—that is no person who have a share in both control and residual earnings. (Hansmann 1996, 228)

6. Notice that the theory we develop in this paragraph explains virtually all charitable exemptions. Charities are exempt from any entity income tax because any net income they might generate will be used exclusively for public purposes. As explained below, charities are exempt from any property tax since the property they own is used exclusively for public purposes, and they are exempt from sales taxes since the goods and services they purchase will be used exclusively for public purposes. Finally, this theory explains the charitable-contribution deduction, since the monies contributed by donors to charities have been forever given up for personal uses and irrevocably transferred for use of the public. Private uses have been curtailed to make economic resources available for public use.

7. There is nothing in the legislative history of the charitable exemption to provide any indication of whether the legislators who first enacted these provisions thought of them as refinements of the tax base or, for example, tax expenditures. Thus, it is more or less up to us to decide which is the better way of viewing these provisions.

8. Charities are in effect held in trust by the directors of nonprofit corporations or trustees of charitable trusts for the equitable benefit of the entire public (see note 6).

9. To expand the argument fully, we would have to show that we would not choose to have the tax fall on the charities' beneficiaries or those who work for the charity, and that in fact it would not fall on the charities' suppliers. Finally, it would be noted that most charities do not charge for their services; those that do (e.g., schools charging tuition or performing arts groups selling tickets) almost by definition choose not to charge prices equal to the cost of producing the goods consumed by the organizations' recipients. This last point has been well stated by William Baumol and William Bowen in explaining the economic nature of nonprofit organizations:

> The concern of the typical nonprofit organization for the size and composition of its clientele often causes operating revenue to be lower than would be the case if services were priced to satisfy a simple profit-maximization goal. Since such a group normally considers itself to be a supplier of virtue, it is natural that it should seek to distribute its bounty as widely and as equitably as possible. The group is usually determined to prevent income and wealth alone from deciding who is to have priority in the consumption of its services. It wishes to offer its products to the needy and deserving—to students, to the impecunious, to those initially not interested in consuming them, and to a variety of others to whom high prices would serve as an effective deterrent to consumption. (Baumol and Bowen 1965, 495)

Thus, we find that in most cases, those who contribute to charities would bear the brunt of the property tax if the exemption were removed.

10. The suggestion that charitable tax exemptions are best understood as a means of defining the tax base applies only to general taxes and not to taxes imposed to defray the costs of government services that may have increased because the services were provided to exempt organizations. The distinction is between general government services, such as schooling or safety-net provision, which charities do not make more expensive (indeed, in many cases they operate to reduce their costs), and services such as garbage pickup or supplying water, whose costs increase when they are provided to charities. In

New York, about 70 percent of the revenue collected by the property tax is used to defray general government services (see Swords 1981, 42–47).

11. It would likely be part of the only second category, since the second category includes wealth held by the government and it would be illogical for the government to tax itself. Indeed, the part of the second category that would be included in the tax base would be wealth held by or contributed to charities.

12. Assume that the jurisdiction in question has $1,000 of first-category assets and $200 of nongovernment second-category assets, and needs $50 for government uses. If only the assets in the first category were in the tax base, the tax rate would need to be set at .05. If the assets in both the first and second category were included, the tax rate could be reduced to .0416667.

13. At this point in the analysis, tax policy merges to some degree with democratic theory. Some people will argue that since the effect of charitable exemptions is to increase taxes, private individuals operating outside of the normal legislative process are making decisions about what public goods and services should be provided and thus, to some extent, forcing people to pay for services they do not support.

14. In considering this issue, it may be relevant to take into account the amount of private wealth that is available for taxation. In a country with very little private wealth and, therefore, a very small tax base, it might make good sense not to narrow an already thin tax base by providing charitable exemptions. But in a country as rich as the United States, which has a huge tax base of private wealth, the very small increase in taxation on that base caused by charitable exemptions may seem entirely tolerable.

REFERENCES

Andrews, W.D. 1972. "Personal Deductions in an Ideal Income Tax." *Harvard Law Review* 86: 309–85.

Baumol, William, and W.G. Bowen. 1965. "On the Performing Arts: The Anatomy of Their Economic Problems." *American Economic Review* 55: 495–502.

Bittker, Boris. 1968. "Churches, Taxes, and the Constitution." *Yale Law Journal* 78: 1285–1310.

Hansmann, H. 1996. *The Ownership of Enterprise.* Cambridge, Mass.: Harvard University Press.

Swords, P. 1981. *Charitable Real Property Exemptions in New York State: Menace or Measure of Social Progress?* New York: Association of the Bar of the City of New York (distributed by Columbia University Press).

The Collision between Nonprofits and Cities over the Property Tax

Possible Solutions

Richard D. Pomp

Nick Carbone, former deputy mayor of Hartford, Connecticut, is a brilliant strategist and an indefatigable community organizer. His success in Hartford has not been widely emulated elsewhere, simply because there are not enough Nick Carbones to go around. As the consummate power broker in the city, Nick lived every day with the consequences of the loss of property-tax revenue that the city experienced as nonprofits continued to expand and remove property from the tax base. Nick worked tirelessly to implement his vision of a solution.

I was privileged to be a bit player in the solution. In hindsight, I provided the intellectual cover that was needed as the political chess pieces were moved into their strategic positions. Nick has told that story in his typically understated fashion, not taking the credit he deserves for accomplishing what no one else had been able to do. Since politicians usually overstate their accomplishments, rather than understating them, his modesty tells you a lot about Nick.

Nick's story suggests that the subject of the proper treatment of tax-exempt property can be broken down into three questions: whether the existing exemptions ought to be continued and, if so, for which activities; which level of government ought to bear the costs of the exemption; and what alternatives exist for subsidizing the activities of organizations that the state wishes to encourage.

Some people will object to the word "subsidize," arguing that certain organizations are not properly taxable because they are nonprofits. The lack of a normative model of the property tax makes it difficult to debate this issue. Compared to the income tax, where there is general agreement about the Haig-Simons normative model (which enables us to talk meaningfully about "subsidies" such as tax expenditures), debate about the property tax suffers from lack of any comparable consensus. One of the greatest contributions that can be made to the property-tax literature is the development of a normative model, and I applaud Evelyn Brody's and Joan Youngman's efforts to do just that.

For the present, we need not get bogged down in semantics. However they are phrased, the fundamental issues are to determine the appropriate contribution for these properties to make toward the costs of local government, and how best to accommodate and balance the interest of the cities or other jurisdictions that contain a disproportionate percentage of tax-exempt properties.

The first question, whether the existing exemptions ought to be continued and, if so, for which activities, is obviously controversial. It does, however, have a noncontroversial aspect. Even if the state is content to continue the existing general pattern of statutory exemptions for nonprofits, a number of ambiguities in the law could be eliminated through better drafting, and are well-identified in the legal literature (see, e.g., *Property Tax Exemptions for Nonprofit Institutions* 1978). A systematic distillation of situations encountered by assessors would also help focus on troublesome issues. Many of the problems could be corrected administratively, through the promulgation of regulations similar to those issued under most state corporate income taxes or sales taxes.

Our experience with the federal income tax, however, indicates that continual vigilance is necessary to prevent circumvention of the law. Again, the property tax is no exception. Once an exemption is provided by law, taxpayers will restructure their transactions to bring themselves within the exempt category. The stakes are high, so definitional lines come under enormous pressure. The greater sophistication of the tax bar today means that definitions of nonprofits adopted in the 19th and 20th centuries must have a meaningful review.

Resolving ambiguities in the statute is of course desirable, but what really is necessary is a wholesale evaluation of the scope of existing exemptions. When tax rates were low and cities were thriving, broad, generous, wide-reaching exemptions were acceptable. They are not so today. If I were a legislator, I would grant an exemption only if the activity or service were one that the state would have to perform if a private entity did not, and, even then, only if the exemption were required in order to provide the service to all needy members of the public. I realize that representatives of nonprofits will find my criteria too narrow for their tastes, but as long as cities are going to finance the exemption, I think a narrow test is entirely justified. I would be content with a broader test if cities were to be compensated adequately for their lost revenue. In any event, I think that most people would agree that the case for an exemption becomes weaker if the activity in question can command sufficient fees to pay for local services, lacks quasi-public features, and is directed toward middle- and upper-income individuals. If such activities are exempt, then the state is effectively redistributing income away from the poor.

Of course, opinions will differ about where on a continuum particular activities fall. Strong candidates for exemption under my criteria, for example, would be the Red Cross, the Salvation Army, hospitals that treated the indigent, or libraries; strong candidates for denial might include property owned by medical, dental, or bar associations. An apartment building owned by a hospital and rented to interns and residents would not, under my criteria, present a very strong case for exemption, though such buildings are currently exempt in some states, including Connecticut.

Assuming that some subsidy is in order, the next question is to decide which level of government should provide it. I have already suggested that many exempt properties provide general and diffuse benefits to areas beyond the jurisdiction where they are located. This is clear for the Capitol and other state-owned buildings, but is also true for many other properties. For example, a recent study found that less than half the patients treated in tax-exempt hospitals in Bridgeport, Hartford, New Haven, and New London actually lived in those cities. The results were even more pronounced for colleges and universities located in those cities.

Perhaps there was more of an overlap during the 1800s between the jurisdiction where the property was located and the jurisdiction where the beneficiaries lived. But the growth of the suburbs and individuals' increased mobility have produced a situation in which many of the benefits and services generated by tax-exempt organizations are provided to residents of other jurisdictions. Where is the justice in a state law that forces a city to subsidize those who live in the suburbs?

This injustice is recognized for state-owned property by a payment in lieu of taxes (PILOT) program, which exists in some states. Under PILOT programs, the state provides municipalities with payments intended to offset the revenue lost because of state-owned property. Although these payments may represent only a small percentage of the lost property-tax revenue, the state at least recognizes the unfairness of forcing certain municipalities to subsidize state government. Why not recognize the unfairness of forcing certain municipalities to subsidize another state objective—the encouragement of nonprofit activities?

If a subsidy is to be provided to certain organizations, what form should it take? The present treatment, an exemption from property taxes, is probably one of the least rational methods. Consider, for instance, two organizations, X and Y. X is a young organization, struggling financially, and can afford only to rent office space. Y, on the other hand, is well established and known for its generous salaries and opulent headquarters on prime downtown real estate. Has the state consciously chosen to ignore X, the struggling organization, but to grant benefits to Y, the less needy organization? Has the state consciously chosen to increase its subsidy in proportion to the land and buildings an organization owns? In a period of high unemployment, would it not make more sense to provide a subsidy on the basis of the number of persons employed by a charitable organization, rather than the value of its real estate?

To point up yet another irrationality, suppose that X is located in a jurisdiction that makes wide use of service charges, and that X and Y use the same amount of water, sewer services, refuse services, and so forth. X pays a service charge for these services, whereas Y's jurisdiction finances these services through its property tax. Has the state intentionally decided that Y is to be insulated from costs that X bears? To put it yet another way, if the state were to grant cash subsidies to organizations that are presently exempt, would it purposely adopt a program that gave nothing to organizations so poor that they could not afford to own real estate, and, instead, distributed money on the basis of how much real property they owned? That is the effect of the existing law, except that local jurisdictions, rather than the state, grant the cash subsidies by not collecting the property tax they otherwise would.

Because of these irrationalities, I would prefer to replace property-tax exemptions with an explicit cash subsidy. (The exemption could be continued for religious organizations, because giving them a cash subsidy would be constitutionally suspect.) If a system of cash grants were adopted, I have no doubt that the state would narrow the existing law in order to channel money only to the neediest organizations. But if the state would not be willing to grant a cash subsidy in the same amount and to the same organizations that are now benefiting from the statutory exemptions, why should the existing system be continued? Is it because the local jurisdictions are footing the bill?

I have no illusions about a wholesale change in the law, but understanding the defects in the existing system helps identify areas in which a better balance can be reached among the interests of the tax-exempt organizations, cities, and states. The following options attempt to strike a better balance while staying within the present structure.

Option 1: Require the permission of the local jurisdiction before any taxable property can be bought by a tax-exempt organization. Nick Carbone used this approach in Hartford to bring the nonprofits to the table and force them to help fashion a program that would reduce the financial pressures on the cities. This approach gives decisionmaking power to the level of government that bears the cost of the exemption. Option 1 is hardly radical—it is the very approach used with respect to industrial and commercial property. At present, jurisdictions have the power to grant property-tax exemptions in order to attract industrial and commercial property. Before granting an exemption, a jurisdiction must evaluate whether the benefits of having such property outweigh the loss of tax revenue, and be certain that the business would not locate within the jurisdiction without the exemption. Option 1 merely extends this approach to nonprofit property currently exempt under state law.

A municipality would be free to evaluate whether the presence of a particular institution was worth granting an exemption. The analogy with commercial property is useful in highlighting another similarity. States have a valid interest in both industrial property and tax-exempt property. States also have an interest in encouraging nonprofit activities and in attracting new industry; yet most states do not require local jurisdictions to exempt new businesses moving into the state. That decision is left to the local jurisdictions. A state is not helpless in attracting industry, because it has a wide variety of incentives and inducements that can be offered as part of a package, but the state must pay for these incentives and inducements. Why should a similar approach not be used for hospitals, colleges, museums, and other quasi-public organizations?

Option 1 also allows the local jurisdiction to offset the leverage that a tax-exempt organization has in bidding against other potential purchasers of land. Because a tax-exempt organization does not have to pay property tax—one of the carrying costs associated with the ownership of property that all other purchasers must take into account—the organization can afford a higher purchase price and thus outbid other potential buyers. In a jurisdiction with high property taxes, typically a city, this leverage is increased. Option 1, however, allows jurisdictions to offset this advantage.

Moreover, Option 1 allows jurisdictions to exercise rational land-use planning. For example, a city could refuse to allow a tax-exempt organization to buy property in the heart of the financial or shopping district, but welcome expansion into an area undergoing urban renewal. Furthermore, permission to expand could be conditioned on a host of subsidiary agreements concerning the creation of new jobs, affirmative action programs, or any other priorities of the city. Proper safeguards could provide that the benefits of the exemption would be paid back to the city if these conditions were not satisfied.

Option 2: Phase in the exemption whenever taxable property is bought by a tax-exempt organization. This option, which cushions a jurisdiction against an abrupt decline in revenue in the year of purchase, is feasible for established organizations and for property being bought by the state. It would be improper to phase in the exemption for property bought by a newly created organization, because it is during the start-up period that the organization is likely to be short of funds and thus most in financial need.

Option 3: Phase out the exemption after a certain period. A time limitation would enable new organizations to get started without the burden of the property tax, and would also recognize the jurisdiction's interest in not being burdened with a perpetual exemption. A specific phase-out date would allow an organization to plan adequately for the eventual imposition of the property tax.

Option 4: Limit the number of acres qualifying for the exemption. Like Option 3, this approach attempts to balance the interests of the tax-exempt organizations against the revenue loss incurred by the jurisdiction. An acreage limitation recognizes that once some reasonable level of property ownership has been exempted, further expansion should not be at the expense of the local government.

Option 5: Set a dollar limit on the amount of property that can be exempt. A dollar ceiling on the exemption is another means of balancing the interests of the tax-exempts with those of the jurisdiction. Owning property in excess of the ceiling indicates that the organization has a level of wealth or ability to pay that does not justify any further exemption.

Option 6: Impose a user charge. A user charge recognizes that tax-exempt organizations consume local services and should, therefore, contribute to the costs of local government. Recall from the earlier discussion that Option 6 exists in jurisdictions that already provide some services, such as supplying water, on a user-charge basis. Applying Option 6 to all tax-exempt organizations, regardless of where they are located, would end the discrimination that currently exists between tax-exempt groups in jurisdictions that have user charges and those in jurisdictions that finance similar services through the property tax. More important, a service charge removes the incentive for a tax-exempt group to hold on to vacant or idle land that it no longer needs, a tendency that a land-starved city can ill afford. A user charge will also curtail the incentive for tax-exempt organizations to overinvest in real estate; Option 6 should therefore result in a more efficient allocation of resources.

A user charge need not involve the elaborate metering of various municipal services, although such a procedure might be feasible in certain situations. A simple means of implementing a user charge is to estimate the percentage of the jurisdiction's total budget that is devoted to supplying property-related services, such as fire and police protection, traffic control, and garbage collection, and then apply that percentage of the mill rate to the value of the tax-exempt property. If 35 percent of the budget were estimated as attributable to the provision of these services, for example, and the mill rate were 60, then the assessed value of the tax-exempts would be subject to a user charge of 21 mills (0.35×60). A circuit breaker could be used to grant relief to organizations that could not afford the increased cost. Tax-exempt groups would still be receiving a subsidy under Option 6, measured by the difference between the user charge and the full mill rate (39 mills difference in the example).

Option 7: State payments to jurisdictions containing tax-exempt property. Option 7 recognizes that it is unfair for a jurisdiction to bear the entire loss in property taxes attributable to the presence of tax-exempt property. Option 7 extends the state's PILOT program to property not owned by the state, on the theory that the exemption from the property tax implements state objectives and goals. In order to channel state funds where they are needed most, payments might be made only to jurisdictions having more than the statewide average of tax-exempt property. Alternatively, jurisdictions might be reimbursed not for all their tax-exempt property, but only for the amount in excess of the statewide average.

The above options are not mutually exclusive; various combinations could be adopted to deal with special situations. Nor is there any reason to apply the same approach to all categories of property. For example, Option 4, an acreage limitation, might be more suitable for some types of organizations, such as cemeteries, than for others. Or a different acreage limitation could be applied to different categories of property. Similar flexibility exists in the other approaches. Payment by the state, Option 7, could be combined easily with any of the other approaches. A different combination of approaches would allow for a different balance in sharing the costs of the exemption. The user-charge option, for instance, could be adopted in conjunction with a state contribution to the jurisdiction that was equal to a percentage of the difference between the user charge and the full property tax. The percentage contributed by the state could vary from a nominal amount to 100 percent: If the tax-exempt organization provided benefits that were spread throughout the entire state, the percentage would be closer to 100 percent; if most of the benefits were distributed to residents of the jurisdiction, the percentage could be reduced accordingly.

A combination of approaches introduces a degree of sophistication and balancing of competing interests that is unattainable under the present system. Indeed, in view of the flexibility that is possible with the various options, the existing statutory scheme of exemptions is a crude and inequitable approach to a difficult problem.

As Nick Carbone indicated, he had placed the nonprofits in a defensive posture, in which they feared the worst. They embraced the PILOT program with a great sense of relief, because it freed both the institutions and the cities from their previous adversary roles. Both parties had been on a collision course, as revenue-starved mayors eyed the exempt institutions as a source of untapped revenue. By placing the issue in its proper statewide context, the PILOT program for tax-exempt groups allowed the parties to form a new partnership and work together at solving social problems. The issue of tax-exempt property had driven a wedge between groups that should have been working together, and Carbone skillfully removed that wedge with the PILOT program.

REFERENCE

Property-Tax Exemptions for Nonprofit Institutions: Problems and Proposals. 1978. Hartford: Hartford Chamber of Commerce.

About the Editor

Evelyn Brody is a professor of law at Chicago-Kent College of Law, Illinois Institute of Technology, and a visiting professor of law at Duke (fall 2001) and NYU (spring 2002), as well as an associate scholar with the Urban Institute's Center on Nonprofits and Philanthropy. She teaches courses on taxation and nonprofit law. Her publications have examined the similarities between nonprofit and for-profit organizations; the ramifications of charitable endowments; the possible effects of tax reform on charities; and the limits of nonprofit fiduciary law. She is contributing a chapter on nonprofit accountability to *The State of America's Nonprofit Sector* (Lester Salamon, editor; forthcoming), and a chapter on the legal framework for nonprofits to the second edition of *The Nonprofit Sector: A Research Handbook* (Walter W. Powell and Richard Steinberg, editors; forthcoming). Long active with the American Bar Association's Section on Taxation, Professor Brody is also working on nonprofit law revision projects with the American Law Institute and the ABA Business Law Section. She has been appointed a co-reporter of the American Law Institute's new project on the law of nonprofit organizations.

About the Contributors

Woods Bowman has had a varied career in state and local government, nonprofit administration, and academia. He is associate professor in the Graduate Program in Public Service Management at DePaul University. For 14 years he was an elected member of the Illinois House of Representatives, where he chaired an Appropriations Committee. His district included Evanston, home to Northwestern University, where property-tax exemption is a much-discussed issue. His other experience includes work as chief financial officer of Cook County and interim president of Goodwill Industries of Metropolitan Chicago.

Nicholas R. Carbone is the president of the Connecticut Institute for Municipal Studies, Inc., a nonprofit organization created in 1992 to develop strategies to revitalize communities in crisis and eliminate duplicative public services. As president, Mr. Carbone helps identify projects focusing on critical issues facing Connecticut's communities in crisis. Prior to joining CIMS, Mr. Carbone was a member of First Central Bank's board of directors and was vice president of Largo/Hartford, Inc., which served as a development manager for a 33-acre mixed-use project in Hartford. Mr. Carbone has served as cochairman of the Hartford Housing Partnership for the City of Hartford and as chairman of the Mayor's Task Force on Crime. He has also served on Hartford's City Council.

Joseph J. Cordes is an associate scholar with the Center for Nonprofits and Philanthropy at the Urban Institute and a professor of economics and the director of the graduate program in public policy at George Washington University. His research interests include tax and regulatory policy, benefit-cost analysis, and the economic behavior of nonprofit organizations, with a special emphasis on the incentives that nonprofit organizations face to seek out commercial sources of revenue. He co-edited the *Encyclopedia of Taxation and Tax Policy* (Urban Institute Press, 1999) with Robert Ebel and Jane Gravelle.

Deirdre Dessingue is associate general counsel of the United States Catholic Conference (USCC), specializing in the law of tax-exempt organizations. From 1993 to 1999, Ms. Dessingue served on the board of overseers of the Pontifical Faculty of the Dominican House of Studies. Ms. Dessingue served as assistant general counsel of USCC from 1981 to 1985, and prior to that spent five years as an attorney in the Exempt Organizations Tax Review, as cochair of the Religious Organizations Subcommittee of the ABA Tax Section's Exempt Organizations Committee, and as a member of the IRS Advisory Committee on Tax Exempt and Government Entities.

Stephen Diamond is a professor at the University of Miami School of Law. He has written and continues to work on the history of taxation in the United States. He also teaches and does research on the history of food and alcoholic beverage law in the United States and the European Union.

Janne Gallagher is deputy general counsel of the Council on Foundations. Prior to joining the Council, Ms. Gallagher was part of the exempt organizations practice group at the Washington, D.C., law firm of Caplin & Drysdale. Ms. Gallagher served as editor of *State Tax Trends for Nonprofits* from 1989 to 1998, and is a frequent speaker and author on issues of concern to tax-exempt organizations.

Marie Gantz was a research associate with the Urban Institute's Center on Nonprofits and Philanthropy when this book was written. She worked on a number of publications analyzing the finances of nonprofit organizations, including a comparison of nonprofit nursing home finances that had been self-reported to the Internal Revenue Service and the Health Care Financing Administration, and an analysis of executive salaries and benefits reported on IRS Forms 990. She also examined regional levels of charitable giving using data from the IRS Statistics of Income Bulletin. She is currently pursuing a Ph.D. in statistics at the University of Kentucky.

David B. Glancey is the chairman of the Philadelphia Board of Revision of Taxes, which is the Real Property Assessment and Appeals Office for the City of Philadelphia. Mr. Glancey was vice chairman of the panel from 1983 to 1988, and since the beginning of 1989 has been the chairman of the board. Previously, Mr. Glancey was counsel to the Committee on Local Government for the Senate of Pennsylvania. From 1978 to 1984, he was also associated with the law firm of Dilworth, Paxson, Kalish & Kauffman, where he was a member of the firm's litigation department.

Robert T. Grimm, Jr., is the research director of the American Philanthropists Project at the Center on Philanthropy at Indiana University, and is a faculty member in philanthropic studies and history at Indiana University. He is also the editor of the forthcoming *Notable American Philanthropists: Biographies of Giving and Volunteering* (Greenwood and Oryx, 2002), an Earhart Fellow, and a regular columnist for the Council on Foundations' *Foundation News & Commentary*. Currently, he is conducting research on the history of Goodwill Industries and Americans with disabilities in the twentieth century.

Peter Dobkin Hall is Hauser Lecturer on Nonprofit Organizations at the Kennedy School of Government, Harvard University, and is a research fellow at the Yale Divinity School. He is the author or editor of many books and articles on topics relating to philanthropy, voluntarism, and nonprofit organizations, including *Sacred Companies: Organizational Aspects of Religion and Religious Aspects of Organizations* (coedited with N. J. Demerath III, Terry Schmitt, and Rhys H. Williams; Oxford University Press, 1998), *Inventing the Nonprofit Sector* (Johns Hopkins University Press, 1992), and *Lives in Trust: The Fortunes of Dynastic Families in Late Twentieth Century America* (with George E. Marcus; Westview Press, 1992).

Pamela Leland is currently serving as the interim director of the Center for Community Development and Family Policy (CCDFP) in the College of Human Services, Education, and Public Policy at the University of Delaware. As a member of CCDFP, she serves as executive director of the Urban Affairs Association. She is also a faculty member in the School of Urban Affairs and Public Policy, teaching nonprofit management and public administration and providing an array of technical assistance and management support to nonprofit organizations. Prior to joining the University of Delaware, Dr. Leland served on the faculties of Seton Hall University and Marywood University.

Dick Netzer is professor of economics and public administration at the Wagner Graduate School of Public Service, New York University, where he has taught since 1961. For the past fifty years, he has been doing research on and writing about the property tax, and on other aspects of subnational public finance. His current projects include a comprehensive re-evaluation of the taxation of business property in the United States; evaluating the feasibility and relevance of land value taxation in developed and developing countries in the contemporary world; and the preservation of cultural heritage.

Thomas Pollak is assistant director of the National Center for Charitable Statistics at the Urban Institute. Areas of interest include nonprofit organization finance and arts organizations. Mr. Pollak earned his law degree from Georgetown University.

Richard D. Pomp is the Alva P. Loiselle professor of law at the University of Connecticut. He has taught at Harvard, NYU, Texas, and Boston College. In addition, he has been a distinguished professor in residence, Chulalongkorn Law School, Bangkok, Thailand, and a visiting scholar at the University of Tokyo Law School. From 1981 to 1987, Professor Pomp was director of the New York Tax Study Commission, a period during which New York restructured its personal and corporate income tax and created an independent tax tribunal. He is currently a consultant to the U.S. Treasury on state taxation of electronic commerce.

Daniel Salomone joined the Minnesota Taxpayers Association as executive director in April 1991. Prior to joining the association, he served as the research director for the Minnesota Department of Revenue and the

Minnesota Senate Counsel and Research Office. While in the Department of Revenue, he introduced computer modeling and tax return sampling in the analysis of legislative tax proposals. At the Senate, he led a multi-agency study of the effectiveness of state aid to Minnesota cities. He is currently an adjunct faculty member at Hamline University, where he teaches a course in Public Fiscal Management. He serves on the boards of the National Tax Association, the National Taxpayers Conference, and the Governmental Research Association.

David L. Sjoquist is professor of economics, senior associate in the Policy Research Center, director of domestic studies program in the Andrew Young School of Policy Studies, and director of the fiscal research program at Georgia State University. Dr. Sjoquist is a specialist in public finance, particularly state and local public finance, but also has an extensive interest in urban economics, especially local economic development and central city poverty. He is a member of the National Tax Association, of which he is a past member of the board of directors, and serves on the board of editors of the *National Tax Journal.*

Peter Swords is the former president of the Nonprofit Coordinating Committee of New York (NPCC), an umbrella group of New York Section 501(c)(3) organizations that is devoted to improving and protecting the City's nonprofit sector. Prior to becoming president of NPCC, Mr. Swords was an associate dean at the Columbia Law School. He continues to teach courses at Columbia on nonprofit institutions at the School of Law and at Teachers College. He is currently working on a project designed to help people understand the Form 990. Mr. Swords lectures in the area of nonprofit law and liability insurance. He serves on the boards of the Center for the Study of Philanthropy (Graduate Center, CUNY), and is a member of NPCC's Government Relations Committee. Mr. Swords is the author of the book *Charitable Real Property Tax Exemptions in New York State.*

Joan M. Youngman is a senior fellow at the Lincoln Institute of Land Policy, where she chairs the department of valuation and taxation. Ms. Youngman has practiced tax law with the Boston firm of Hale and Dorr and served as a research associate with the Harvard Law School International Tax Program, where she is currently a research fellow. She is the author of several articles on taxation, coauthor of *An International*

Survey of Taxes on Land and Buildings (Kluwer, 1994), and author of *Legal Issues in Property Valuation and Taxation* (International Association of Assessing Officers, 1994).

Edward A. Zelinsky is professor of law at the Benjamin N. Cardozo School of Law of Yeshiva University. He was the first Yale student elected to the New Haven Board of Aldermen, on which he served for fourteen years.

Index